AMBIGUOUS ANTIDOTES: VIRTUE AS VACCINE FOR VICE IN EARLY MODERN SPAIN

Ambiguous Antidotes: Virtue as Vaccine for Vice in Early Modern Spain

HILAIRE KALLENDORF

UNIVERSITY OF TORONTO PRESS
Toronto Buffalo London

Toronto Buffalo London
www.utorontopress.com

ISBN 978-1-4875-0213-3

Library and Archives Canada Cataloguing in Publication

Kallendorf, Hilaire, author
Ambiguous antidotes : virtue as vaccine for vice in early modern Spain / Hilaire Kallendorf.

(Toronto Iberic ; 30)
Includes bibliographical references and indexes.
ISBN 978-1-4875-0213-3 (cloth)

1. Spanish drama – Classical period, 1500–1700 – History and criticism. 2. Virtues in literature. I. Title. II. Series: Toronto Iberic ; 30

PQ6105.K35 2017 862′.309 C2017-904286-6

University of Toronto Press acknowledges the financial assistance to its publishing program of the Canada Council for the Arts and the Ontario Arts Council, an agency of the Government of Ontario.

Funded by the Government of Canada
Financé par le gouvernement du Canada
Canadä

For my grandmother,
who tried to teach me
the way of Virtue

Virtue? A fig!

– William Shakespeare

Virtue itself turns vice, being misapplied,
And vice sometime by action dignified.

– William Shakespeare

All virtues are historical . . .
Morality is first artifice, then artifact.

– André Comte-Sponville

Nec cessat naufraga virtus.

[Nor does virtue cease, though shipwrecked.]

– Lucan

Contents

List of Figures xi

Prologue: Virtuous Genealogies xiii

Acknowledgments xix

Introduction 3

I *Virtue as a Medical Metaphor* 4
II *Correspondences of Virtue to Vice* 10
III *Antidotes* 12
IV Pharmakon 22
V *The Golden Mean* 29

1 Blind Justice 37

2 Fleeting Fortitude 69

3 Charity as Greed 84

4 Loose Chastity 106

5 Prudence: Panacea or Placebo? 126

6 Class Trumps Sex: The (En)gendering of Virtue 145

Conclusion 164

I *(Not Just) the Veneer of Virtue* 164
II Virtus *or Virus?* 167
III *Historical / Literary Roots* 171
IV *Machiavellian* Virtù 173
V *Erasmus at the Theatre* 181

Epilogue: Virtual Virtue 190

Notes 199

Bibliography 263

Index of Comedias 295

Index 309

Figures

1 "Chastity impales Lust with a sword" (Pudicitia Libidinem gladio) from Prudentius, *Psychomachia*, 10th century. Brussels, Bibliothèque royale, MS 10066–77, fol. 116v. 4

2 *Rosmarinus coronarium* (rosemary) woodcut engraving from Andrés de Laguna, *Pedacio Diascórides Anazarbeo* (1555), fol. 320, in a hand-coloured exemplar prepared specially for King Philip II (R/8514, Biblioteca Nacional de España, Madrid). 8

3 (a & b) A matching pair of a tree of Vices and a tree of Virtues, from a manuscript of *Speculum Virginum* (Walters Art Museum MS W. 72, fols 25v–26r, ca. 1200). 11

4 Title page, *Concordia apothecariorum Barchinonensium* (1511) (photo courtesy of Museu de la Farmàcia Catalana, Universitat de Barcelona). 13

5 Title page, Nicolás Monardes, *Primera y Segunda y Tercera Partes de la Historia Medicinal* (Seville: Alonso Escribano, 1574) (R.Micro/6026, Biblioteca Nacional de España, Madrid). 15

6 Pharmacy jar (*albarelo*) with Jesuit emblem, Farmacia del Palacio Real de Madrid, número inv. 10031653 (first half of 18th century) (© Patrimonio Nacional). 17

7 Title page, Andrés de Laguna, *Pedacio Dioscórides Anazarbeo, acerca de la materia medicinal y de los venenos mortíferos* (Salamanca, 1566) (R.Micro/17685, Biblioteca Nacional de España, Madrid). 19

8 Estéban March, *Moisés y la serpiente de metal* (ca. 1650), Colección Banco Santander, Madrid. 27

9 Fortitude between Fierceness and Cowardice. The Hague, Museum Meermanno-Westreenianum, 10 D 1, fol. 37r, Book 3. 27

10 Temperance between Insensitivity and Intemperance. The Hague, Museum Meermanno-Westreenianum, 10 D 1, fol. 37r, Book 3. 27
11 Michael Pacher, *The Devil Presenting St. Augustine with the Book of Vices* (1483) (photo courtesy of Art Resource). 45
12 Inquisitorial coat of arms on a 1678 document from the Tribunal of Toledo, now held at the University of Notre Dame (Inquisition 106), naming Francisco de Aranda Quintanilla a familiar of the Inquisition; the sword and the olive branch represent Justice and Mercy, respectively (reproduced from the original held by the Department of Special Collections of the Hesburgh Libraries of Notre Dame). 67
13 Archangel Michael (symbol of Fortitude) dressed for battle, defeating Satan: Juan Fernández Navarrete ("El Mudo"), *San Miguel* (1565), Parish church of Briones, Rioja, Spain (photo courtesy of Art Resource). 74
14 Antonio Corradini's allegorical statue of *Pudicizia*, or modesty, in the Sansevero Chapel of what was historically the Spanish kingdom of Naples (1751) (photo courtesy of Art Resource). 124
15 Francisco de Zurbarán, *Saint Jerome in the Company of Saint Paula and Saint Eustoquia*, National Gallery of Art, Washington, DC (ca. 1640–50). 149
16 Goddess Virtus appearing on a gold coin minted in Spain in 68 AD to commemorate the Roman emperor Galba, who was governor of Hispania Tarraconensis (Tarragona, Spain) (photo © The Trustees of the British Museum). 151
17 Goddess Virtus on Virginia treasury bill issued by the US Continental Congress in 1777, worth "four Spanish milled dollars" (The Colonial Williamsburg Foundation, Gift of the Lasser family). 151
18 Goddess Virtus on Virginia's state flag. 151
19 A translation of Machiavelli's *Discourses on Livy* by Juan Lorenzo Otevante dedicated to Philip II (1555), this censored copy of which may be found at the Escorial (© Patrimonio Nacional). 176
20 Valencia, 1528 edition of the Spanish translation of Erasmus, *Enquiridion, o manual del caballero cristiano*, printed by Juan Joffre; the word *Virtus* adorns the knight's horse's garment at the far left in the engraving (77.Dd.24 PS, Österreichische Nationalbibliothek, Vienna). 185

Prologue: Virtuous Genealogies

This book began when I was a child. I used to sit in my grandmother's kitchen and reflect upon a framed picture she had hanging there on the wall. It was titled *Spectrum of Love*. Beneath this heading were listed out Patience, Kindness, Generosity, Humility, Courtesy, Unselfishness, Good Temper, Guilelessness, and Sincerity, complete with a hand-drawn dove and flowers, along with descriptions for each. A table of Virtues, of sorts. At a very young age I was so attracted to this list that (with her permission) I grabbed the picture off the wall, took a pen and scrawled in large, childish letters: "This is mine – Hilaire," indicating my request to inherit that object. Not wanting to make me wait for her death, she gave it to me when I was old enough to have a house of my own. It still hangs in my home office, where I am sitting as I write these words. She was the single greatest source for spiritual instruction in my life. No doubt, my grandmother wanted to encourage me in the way of Virtue.

Fast forward a decade or more. The next snapshot in this collage is dated 1993, when I was a university student and William J. Bennett published *The Book of Virtues*. It was given to me by my boyfriend's mother as a Christmas gift (subtle hint). Imagine my chagrin when, a decade later, controversy erupted over the news that Bennett himself was an inveterate gambler who had lost millions at the casinos in Las Vegas. The scandal was that this alleged hypocrisy undercut his public message of self-discipline. Perhaps the Virtues were not so straightforward after all.

Fast forward to the present day. The year of sabbatical leave in which I have written the bulk of this manuscript has coincidentally also been my first year to undergo allergy immunotherapy, a painful process in which raging allergens are injected into both hips every week, making it hurt even to sit down. The angry, red, itchy reaction I experience each time serves as a vivid reminder of the troubling similarity between disease and vaccine. Sometimes a small amount of the disease must be injected to make the body grow stronger – i.e., literally more virtuous.

These are some of the personal reasons I am attracted to this subject matter. The professional ones are more obvious. This book in some ways participates in recent trends such as the growth industry in Virtue Ethics, as well as what one scholar has called the "ethical turn" in literary scholarship.[1] It bears traces of my participation in the First Global Conference on Sins, Vices, and Virtues in Prague, Czech Republic, in March 2012, as well as my membership in the University of Chicago's Arete Initiative / Wisdom Research Network, sponsored by the John Templeton Foundation. Its foremost intellectual debt is owed to Richard Newhauser, who taught me in a National Endowment for the Humanities summer seminar at Cambridge University on the Seven Deadly Sins. Our main take-away from those weeks of intense discussion was that the Vices (as well as the Virtues) are consummately ambiguous. Finally, in 2013 the University of Toronto published my *Sins of the Fathers: Moral Economies in Early Modern Spain*, to which the present volume in some sense forms a companion. That book in turn was a sequel to my *Conscience on Stage* (University of Toronto Press, 2007), in which I first established my methodology of mining 800 digitalized Renaissance stage plays from Spain that together form a corpus of moral knowledge from the early modern period. In a review essay titled "Hispanic Casuistry Studies: Room to Grow" and appearing in *Hispanic Review*, William Childers declared that this book – along with my friend Elena del Río Parra's *Cartografías de conciencia* – had inaugurated a new field: the study of early modern Hispanic casuistry, or case morality.[2] If he is right, then the present book may be seen as the next installment in that body of work.

The Spanish word for Virtue, *Virtud*, stems directly from its Latin ancestor *Virtus*. This word was the Romans' translation of a concept known as *arete* which they had inherited from the ancient Greeks.[3] Bearing agonistic resonance due to its association with stadium athletes,[4] this word eventually came to mean excellence in the moral realm. Owing in part to the paucity of the Latin language, which lacked a more appropriate word to convey the full weight of the Greek original, what was once a rich ethical complex of ideas was reduced to the blatantly martial-sounding *Virtus*.[5] As scholars have noted, this is a fascinating case where linguistic change reflects a shift in cultural ideals.[6] We shall explore the ramifications of Virtue – a word unmistakeably tied to *vir*, the Latin word for man – for gender studies in our sixth chapter.

From these overtly pagan origins, Virtue took a bizarre journey as convoluted as that of Odysseus. Appropriated by figures within the early Christian church, most notably the fifth-century Latin poet Prudentius (who was born in Spain),[7] any unified notion of Virtue splintered off into competing lists of specific Virtues organized into neat Scholastic schemes. The Cardinal Virtues, so named because together they formed the "hinge" upon which moral life turned, were a list developed first by the pagan philosopher Plato.[8] Only later did they become Christianized, after further modification by Cicero, Saint Augustine, and Saint Thomas Aquinas.[9] (The Cardinal Virtues are Justice, Fortitude, Prudence, and Temperance.)[10] The Theological Virtues, by contrast, were more biblical; however, they were fewer in number (three instead of four) and derived from the thirteenth verse of the thirteenth chapter of Saint Paul's first letter to the Corinthians: "And now there remain faith, hope and charity, these three: but the greatest of these is charity" (1 Corinthians 13:13). These three Virtues were joined to the Cardinal four to add up to the number symbolizing heavenly perfection, i.e., seven.

These various taxonomies and organizational schemes were well known to Renaissance Spain. For example, the Jesuit Francisco Suárez wrote a treatise on the three Theological Virtues, while the Cardinal Virtues enjoyed a place of prominence in Juan de Mena's medieval masterpiece *Laberinto de Fortuna*.[11] These borrowings, continuities, and discontinuities with tradition we might have expected. What is somewhat surprising is that we encounter a veritable obsession with Virtue and its nature in Spain's early modern popular drama. Lope de Vega highlights Virtue and virtuous action as particularly attractive to audiences in his *Arte nuevo de hacer comedias en este tiempo* (1609):

> Los casos de la honra son mejores
> porque mueven con fuerza a toda gente,
> con ellas las acciones virtuosas,
> que la virtud es dondequiera amada.[12]

Even a cursory glance shows that titles of plays from this period reflect this concern. From Lope's own *La mayor virtud de un rey* and *Virtud, pobreza y mujer*; to Tirso de Molina's *La elección por la virtud*; to Luis Vélez de Guevara's *Virtudes vencen señales*; to the anonymous burlesque comedy *El premio de la virtud y castigo en la mentira*, these playwrights (and their audiences) never seem to tire of mulling over or re-hashing questions such as, "which is the greatest Virtue?" or "what are Virtue's rewards?" Contemporaneous novelists, too, devoted short stories to Virtue, such as María de Zayas's *El desengaño amado y premio de la virtud* or Diego de Ágreda y Vargas's *El premio de la virtud y castigo del vicio*. If we include the eighteenth century – which is too late for the scope of this study – theatrical examples only multiply, giving rise to titles such as the anonymous *La virtud consiste en medio, el pródigo y rico avariento*; Tomás de Añorbe y Corregel's *La virtud vence al destino*; Álvaro Cubillo de Aragón's *De el engaño hacer virtud*; and Luis Moncín's *La virtud premiada*. Interest in these questions seems to speed up as time goes by, not slow down. Not to mention that for the period which is covered by this study (roughly 1550 to 1700), plays devoted to specific Virtues also abound, such as Guillén de Castro's *La humildad soberbia*, *La justicia en la piedad*, and *La piedad en la justicia*; Lope de Vega's *El triunfo de la humildad, y soberbia abatida*, complemented by his *Loa en alabanza de la humildad*; Tirso de Molina's *La prudencia en la mujer*; Francisco de Quevedo's *Dios hace justicia a todos*; and Calderón's *Las tres justicias en una*, to name only some of many.

A fairly detailed knowledge of Virtue's taxonomies is also revealed in these plays; in a typical example, Calderón makes reference to "las cuatro Virtudes, prometiéndose anteverla la Fortaleza, y Templanza, la Justicia, y la Prudencia."[13] Iconographical symbols for the Virtues are also included; for instance, in another of Calderón's sacramental dramas a sword is described, the different parts of which represent the Cardinal Virtues through their symbols:

> Se significan en ella
> las cuatro Virtudes juntas:
> la Hoja es la Justicia; el Pomo,
> la Fortaleza, y si se aúnan
> en ser la Templanza el Puño,
> y la Vaina la Cordura.[14]

All of this simply goes to show that it is not in any way a "stretch" to propose to study Virtues as they were conceived in early modern Spain through its theatre, nor is there a lack of source materials. (On the contrary, we are faced with an embarrassment of riches.) A word about method: I have modernized all spelling to facilitate online searches of the digital version of this book, and all citations to plays are taken from their digital versions collected together in the Teatro Español del Siglo de Oro database, distributed by ProQuest. Hard-copy scholarly editions of plays have often been consulted when these were available (for many plays cited in these pages, no modern edition exists yet). For any readers who might be curious about the kind of digital humanities scholarship to be found within these pages, I refer them to the prologue of my last book, which contains some reflections on the interplay between archive and repertoire.[15] Methodologically, this study puts into practice a modified version of the model developed theoretically by Franco Moretti in *Distant Reading* – modified in the sense that it combines old-style philology or "close reading" and historical contextualization with large-scale quantitative analysis. In response to the question "why these Virtues and not others?" I would respond that I started out by collecting data on many more Virtues than these. No university or trade press in the world would publish all the material available on this topic. I narrowed down my own list of Virtues to be covered in individual chapters by following where the evidence led me and seeing which Virtues seemed to stand out by looming largest on this particular cultural landscape. To borrow a phrase from *Sins of the Fathers*, these are the Virtues which generated the largest nodes of cultural anxiety regarding their definition, breach, and execution.[16] I would encourage future researchers to continue this work by looking more in depth at some of the many other Virtues not treated here in detail. This "new field" of early modern casuistry studies is wide open.

Acknowledgments

This project was funded by the Academy for the Visual and Performing Arts, the Program to Enhance Scholarly and Creative Activities, a Cornerstone Faculty Fellowship from the College of Liberal Arts, and a Faculty Development Leave, all at Texas A&M University, as well as Publication Support Grants from both the Department of Hispanic Studies and the Melbern G. Glasscock Center for Humanities Research. Part of chapter 3 was published previously as "Abject Antidotes: Charity as Greed in Early Modern Spanish Drama," in *Hispania felix: Revista rumano-española de cultura y civilización de los Siglos de Oro* (2017): 173–92. I wish to thank my research assistant, Brittany Henry, who performed diligent word searches on the Virtues and their variants, and to my husband Craig Kallendorf for being my first and best critic. Thanks also to Suzanne Rancourt, Barb Porter, and Miriam Skey at the University of Toronto Press for many years of nurturing me as a writer. My greatest intellectual debt for this book and its subject matter is to Richard Newhauser, a.k.a. "King of Vice."

AMBIGUOUS ANTIDOTES

Introduction

And with some sweet oblivious antidote
cleanse the stuff'd bosom of that perilous stuff
which weighs upon the heart?

– William Shakespeare[1]

Every virtue is a summit between two vices, a crest between two chasms.

– André Comte-Sponville[2]

Traditionally, the classic relationship of Virtues to Vices followed an agonistic model based upon Prudentius's *Psychomachia*, or *Conflict of the Soul*, a medieval Latin allegorical poem in which female personifications of the Virtues battle against and defeat the (likewise female) corresponding Vices (Figure 1). Prudentius himself was born in 348 AD in northern Spain, and his legacy was carried on into the early modern period by such Golden Age authors as Pedro Pablo de Acevedo, a Jesuit schoolmaster and author of the student drama *Bellum virtutum et vitiorum*. The *psychomachia* model, likewise, does appear in more mainstream Spanish stage plays, particularly the *autos sacramentales*,[3] as in the lines "portentos de batalla, en que andan Vicios, y Virtudes compitiendo."[4] In Calderón de la Barca's sacramental drama *Amar y ser amado, y divina Philotea*, there is a battle scene onstage where Virtue leads the charge, backed by an entire army, against an opposing army of the Vices. Her battle cry is "A ellos, mueran todos." An editorializing comment appears from one of the Vices later in the play: "segunda vez de vencida, roto el Ejército nuestro: no hay virtud, que victoriosa no blasone de su opuesto."[5] Thus we see that the agonistic model was not absent from Golden Age theatre, and that the Virtues, predictably, emerged victorious from these onstage battles.

Figure 1. "Chastity impales Lust with a sword" ("Pudicitia Libidinem gladio") from Prudentius' *Psychomachia*, 10th century, Brussels, Bibliothèque royale, Ms. 10066–77, fol. 116v.

The traditional model, however, was not the only one available for playwrights looking to describe the relationship between Virtue and Vice. Other models coexisted with the martial, agonistic kind, and it is to one of these in particular that we shall turn our attention here. The model in question is of the medical variety, in which Virtue was seen to serve as a vaccine or antidote for Vice. This paradigm ultimately derives from Plato and Aristotle, whose father was a medical doctor, and who self-consciously modelled the method for his philosophy after the art of medicine.[6] There is ample precedent for this connection to be found in the literature – and even the architecture – typical of early modern Spanish cultural production. We shall begin by looking at Virtue during this time period in Spain when it appears as a medical metaphor.

I Virtue as a Medical Metaphor

The sixteenth-century Hospital Tavera in Toledo bears the following Latin inscription above the entrance to its pharmacy:

> Prudentiae et Temperantiae eximius.
> Aegrae valetudinis oppugnacula medicamina
> eorumque materies hic asservantor.
>
> [The best Prudence and Temperance.
> Medicines are the attacks on a sick body
> and their substances are preserved here.]

Similarly, at the seventeenth-century Hospital de la Misericordia in Salvador de Bahia, Brazil, the Sala Nobre has painted on the ceiling depictions of the following Virtues: *Concordia* (Harmony), *Charitas* (Charity), *Fidelitas* (Loyalty), *Liberalitas* (Generosity), *Honor* (Honour), and *Ratio* (Reason). Many more examples could be adduced. In early modern Iberia, as well as its colonies, the care of the sick was a charitable enterprise,[7] and as such relied upon the virtuous behaviour of health practitioners. But as we shall see, there is more to this relationship of Virtue to medicine than immediately meets the eye.

Virtue appears in connection with health also in Spain's popular stage plays.[8] Many theatres in Madrid were operated by hospitals or their confraternities for the specific purpose of raising money to provide medical care for the poor.[9] This "hidden origin" or context of medicine linked to Virtue for Spain's national dramatic tradition is reflected in the plays themselves.[10] We find lines linking these two concepts explicitly with humorous wordplay, as in "Esto tengo de virtud, de que estimo mi salud"[11] (hey – it even rhymes!). Indeed, Virtue *is* health in this world view, albeit divinely granted: "Espera en Dios, y con rara fe confiesa su virtud, que es de la vida salud."[12] Virtue brings health to the sick, as when a person "tiene virtud de dar la vida y salud."[13] A virtuous person wields power to impart health to another, as when Antón Martín says of a sick woman being cared for by Saint John of God: "mas yo sé, que en su virtud, tendrá muy presto salud, aunque más sin ella esté."[14] In some cases spiritual Virtues are said to effect a physical cure; in this same play, the same woman says in the next act regarding the reputation of this holy saint: "Bien pudiera en mi casa curarme, hermano mío, pero la relación de sus virtudes me dio esperanza de salud."[15] She has come seeking help from holy men in what is clearly a metaphorical comparison of spiritual with physical health.

But the word *Virtud* appears in the *comedias* also in the non-moral context of purely medical remedy. One character, referring to a proposed medicine, asks "¿Y de qué enfermedad cura?" The answer comes that this particular remedy will whet the appetite: "Sus virtudes son muy sanas, abre de comer las ganas."[16] This medicine presumably functions as an *aperitif*. Other remedies were formulated to act against a specific disease, such as the plague, which so threatened Madrid from 1647 to 1649 that guards were stationed at entrances to the city to prevent infected travellers from entering. We see this trend in the line from Tirso de Molina's *El amor médico*, "olla, boñigas, y clavos ... deben de tener virtud (sin duda) contra la peste."[17] Given that *boñigas* refers to animal excrement, this does not sound like a very savoury mixture.

As we might have anticipated for a comic genre, it is not uncommon to find jokes in these plays about pairs of lovers "playing doctor" and using their "Virtue" to cure one another. Thus we find "La virtud de Pedro, en ser de Belisa medicina" in Lope de Vega's *Los melindres de Belisa*.[18] In like fashion, another of Lope's plays incorporates the truism that "la dama, a los males de quien ama, es milagrosa virtud: aquí está el Doctor."[19] These scenes are similar in some ways to the lovers' ruse we find in comic literature written about demonic possession, in which the woman pretends to be "possessed" by a demon (really, she has just fallen in love with a boy), with her suitor posing as the exorcist who knows the secret to curing her affliction.[20] Such episodes bear the additional resonance of Virtue as sexual potency or virility, a linkage we shall explore later in our conclusion to this study.

Virtue is not only connected with medicine in these stage plays, but metaphorically with medical botany – a relationship made explicit, for example, in an early modern English treatise titled *Vertues off Herbes*.[21] In the *comedias* we find lines such as "en las plantas piensa hallar virtudes con que curar"[22] as well as allusions to "aceites y ungüentos y hierbas de gran virtud."[23] One character lists out names of specific herbs and their powers: "el polipodio, el frago, la mandrágora, y otras de mil virtudes esquisitas."[24] Two of the herbs mentioned here are calaguala and mandrake. The word *Virtud* is further associated with homeopathic remedies and *curanderas*: "Es mujer de escapulario con más botes de virtudes, aguas, hierbas, y saludes."[25] Specifically, plants are referred to as remedies ("¿o qué planta diera al enfermo salud, si negara la virtud con que a esas otras se adelanta?")[26] which produce foreseeable effects such as chills, hiccups, and sweating: "algunas hierbas, cuya virtud natural, causa frío, hipo, y sudor."[27] These lines are from Antonio Zamora's *El hechizado por fuerza*, about a false bewitchment brought on by the clever use of herbs to provoke these symptoms. Here Virtue is the juice squeezed out of a plant: "hermoso Racimo ... exprimiéndole avariento, su licor bebe sediento: ¿Qué Virtud habrá escondida en esta Planta florida?"[28]

Recipes for these remedies appeared in *antidotarios*, or remedy books:

> CONDE DON PEDRO: ¿En las hierbas no hay virtud?
> MARCELO [CRIADO, PAJE DEL CONDE]: De remedios está lleno su libro.[29]

A familiar example of one of these recipes employed to maximum dramatic effect is the potion given to Segismundo in Calderón de la Barca's *La vida es sueño* in order to cast him into a deep sleep for the purpose of transporting him from the tower to the palace, so he will believe later that his time there was only a dream. This concoction is described by Clotaldo to Basilio as "bebida que de confecciones llena hacer mandaste, mezclando la virtud de algunas hierbas, cuyo tirano poder, y cuya secreta fuerza, así el humano discurso priva, roba, y enajena."[30] This is an example of "virtuous" or powerful herbs being used theatrically to not-so-virtuous ends.

By the time of the Golden Age, this metaphorical and linguistic connection between medicinal herbs and human Virtue had become so solidified in the minds of playwrights and their audiences that specific herbs such as rosemary were being referenced as symbols of the Virtues: "Entre las plantas, que produce el prado, / Es de virtudes símbolo el Romero."[31] Here we see that rosemary specifically came to be seen as emblematic of all the Virtues (Figure 2). In "Medieval Plantsmanship in England: The Culture of Rosemary," John H. Harvey explains that this plant is Mediterranean in origin, which places it in Spain, and that from earliest times its medicinal properties were recognized, including by the very first medical school at Salerno.[32] Harvey has examined several manuscripts of a text called the *Little Book of the Virtues of Rosemary* (ca. 1440), translated by a Dominican friar named Henry Daniel, who considered it to be a sort of holy herb.[33] George R. Keiser confirms that this plant, used in rituals at both weddings and funerals, bore sacred or "virtuous" connotations. He cites a broadside (ca. 1615) titled *The admirable vertue, property and operation of the quintessence of Rosemary flowers, and the meanes to use it for the sicknesses and diseases herein mentioned.*[34] These properties of rosemary were known in Spain, as is demonstrated by a manuscript held at the University of Salamanca, titled simply *Propiedades del romero*, which has been analysed by Marcela López.[35]

It may come as a surprise to some readers to find technical medical language concerning medicine and its application employed in an

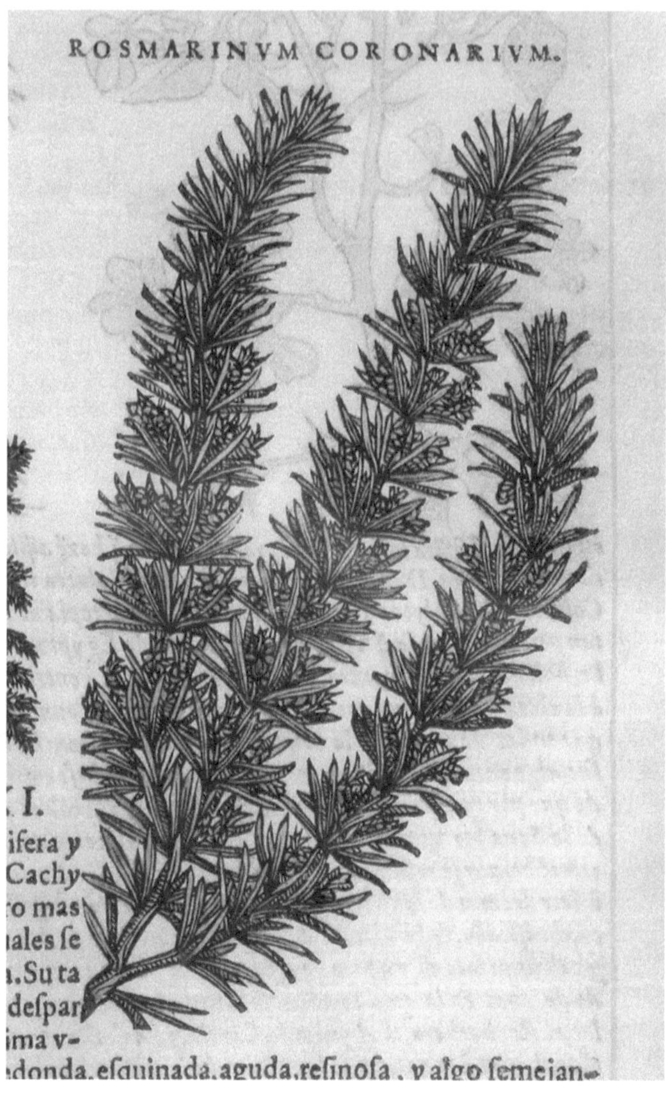

Figure 2. *Rosmarinus coronarium* (rosemary) woodcut engraving from Andrés de Laguna, *Pedacio Diascórides Anazarbeo* (1555), fol. 320, in a hand-coloured exemplar prepared specially for King Philip II (R/8514, Biblioteca Nacional de España, Madrid).

explicitly moral context. Witness this exchange from Calderón de la Barca's *La exaltación de la Cruz*:

ZACARIAS: Siendo la ley verdadera,
¿quien puede dudar que es Dios
Divina Jurisprudencia?
ANASTASIO: ¿Hay Medicina?
ZACARIAS: No solo
como Autor della, la engendra;
pero aplica los remedios
de vida, y salud eterna.[36]

Here God appears as divine Doctor as well as divine Judge. This characterization becomes more understandable when we realize that according to the statutes passed by the Fourth Lateran Council (1215), sin could be responsible for producing literal physical disease:

> Infirmity of the body sometimes derives from sin, as Our Lord said to the sick man he had healed, "Go and sin no more, that worse not happen to you" [John 5:14]. Thus with the present decree we establish and severely command the physicians of the body that, when they are called by the sick, they should first of all admonish and induce them to call the physicians of the soul, so that, after the spiritual health [*salus*] of the sick has been attended to, recourse can be had to the remedies of corporeal medicine with greater efficacy; for, in fact, when the cause is taken away, the effect ceases as well [*cum causa cessante cesset effectus*].[37]

According to Anthony Cascardi, this supernatural causation for natural illness extends in multiple discourses of Golden Age Spain beyond the physical body of the individual believer to the health of the body politic:

> The question of the health of the republic draws as well on a range of contemporary thinkers who deploy medical language in order to establish parallels between the health of the individual and the health of the state. Concerns over the spiritual health of readers were prominent in the writings of Alfonso de Madrigal (especially in *De optima politia* [*The Ideal Government*]), Miguel Sabuco, Juan Huarte de San Juan, Gallego de la Serna, and Antonio de Guevara.[38]

I have examined a similar phenomenon, adjusted slightly to accommodate an additional layer of discourse from treatises on demonic possession, in "Exorcizing the Body Politic."[39]

Within this broader context connecting Virtue metaphorically to medicine – and, by extension, medicine to politics – specific correspondences were established by means of which a select Virtue became the designated antidote for a certain Vice. We shall now turn to this specific subcategory of moral (as it was conflated with medical) discourse.

II Correspondences of Virtue to Vice

As portrayed in early modern Spanish stage plays, even "secular" ones, the job of the Virtues is to repress Vice – for example, Greed – as in the line where an erstwhile grifter confesses, "yo fuera ladrón, pero he reprimido el vicio con la virtud."[40] Virtues reprimand and punish the Vices' unrestrained freedom ("Políticas, y Morales Virtudes, que reprehenden, y castigan la desahogada libertad de los vicios"),[41] ultimately wiping out sin with heavenly power: "Así muerte al vicio doy con la virtud celestial."[42] In some *comedias* each Vice has a corresponding Virtue, for example: "a la ira la templanza, y a la crueldad la prudencia."[43] Likewise, in Calderón de la Barca's *La primer flor del Carmelo*, the young David, future king of Israel, cries, "venza mi humildad de Saúl la ira."[44] At first glance, these pairings appear to be mathematically precise: "hay contra siete Vicios, siete Virtudes."[45] This neat, orderly scheme echoes iconographical programs such as an illuminated manuscript of *Speculum Virginum* in the Walters Art Museum in Baltimore which shows a matching pair of a tree of Vices and a tree of Virtues on facing pages (Figure 3 a and b).

The very titles of some early modern Spanish stage plays illustrate these pairings of a Virtue with its corresponding Vice. This occurs, for example, with Pride and Humility in Lope de Vega's *El triunfo de la humildad, y soberbia abatida*. The same is true for Tirso de Molina's *La lealtad contra la envidia*, the third and final part of Tirso's Pizarro trilogy based on the Pizarro brothers' conquest of Peru. The "Envy" of the title arises in the first act when Gonzalo Vivero and Fernando Pizarro are enamoured of the same woman, Isabel Mercado. Gonzalo challenges Fernando to a duel but is won over by his chivalry, courtesy, and Prudence and decides to accompany him to Peru instead. He renounces their dispute, and the two become fast friends. This play, which thematizes Loyalty as antidote for Envy, ends on a note of wishful thinking:

Figure 3. (a and b) A matching pair of a tree of Vices and a tree of Virtues, from a manuscript of *Speculum Virginum* (Walters Art Museum ms. W. 72, fols 25v–26r, ca. 1200).

"pues vence la lealtad siempre a la embidia."[46] Would that things were really that simple.

In point of fact, there seems to be no agreement regarding which Virtue might serve as a suitable antidote for a given Vice. The "necessary" or accepted medieval correspondence between specific Virtues and Vices must be called into question for the early modern period. Is Patience really the only available antidote for Anger? Would not Temperance work as well? Is one Virtue sometimes needed to balance out another one, as with the scales of Justice and Mercy which appear as a symbol carved in stone outside the United States Supreme Court? This literary ambiguity finds a parallel in early modern medicine, as it was debated among doctors whether a remedy prescribed for one patient would ever mirror exactly the solution stipulated for another. In the words of medical doctor and Augustinian priest Agustín Farfán, author of *Tratado breve de Medicina* (1579): "Y como las complexiones de los hombres son diversas, así con diversos remedios se han de curar."[47]

At this point it will be helpful to look at actual early modern remedies, or antidotes, and their prescriptions to see both how they were formulated and by whom. Just how precise were these recipes? In the process we can hope to learn something about early modern mindsets regarding problem-solving in the medical as well as moral arenas.

III Antidotes

Existing records of actual antidotes from the early modern period in Spain range from stand-alone works, such as Álvaro de Castro's *Antidotarium*, written ca. 1500–20 by a Jewish *converso* medical doctor from Toledo and grounded in Arabic tradition, to chapters on antidotes that formed a part of more general treatises on medicine. For example, Bernardino de Laredo's *Modus faciendi cum ordine medicandi* (1527) contains an ample *antidotario*, while Luis Lobera's "Antidotario muy singular" in his *Remedio de cuerpos humanos* (1542) contains some 300 recipes with exact ingredients and dosage information. Eventually these isolated chapters led to genuine works of pharmacology published under the label of *concordias*.[48]

Illustrative of this trend is the *Concordia apothecariorum Barchinonensium* (1511), an early recipe book for apothecaries which could be considered the first Spanish pharmacopia (Figure 4).[49] Further instalments in this genre included Pedro Benet Mateu's *Liber in examen apothecariorum* (1521), Nicolás Monardes's *Diálogo llamado pharmacodilosis* (1536),

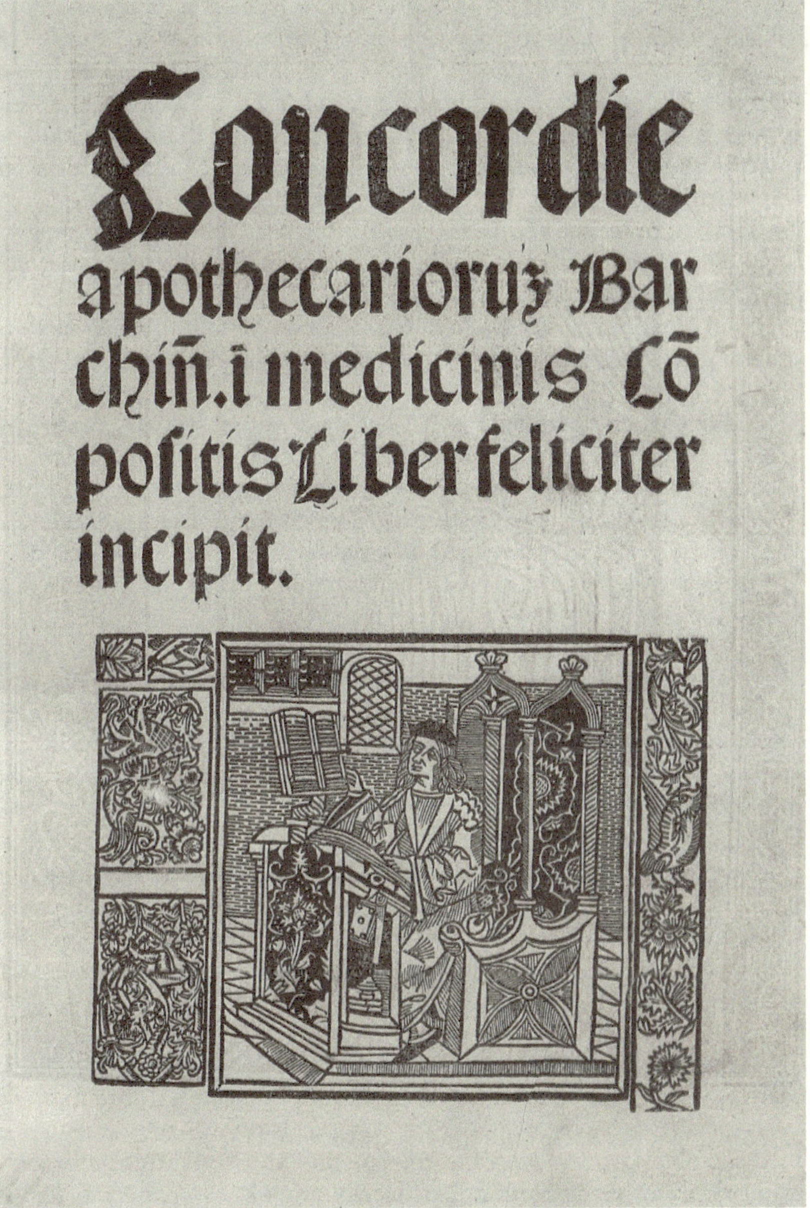

Concordie
apothecarioruʒ Bar
chiñ. ĩ medicinis Cō
positis Liber feliciter
incipit.

Figure 4. Title page, *Concordia apothecariorum Barchinonensium* (1511) (photo courtesy of Museu de la Farmàcia Catalana, Universitat de Barcelona).

Luis de Oviedo's *Méthodo de la colección y reposición de las medicinas simples, y de su corrección y preparación* (1581), Simón de Tovar's *De compositorum medicamentorum examine novum methodum* (1586), and Antonio Castell's *Theórica y práctica de boticarios* (1592). Interestingly for our purposes here, the word *Virtue* appears in these medical and pharmaceutical treatises to refer to the potency or effectiveness of a medicine, as in the phrases *virtudes curativas* or *virtudes medicinales*. For example, see the title page of Nicolás Monardes's *Primera y Segunda y Tercera Partes de la Historia Medicinal* (Seville: Alonso Escribano, 1574) (Figure 5).

Ángel Martínez describes how these books came into being right at the point where pharmacology was organizing itself as a profession:

> Constituídos en la segunda mitad del siglo XIII en distintas regiones españolas los Gremios de Boticarios y Especieros, que no fueron suficientes para ordenar la labor profesional, ciertamente anárquica en aquellos tiempos, se transformaron a mediados del siglo XV en Colegios (Collegium Apothecariorum), que alcanzaron especialmente en el entonces Reino de Cataluña y Aragón elevado nivel científicoprofesional, al que no llegaron, salvo rara excepción, los escasos coetáneos extranjeros.[50]

He infers how primitive pharmacists, working before the age of print, had relied on manuscript *antidotarios* or *recetarios*, of which he mentions several.[51] Martínez describes the freedom with which the authors and users of these treatises tweaked existing recipes, much the way we might do with Grandma's cookbook:

> Al componer sus fórmulas el farmacéutico gozaba de cierta libertad, haciéndolo según su particular apego a uno u otro afamado autor, y llegando incluso a modificarlas según criterio propio, como puede observarse por las abundantes notas marginales y correcciones que se encuentran en recetarios antiguos.[52]

Part of the problem was that at least until the late sixteenth century, there was no uniform system of weights and measures in use in Spain even for quantities of substances where precision was needed, such as medicines.[53] Martínez describes the reaction of distrust this haphazard improvisation on the part of pharmacists provoked in patients: "lo que traía aparejada una desconfianza del enfermo y del médico contra el boticario y sus pócimas, debido a la frecuencia de los desiguales efectos de éstas."[54] This chaotic situation was what led the recently constituted

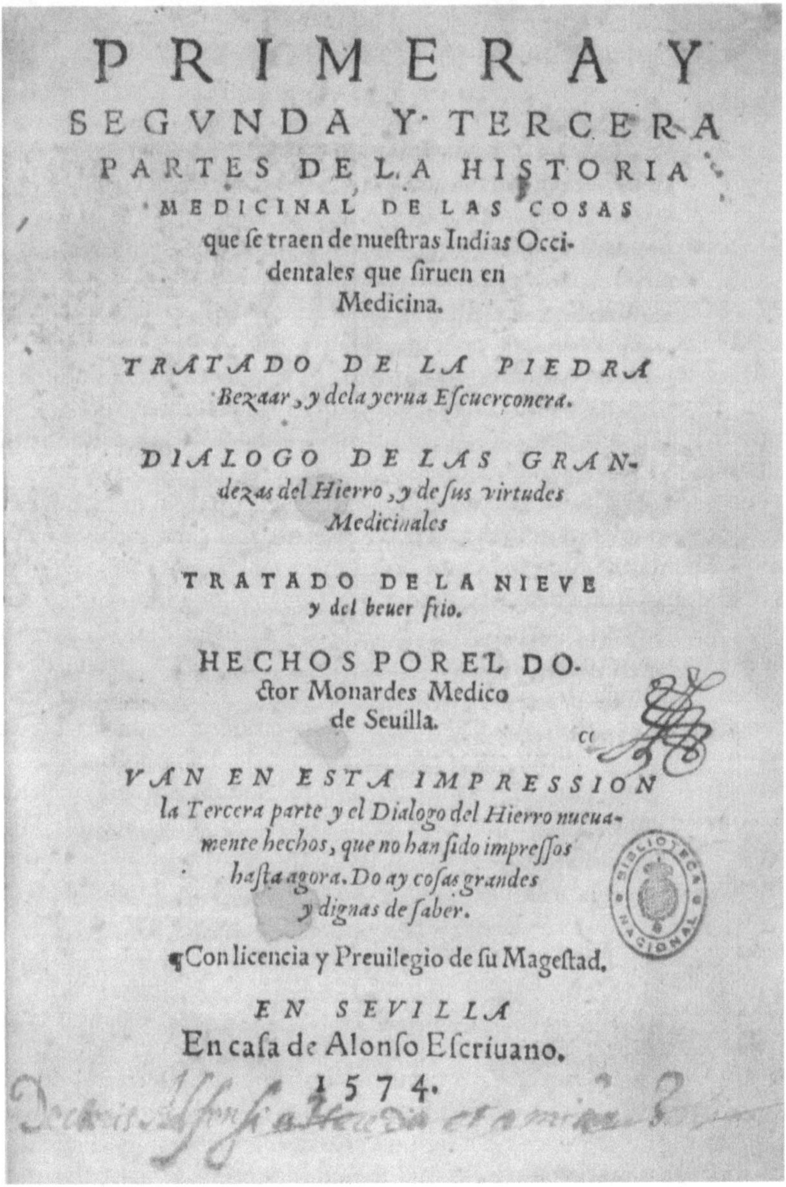

PRIMERA Y SEGVNDA Y TERCERA PARTES DE LA HISTORIA MEDICINAL DE LAS COSAS que ſe traen de nueſtras Indias Occidentales que ſiruen en Medicina.

TRATADO DE LA PIEDRA Bezaar, y dela yerua Eſcuerçonera.

DIALOGO DE LAS GRANdezas del Hierro, y de ſus virtudes Medicinales

TRATADO DE LA NIEVE y del beuer frio.

HECHOS POR EL DOctor Monardes Medico de Seuilla.

VAN EN ESTA IMPRESSION la Tercera parte y el Dialogo del Hierro nueuamente hechos, que no han ſido impreſſos haſta agora. Do ay coſas grandes y dignas de ſaber.

¶Con licencia y Preuilegio de ſu Mageſtad.

EN SEVILLA
En caſa de Alonſo Eſcriuano.
1574.

Figure 5. Title page, Nicolás Monardes *Primera y Segunda y Tercera Partes de la Historia Medicinal* (Seville: Alonso Escribano, 1574) (R.Micro/6026, Biblioteca Nacional de España, Madrid).

Colleges of Apothecaries to commission these manuscripts – later often printed in multiple editions – in the first place:

> Este desorden determinó a los Cónsules o directivos de los recién constituidos "Collegium Apothecariorum," allá por fines del siglo XV y principios del XVI, a encargar a uno o varios de sus miembros la confección de un libro con el conjunto de fórmulas de más aprecio y uso en la época, así como reconocimiento de materiales y sus falsificaciones.[55]

The recognized potential for falsification here is disturbing, given the possible consequences for patients' health. The scarcity or prohibitive cost[56] of ingredients offers only limited excuse; in all likelihood, charlatan practitioners would have been guilty of deliberately altering the ingredients of a recipe for a given drug,[57] either with or without the intention to harm its intended recipient.[58]

The perusal of these medico-cultural artefacts is fascinating, but who used these books in actual practice? Records from the archive of the Gran Hospital Real de Santiago de Compostela, for example, contain verifications of blood purity (*limpieza de sangre*) for individuals occupying the post of pharmacist (*boticario*) at that institution during the seventeenth and eighteenth centuries.[59] For instance, a certain Pedro Fernández y Romero is recorded as having practised the art of pharmacy there by assisting the main pharmacist Alonso Rodríguez in "dispensar y conseguir los medicamentos necesarios para la dicha Botica."[60] Such individuals were known personally to some Golden Age playwrights, as we see from the fact that the father of Joseph de Villaizán (d. 1633), a minor poet of Calderón de la Barca's generation who perhaps studied with him in school, was a pharmacist or *boticario* by profession.[61]

One interesting and possibly unanticipated conflation we find in these documents of moral with medical roles played in society is the practice of pharmacy by monks and /or priests. For example, in the eighteenth century Juan García Cuervo was a *boticario* in the monastery of Cornellana along with Fray Mauro Fernández, chief pharmacist for that institution.[62] This trend is confirmed in surviving objects from material culture such as pharmacy jars marked with the symbol or coat of arms for specific religious orders like the Jesuits (Figure 6). Yet another unanticipated twist is the conflation of at least the rudiments of humanistic education in grammar, rhetoric, etc. with practical training for the future dispensers of drugs. As an illustration, a certain Antonio Ramos Solís was apprenticed by his parents to Fray Thomas González, *monje profesor* and pharmacist at the Real Monasterio de

Figure 6. Pharmacy jar (*albarelo*) with Jesuit emblem, Farmacia del Palacio Real de Madrid, número inv. 10031653 (first half of 18th century) (© Patrimonio Nacional).

Sobrado (Order of Saint Bernard) before moving to Orense, where he studied grammar and continued his apprenticeship under the tutelage of a different, unnamed pharmacist. From there he went to Madrid, where he passed his pharmacy exam. He later went on to apply for the job of chief pharmacist at the Boticario del Real Hospital in Santiago de Compostela, which had been left vacant by the death of his father-in-law Juan López.[63] We may extrapolate from his career path that at least a minimum of grammar school education[64] was necessary for a pharmacist in order to be able to read recipes for mixing medicines together.

In addition to pharmacists / *boticarios*, it is important to examine the practice of actual doctors. Foremost among these was Andrés de Laguna, a medical doctor and humanist who wrote a treatise on the moral Virtues, a gloss on Aristotle titled *De virtutibus*. Laguna (1499–1560), a *converso* born in Segovia, served as personal physician to both Carlos I and Philip II. He was responsible for the translation of Dioscorides's *Materia medica* from Greek into Spanish (Figure 7). In his dedicatory letter to King Philip II, he urges him to patronize the design of a botanical garden where plants might be grown for medicinal purposes, as some of the princes in Italy had already done.[65] King Philip followed his advice, establishing Spain's first botanical garden in Aranjuez,[66] the plants from which he ultimately used to stock the shelves of royal pharmacies, like the new one he was building at the Escorial.[67]

The shrewd Laguna understood the dangers of ambiguous antidotes. The preface to his Spanish translation of Dioscorides has been further translated into English by V. Peset and is worth citing here at some length:

> Therefore, as a grammarian cannot form or understand a sentence without first having a perfect acquaintance with the elements and parts which go to form that sentence, in the same way it is impossible for a physician to prepare any compound medicine which could be of use to bodily health, or even make convenient use of it, if he be not acquainted and experienced in the use of the simple medicines from which the compound ones are derived.[68]

Laguna complains of the "important mistakes which, because of a printer's error, are often found in the prescriptions of the ancients" for mixing compound drugs from simple ingredients and proffers the following concrete examples:

> [L]et us consider the warm Diamargariton which was prescribed by Avicenna and which to this day has cost many lives through its preparation ... If drunk, it is potent enough to kill the strongest elephant ... [*He then*

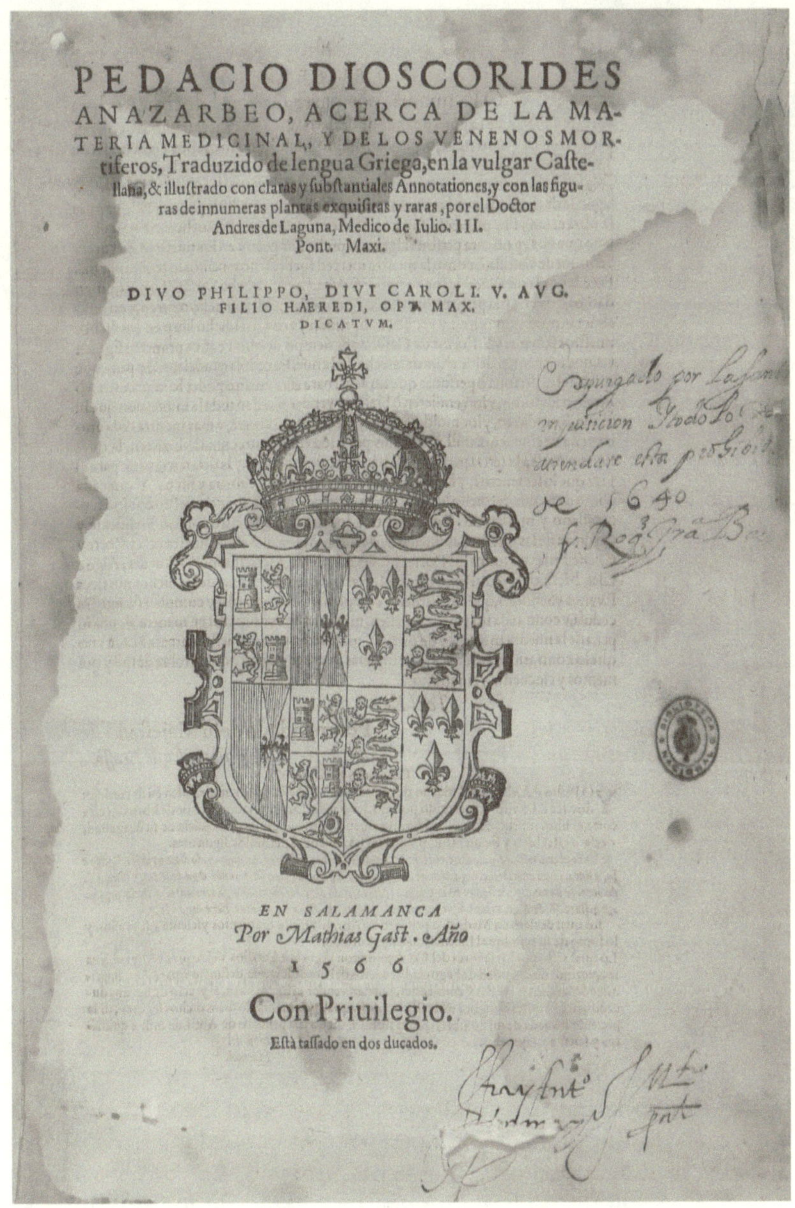

PEDACIO DIOSCORIDES
ANAZARBEO, ACERCA DE LA MA-
TERIA MEDICINAL, Y DE LOS VENENOS MOR-
tiferos, Traduzido de lengua Griega, en la vulgar Caſte-
llana, & illuſtrado con claras y ſubſtantiales Annotationes, y con las figu-
ras de innumeras plantas exquiſitas y raras, por el Doctor
Andres de Laguna, Medico de Iulio. III.
Pont. Maxi.

DIVO PHILIPPO, DIVI CAROLI. V. AVG.
FILIO HAEREDI, OPT. MAX.
DICATVM.

EN SALAMANCA
Por Mathias Gaſt. Año
1 5 6 6

Con Priuilegio.
Eſtà taſſado en dos ducados.

Figure 7. Title page, Andrés de Laguna's *Pedacio Dioscórides Anazarbeo, acerca de la materia medicinal y de los venenos mortíferos* (Salamanca, 1566) (R.Micro/17685, Biblioteca Nacional de España, Madrid).

> *moves on to a drug named Thapsia.*] [I]n certain desperate cases Dioscorides ordains that it should be taken orally when one's disposition is strong enough, so that it will act as a laxative on obstinate and serious humours. Nevertheless, by its nature, it is such a corrosive and effective medicine, that ... once a cunning servant who had no desire to follow his master on his journey but wished to remain near his young lady, sought therefore an excuse and placed this medicine on his leg which in time hardened and swelled up like a boot; of course he succeeded in staying behind ... [I]t did not make sense that such a strong and corrosive medicine that irritated and caused inflammation when used externally could be used to cure internal sickness ... [A]fter having consulted old books, we came across an abandoned manuscript which had been discovered by Maestro Vicenzio, an honorable apothecary of Rome ... [I]n this manuscript, instead of finding Thapsia, we read Capsia [i.e., cinnamon] ... So you can understand in what danger our lives are when they depend on the will of certain idiots who, instead of giving you the antidote that can heal, give you a very strong poison.[69]

Here we find a real-life example of an ambiguous antidote. Although drawn from actual medical practice, this discourse by a renowned medical doctor displays what can only be termed an irresistible narrative drift into the picaresque.

Literary examples of illegible or confusing pharmaceutical recipes may also be found, as in Lope de Vega's *Pobreza no es vileza*, where he satirizes the macaronic Latin typical of these compilations:

> Un latín remendado
> que ningún hombre lo entienda,
> y que a cualquier boticario
> pueda servir de recetas.[70]

The anonymous comic interlude *El hospital de los podridos* speaks of the unfortunate "yerros de médicos y boticarios" caused by these ambiguous recipes, with negative consequences for both health and life.[71] Incompetent pharmacists are likewise satirized in the second colloquy of Antonio de Torquemada, "En que se trata lo que los médicos y boticarios están obligados a hacer para cumplir con sus oficios, y así mismo se ponen las faltas que hay en ellos para daño de los enfermos, con muchos avisos necesarios y provechosos."[72] Further satire of the pharmaceutical profession may be found in Luis Quiñones de Benavente's comic interlude "El Boticario."

These literary artefacts full of scabrous humour may strike us as funny today, but the consequences of irresponsible pharmacists' negligence could be deadly serious. In recognition of this danger, Spanish monarchs as early as Charles V had attempted to regulate the sale of controlled substances:

> The government of Castile forbade the sale of venoms, poisons, or herbs known to be mortally toxic. Some substances, such as scammony, might be sold because they lost their poisonous quality when mixed with other drugs under the expert eye of the apothecary. Throughout the sixteenth century, the crown added items to the list of dangerous substances to be kept out of the public market. Charles V forbade apothecaries and spice merchants from selling soliman and other dangerous substances without a physician's approval. Apothecaries were later prohibited from selling the dangerous substance in any quantity greater than what was necessary for one person. For the sale of other potentially dangerous substances, particularly those involving opiates and preparations of hyacinth, apothecaries were required to mark the containers and "sign the lid of the glass jar, noting the day, month and year when the compound was mixed." Failure to do so would result in a 6,000 *maravedís* fine each time a container was improperly marked.[73]

Further punishment might include banishment of the offending pharmacist from the kingdom for a full year, revocation of his licence to practice pharmacy, or even public burning of illicit drugs in the town square.[74] Official visitations of pharmacies by agents of government oversight were designed to ensure that these rules were followed,[75] although abuses ranged from a pharmacist's conveniently absenting himself on the day of the visitation, to hiding illicit poisons, to even borrowing medicines he might be lacking from another pharmacist to make it look like he had a well-stocked pharmacy and returning them later.[76] Sometimes pharmacists attempted to elude scrutiny by passing the buck: in a 1588 lawsuit in Madrid, local apothecaries filed a complaint against wholesale drug traders before the Tribunal del Protomedicato in which they charged that the traders were selling dangerous substances without a physician's license.[77] But the Spanish government was well aware that the scope of the problem was not limited to the wholesale drug industry. A royal *pragmática* from this time period accuses pharmacists themselves of culpable behaviour: "para que hagan polvos o tabletas purgativas, ni receten, no siendo Médicos aprobados, porque los ignorantes suelen dar estas cosas sin comunicarlo con Médicos y se han visto, y ven muchas muertes, y malos sucesos."[78] In 1563 the Cortes de Madrid gave an unvarnished assessment of this deplorable situation: "en las boticas de estos reinos hay gran descuidado en el hacer y componer las medicinas y se hallan cada día compuestos muy falsos y hay mal recaudo generalmente en las dichas boticas, y pues en ello van las vidas y saludes de las gentes."[79] This judgment merely echoed a complaint lodged in Valladolid in 1548 that the pharmacists "dan unas medicinas por otras, y hacen otros errores de que se sigue gran daño a los que toman las tales medicinas."[80]

Now that we have established the historical reality of ambiguous antidotes, let us explore briefly the duality of poison / cure as explicated by French deconstructionist Jacques Derrida through the Platonic notion of *pharmakon*.

IV *Pharmakon*

In his often-cited work "Plato's Pharmacy," Derrida offers a detailed analysis of the multiple meanings of the Greek word *pharmakon* as it appears in the thought of this ancient philosopher:

> This *pharmakon*, this "medicine," this philter, which acts as both remedy and poison, already introduces itself into the body of the discourse with all its ambivalence. This charm, this spellbinding virtue, this power of fascination, can be – alternatively or simultaneously – beneficent or maleficent. The *pharmakon* would be a *substance* – with all that that word can connote in terms of matter with occult virtues, cryptic depths refusing to submit their ambivalence to analysis, already paving the way for alchemy – if we didn't have eventually to come to recognize it as antisubstance itself.[81]

The ambivalence of the term, as Derrida explains, causes it steadfastly to resist all attempts at translation. The same word used to denote the hemlock drunk by Socrates in order to commit suicide,[82] *pharmakon* has been rendered in various translations *remedy, recipe, poison,* or *drug.*[83] Derrida makes clear that the ambivalence he recognizes in the word as a deconstructionist is not a case of his imposing postmodern undecidability onto an ancient text; rather, the ambiguity is already there due to Plato's own ambivalence:

> The remedy is disturbing in itself. One must indeed be aware of the fact that Plato is suspicious of the *pharmakon* in general, even in the case of

> drugs used exclusively for therapeutic ends, even when they are wielded with good intentions, and even when they are effective. *There is no such thing as a harmless remedy.*[84]

He goes on to describe – with ample grounding in ancient medicine – how any drug was seen to interfere with the body's natural function and was therefore viewed as foreign or alien to good health.[85] It goes without saying that according to this theory, the same exact drug, applied in different quantities or in different contexts, may on two separate occasions produce very different (even opposite) results. *Pharmakon* is an ancient concept employed by Plato, Derrida, and other philosophers[86] to describe processes operating within classical medicine but also, metaphorically, such varied activities as writing, masturbating,[87] or committing suicide.

We do not have to look far within the early modern period to find ambivalent substances understood in terms of the *pharmakon* – the ultimate ambiguous antidote.[88] Our efforts to do so should not be judged anachronistic, considering the fact that Plato's ideas were hugely popular in Renaissance Spain.[89] A common Spanish proverb to this day states that "todo mal se cura con otro semejante," and this aphorism was repeated during the Golden Age.[90] One specific example discussed previously in this chapter, the herb rosemary, was believed to possess curative properties,[91] such as healing a snake's bite, but could also kill an adder if placed inside its hole.[92] Supposedly a branch of rosemary placed above a door's lintel could prevent snakes and scorpions from entering one's house.[93] The pharmacopias we referenced earlier contained recipes for poisons as well as medicines; for example, the doctor we met previously, Andrés de Laguna, makes allusion to both substances on the title page for his *Pedacio Dioscórides Anazarbeo, acerca de la materia medicinal y de los venenos mortíferos* (Salamanca, 1566) (see again Figure 7). In this treatise, Laguna specifically acknowledges the fine line between poison and antidote when he laments the danger of administering excessive doses of a prescribed medicine. He says of doctors who do this, "no menos se debe huir [de ellos] que de la pestilencia."[94]

These ideas find their way likewise into early modern drama. In Shakespeare's *Romeo and Juliet*, Friar Lawrence delivers the following speech about medicinal properties of herbs:

> Within the infant rind of this weak flower
> poison hath residence and medicine power;
> for this, being smelt, with that part cheers each part,

being tasted, stays all senses with the heart.
Two such opposed kings encamp them still
in man as well as herbs, grace and rude will;
and where the worser is predominant,
full soon the canker death eats up that plant.[95]

We should recall that this same Friar Lawrence was the source of the sleeping potion drunk by Juliet, though not of the poison swallowed by Romeo (the source for this was an unnamed Apothecary, a shadowy figure to whom both Plato and Derrida would have attributed the similarly ambiguous term *pharmakos*).[96]

In Spanish drama, too, we find multiple permutations of the *pharmakon*, as when Eco in Calderón de la Barca's *Eco y Narciso* declares, "lo que fue veneno en ellos será medicina en él."[97] This line shows the acute recognition that what could be poison for one patient might prove to be salutiferous medicine for another. Likewise, in Calderón de la Barca's *Las tres justicias en una* we find a description of a rare and exotic plant which boasts the strange property of healing a wound if there is one, or producing a wound if there was not one before:

Una planta oí que nace
tan rara y tan exquisita,
que donde hay llaga, la quita,
y donde no la hay, la hace.[98]

This same plant is mentioned in at least one of Calderón de la Barca's other plays, *El galán fantasma*.[99]

Such lines bespeak the very real possibility that Virtue may turn to venom: "tan alta Virtud, en vez de antídoto, ser veneno."[100] There is not just the danger that medicinal substances or antidotes will be mistaken, but that they will actually produce the opposite effect of the one desired: "con él hierba animada, que infiel *le vicie de su Virtud*."[101] This last line contains within it grammatically the infiltration of Virtue by Vice.

With such confusion reigning about ambiguous antidotes, it should come as no surprise to find playwrights exploiting the dramatic potential of medicine which actually makes the patient more ill. A prime example is the play *Enfermar con el remedio*, printed as a *suelta* (Valladolid: A. del Riego, 1730[?]) and currently held by the Wilson Rare Books Library at the University of Minnesota. The title page indicates collaborative authorship with the phrase "de tres ingenios," but Don Cruickshank confirms that Calderón de la Barca wrote Act 1, Luis Vélez de Guevara wrote Act 2, and Jerónimo Cáncer wrote Act 3.[102] This single play by itself demonstrates the prevalence of this theme and knowledge of its particulars by at least three mainstream dramatists. Lope de Vega had rehearsed this trope earlier in *La francesilla*: "Mira lo que haces, / que a veces el antídoto es veneno."[103] Likewise, in Tirso's *La lealtad contra la envidia* we see the concept of the antidote causing more damage than the original illness when Fernando says, "tal vez en la enfermedad / hace el remedio más daño."[104]

The notion of *pharmakon* held special resonance for an era in which actual poisonings were known to have taken place, particularly to be rid of a political rival or an unwanted heir to the throne.[105] In his biography of Golden Age playwright Pedro Calderón de la Barca, Don Cruickshank recalls rumours that King Philip IV's favourite, the Count-Duke of Olivares, had poisoned the monarch's younger brother, prince Carlos:

> Another of the events of 1632 was the unexpected death, on 31 July, of the Infante Don Carlos, a docile and inneffectual young man who, while Philip IV had no child, could have been Spain's next monarch. Ineffectual he may have been, but he was seen by the anti-Olivares faction as a potential leader, so much so that gossip held that Olivares had had him poisoned.[106]

Whether or not the rumours were true is, for our purposes, irrelevant: their very existence shows a cultural preoccupation with a phenomenon we might reasonably call an early modern form of substance abuse.

As any casual visitor to the pharmacy knew, strong poisons were readily available: "ponzoñas, de tal virtud y poder, que maten a sangre fría."[107] Poison could be imbibed through drinking or else weaponized by placing it on the tips of arrows: "En la hierba de tu flecha hay virtud."[108] The fact that the word *Virtud* is used in these plays to describe the power of venom, or poison, only adds another layer of moral / medical ambiguity: "de repente mata, tal vez un veneno fuerte quita con virtud crecida en un instante la vida."[109]

But a fascinating twist to this slippage between moral and medical language arises with the possibility that a poison might actually *become* a cure, as in the case of "aquel, que está herido de un veneno y otro veneno le cura."[110] For example, the antidote for a snake's bite was actually thought to be a substance found within the vipers themselves: "de víboras se hace triaca para el veneno."[111] In Calderón de la Barca et al.'s *El monstruo de la fortuna* (Juan Pérez de Montalbán wrote only Act II), Felipa explains that she read how a king, who had been warned by astrologers that he risked being poisoned, gradually became accustomed to ingesting poison on purpose in small doses. The unintended result was his addiction.[112] There still exists in Italy today the tradition of the Mithraditic cure, whereby King Mithradites drank a small amount of poison each day to immunize himself because he was afraid of being poisoned.[113] For his part, Jacques Derrida fully anticipated

> this transmutation of the drug into a remedy, of the poison into a counterpoison. Such an operation would not be possible if the *pharmakologos* did not already harbor within itself that complicity of contrary values, and if the *pharmakon* in general were not, prior to any distinction-making, that which, presenting itself as a poison, may turn out to be a cure, may retrospectively reveal itself in the truth of its curative power.[114]

A contributing factor to the popularity of this paradox – a rhetorical trope of which the Baroque age was enamoured anyway[115] – was the appearance of a related story in the Bible. Early modern theatregoers would have found a parallel in the symbolism of the bronze snake lifted up on a staff by Moses at God's command to heal the snake-bitten Israelites who looked at it.[116] *Poison by poison is cured*. This Old Testament episode is thematized by Calderón de la Barca in *La serpiente de metal*, a dramatic meditation on the symbol which, by some accounts, is still used today to represent the medical profession (Figure 8).[117] Then as now, the Old Testament was understood to be a foreshadowing of the New, and Moses' bronze serpent on a pole was a sign of Christ's future crucifixion – a horrible death, or poison, which would nonetheless bring health, or salvation. The ultimate antidote was seen to be Christ's Holy Cross: "la Inmensa crueldad de un Leño. En virtud de sus Virtudes postrar podrás sus Venenos, que no tendrán fuerza alguna."[118] The contorted syntax of these lines labours to express the complicated relationship of Virtue to venom.

An important variation on this theme is the combination of extracts from two different plants which, if taken separately, are poisons; if taken together, however, they blend to form good medicine:

> También de dos peregrinas
> hierbas oí, que en sus senos,
> apartadas son venenos,
> y juntas son medicinas.[119]

Figure 8. Estéban March, *Moisés y la serpiente de metal* (ca. 1650), Colección Banco Santander, Madrid.

Figure 9. Fortitude between Fierceness and Cowardice. The Hague, Museum Meermanno-Westreenianum, 10 D 1, fol. 37r, Book 3.

Figure 10. Temperance between Insensitivity and Intemperance. The Hague, Museum Meermanno-Westreenianum, 10 D 1, fol. 37r, Book 3.

These same two plants resurface again in Calderón de la Barca's *La gran Cenobia*: "Dos plantas hay con divina virtud, que sin duda alguna son veneno cada una, y juntas son medicina."[120] A more extensive passage is devoted to them in the same playwright's *Agradecer y no amar*:

De dos plantas dos venenos
nacen, cada cual impío,
uno ardiente, y otro frío,
están de ponzoña llenos:
si estos se aplican mezclados,
no sólo del corazón
tósigo, epitictima son,
uno con otro templados.[121]

Once again, we find a similar speech in the second part of his *La hija del aire*:

Bien así como dos plantas,
que los naturales cuentan,
que son cada una un veneno,
y estando juntas se templan,
de suerte, que son entonces
la medicina más cierta.[122]

And finally, in his *Peor está que estaba*:

Escriben los naturales
de dos plantas diferentes,
que son venenos, y estando
juntas las dos, de tal suerte
se templan, que son sustento.[123]

This medical topos is starting to look like a literary preoccupation during this time period. Could it be that similar language finds its way into the moral realm? To explore this and other questions, it will be necessary to establish one final key principle that will prove foundational to this discourse: the *aurea mediocritas*, otherwise known to history as the Golden Mean. Its vexed relationship to the *pharmakon* will soon become apparent.

V The Golden Mean

The Golden Mean is an ancient concept which has found its way into the discourse of fields so varied as music, mathematics, journalism, architecture, medicine, psychotherapy, mass media ethics, and the fine arts.[124] The main sources for this classical notion are the Greek philosopher Aristotle and the Roman poet Horace. Aristotle explains the Doctrine of the Mean in his *Nicomachean Ethics*:

> Virtue, then, is a kind of moderation inasmuch as it aims at the mean or moderate amount ... It is a moderation, firstly, inasmuch as it comes in the middle or mean between two vices, one on the side of excess, the other on the side of defect; and secondly, inasmuch as, while these vices fall short of or exceed the due measure in feeling and in action, it finds and chooses the mean, middling, or moderate amount ... The mean as concerns fear and confidence is courage: those that exceed in fearlessness are foolhardy, while those who exceed in fear are cowardly. The mean in respect to certain pleasures and pains is called temperance, while the excess is called profligacy ... In the matter of giving and earning money, the mean is liberality, excess and deficiency are prodigality and miserliness ... With respect to honor and disgrace, the mean is "high-mindedness," the excess might be called vanity, and the deficiency might be called humility or small-mindedness ... We may take the term "wrathful" for the one who is angry in excess, and "timid" for the one who is deficient in anger.[125]

According to this doctrine – which also relates to *eudaimonia* or happiness – Virtue exists as a midpoint between opposing Vices on a continuum or spectrum which is by definition a *pharmakon*, since it encompasses both poison and cure. For example, the quality of being courageous (Fortitude) falls somewhere between "rash" (an excess of courage) and "timid" (not enough courage, which would be a defect). This scheme is surprising because it defies the dualism normally typical of Aristotle and the Scholastics. At least through postmodern lenses, one might even be tempted to see in this search for a "third term" or *aporia* a primitive form of proto-deconstruction.

Another classical source[126] for a variation on this concept is the Roman poet Horace. His *Ode* II.10 immortalized the Golden Mean:

> You will keep your life on a straighter course, Licinius, if you neither push continually out to sea, nor, while cautiously avoiding the storms, hug the

> dangerous shore too closely. The man who cherishes the golden mean maintains a safe position: he escapes the squalor of a tumble-down house and also escapes, because of his moderation, the resentment caused by a mansion. It is more often the tall pine that is shaken by the wind; the collapse is more devastating when high towers fall, and it is the mountain peaks that are struck by lightning. In adversity the well-prepared mind hopes for the opposite situation, is on guard against it in prosperity ... In dire straits show yourself spirited and brave; you will also be wise to shorten your sail when it swells before too favourable a breeze.[127]

This famous formulation by Horace is often referred to by its Latin name, much-debated and frequently misunderstood, which is *aurea mediocritas*.[128]

The third related classical concept which is relevant for our discussion here is Plato's theory of the unity of the Virtues. Virtue conceived as a midpoint between two Vices entails – keeping in mind the correspondences of specific Vices to specific Virtues, noted above – at least two Virtues cooperating with each other to combat each of the Vices at opposite ends of the spectrum. Plato identifies the possibility for this unity:

> The question ... was ... Are the five names of wisdom, temperance, courage, justice, and holiness attached to one thing, or underlying each of these names is there a distinct existence or thing that has its own particular function, each thing being different from the others? ... Each of these names applies to a distinct thing, and ... all these are parts of virtue; not like the parts of gold, which are similar to each other and to the whole of which they are parts, but like the parts of the face, dissimilar to the whole of which they are parts and to each other, and each having a distinct function.[129]

In reference to Golden Age Spain, Cascardi summarizes Plato's position on this question: "there can be no exercise of any one virtue that would ... obviate the others. The unity of the virtues is required."[130] In other words, the Virtues should work harmoniously in concert with one another.

These ideas found much currency in a wide variety of discourses produced during Spain's Golden Age. In his *Empresas políticas*, the political philosopher Diego Saavedra Fajardo makes specific reference to Aristotle's Doctrine of the Mean: "A ella se reduce toda la sciencia de reinar, que huye de las extremidades, y consiste en el medio de las cosas, donde tienen su esfera las virtudes."[131] The satirist and lyric poet Francisco de Quevedo does the same in his *Sueño del alguacil endemoniado*, where he writes: "Todo el infierno es figuras, y hay muchos porque el sumo poder, libertad y mando les hace sacar a las virtudes de su medio y llegar los vicios a su extremo."[132] The Jesuit allegorist Baltasar Gracián, often called the theorist of Baroque literary *conceptismo*, employs similar language in his *Agudeza y arte de ingenio* to describe the coincidence of opposites, or *coincidentia oppositorum*. For him the goal is to "hallar correspondencia y materia de concordar los extremos repugnantes ... unir a fuerza de discurso dos contradictorios extremos."[133] Jeremy Robbins notes that the Golden Mean makes an even more explicit appearance in Gracián's creative work *El Criticón*, including a scene where the travelling characters Critilo and Andrenio come to the juncture of three roads and decide to take the middle path:

> The Aristotelian view expounded in the *Nicomachean Ethics* of virtue as lying between two extremes is raised explicitly in this episode from the "Entrada del Mundo," with "fortaleza" being the middle way between the two opposing vices, "temeridad" and "cobardía."[134]

Finally, this discourse of the Golden Mean was also present in specifically spiritual contexts, such as the (also Jesuit) Francisco Núñez de Cepeda's *Idea de el buen pastor*. In this text, we find an impassioned plea for the unity of the Virtues in a well-ordered republic:

> Forma la República bien concertada de las *virtudes* un coro suave, y armonioso de voces, tanto más sonoro a los oídos divinos, cuanto tienen entre sí mayor correspondencia; y como las cuerdas bien templadas del instrumento una sola que se toque, resuenan todas, así al compás del ejercicio de una *virtud*, echan las otras sus voces, resuena cada una en su proporción, y de todas juntas resulta una música agradable.[135]

Thus we see that Virtue was conceived at least in part according to classical ideals by a wide variety of authors in early modern Spain.

It is logical, then, to find references to classical, pagan notions of Virtue in Spain's early modern drama. The foremost Spanish playwright Lope de Vega even alludes to the Golden Mean in his *Arte nuevo de hacer comedias*:

> Que dorando el error del vulgo quiero
> deciros de qué modo las querría,
> ya que seguir el arte no hay remedio
> *en estos dos extremos dando un medio.*[136]

We encounter multiple instances in the plays themselves where explicit mention is made of this *medio*, or Golden Mean. For instance, in Lope de Vega's *El perro del hortelano* and *El verdadero amante* we find the phrases "da un medio a tantos extremos" and "buen medio queréis hacer de dos extremos viciosos."[137] In case we were confused about the context, many plays repeat this language specifically with regard to ethics and moral notions of Virtue and Vice. For example, "En medio está la virtud, si son vicios los extremos," and "si en estos peligros dos quieres hallar el remedio, la virtud consiste en medio."[138] The *comedias* point to the Golden Mean as a place of rest and tranquility, as when one character says to another: "Tu virtud el medio sea en que mi descanso viva."[139] Sometimes the Golden Mean is represented by a specific action, such as marriage: "que sea el medio de estos extremos el casarnos, que es virtud."[140]

The surprising ramification of this concept is that in the case of Virtue, it is literally possible to have too much of a good thing, "de lo que es virtud hacer exceso."[141] This line occurs in a play whose very title is illustrative of the Golden Mean, Guillén de Castro's paradoxical *La justicia en la piedad*. We find this idea repeated in the lines "Es más que virtud, extremo" and "No es bien, que sea virtud a tales extremos."[142] The plays warn repeatedly of negative consequences if this balance is not respected: "Porque todos los extremos la virtud dañan y alteran."[143] Any type of extreme has the potential to damage and alter Virtue. Golden Age theatregoers were urged to avoid this scenario: "huye excesos, pues que con la virtud podrás templarlos."[144] *Comedia* characters even make reference to ancient philosophers to support this idea; one of them asks, "¿No dicen los Filósofos que tiene el medio la virtud, si son viciosos los dos extremos?"[145]

Addicted to Baroque displays of ingenuity, early modern Spanish playwrights appeared to enjoy playing with the dualism implicit in this formulation. At times the two poles of Vices metaphorically became the two worlds of Spain's empire: "Dos mundos tiene por extremos la virtud, que en ella véis."[146] But this math only works with two Vices assumed to be polar opposites; introduce a third Vice, and the equation falters: "Aunque sois tres, sois tres extremos, cuya virtud nunca vimos."[147] There can be no middle if the endpoints are three. In order to adjust the proportions, dramatists had recourse to the ideal of balance as it could be measured with a scale, as in "sienten conmigo cuantos con desapasionado juicio miran y censuran las virtudes con la balanza de la razón."[148] Who knew that Virtues could be censured?

This verbal picture is repeated in early modern dramas from other European countries, as when Iago says to Roderigo in Shakespeare's *Othello*:

> If the [beam] of our lives had not one scale of reason to poise another of sensuality, the blood and baseness of our natures would conduct us to most prepost'rous conclusions.[149]

What seems desirable here is some combination – just the right mixture – of Virtue with Vice.

The embrace by Golden Age playwrights of these pagan ideas led to some bizarre oxymorons, which once again fit right in with the Baroque age's love of paradox.[150] The yoking of opposite qualities together, where a Virtue modifies or moderates a Vice to which it is neighbour, is evident is such expressions as "pereza diligente."[151] Some of these oxymorons even appear in the titles to these plays, such as Guillén de Castro's afore-mentioned *La justicia en la piedad* or the same dramatist's *La humildad soberbia*. Specific pairings seem to gain currency as we see Virtues accompanied by their "antidotal" Vice; for example, "pues a un tiempo mismo mezclas a la ira la templanza, y a la crueldad la prudencia."[152] These lines appear in Francisco de Rojas Zorrilla's *El más impropio verdugo por la más justa venganza*, a play whose very title carries within it the paradox of a "just" revenge. Some lines from these plays even suggest that this recipe for Virtue seasoned by Vice is a uniquely Spanish combination: "pero el que de España veo pone al deseo templanza, al amor desconfianza, y al valor tal cobardía."[153] What are we to make of these unseemly juxtapositions?

A method to this madness may be found in the contention that Vice makes Virtue shine more brightly by comparison, like a foil. We see this paradigm at work in the lines,

> No cabrán en mis palabras
> afectos para decir
> la merecida alabanza
> de este Príncipe, el valor,
> la osadía, la templanza,
> el arrojo, la cordura,
> la modestia, la arrogancia;
> mezcladas unas con otras,
> que hacen la virtud más clara.[154]

So – arrogance actually makes modesty shine all the more brightly? We might be tempted to think this playwright made a mistake, or that this characterization of Virtue was merely an aberration, until we discover that the same formulation is repeated in multiple contexts by many different dramatists. For example, "Todos los opuestos lucen de los opuestos al viso, la virtud virtud no fuera, a no ser contrario el vicio."[155] Virtue and Vice need each other. If there were no dark night, the sun would not shine: "si no hubiera noche oscura no fuera el Sol estimado, la virtud a no haber vicios, ¿tuviera quilates tantos?"[156] One character even declares bluntly, "no hay virtud sin contrastes."[157]

The Golden Mean makes its way into *comedia* titles too, such as Guillén de Castro's *El vicio en los extremos*. This play contains numerous instances of the application of this principle: "Virtud es vencerse a sí, mas ni tanto, ni tan poco"; "la virtud se aparta de los extremos"; and "consiste en el medio la virtud."[158] Interestingly, this work also contains an exception to this rule, namely the case of paternal love: "en el amor paternal cualquier extremo es virtud."[159] Apparently one can never love a child too much.

Aware of the theatrical implications of this philosophy in terms of its inherent visual appeal, playwrights exploited to full effect the Golden Mean's ekphrastic potential. One particularly inventive character declares that he wants to have the Golden Mean placed as a motto upon his coat of arms:

> CONDE DE PALMA: El medio busco yo.
> DIEGO DE LA CERDA: Virtud es ésa.
> CONDE DE PALMA: Éste quiero en la corte por empresa.[160]

We need look no further than contemporaneous iconography to guess what his proposed coat of arms might have looked like. It is common to find in manuscript illuminations a visual depiction of a specific Virtue between two Vices, such as Fortitude between Fierceness and Cowardice (Figure 9) or Temperance between Insensitivity and Intemperance (Figure 10).

As also happened in other intersections of theatrical practice with the graphic arts – for example, the appearance of costumes derived from specific emblem books in the *autos sacramentales* – [161] these playwrights anchored their directions for placement of characters on the stage within established iconographical depictions of the Virtues. For instance, Calderón de la Barca's *¿Quién hallará mujer fuerte?* shows a visual picture of Virtues balancing one another. The stage directions read, "una parte, lo más distante que puedan, Debora, Justicia, y Prudencia; y a otro Jaél, Fortaleza, y Templanza, y en medio la Sabiduría." In the same play we are supposed to see the typical system of moveable carts: "Carros, y veénse en el uno la Justicia, y la Prudencia, y en el otro la Templanza, y la Fortaleza."[162] Riding in these carts are two pairs of Virtues, clearly designed to balance each another out.

This same dramatic technique occurs also in less serious or religious works to indicate the placement of characters onstage. In Lope de Vega's *El anzuelo de Fenisa*, witness this exchange among Celia, Fabio and Bernardo:

> CELIA: Los medios son bien honrosos.
> BERNARDO: Somos extremos viciosos, y nuestra virtud te hacemos.

The clear implication is that she is to stand between the two men. In case there was any doubt, the stage directions specify, "Cógenla en medio."[163] A humorous variant of this scenario occurs when one character says to another, "tú eres la virtud, el medio, y yo el extremo vicioso."[164] These implied stage directions likewise would have indicated the placement of characters onstage. In similar fashion, in Calderón de la Barca's *loa* for *El diablo mudo* we find a staging of the Supreme Tribunal where the allegorical figures Justice and Pity will both hear a given case. A line from the *loa* explains, "que rigor sumo se llama el sumo derecho de la Justicia, y que debe templarse con los afectos de la Piedad."[165] Once again we are confronted with a verbal / visual depiction of the Golden Mean: "quede la Piedad en medio."[166]

These playwrights reinforced their message with a visual picture just in case it was not clear enough: the place for Virtue is in the middle. Virtue should not be too extreme. But how can one find the midpoint between two Vices with absolutely mathematical precision? Is it not feasible that most attempts at virtuous action would err on one side or the other? And does that not make Virtue potentially a *pharmakon*, or ambiguous antidote – at once poison and cure?

It is my contention that Virtue is portrayed so ambiguously in early modern Spanish drama that the notion of *pharmakon* is not merely one possible way to characterize it, but in fact the only one that makes sense, given the overwhelming preponderance of evidence. Now that we have examined metaphors for Virtue in a medical context, more-or-less exact correspondences of Virtues as antidotes for specific Vices, the ambiguity of antidotes in their conceptualization as *pharmakon*, and classical / pagan notions of Virtue epitomized by the Golden Mean, let us turn to some specific Virtues and their representations on the early modern Spanish stage. Individual chapters devoted to Justice, Fortitude, Charity, Chastity, and Prudence will allow us to explore the inner workings of this moral / medical model as it was deployed within actual theatrical practice. In the process, we can hope to learn something about early modern morality and more specifically, the incursion of pagan notions of Virtue into the Christian humanist synthesis. This, in turn, will enable us to explore larger questions in our conclusion about Spain's surprisingly active participation in the recuperation of secular, classical ethics which has come to be considered a hallmark of the larger European Renaissance.

1 Blind Justice

Justice ... is not a virtue like the others. Rather, it is the boundary that defines them, the principle that allows them to coexist.

– André Comte-Sponville[1]

Many thinkers throughout history have claimed for Justice a certain pride of place among the Virtues – a position I share, which is why I have chosen to treat it first. But there seems to be no consensus about exactly why Justice is so special. Elaine Scarry sees justice or fairness as related to beauty in its "symmetry of everyone's relation to one another"[2] and makes reference to a statement inspired by Aristotle that justice is like a perfect cube – i.e., equal in all directions. André Comte-Sponville suggests property is not the sole object of justice, as Hume thinks, but instead quotes Spinoza in claiming that "Justice consists in the habitual rendering to every man his lawful due."[3] In 1525 an Italian writer and future ambassador named Galeazzo Flavio Capra made the odd, even diabolical comparison: "la iustizia, quale così tra le virtù tiene il primo luogo come faccia tra le minori stelle el risplendente Lucifero."[4] Considering that the comparison is to Lucifer's leadership of the rebel angels, this is hardly the unambiguously positive endorsement we might have expected.

Most theorists agree that there are at least two kinds of Justice: conformity to the law (*jus* in Latin) and equality or proportionality. To pose this problem in terms already familiar to readers of my book *Sins of the Fathers*, legality is Justice in its more communal form (for the *polis*), while equality works to promote Justice among individuals.[5] Aside from its proliferating forms or subcategories, there is another very good reason to consider Justice first in this analysis – namely, that early modern Spaniards also did so. As Don Cruickshank notes, "Spanish political philosophers of Calderón de la Barca's day saw Justice as the chief princely virtue."[6] Let us consider, then, both how Justice is portrayed in the drama and what those references can tell us in broader terms about how Justice was conceptualized more generally in Spain during this time period, keeping in mind that literature just as often refracts (as opposed to reflects) the experiences of real people in the course of everyday life.

Justice is intimately associated with law in early modern theatre: "es derecha justicia, si admitidas son las Leyes."[7] In fact, in one literary formulation, Justice is the soul and form of law: "fuerzas de ley, en cuanto participa la razón de la justicia, que es su alma, y forma."[8] Laws are said to have given Justice birth: "leyes el mundo inventó, y de las leyes nació la justicia, que es virtud."[9] We are reminded not so subtly in these lines from a stage play of Justice's status as a moral Virtue.

Law is intimately bound up with a related concept, *derechos*, or rights, which the law is supposed to guarantee against tyranny: "Leyes la justicia escribe, que llama el mundo derechos, y contra tiranos pechos."[10] These rights might include privileges such as primogeniture, which allowed the firstborn to inherit the majority of his father's estate ("De la primogenitura de Jacob conoceréis la justicia que tenéis, viendo que el cielo procura restituirle el derecho"),[11] or the right to rule: "Yo me quito esta corona, porque es razón, y justicia, que corone tu cabeza como a Reina de Castilla."[12] Here a noblewoman named Leonor voluntarily gives up the crown of the title in Lope de Vega's *La corona merecida* because Justice dictates that Sol should rightfully wear it instead.

Literal props appear to accompany the allegorical figure of Justice onstage in order to provide her with some stage business. Thus we find stage directions buried within lines of dialogue, such as "Tú, Justicia, serás quien todas las Cédulas saques," in what was clearly a cue to take out sheaves of documents, perhaps replete with wax seals, upon which laws might appear to be written.[13] This action really happened in Spain whenever the *letrados* were consulted regarding the interpretation of a given law perceived to be in conflict with other laws. In a fact acknowledged onstage which is particularly relevant for our study of Virtue, these learned men were often priests: "ciertos frailes Franciscos [*sic*], y Agustinos que anoche su justicia consultaban, y otros letrados de este nombre dignos."[14]

Specific laws scrutinized by the *letrados* included those which stipulated a certain punishment for a particular crime. Punishments were deemed acceptable as permitted by law, which might mitigate a ruler's harsh tendencies: "corra con todo el severo rigor de Justicia, venga, según conforme a Derecho."[15] Presumably a ruler's power would thus be limited to inflict only those punishments allowed within the scope of legality (although we will see how this theoretical provision was often abrogated in practice). This was especially true for laws governing the death penalty, as in "que muera es justicia, en cuya obligación la otra ley se ejecuta,"[16] or some other punishment for homicide, as in "la muerte de Octavio ... la justicia le castigue conforme las leyes mandan."[17]

Representations of Justice on the early modern Spanish stage do not just involve *letrados* generally, but governing bodies more specifically. One such governing body explicitly invoked was the Senate. While this entity per se did not exist in Spain, it did in other theatrical settings such as classical Rome and republican Venice. Here we find proud echoes of Spain's Roman origins, as in "pienso hacer justicia, como si fuese un Senador Romano."[18] In Lope de Vega's *El piadoso veneciano* Sidonio predicts to Gerardo, "bien sé que la justicia del severo Senado hará muy presto venganza en mi cabeza."[19] Instead of a Senate, in Spain there was a king's council ("justicia es el Consejo de los Reyes") which traditionally had its seat in Valladolid: "pretendo ir a Valladolid, y en el Consejo Real pedir justicia."[20]

Other fora for exacting Justice were the law courts. Jurisprudence presents herself in Calderón de la Barca's casuistically named *A Dios por razón de Estado* as "Yo la gran Jurisprudencia, que de la Justicia vengo apadrinada."[21] Justice is associated not just with jurisprudence in the abstract, but specifically with tribunals in Madrid: "En Madrid, donde reside la Justicia, y la Clemencia, en sus Doctos Tribunales."[22] Each kingdom had a court system, for example the one in Castile, invoked by name in the apostrophe "Castilla, yo llego al Tribunal recto, y santo de tu justicia."[23] Justice was associated with all the technical aspects of processing cases – "testigos, probanzas, defensiones y sentencias, apelaciones, términos jurídicos ... justicia soy,"[24] including lawyers' fees, as we see in the phrase "pido justicia y costas."[25]

Justice was perceived to be a necessary component of lawsuits, often notable by its absence: "Miente el que el pleito sustenta donde no tiene justicia."[26] The literary treatment of Justice in the *comedias* includes a recognition that sometimes laws might conflict or both parties could be deemed in the right, as in "cada cual fundaba en derecho su justicia."[27] In extreme cases, the judge could be deceived or testimony falsified: "engañados jueces, o fingidos testigos, o sentencia contraria a mi justicia."[28] If the situation became unbalanced enough, Justice was said to abandon her scales: "Pleitos, donde la justicia suelta a veces la balanza."[29]

As is still the case today, most lawsuits then were presided over by a judge or judges, also called *oidores*.[30] A character refers explicitly to this figure when he declares, "luego al punto hize llamar un Juez, como Justicia mayor."[31] But judges were not the only public officials associated with Justice. In addition, in these plays we find references to Justice connected to such multifarious figures as confessors, preachers, and teachers: "en las rectas Varas de Justicia, al ir creciendo, arrimos de Confesores, Predicadores, y Maestros."[32]

With all this flurry of activity happening around it, where was Justice perceived to be physically located in the early modern period in Spain, at least as that perception finds voice in its literature? One answer (among others) is, the royal court: "en la Corte hay justicia, y hay castigos."[33] The epicentre of the court was of course the king, as the ability to administer Justice was the very definition of a monarch: "él es Rey, haga justicia, dé ley, por él las causas decidan."[34] Sometimes kings made laws as well, as we see in the line, "el hacer justicia es el oficio de los Reyes, autores de las leyes."[35] Here kings are said to be the authors of their kingdoms' laws (in practice, this was highly improbable, at least in any exclusive sense, as the king himself could not possibly be familiar with all the minutiae of every case and for this task employed an army of *letrados* to study specific questions regarding which new legislation might be needed; nevertheless, in the common perception, the king came symbolically to represent the power to make the laws, even if he was not technically their author). The idealized portrait of a king presented in Agustín Moreto's *El valiente justiciero* theorizes that kings should prefer Justice to all other Virtues, starting from birth: "en naciendo / Han de saber los Reyes, / A las demás virtudes prefiriendo / La justicia, que a obrar lo justo obliga."[36] Kings are reminded frequently of this obligation in the words of counsellor figures such as, "Véncete, Rey, a ti mismo, la justicia a la pasión se anteponga."[37] Here a king is urged to place Justice before his passions, thereby conquering himself and his desires. This is the ideal recipe for rule, even if a king must kill his own son, as when Roldán asks Emperor Carlos, "¿Matar tu hijo puede ser justicia?" to which the Emperor replies, "Pues más me toca, si ese ejemplo llevo hacer justicia, siendo Rey Cristiano."[38]

This principle finds its most memorable illustration in Calderón de la Barca's biblically based *Los cabellos de Absalón*, a radical reworking of Tirso de Molina's *La venganza de Tamar*, where King David (in the Calderón de la Barca version) delivers the following speech upon realizing he must punish his incestuously rapacious son with death:

> No ha de poder la justicia
> aquí más, que la afición;
> soy padre, también soy Rey;
> es mi hijo, fue agresor;
> piedad sus ojos me piden,
> la Infanta satisfacción;
> prenderéle en escarmiento
> de este insulto; pero no,
> levántase de la cama,
> de su pálido color
> sus temores conjeturo;
> pero ¿qué es de mi valor?
> ¿Qué dirá de mí Israel
> con tan necia remisión?
> Viva la justicia, y muera
> el Príncipe violador.[39]

The King in Juan de la Cueva's *Comedia del príncipe tirano* echoes this sentiment when he says, "entenderán de mi justicia / que aun a mi propio hijo no perdona."[40] The fact that his son is the tyrannical prince of the play's title lends further support to his decision not to grant him special privileges.

Kings are adamant onstage that in the administration of Justice there is to be no exception of persons. One King declares that this principle is the very foundation of his rule: "mi corona fundo, en tener la malicia refrenada, en mi justicia no hay excepción de persona."[41] In fact, the argument might be made that Justice is more exemplary if it hits close to home: "porque propia sangre, más ejemplo sea, dando a la justicia Majestad severa."[42] The result of a king's not sparing the life of his own kin is to create an aura of severe majesty around the monarch. The consequences for this decision were perceived to reflect the royal family's status, even their purity of blood: "juro a los Cielos, que administre justicia en mi propria sangre, tan limpia desde su origen."[43] We find here an implied racism in the idea that Spaniards who were not Old Christians, or not of pure blood, might adhere to alien cultural codes which could prioritize family loyalty over consistent application of the law. The bottom line here is that Justice must be fair and impartial: "Que iguales al grande, y chico en la justicia, que premies al bueno, que des castigo al malo."[44] The element which must be removed from the equation in order to preserve fairness is that of emotion: "sed juez, y escuchad el cargo, porque erraréis la justicia en estando apasionado."[45]

All of this provides an adequate literary picture of the theory of how a good king should act. But what happens onstage when a king is not just? "Si agravia el Rey la justicia, ¿quién habrá que la defienda?"[46] If Justice is not upheld by the king, who will uphold it? Sometimes kings get it wrong, as when a loyal theatrical subject asks, "¿Cómo, magnánimo Rey, tanto a tu justicia faltas, que das premio, y no castigo?"[47] Characters debate onstage about whether to give the king what he wants in order to appease him, or else honour the letter of the law and make no exceptions, even for him:

> CARLOTO: Que al Rey es mucha justicia darle aquello que codicia.
> RODULFO: Cuando codicia lo injusto, no es justicia hacerlo justo, sino pecado, y malicia.[48]

The ultimate solution for this dilemma is of course tyrannicide, explored forcefully in Lope's *Fuenteovejuna* and studied extensively by A. Robert Lauer in *Tyrannicide and Drama*. Lines in these plays appear to defend the use of tyrannicide when warranted: "por mi mano muera el injusto tirano, y viva nuestra justicia."[49] Here Justice is problematized with the notion that "our justice" (nuestra justicia) might supersede the stated laws of the realm. What we find implied is nothing less than a subversive defence of civil disobedience.[50] However, these exceptions tend to be couched between careful disclaimers and defences of the legitimacy of monarchy, as well as mournful laments for having exiled a rightful ruler, as in "culpen la poca justicia con que han querido quitarle a un Rey legítimo el Reino, noble herencia de sus padres"[51] and "Desterramos nuestro Rey con sus hijos sin justicia, movidos de tu malicia, y contra derecho y ley."

It may intrigue even some Golden Age scholars to find portrayed onstage within this hegemonic culture a debate about rights and the laws' legitimacy: "viendo entre las tres suspenso, cuanto litigan iguales de su justicia el derecho."[52] In this instance we see three characters all claiming to be in the right, with the result being a "suspension" of the final decision which keeps the audience, likewise, in suspense until the play draws to a close. I have explored the function of casuistical *dilatio* and the suspension of a play's resolution within the larger context of a poetics for the *comedia* based upon casuistry elsewhere.[53] These plays literally leave the door open to other points of view. In fact, open doors become metaphors for a ruler's willingness to hear a subject's case presented: "al que pide justicia no ha de haber puerta cerrada."[54] To the contrary, one anguished supplicant asks, "¿A mi justicia tenéis, señor, la puerta cerrada?"[55] A just king is obligated to keep his doors open: "las puertas ha de tener siempre abiertas un Rey que justicia guarda."[56]

In addition to doors, another physical object frequently associated with Justice is a balance, or scales. Stage props are stipulated in stage directions: "sale la Justicia con un Peso pequeño"[57] or "al lado de la Justicia habrá unas balanzas."[58] The scales must be evenly balanced and accurate, as in "pesará más en la recta balanza de mi justicia."[59] The two sides of the scale represent either Justice and Grace, respectively ("iguales, como ser en una misma balanza, detenido a la Justicia, y liberal a la Gracia")[60] or else Justice and rigour: "gran señor que tienes el rigor y justicia en la balanza."[61] One suspects that all three of these qualities might be present on the same spectrum, with Grace on one end, rigour on the other, and Justice in the middle.

The allegorical figure of Justice uses these scales to measure and "tax" certain deeds: "la Piedad en su Oliva las premia, y la Justicia en su peso las tasa." For example, one act of contrition is equated to the carat weight of a precious gemstone such as amethyst:

GRACIA: ¿Qué tasa tiene esta Amatista?
JUSTICIA: Un Acto de Contrición, en que abraza un solo quilate.[62]

Presumably, more acts of repentance taken together would constitute more precious stones, such as diamonds, or at least a higher carat weight of the same stones. On a more abstract level, the scales can also represent a suitable recompense on the one side for a wrong committed on the other: "igualándose en justicia la Culpa, y la recompensa."[63]

In the absence of an actual object such as a scale used as a stage prop, a person's two hands could serve a similar function, as when one character says to another: "en tu mano está su vida, escoge; pues tengo yo la justicia en la una mano, y en la otra mano el perdón."[64] Here an actor with outstretched arms extended to either side could serve as a visual symbol of Justice weighing both sides of a question. In this case, specific hands are sometimes designated: "el castigo es mano izquierda, mano derecha el perdón."[65] In the ideal situation the two sides of the scale should remain evenly balanced: "El premio, y castigo libre igual de justicia el peso."[66]

Yet another visual image for Justice appears in the form of ledgers, folios, and account books. This staged representation was true to life, as we see in Richard Kagan's description of reams of paper used in lawsuits in his *Lawsuits and Litigants in Castile, 1500–1700*:

> Insistence on written procedures meant also that most lawsuits consumed reams of paper, or as one royal visitor to the *chancillería* of Valladolid put it: "There are *pleitos* of ten thousand and twenty thousand pages whereas three thousand to four thousand pages are the rule; more is written in a single lawsuit than in all of the histories of Spain, France, and Italy and in those of the nations of the Greek and Roman world."[67]

These books are often specified as props to appear in Justice's hands whenever she as an allegorical figure first appears onstage: "La Justicia del propio conocimiento, con las cuentas en la mano."[68] Stage directions even stipulate the concrete form these props are supposed to take: "Salga el Justicia con un papel, pluma, y tinta."[69] Apparently, God as Judge possesses a divine ledger keeping track of every sin committed by human beings: "Culpas sin suma, la justicia de Dios es libro y pluma."[70] This book is actually pictured in a roughly contemporaneous painting, namely Michael Pacher's *The Devil Presenting St. Augustine with the Book of Vices* (1483) (Figure 11).

Not surprisingly, given these resonances, the allegorical figure of Justice appears onstage most often as a ruler bearing symbols of authority. Her additional props include a rod or sceptre, conventional images used to denote sovereignty. There is a moment of apotheosis, which would have been staged spectacularly, in which Justice emerges from a *carro* or moveable cart in lavish costume carrying bedazzling props appropriate to her stature: "ábrese un Carro, y se ve en él la Justicia, Dama bizarra, con una Vara dorada en una Mano."[71] This scene is repeated in royal processions even in the "secular" *comedias*, albeit with human rulers, as in "vase en un trono Carlos con una vara de Justicia dorada en la mano."[72] The sceptre is a symbol so ancient and pervasive that it can be traced back to medieval Spanish literature. Juan de Mena devoted an entire stanza of his *Laberinto de Fortuna* to defining Justice, and in this depiction, the sceptre is the first symbol mentioned:

> Justicia es un çeptro que el cielo crió,
> que el grand universo nos faze seguro,
> ábito rico del ánimo puro,

Figure 11. Michael Pacher, *The Devil Presenting St. Augustine with the Book of Vices* (1483) (photo courtesy of Art Resource).

introduzido por público pro;
e por igual peso jamás conservó
todos estados en los sus ofiçios;
es más açote que pune los viçios,
non corruptible por sí nin por no.[73]

Justice is seen here as a divine sceptre as well as a whip that lashes vices into submission. We see in this stanza several themes introduced in this chapter: the scales / balance to weigh actions ("igual peso"), the exemplary punishment of vice, and the possibility raised that Justice might be corruptible, which we shall see momentarily (here Mena claims that it is not, but the very fact that he feels the need to clarify this tells us something about its perceived vulnerability).

We see an interesting corollary to the sceptre symbolism in staged ceremonies of relinquishing the rod. Whenever one ruler cedes power to another, he symbolically hands over his rod or sceptre representing Justice to the new ruler designated to assume his authority. In Lope de Vega's *El postrer godo de España*, Tarife declares, "el grande Almanzor ha entregado a mi valor, de su justicia la vara." As students of Spanish history may remember, Almanzor ruled Muslim Spain in the late tenth and early eleventh centuries, at a time when al-Andalus was at its pinnacle. Even when a theatrical minister of Justice merely enters a house, he symbolically lays down his rod as a sign that he does not mean to exercise his judiciary function by prosecuting anyone who lives there: "suele dejar el ministro de justicia la vara, cuando codicia la casa donde entra honrar."[74] This symbolic gesture brought honour to the house where it was performed – at least onstage – because presumably it served as a public declaration that all the house's inhabitants were blameless in the eyes of the law.

The symbolism of Justice in the *comedias* and *autos sacramentales* includes not only props such as rods or sceptres, but also moveable scenery such as chairs or thrones. A throne denotes ultimate authority, as we are reminded by Giorgio Agamben: "Nell'iconografia del potere, tanto profano che religioso, questa vacuità centrale della gloria, questa intimità di maestà e inoperosità, ha trovato un simbolo esemplare nell' *hetoimasia tou thronou*, cioè nell'immagine del trono vuoto."[75] The throne appears literally onstage as a moveable prop in the sacramental dramas, where the stage directions read, "Las Chirimías, y vuélvese a ver el Trono de la Justicia."[76] The allegorical figure performs the symbolic action of descending from this throne, as when Springtime announces, "Ya del Trono desciende la Justicia a su Sala," to which the Demon replies, "Bien se entiende en esto la noticia de que viene del Cielo la Justicia."[77] In this explication, the throne placed on high – probably on a dais or other raised part of the stage – bore a further symbolic connotation for Justice's high place of origin, i.e., heaven. This physical location for Justice meshes well with the spatial layout of many Spanish towns such as Toledo, where the Alcázar dominates the surrounding territory from its placement on a high hill. This spatial allocation served the dual or even triple function of denoting majesty, creating an impregnable fortress, and catching the mountain-top breezes in the days before air conditioning. Justice's domain is thus imagined in the theatre as an Alcázar like those inhabited at one time by Muslim rulers of Spain and then by Catholic monarchs: "La Divina Justicia el estrago viendo, baja de su Real Alcázar."[78]

To reverse the direction of this movement, in a steady ascendance, Justice moves from the tops of mountains, to the sky, and finally to heaven itself. Justice is referred to as the sun which banishes clouds: "saldrá el sol de la justicia, y esparcirá los nublados."[79] In this figuration, both clouds and shadows are intimately associated with sin and guilt: "ahora que entre reflejos se mira el Sol de Justicia, disfrazado en blancos Velos, que destierra de las Sombras los pavorosos, funestos golfos de la Culpa."[80] Justice's sun is said to sparkle so brightly that it does not need a cold, clear night to shine forth: "Sol de Justicia, cuya indeficiente Luz no ha menester noche fría para alumbrar."[81]

Ultimately – and this should resonate for readers familiar with still-theocentric Golden Age culture – Justice is said to be divine. No one can escape the wrath of God's Justice, as when one character asks rhetorically in the tradition of the Psalmist: "¿Adónde de tu Justicia seguro estaré, Señor?"[82] Other plays repeat this theme, as in "¿Quién (¡Cielos!) podrá huir de la Justicia de Dios?"[83] The Justice of God was said to condemn to the depths of the ocean any human being who might act maliciously: "en Piélagos Humanos la Divina Justicia de Dios condena al Hombre, y su Malicia."[84] Divine Justice would have been sonorously and visually represented onstage by special effects such as thunder and lightning.[85] More spectacular examples include rocks falling from the sky, covered in blood: "en fe de su justicia caerán del cielo piedras, envueltas en la sangre, que verterán."[86] Divine Justice chases delinquents into hell, which could be symbolized in some of the period's plays by a trap door: "con espadas ardientes, de la divina justicia, hasta el Infierno los meten."[87]

Biblical episodes mentioned in the context of divine Justice include the plagues cast upon Egypt after Pharaoh disobeyed God's command to set the Hebrew slaves free. In a direct theatrical echo of this story, the character Moses is begged to intervene in order to stay the beating delivered by God's harsh whip: "Moisés, suspende el severo azote de la Justicia de Dios."[88] Indeed, Moses' rod raised in response to God's command to part the waters of the Red Sea is emblematic of the rod of Justice itself, the symbolism of which we have already seen.[89] But does the rod represent Justice or Mercy? These lines bear within them like a holograph or watermark the ambiguity of Virtue and its status as *pharmakon*.

Even in non-Christian contexts, deities were called upon to act justly to right human wrongs, as when an unnamed woman says to Cleopatra in Rojas Zorrilla's *Los áspides de Cleopatra*, "El cielo ... con justicia soberana, permita Reina tirana, que te mate un áspid fiero"[90] (and that is in fact how she died, which makes these words prophetic in hindsight). Early modern Spaniards believed they were ministers of divine Justice, as in "Llega, ya que ser nos toca Ministros de la Divina Justicia, que te condena."[91] The King in Guillén de Castro's *La justicia en la piedad* invokes the divine right of kings[92] to emulate God's righteous anger: "mi severa justicia corresponde a la de Dios, a quien ahora imito."[93] In this world view, it was not a stretch to believe that human beings could be God's instruments: "yo aquí para con vos de la justicia de Dios soy un humano instrumento."[94]

Just as God had given kings a divine right to rule, in this belief system, he had also called upon Spain to conquer distant empires. In the *comedias* we find repeated references to the Justice of empire as divinely bestowed upon those worthy to administer it, as in "el imperio con justicia tienes" (this from Lope de Vega's *La imperial de Otón*) and "tienen al Asia, y Turingia [northern England] la justicia hereditaria, que les dio el Cielo."[95] A prince's aspirations to conquest are seen as entirely justified, as it were, through this concept of hereditary Justice: "Príncipe de Persia, y Media, y de ver, con que justicia tan grande Imperio pretendas."[96] These lines are spoken in the context of Ciro's pretensions to empire in what is now the Middle East.

Closely related to this ethos of conquest in connection with Justice is the notion of the just war.[97] Buried within most arguments in favour of empire were philosophical debates going back to antiquity about what does and does not constitute an adequate justification for making war on a people or country. Not surprisingly, given all we know about

Spain's participation in the larger European Renaissance and its accompanying revival of the classics, this trope too appears in the *comedias*, as in "fundarse en buena guerra tu justicia" and "con la razón, la guerra es justa."[98]

However, debates regarding Justice did not tend to anticipate inflammatory actions such as invasion, but instead occurred all too frequently after the fact, to justify such actions retrospectively. At that point, these discussions were more likely to take the form of reasoning over the best way to remedy a bad situation, or repay a debt. We encounter this stance in the line, "de conciencia, y de justicia les debo restituir cuánto me ofrecen y aplican,"[99] in which a character acknowledges personal responsibility for restitution. *Restitución* is a buzzword appearing even in the titles of some casuistical treatises on the topic.[100] In these treatises as well as some stage plays, Justice is often invoked as the reason why money must be paid or recompense offered.

We start to see here a larger pattern of commutative Justice, or what might be termed situations of redress. These begin with simple speeches such as, "Ante vos pido justicia de quien me agravia,"[101] or more complicated ones, like "hoy a tus plantas me arrojo, justicia, señor, justicia de esta afrenta, de este oprobio, de este agravio, de esta injuria."[102] The most common word used to describe the action for which recompense or restitution is required is *agravios*, as in "Madrid, Madrid, vuestro Rey a haceros justicia viene de agravios."[103] It is common in these plays to find Justice specifically invoked by a damsel in distress, as in "a tus pies pide justicia una infeliz mujer, de un tirano, y de un traidor,"[104] but Justice may also be invoked by a man in cases of honour ("justicia pido de un infame, que me ha hurtado honra").[105] Similar laments are heard following the death of a child[106] or the death of a spouse.[107] These sorrowful cries sound like the mournful complaints of a bird that has lost its nest.[108] Most frequently in these scenarios a woman appeals to a man, or a man appeals to another man, although occasionally the power roles are reversed when the complaint is directed to a female judge, as in the biblically inspired *¿Quién hallará mujer fuerte?* about the Old Testament judge Deborah. Here a female plaintiff addresses herself to her fellow woman: "Divina Debora Bella, de una Querella que tengo a pedir justicia vengo."[109]

Situations where redress was required could vary widely on the popular stage. Redress might be demanded, for example, in a pastoral vein by a shepherd for specific crimes such as killing and eating his sheep. In Calderón de la Barca's *La primer flor del Carmelo*, the shepherd complains, "sin aliento, de una tropa de Soldados a pedir justicia vengo: Un Extranjero Pastor soy."[110] Even a foreigner could seek protection by invoking the laws of the realm. Redress is also exacted for more serious crimes, up to and including theatrical murder: "llegó al campo de Teágenes un hijo, pidiendo justicia de ella por el pasado homicidio."[111] In a biblical echo of the murdered Abel's blood crying out to God for vengeance, if there is no living person available to seek redress, the very blood of the victim cries out to God for Justice.[112]

But it might well be asked: in these cases, what redress is really possible? Often only the death of the offender can compensate, in this mentality, for the death of a loved one: "Rey Úngaro, la sangre de mi primo pide a voces justicia, al Conde preso quiero, denme al Conde, muera el Conde."[113] There were dramatic situations in which the king or other minister of Justice would agree to inflict the death penalty. But there was also at least an implicit statute of limitations on recompense for wrongs committed in the past, as in "de los daños pasados hoy mi justicia severa más satisfacción no espera."[114] If the crimes had already been punished, or simply too much time had gone by, then no more satisfaction could be expected even if the offence was extreme.

The quantity of these references to retributive Justice should not distract us from its distributive form. This subcategory of Justice is all too often equated with the literary definition of the Virtue itself: "la definición de la justicia es dar a cada cual su justa parte."[115] Operative here is the concept of distributive Justice, known in this period by name and referred to as such, as in "de Dios distributiva la Justicia." Calderón de la Barca's *La primer flor del Carmelo* goes to great pains to explain in detail what this concept means: "que nada desampara, y desayuda, haciendo que su Justicia a cada uno distribuya, desde la Hormiga más vil." The stage directions for this *auto* specifically call for an apotheosis of Justice in her distributive form. She describes herself: "La Justicia soy ... sin ser liberal, ni corta."[116] As we shall see presently, this descriptive phrase can only be understood properly as a reference to the Golden Mean.

Distributive Justice demonstrated a special concern for the poor as the logical extension of *noblesse oblige*: "oír las tiernas querellas del pobre ... hacer justicia al humilde que se queja, es del Imperio el oficio."[117] According to this logic, even a person as poor as a slave could expect to receive protection from Justice and the rule of law.[118] Key to a proper understanding of this concept is the notion that poverty was accepted in Golden Age Spain as a normal and necessary part of the natural order: "El Cielo quiso que hubiera Pobres, y Ricos, midiendo su Justicia, porque cuando el uno merezca dando, merezca el otro pidiendo."[119] As Stephanie Fink de Backer explains, the rich and the poor became mutually dependent on each other within the framework of a complex symbiosis: "both rich and poor became mutually dependent upon each other's performance to guarantee both material and spiritual survival."[120]

But we should not be deceived by this literary depiction of Justice as sanguine. Still by far the most frequent deployment of Justice onstage fits its punitive function. The most common crime Justice punishes is the rather catch-all term "malice": "La Justicia, castigar pretendiendo la malicia."[121] In proto-Foucauldian fashion, this urge to punish wins out over more benevolent impulses: "venga de su Justicia movido, a castigar rigoroso, en vez de premiar benigno."[122]

Simple punishment is one thing, but exemplary punishment was often employed in very public fashion both on- and offstage in Spanish Golden Age society to serve as a deterrent. One powerful character declares his intention to do exactly that: "justicia a los dos pretendo hacer, para que el mundo vea."[123] The most likely stage scenario here is for a ruler to show an example to vassals, as when the King in Agustín Moreto's *El valiente justiciero* proclaims: "No solo por mi justicia ha de quedar castigada, para ejemplo a mis vasallos."[124] This exemplary punishment may take the dramatic form of chopping heads off.[125] One noble character commands that after the gruesome deed, villagers' heads be displayed on hooks: "hacer justicia de estos villanos, las dos cabezas poned en dos escarpias."[126] Presumably this is done in order to warn other people from the same village of what will happen if they follow their compatriots' negative example. Another spectacular punishment mentioned is that of being burned alive, a penalty considered for the infamous slanderer of the title in Juan de la Cueva's *El Infamador*: "al mundo con su lengua infama. Mirad vos si es justicia perdonarlo, o si será arrojarlo en viva llama."[127] Or the condemned might be burned in effigy, a punishment favoured by the Inquisition when a heretic could not be found, had already died, or had fled the country: "la deshonesta vida se declara, y dice, si justicia alguna hubiera, de aqueste fuera bien estar quemada la estatua."[128] Even lesser crimes such as slander or theft might garner a more mitigated, but still notably harsh, sentence, for example exile or being condemned to the galleys.[129] Yet another iteration might involve being placed in chains:

ALCALDE: Ponedle bien la cadena.
LAURO: Hazed, señores, justicia ...[130]

The desired effect of these exemplary punishments performed onstage is that an entire kingdom will hear and take note: "El rigor de mi justicia hoy ha de ver Aragón, castigando la intención."[131] (Incidentally, here we see that even intentions can be culpable.) Public spectacles of punishment were frequent also in Spain's colonies, as we see too in literature when Fresia asks in Lope de Vega's *Arauco domado*: "Dime, Español, que Dios guarde, ¿hacen justicia esta tarde del gran General de Chile?"[132]

This public aspect of spectacle produced by exemplary punishments shows a civic-minded tendency which may be said to have originated in Rome, as we see in Renaissance tragedies with a classicizing flavour such as Juan de la Cueva's *La muerte de Virginia y Appio Claudio* when Tucia calls, "Justicia, pueblo Romano, justicia."[133] Indeed, exemplary Romans such as Trajan, Cato, or Augustus and even pagan gods are frequently mentioned in the *comedias* in the context of Justice by name.[134] The cultural memory of these figures was carried to Spain by its Roman conquerors, with the result that public opinion mattered if rulers wanted to keep their jobs for very long: "En cosas del común bien, o justicia en opinión, es bien que satisfacción los Reyes entonces den."[135] There was always a danger of riot when people demanded Justice of a ruler onstage, as we see when a subject says to King Pedro in *El Rey Don Pedro en Madrid*, "Madrid al tenor de éste, y a la voz de tu justicia el pueblo en tumultos viene."[136] This was the same King Pedro whom historians have labelled alternatively *el Justiciero* or *el Cruel*, a historical figure we might accurately label a *pharmakos*.[137] Through public spectacle in both literature and life, rulers could satisfy their subjects' desire for Justice but also (let us be honest here) for entertainment. Exceptions to this rule occurred when Justice was carried out in private, as we see in the lines: "pena de la vida tiene, mi justicia le condena, mas no ejecutar la pena públicamente conviene."[138] Here even the death penalty is exacted in secret so as to avoid the public scandal which might result (and, in theatrical terms, to avoid the staging difficulties implicit in a scene which would require some pre-Hollywood version of special effects such as fake blood).

Whether public or private, the single characteristic most commonly associated with Justice in these plays is harsh rigour: "Repara, que suma justicia es sumo rigor."[139] Justice is the gardener who pulls out the weeds of hidden crimes[140] or trims the tree of infected branches: "Así el Rey de la justicia para que sepa cortar las ramas en que hay malicia."[141] This may involve lopping off a limb such as a hand or a foot, as when a character is left with "nada para correr, que le habían cortado un pie por justicia,"[142] or even an ear, as in "los afrentados por justicia y castigados viven con gran deshonor si fueren desorejados."[143] These punishments were exacted symbolically for crimes involving specific bodily members, but more capricious applications of such penalties are also known to have occurred at the theatre, such as a court jester losing his teeth for failing to make the king laugh.[144] Metaphorically, victims of harsh Justice confide that their goose has been cooked: "Por justicia entre rayos airados, ya cocidos nos llevan, y ya asados."[145] This may or may not be a reference to the live burnings associated with the Inquisitorial *auto de fe*.

When is legitimate rigour too harsh? The *comedias* are rife with protestations that given the right circumstances (such as defence of one's honour), even harsh actions are permissible: "No es rigor, sino justicia, volver un Rey por su honor."[146] However, *comedia* characters resist the notion that Justice must always be implacable, as when one of them rants, "Infame, ¿por qué ha de morir? ¿Por qué? ¿No es justicia intolerable?"[147] If used in excess, Justice bleeds over into either Fortitude, on the one side, or imprudence, on the other:

> la demasiada justicia en sí, es acción heroica; la demasiada justicia con los extraños, es tiranía. ¿Qué es ser demasiado justo? ... muy justo con los extraños en menudencias, deja de ser justicia, y se hace imprudencia.[148]

This passage offers a rather explicit description of undesirable consequences to be anticipated for not respecting the fragile equation which is the Golden Mean.

As we noticed in this last quotation, Justice when not applied properly can resemble imprudence or even cruelty: "es en ti crueldad lo que parece justicia."[149] What if Justice simulates cruel action? The two can look so much alike at the theatre that characters feel the need to clarify which is which, as in "Ya andas pesado, villano, justicia di, y no crueldad."[150] They can also be dished out together, as in "él también medirá igualmente atentas la crueldad con la justicia."[151] Justice is called cruelty when it is administered with relish or even pleasure, resembling a dragon with a fiery mouth.[152] At least in this literary representation, Castile had a particularly low tolerance for judicial harshness. Or

Justice may be maligned as cruelty even when it is not, as King Pedro I in Agustín Moreto's *El valiente justiciero* complains: "¡que me llamen Cruel, por castigar sus excesos!"[153]

Much as Justice can be confused with cruelty, it may also be confused with revenge. Revenge and Justice are not the same thing. Plays make clear this distinction; for example, "Yo te ofrezco, Federico, no vengarte, sino hacerte justicia." Given a choice between the two, Justice is clearly preferable.[154] But they often come together, as in "cuando son parejas la justicia, y la venganza."[155] They can morph into one another, as in "no pretendas hacer venganza de la justicia."[156] They are a pair, a two-for-one special, or perhaps a bargain discount.

The fact remains that the most common motive listed in stage plays for demanding Justice *is* revenge. This happens when no redress is possible and the punishment inflicted cannot possibly restore what the innocent victim has lost.[157] It can also be used as a Plan B if Justice falters, as when a character promises, "justicia espero, o tomaré venganza."[158] The same action might be defined as revenge if taken by the average man, but Justice if taken by a king: "es justicia en los Reyes la venganza."[159] In Guillén de Castro's *Las mocedades del Cid, Comedia segunda,* Don Diego claims that revenge is justified, as it were, as long as it is grounded in Justice: "Fundada está en justicia esta venganza."[160] There is a blurry line between them, as they find themselves at opposite ends of what could only be described as a sliding scale. For example, in Guillén de Castro's significantly titled *La justicia en la piedad,* the King laments, "Tan lastimado quedo, que en mí alcanza la justicia el furor de la venganza."[161] Take Justice, add injury, and the result is a fury of vengeance. The close relationship between revenge and Justice is further shown by the line, "la justicia es la justicia, émulo de la venganza."[162] Here Justice gets the better of her evil twin. Playwrights aim to clarify that a noble character's true motive was *not* revenge: "la justicia del Rey, que es virtud, y no es venganza" – this line appearing in none other than Lope de Vega's *La mayor virtud de un rey.*[163] Or perhaps the definition depends on point of view: "que en ti es justicia, cuando en mí venganza."[164] This means Virtue is situationally determined: what is Virtue for one person might not be for another. It all depends on motive. Or maybe Justice and revenge are possible at the same time. One character cries out for both as she calls for her enemy to be burned: "que vivo muera, y quemado quien tanto insulto comete; justicia pido, justicia, y venganza juntamente."[165] The result is "just" vengeance: "Justa venganza he tomado."[166] Crucial plays for this topic are Lope de

Vega's *El castigo sin venganza* and Francisco de Rojas Zorrilla's *El más impropio verdugo por la más justa venganza.* A key line from the former reads, "ejecutó sin venganza las leyes de la justicia."[167] There is much danger of confusion here, and these two related but distinct concepts may be impossible ever to sort out in a satisfactory manner. This blurring of moral boundaries only adds to the ambiguity of a Virtue we might once have believed to be transparent and self-explanatory.

Whether motivated by vengeance or not, Justice in its harshest form usually appears onstage wielding a sword. Sometimes Justice appears as a shield ("haz con la justicia escudo"),[168] but more often as a sword with a sharp blade.[169] Most frequently we witness an apotheosis of Justice holding a sword in the sacramental dramas, where the previous props we discussed (such as a sceptre or rod) have given way to weapons. Some representative stage directions read: "en un Trono la Justicia con una Espada en la mano derecha."[170] The sword of Justice appears in non-sacramental plays as well. Justice delivers the death sentence in Agustín Moreto's appropriately named *El valiente justiciero.*[171] This sword is wielded against idolatry ("el blanco acero desnudas contra el Idólatra fiero")[172] or heresy: "Yo me maravillo, cómo la sangrienta espada de la Divina Justicia su rigor no desenvaina contra Reinos obstinados a su Fe."[173] Specifically, it is wielded by Spaniards against Jews: "y la sacra Oliva defendéis con el Acero de vuestra Justicia, que tiembla el Hebreo."[174] Even worse than swords, the rods and sceptres we have seen to be so typical of Justice morph nightmarishly into scythes: "justo Ministro de las cóleras de Dios, cuya Vara de Justicia es una guadaña atroz."[175] The *guadaña* was a scythe like the one appearing in traditional depictions of the Grim Reaper. Alternatively, Justice might exact harsh penalties with whips: "la espada de su justicia, y el azote de su mano."[176] In a sign of changing military technology, in this "new" day and age, Justice might even use bullets: "Contra el plomo que ya vuela del tiro de mi justicia, tú, hijo, hiciste rodela."[177]

The inevitable outcome of so much carnage was undoubtedly bloodshed. There is a very good reason why the symbolic colour for Justice is almost universally red: "A las Leyes, la Justicia el rojo color sangriento."[178] Here we see stipulated not only the colour but also the meaning intended, i.e., Justice is supposed to be bloody. One sacramental drama explains why red is the colour customarily used to symbolize law – it represents bloody Justice: "La carmesí, que es color de la Justicia sangrienta, es divisa de las Leyes."[179] Justice is further associated with actual blood, as in "Señor, Señor, detén la mano sangrienta de tu justicia."[180]

Swords, bloodshed, mayhem – all this gory spectacle boils down to one key, consummately theatrical ingredient: fear. As we know from Michel Foucault's *Discipline and Punish*, "A figure had haunted earlier times, that of the monstrous king, the source of all justice and yet besmirched with crime; another fear now appeared, that of some dark, secret understanding between those who enforced the law and those who violated it."[181] The *comedias* affirm unanimously that the effect produced by Justice is fear: "Aquése es efecto propio de la justicia, en quien Dios puso el temor, y el asombro."[182] This line may be found in Calderón de la Barca's *Las tres justicias en una*, in which the King metes out Justice for three crimes simultaneously: Lope's impiety towards his alleged father; Mendo's dishonour of the dead Laura; and Blanca's deceit towards her husband. But the response evoked by all three transactions of Justice is the same: "Temor de Dios Divino, que siempre vive asustado de su Justicia, y Rigor."[183] This sensation of living in fear haunts us as we identify with early modern Spain's persecuted subjects.

Their fear was not just of God, but of anyone in authority, as when a powerful person says, "así de mi justicia tiembla España."[184] If not fear of actual physical harm, then noblemen experienced fear that they would lose their privilege: "pues el miedo de los nobles, es de la justicia el miedo."[185] The context here is a nobleman fleeing the country into exile in order to escape the long arm of Justice. We find lines to the effect that anyone who does *not* fear Justice must not be in his right mind: "la justicia, quien no temerla codicia, ni noble, ni cuerdo es."[186] Fear is so instilled in their collective psyche that even a severe glance can cause the guilty to tremble: "¡No me mires tan severo, que ya, ya de tu Justicia los graves rigores tiemblo!"[187] Or else fear is so internalized that guilty persons might give themselves up voluntarily, as in "por vuestras puertas entro a dar a vuestra justicia sin resistencia mi cuello."[188] Presumably, from the language used, his fate will be either hanging[189] or beheading. The latter is surely the case in a similar dramatic example, where the guilty party waives all right of appeal: "ya no apelo, porque justicia me falta, cortad, cortad, sin recelo, mi cabeza."[190] This line is a striking instance of what Foucault would call internalized *surveillance*.

The all-pervasive experience of fear lived on a daily basis may produce the paranoid impression that someone is following you, as in "huyendo del Furor de la Justicia de Dios, que me va siguiendo."[191] Justice was perceived to be ever-vigilant – in fact, so much so that it was always awake: "Mas la justicia me sigue con bien despierto cuidado."[192] Justice is like a spider's web that will catch the unsuspecting in its trap.[193] Permeated by fear, waiting for Justice to act, we are literally left hanging: "por un instante la justicia se suspenda."[194] Justice is poised like a guillotine whose blade is about to fall: "ves pendiente el brazo de la justicia: honoroso, y vengativo."[195] It hangs over one's head, ready to come crashing down at a moment's notice: "La espada de su justicia sobre tu cuello verás."[196] Metaphors proliferate of blades unsheathed, waiting to strike, as in the command: "levanta el sangriento brazo, de tu justicia levanta los cuchillos afilados del castigo."[197] As we have seen in Foucault's *Discipline and Punish*, power works through fear even in the absence of actual physical violence. Justice's blow is never foreseen until after it is felt: "el golpe de la justicia no se ve hasta que se siente."[198]

But in order to cut cleanly, the blade of Justice must itself be straight as opposed to crooked. From the same Latin root for *recto*, or straight, we get the English word *rectitude*. This is the theory of how Justice should operate, as in "aquí está el señor Alcalde, que les hará justicia rectamente."[199] Justice's duty is to cut short anyone who veers off the path: "Justicia es cortar el paso a una vida que va errada."[200] In theory Justice should never be twisted, as in "guardando el rigor de la justicia nunca torcida en mi mano."[201] But in practice, Justice can prove mischievous or even transgressive; in this vein, we find such surprising lines as, "es la justicia traviesa."[202] Some things that can twist Justice are love or perhaps greed ("mas la justicia / No ha de torcer amor, ni otra codicia"),[203] or even friendship ("no torcer justicia, por amistad").[204] One character protests that even the prize of kingdoms could not tempt him to be swayed or allow his sense of Justice to become distorted: "por mil Romas, y Milanes no torceré la justicia."[205]

In similar fashion, a different set of adjectives is employed in these plays to describe Justice as narrow rather than wide. César declares to the King's nephew, "No es llana vuestra justicia, a lo que yo imagino, que del Rey sois sobrino."[206] In contrast, Tomassa in Tirso's *La huerta de Juan Fernández* boasts in the context of romantic love, "la justicia tengo llana." As I have shown in my first book-length study of casuistical reasoning in the dramas, *Conscience on Stage*, similar language is used to describe the condition of moral laxity, or having a "wide" conscience, with results which are similarly prejudicial.[207]

If Justice is twisted rather than straight, or wide as opposed to narrow, then it is most likely susceptible to a bribe. Synonyms for bribes appear in these plays in the context of Justicia, such as *cohecho*: "tomamos el cohecho, por fuerza se ha de torcer la justicia."[208] There also appears the word *dádiva*, roughly equivalent to *soborno*: "ni dádiva que nos ligue, por quien la justicia tuerza."[209] If it is egregious enough, a bribe can amount to outright fraud:

SOLDADO 1: No más que el de sobornarse en la Justicia.
FISBERTO: Bien obra al acumulado fraude.[210]

We find these issues wrapped up inextricably with the word *interés* (interest), which can interfere with Justice being served properly: "Tienen aquí los pobres esta usanza, cuando alguno a pedir justicia viene, que solo el interés es quien la alcanza."[211] In other words, only the wealthy can buy Justice. In a characteristic image, the rod of *interés* is said to twist or make crooked the straight one of Justice: "avaricia, que la vara de interés tuerce la de la justicia."[212] It is telling that this example is mentioned in the same breath with the Deadly Sin of Avarice. As one *comedia* character opines cynically, "nunca justicia falta, a quien el dinero sobra."[213] Justice can be bought, apparently, for the right price. Judges and other court officials as portrayed onstage were susceptible to bribery: "que el juez, que por interés tuerce la justicia, es espada con muchas vueltas."[214] In the current jargon, the corrupt judge not only stabs you in the back, but also twists the blade. In fact, this problem appears to have been so prevalent, at least in its literary representation, that money is called a sieve through which Justice leaks: "el dinero es aguijón con que corre la justicia."[215] Even when there is no actual bribe involved, there is always the danger that there will be suspicion of same.[216] At the very least, rich people will be treated differently. A Jewish character named Jacob critiques the Christian "Justice" system, saying "Mal conocéis justicia de Cristianos; cuando miran, que es hombre de provecho, échanle mano, por henchir las manos."[217] These apparently widespread practices (or at least perceptions of practices) are hard to reconcile with idealized portraits of distributive Justice seen in previous examples.

Whether as a solution to bribery or *soborno*, or simply an accommodation for the inability to meet its own impossibly high standards, there is a sentiment expressed in the *comedias* that Justice ought to be more flexible. In Calderón de la Barca's famous play *El alcalde de Zalamea*, Crespo makes the crisp pronouncement: "A mi parecer, la justicia ha menester más licencia."[218] In other words, Justice needs more leeway. Its sentences can be revoked, as when the King admits, "Bien pueden revocar sentencias tales."[219] Here we find an acknowledgment that sometimes

Justice must give way to reason of state: "bien mirado, alguna vez el rigor de la justicia, señor, cede a la razón de estado."[220] For every rule, there should be exceptions: "Que aunque es la justicia igual, es justo que haya excepción."[221] In its more agile, less stodgy iteration, Justice seizes the forelock of Occasion, much like opportunistic courtiers were urged to do in order to spin a situation to their best advantage: "que también coge el cabello la justicia a la ocasión."[222]

But if Justice becomes too flexible, it can bend to the point of breaking. It loses it edge: "Cuando pierde de su punto la justicia, no se acierta en admitir la piedad."[223] It wields the pen instead of the sword, and in so doing, it becomes lazy. All these sentiments and more are packed into these burlesque lines from Tirso's *Santo y sastre*: "nunca es valiente la Jurispericia [sic]; plumas, no espadas juega la Justicia."[224] Here a clever pun on *jurisprudencia* and *pericia* (Sloth) conflates these two terms to express how slow-moving and sluggish Spain's legal system had become.[225] It is hard to escape the impression that in some of these plays Justice has turned weak or debilitated, as in "aun cuando tenga en tu mano perezosa la justicia, los poderes limitados."[226] Here Justice is referred to outright as lazy, or with limited powers. Justice even seems to be fainting, as when Icilio says, "mi justicia así desmaya."[227] At other times it appears mute, as in "Cuando enmudece la justicia, es necio el que la pide."[228] Here the person who takes the trouble to appeal to mute Justice is called foolish.

Still a more common characterization we encounter is of Justice as blind. In the crisis of Baroque society, "va la razón sin oídos, y la justicia sin ojos."[229] This is the upside-down world decried by satirists like Francisco de Quevedo. The result of Justice's blindness is to stumble around in the dark: "Cuando es grave la ocasión, la justicia a oscuras anda."[230] Ministers of Justice such as judges were likewise characterized as blind, which did not necessarily mean impartial: "no siempre guarda justicia el juez que ciego sentencia."[231] Factors that could blind Justice include flattery, love, obligation, and fear.[232] Here we see a darker, seamy underside to the shining myth of Justice with her sceptre, seated on a golden throne. A blind judge could also be relied upon to twist the verdict, and with it, his own rectitude, symbolized by the straightness of his rod: "el juez ciego torcerá la vara."[233]

We find repeatedly in these plays a recognition that even in the presence of a just judge, still Justice can falter.[234] This happens particularly when it wavers and hesitates to decide: "la justicia indecisa se remite, y no sentencia."[235] Justice falters especially for those who do not share the belief systems in which Christian Justice is grounded: "justicia del cielo perro, el Judío replicaba."[236] Here we see a clash of world views as Jewish and Christian ideas of Justice do not coincide. In what can only be termed a supremely cynical picture, the real equalizer between incompatible people groups is said to be not Justice, but death: "un sabio decía, que en la muerte sola había justicia a todos igual."[237] We are beginning to see a rather dark vision emerge of Justice as flexible to the point of being corruptible, and partial as opposed to impartial, except when one's time on earth is used up.

Regardless of the reasons one might accumulate, the theatrical verdict would appear to be that Justice is insufficient, at least if acting alone.[238] This squares with Kagan's perception of historical Justice as a "Cretan labyrinth" in his landmark study *Lawsuits and Litigants in Castile, 1500–1700*:

> Together, ambiguous laws, conflicting *fueros*, and special juridical privileges helped to fashion a legal order which one historian has compared to the Cretan labyrinth. The image is apt. Castilian justice in the sixteenth and seventeenth centuries was a hodgepodge of confused laws and competing jurisdictions that crafty litigants exploited to their own advantage. According to long-established juridical principles, law was supposed to promote justice, but, as many saw it, Castile's law was so confused that it allowed "many unscrupulous and empassioned individuals to instigate unjust cases and to weaken their opponents."[239]

At the very least, Justice in the *comedias* is insufficient if not backed up by weapons: "Tal vez suele no valer sin las armas la justicia."[240] Kings in particular were said to fall back on the principle, old as Thrasymachus, that might makes right: "en su milicia nuestros Reyes alientan su justicia."[241] As a ruler says to his subjects, "pues oid, vasallos, las armas serán los votos de la justicia que tengo."[242] Lines such as these reaffirm the old warrior ethos of the Reconquest.[243]

When Justice falters, Golden Age subjects fall back upon time-tested medieval ways of settling disputes – namely, duels. In the *comedias* we find some areas of social life which are off-limits to conventional Justice, such as the duel of honour, which incidentally also makes for great staging possibilities. As one character states categorically, "en el duelo de honor nunca la Justicia ha entrado."[244] For honour-obsessed Spanish stage characters, there is no time for Scholastic *quaestiones* about the finer points of legal doctrine; why not just settle things more efficiently in the "campo con los aceros, a donde la verdad de la justicia no se deduce a questiones, sino a fuerzas"?[245] At the theatre also we hear lines which redefine morality, including this Virtue, as when the King in Agustín Moreto's *El valiente justiciero* declares, "No va contra la justicia el que defiende a su esposa."[246] In extreme cases, alternative forms of Justice are the only ones these stage characters will accept, as when Julio proclaims boldly, "Yo solamente en mi acero fundo mi justicia."[247] This type of rogue Justice is apparently celebrated in Lope de Vega's *El acero de Madrid*, where Prudencio boasts: "pues oye, caballero soy honrado, yo no he de traer justicia, la que tengo son mis manos. Para ti bien basto."[248] A Texan cowboy could not have said it any better.

But wait a second – how did we get here? What has led to this near-total breakdown of Justice as the rule of law? How did Golden Age Spaniards arrive at the point where distrust of the official legal system was so intense that – in their stage plays, at least – they felt compelled to take matters into their own hands?

The answer may be found, curiously, in a concept known as Original Justice. This idea may be unfamiliar to modern readers, but it was certainly well understood back then. Original Justice is the lost innocence prior to Original Sin. According to Saint Anselm, who is cited by name in the *comedias*, Original Sin can be defined as the deprivation of Original Justice: "El pecado original (por definición de Anselmo) es privación de justicia original."[249] In other words, Justice now appears as weak because it is a pale shadow of what it used to be. Original Justice, by contrast, is idealized in these dramas through phrases such as "Yugo sencillo de la Original Justicia."[250] This *yugo* or yoke is reminiscent of Christ's command, "Take my yoke upon you and learn of me, because I am meek, and humble of heart: and you shall find rest to your souls."[251] True or Original Justice is defined as a primitive state of nature.[252] The ghost of this lost originary Justice appears in apotheosis in Calderón de la Barca's *La cura y la enfermedad* ("Mira, yo soy la Inocencia de la Original Justicia"), to which Sombra replies ominously, "Yo te haré presto Malicia."[253]

In fact, we see in the sacramental dramas a very legalistic conception of Original Justice as opposed to Original Sin. In Calderón de la Barca's *La hidalga del valle*, Furor asks Culpa, "¿Dónde está el Privilegio, que tu Justicia sustenta?" to which Culpa replies, "En el Génesis está."[254] It requires a significant amount of mental gymnastics to wrap our minds around the idea that the Book of Genesis could actually supply justification for the privilege of Fault. In another of Calderón de la Barca's *autos*, Simplicity speaks the line, "En el Paraíso nací, de la Original Justicia desterróme la malicia, y a los Cielos me subí."[255] This scenario is repeated almost verbatim in *La segunda esposa, y triunfar muriendo* when Death explains, "mi principio fue en el hermoso Jardín de la Original Justicia, a donde engendrada fui de la voz de la Serpiente."[256] These same notions are echoed in Calderón de la Barca's *El diablo mudo*.[257] Similar ideas are repeated likewise in his less allegorical *comedias*. In *El gran príncipe de Fez*, Saint Ignatius explains: "cuando criándole en justicia original Dios, perdió por las traidoras insidias de un áspid la gracia."[258]

The ultimate effect of this doctrine is extremely destabilizing, as early modern dramatist / theologians themselves surely realized. Culpa states baldly in a representative sacramental drama by Calderón de la Barca, "aunque soy la Culpa, la Fe de tu Justicia me disculpa."[259] So Justice exculpates Fault? The effect is dizzying. One character in a play by Lope de Vega even has the audacity to ask how human beings can be expected to follow a precept (Justice) that was essentially never given to us, since we were born into Original Sin: "Mas si de guardar Adán no le tuvo puesto la justicia original, ¿cómo sujetos nacemos a guardar precisamente precepto que no nos dieron, pues que privados nacimos de esa justicia?"[260] In other words: how can we hook up the stereo sytem when we were never given the manual?

It is hard to escape the impression in the *comedias* that Justice depends on point of view.[261] Each person can define Justice for him- or herself, as long as they stay more or less within the boundaries of law: "a cada cual su justicia, conforme a ley de derecho."[262] Sometimes Justice can be unjust, as in "ha muerto un hijo *injusta justicia*, pues fue por ajeno delito."[263] It can even amount to injury ("la Suma Justicia, es suma injuria") or affront: "Mas tu afrenta no es afrenta porque es la misma justicia."[264] The first of these lines comes from a play we have already noted as being particularly relevant for the notion of *pharmakon*, Calderón de la Barca's *La serpiente de metal*. Even when Justice is just, there is always the danger that it will appear otherwise.[265] What is really malice can appear draped in the cloak of Justice, as in "poniendo en su malicia riguridad con capa de justicia." This example occurs in the context of bearing false witness. In the same play, Justice is called the bawd or pimp of kings who go to her to obtain their illicit desires. The King himself asks: "¿Es digna hazaña el tener por tercera a la justicia de sus injustos deseos los Reyes que la administran?"[266] We are by now fairly far removed from the glittering figure of Justice appearing in apotheosis in the sacramental plays.

The consensus seems to be that the definition of Justice is up for grabs until we see how the action plays out: "la justicia se mide con la ventura."[267] Characters jostle with each other to be the one to define a given action, knowing that the first to get there wins the prize: "Astrea, yo te maté, por traidor, por engañosa; no traición, justicia fue; no tiranía, piedad te ha dado la muerte."[268] Huh? When did treason become Justice? And since when does compassion prove deadly? Sometimes characters onstage confess themselves mystified before this undefinable quotient: "Rey, ni sé si es violencia, o Ley, si es justicia, o si es rigor."[269] Apparently a given action could be any of those things, depending on the circumstance.

A messy picture emerges here of Virtues in frank competition with one another: "lo que era gracia, ha hecho justicia la competencia."[270] Instead of the traditional *psychomachia* in which Virtue opposes Vice, here the Virtues resist one another in agonistic contest. As the King confesses in Guillén de Castro's *La justicia en la piedad*, "es la justicia en mí la primera causa que resiste a mi piedad."[271] Justice and Mercy strive with one another, each revoking the other one's decisions, almost like the President and Congress of the United States threatening each other with a veto: "Revoque, pues, la piedad lo que la justicia manda."[272] In some of the plays Justice turns frankly demonic, as in Calderón de la Barca's *Los alimentos del hombre*, where the Demon claims this "Virtue" as his territory:

> ÁNGEL: No por Armas hoy solicito vencerte, sino en Justicia.
> DEMONIO: ¿En Justicia? Mi mejor partido es ése. Reo de culpa Infinita ...[273]

Justice has literally gone over to the dark side in this obscure vision of moral depravity.

~

How are we to reconcile these ambiguities? The plays themselves are unanimous in this regard: the solution may be found in the ever-elusive Golden Mean. Different pairings of Virtues are proposed in combination with Justice to arrive at a mysterious equilibrium: for example, Temperance ("mas usarse ha con templanza de la justicia")[274] or Prudence:

"aunque razones tengan en la justicia fundadas, tal vez debe la prudencia moderar a la justicia."[275] King Solomon says wisely to the Queen of Sheba in Calderón de la Barca's *La sibila del Oriente*, "justicia, y piedad en igual línea se ven, que son virtudes las dos que no pueden exceder una de otra."[276] Here once again we find a verbal / visual picture of the *igual línea*, or equal line, which is a specific reference to a spectrum, the midpoint of which is the Golden Mean. Of these two, the dramas make it clear that either Virtue without the other will not suffice: "Señor, ¿qué es esto? Si todo es misericordia, la justicia ¿qué se ha hecho?"[277] But in an alternative combination, Temperance is the means by which Justice gains the respect it deserves: "Digo que el ejemplo, y el castigo importan a la templanza, con que la justicia alcanza el respeto que se debe."[278] In fact, for Justice to be effective, it must be mediated by Temperance, as in the case of a duel.[279] Plato would say here that the unity of the Virtues is required.

What we find is a formula for the Virtues to work in concert with one another, as in "que ya de la Prudencia viene hollando la senda la Justicia."[280] Justice personified treads the path of Prudence. Like the demon on one shoulder and the angel on the other from artistic renditions of deathbed scenes,[281] the two Virtues take turns whispering into the ear of the judge, alternating from one day to the next: "justiciero, de ser piadoso te precias; ayer te habló la justicia, y ahora el perdón te ruega."[282] These concrete examples of cooperation among the Virtues remind us of Comte-Sponville's formulation that "Justice resides in ... equilibrium or proportion."[283]

The inevitable result of this cooperation ends up being a conflation of Justice with certain key other Virtues. The boundaries blur between them until they become indistinct. In Guillén de Castro's paradoxically titled *La justicia en la piedad*, the Prince declares happily, "Soy dichoso, esta justicia es piedad." He refers here to his father's decision to pardon him after his incarceration for rape.[284] Supplicants cleverly exploit this ambiguity when they approach a monarch, as in "a los pies de tu piedad pido justicia" and "pide a tu clemencia Real justicia."[285] One might well ask, so which is it? Is it Justice they want here, or clemency? Not only are the Virtues conflated, but also their symbols; for example, "el Cetro de la Prudencia es Vara de la Justicia."[286] It is curious to think about whether these props were somehow actually transformed (such as with removable outer casings, like Chinese boxes or Russian nesting dolls) onstage. In the case of the allegorical *autos sacramentales*, given the elaborate special effects used in their staging, such a visible transformation remains a distinct possibility. There is not much left for these Virtues to do but morph into one another, and that is in fact exactly what happens: "Lo que era hasta aquí Misericordia, en Justicia se convierta."[287] And why not? These supposedly opposite qualities have already been revealed as flip sides of the same coin anyhow.

It is tempting simply to leave the matter there, mired in hopeless confusion. But any responsible treatment of this subject matter is forced to ask: when these Virtues remain at all distinct, what is their exact relationship to each other? The dramas offer abundant metaphors to help us answer that question. Justice shines more brightly when couched in Pity, like the foil that makes a gemstone sparkle: "la justicia por la piedad resplandece."[288] Justice is the hand, while Pity is the arm that moves it: "que es la mano la justicia del brazo de la piedad."[289]

Once we begin to study these complex examples more carefully, we are able to discern a sequential ordering that takes place with the changing of the guard. When a new policeman is appointed, when a new sheriff comes to town, he must engage in a flurry of activity to show everyone he means business. After that, he can take his foot off the accelerator a bit: "justicia nueva, que entrar furiosa procura, y después con más blandura con los vecinos se lleva."[290] The result is a type of cyclical action: stern rigour followed by soft pity followed by stern rigour, etc. It all depends on where you freeze the frame as to which point in the cycle you will happen to see.

Perhaps in the end Justice and Mercy are really the same thing. They just go by a different name: "tener piedad, es hacer justicia con otro nombre."[291] An exchange between Justice and Mercy in Calderón de la Barca's appropriately named *El indulto general* (The General Pardon) illustrates the impasse here:

> JUSTICIA: Fuerza es que Justicia haya.
> MISERICORDIA: Sí, mas Justicia hay en quien tiene su lugar la Gracia.

In the course of this dialogue, there is some doubt as to whether these two sovereign entities will be able to resolve the tensions between them. Justice comes out onstage bearing an unsheathed sword upon her shoulder, while Mercy appears bearing her emblematic symbol, the olive branch. Mercy wants to offer pardon to the sinner (Adam), while

Justice insists that his debt must be paid: "Justicia es, que quien debe, pague."[292] The deadlock is only resolved satisfactorily with the intervention of a deus ex machina, or – in this case – an Angel offering the general pardon of the play's title.[293]

Calderón de la Barca's *Los alimentos del hombre*, which has been analysed persuasively in a juridical context by Kátherin Valdés Pozueco,[294] provides the clearest example of the delicate balancing act between Justice and Clemency, with two musical choirs clamouring alternately "Justicia, Justicia" or "Clemencia, Clemencia." In this sacramental drama, the sinful Adam is disinherited by his Father (God), who instead bequeaths the primogeniture to his second son, Emmanuel (Christ). Adam appeals to the heavenly court for sustenance on the grounds of illness, because of which he is unable to feed himself. When Emmanuel intercedes for his brother, God relents, and Adam is provisioned with oil, wine, bread, and meat. At the end of the play, a musical refrain is heard: "Vengan todos a tan piadosa Audiencia, que empieza en Justicia, y acaba en Clemencia."[295] Here we see once more the cyclical action with which we are already familiar.

In a striking variation on this theme, in Calderón de la Barca's *La inmunidad del sagrado*, Justice and Mercy appear as twin sisters, "Hermanas de un parto." The instructions are clear that in their competition with one another, each of them will occupy a full half of the stage: "a la Misericordia, y Justicia invocan ambas, siendo, como son Justicia, y Misericordia, en Sala de Competencias, cada una entera mitad." Ultimately they concur with each other as they render their verdict: "la Misericordia, y la Justicia concurren ya," in all probability because they have both called on God at the exact same moment. In what may seem to some an alarming denouement, these two Virtues join together to form a stunning visual representation – the coat of arms for none other than the Inquisition: "la Justicia, y la Misericordia triunfando, forman las Armas de la Inquisición."[296] A scrutiny of available iconography reveals that these two Virtues do, in fact, appear together, represented by the sword and the olive branch on either side of a cross, on the coat of arms for the Holy Office (see colour drawing on a 1678 document from the Tribunal of Toledo, now held at the University of Notre Dame, naming Francisco de Aranda Quintanilla a familiar of the Inquisition [Figure 12]).[297] A line from the play explains how these two apparently contradictory terms can be reconciled: "al bueno es Misericordia, bien como Justicia al malo."[298] There could be no more appropriate illustration of how these two concepts fit together within early modern Spaniards' moral imagination.

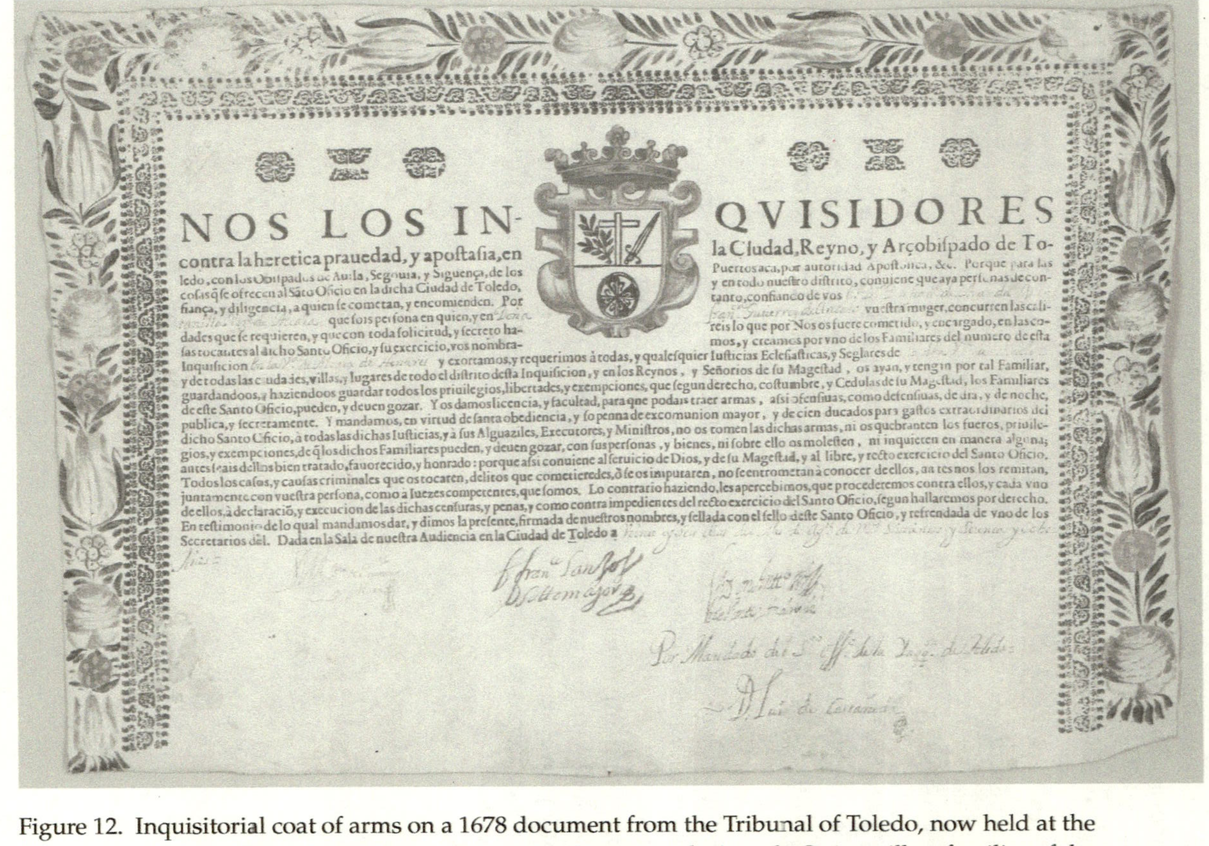

NOS LOS IN- QVISIDORES

contra la heretica prauedad, y apoſtaſia, en la Ciudad, Reyno, y Arçobiſpado de To-
ledo, con los Obiſpados de Auila, Segouia, y Siguença, de los Puertos aca, por autoridad Apoſtolica, &c. Porque para las
coſas q̃ ſe ofrecen al Sãto Oficio en la dicha Ciudad de Toledo, y en todo nueſtro diſtrito, conuiene que aya perſonas de con-
fiança, y diligencia, a quien ſe cometan, y encomienden. Por tanto, confiando de vos
que ſois perſona en quien, y en vueſtra muger, concurren las cali-
dades que ſe requieren, y que con toda ſolicitud, y ſecreto ha- reis lo que por Nos os fuere cometido, y encargado, en las coſas tocantes al dicho Santo Oficio, y ſu exercicio, vos nombra- mos, y creamos por vno de los Familiares del numero de eſta
Inquiſicion y exortamos, y requerimos à todas, y qualeſquier Iuſticias Eclesiaſticas, y Seglares de
y de todas las ciudades, villas, y lugares de todo el diſtrito deſta Inquiſicion, y en los Reynos, y Señorios de ſu Mageſtad, os ayan, y tengan por tal Familiar,
guardandoos, y haziendoos guardar todos los priuilegios, libertades, y exempciones, que ſegun derecho, coſtumbre, y Cedulas de ſu Mageſtad, los Familiares
de eſte Santo Oficio, pueden, y deuen gozar. Y os damos licencia, y facultad, para que podais traer armas, aſsi ofenſiuas, como defenſiuas, de dia, y de noche,
publica, y ſecretamente. Y mandamos, en virtud de ſanta obediencia, y ſo penna de excomunion mayor, y de cien ducados para gaſtos extraordinarios del
dicho Santo Oficio, à todas las dichas Iuſticias, y à ſus Alguaziles, Executores, y Miniſtros, no os tomen las dichas armas, ni os quebranten los fueros, priuilegios, y exempciones, de q̃ los dichos Familiares pueden, y deuen gozar, con ſus perſonas, y bienes, ni ſobre ello os moleſten, ni inquieten en manera alguna;
antes ſeais dellos bien tratado, fauorecido, y honrado: porque aſsi conuiene al ſeruicio de Dios, y de ſu Mageſtad, y al libre, y recto exercicio del Santo Oficio.
Todos los caſos, y cauſas criminales que os tocaren, delitos que cometieredes, ò ſe os imputaren, no ſe entrometan à conocer dellos, antes nos los remitan,
juntamente con vueſtra perſona, como à Iuezes competentes, que ſomos. Lo contrario haziendo, les apercebimos, que procederemos contra ellos, y cada vno
dellos, à declaraciõ, y execucion de las dichas cenſuras, y penas, y como contra impedientes del recto exercicio del Santo Oficio, ſegun hallaremos por derecho.
En teſtimonio de lo qual mandamos dar, y dimos la preſente, firmada de nueſtros nombres, y ſellada con el ſello deſte Santo Oficio, y refrendada de vno de los
Secretarios del. Dada en la Sala de nueſtra Audiencia en la Ciudad de Toledo a

Figure 12. Inquisitorial coat of arms on a 1678 document from the Tribunal of Toledo, now held at the University of Notre Dame (Inquisition 106), naming Francisco de Aranda Quintanilla a familiar of the Inquisition; the sword and the olive branch represent Justice and Mercy, respectively (reproduced from the original held by the Department of Special Collections of the Hesburgh Libraries of Notre Dame).

To conclude, Justice on the early modern Spanish stage was unquestionably violent, and indeed that was what gave it much of its theatrical appeal. But the plays themselves insist that this is sacred violence, "la sacra violencia de la justicia,"[299] a line which uncannily foreshadows René Girard's famous study *Violence and the Sacred*. As Girard himself states,

> Violence and the sacred are inseparable. But the covert appropriation by sacrifice of certain properties of violence – particularly the ability of violence to move from one object to another – is hidden from sight by the awesome machinery of ritual.[300]

This holds true whether the ritual involved is a trial in a courtroom, an interrogation in the Inquisitorial torture chamber, a public execution, a Corpus Christi procession, a royal investiture ceremony, or something so apparently innocuous as the performance of a play about Justice in the *corral*.[301]

But as we shall see, the sacred violence of Justice is only one of the ways in which early modern Virtues were conceptualized as ambiguous. Let us now move on to Fortitude, another Virtue imagined as predominantly "male," to see how even this generalization about gender and Virtue – i.e., that men were more virtuously strong – eventually proved impossible to sustain. In the course of our journey, we too may be forced to leave many of our preconceptions about Virtue by the wayside.

2 Fleeting Fortitude

Of all the virtues, courage is no doubt the most universally admired ... Courage is the virtue of heroes, and who doesn't admire heroes?

– André Comte-Sponville[1]

Chapter IV of Part Three of Honoré Bouvet's *Arbre des Batailles* (1387) provides the perfect segue to move from talking about Justice to thinking about Fortitude, which is the next Cardinal Virtue we shall discuss here. The section is titled "How We May Recognise Whether a Man Has in Him the Cardinal Virtue of Strength." The text reads thus:

> Now we must consider how we may recognise whether a man has in him this virtue of strength, which in Latin is called *fortitudo.* As a first sign you will observe that he finds all his pleasure and all his delight in being in arms, and in *just* wars, and in defending all *just* causes, quarrels, and holy arguments. The second sign is that a man, seeing the great ill and peril incurred in making such a war, or maintaining such quarrel, should yet not quit his purpose, nor for any labour or travail fear to expose his body to fair fight and strict *Justice.*[2]

Several things are notable about this text. First, it aligns Virtue with pleasure and delight – not a given for proponents of joyless, ascetic morality. Second, it overlaps with some of the specific subject areas we looked at previously in the chapter on Justice, namely, the concept of a just war, as well as zealotry or "holy arguments." Third, this text presupposes that the individual who exercises this Virtue must by necessity be male. We shall return to this assumption, and the debates it (en) genders, once towards the end of this chapter and then again in the chapter "Class Trumps Sex."

In its most basic definition, Fortitude may be described as strength or potency, a characterization which could be extended to Virtue more broadly. In medieval Spain, Juan de Mena writing in 1444 devoted the following stanza to defining Fortitude:

> Es fortaleza un grande denuedo
> que sufre las prósperas y las molestas;
> salvo las cosas que son desonestas,
> otras ningunas non le fazen miedo;
> fuye, desdeña, depártese çedo
> de las que diformes por vicio se fazen;
> las grandes virtudes inmenso le plazen;
> fazen el ánimo firme ser quedo.[3]

Here we see that Fortitude is equated to fearlessness, a formula repeated by André Comte-Sponville: "courage is primarily a low sensitivity to fear."[4] As such, Fortitude conquers Fortune, as Lope de Vega states alliteratively: "La fortaleza vence a la fortuna."[5]

In their search for models of Fortitude, Golden Age playwrights needed to look no further than the natural world. Diamond was said to be the hardest stone, and as such it was thought to symbolize strength: "yo fijo por última Piedra ufana, Diamante en quien Fortaleza se explica, y perseverancia."[6] Among the animals, the lion was considered to be the strongest, and thus the most emblematic of this Virtue.[7] Natural realms such as mountains were thought to teach their beastly as well as human inhabitants a certain fierceness typical of Fortitude, as when a mountain man speaks the lines: "soy de estas montañas, y con su misma fiereza, conservo la fortaleza que saqué de sus entrañas."[8]

Further examples of this Virtue could be found in biblical, mythological, and historical figures. A common entity mentioned in relation to this Virtue is the god Mars: "valeroso Marte, Símbolo militar de fortaleza, allí el ingenio, la experiencia, el arte mostraron su valor."[9] This passage from Lope de Vega's egalitarian *Pobreza no es vileza* echoes a portion of another stanza from medieval author Juan de Mena:

> La rueda de Mares presenta
> los que por fuertes virtud representa,[10]

in which the god / planet Mars represents the Virtue of Fortitude, here equated with strength. Known for his great strength likewise was Hercules, also called Alcides, as in "de Alcides la fortaleza."[11]

Fortitude was not limited to the province of the gods. Mere mortals were also deemed capable of this Virtue, as in Lope's *Las grandezas de Alejandro* about the exploits of Alexander the Great: "primero Menón Griego de insigne fortaleza."[12] Here the ancient hero Memnon of Rhodes, the commander of Greek mercenary forces under the Persian King Darius III at the time of Alexander's invasion of Persia in 334 BC, proved to be (at least potentially) a formidable adversary. Examples of Greek valour were later imitated by Roman heroes, as in Juan de la Cueva's *La muerte de Virginia y Appio Claudio*: "La constante virtud, la fortaleza, / de aquel valor heróico, poderoso."[13] These words are spoken by Marco Oracio, deputized by the Roman Senate to judge a specific case, in reference to Virginio, father of the girl Virginia of the play's title, as he argues for the old man to be released from prison (he had been thrown into jail after defending his daughter's honour with a dagger). Another Roman whose name is mentioned in the same breath with Fortitude is Mucius Scaevola, a young citizen who became famous for his bravery in 508 BC when Clusium attacked Rome. With the approval of the Roman Senate, he sneaked into the Etruscan camp, intending to murder its Etruscan leader. His memory is recalled onstage when one character refers to another in laudatory fashion as "Mucio en fortaleza."[14]

Other lines from these plays clearly refer to Fortitude, if not by name, as in "a ti te importan esos ejemplos a mi Rey, las virtudes heroicas de Scipión, y Alejandro."[15] The classical heroes referenced here are Scipio Africanus, who defeated Hannibal in the Second Punic War, and Alexander the Great, who spearheaded the Greek conquest of Persia. Alexander's bodyguard and successor Lysimachus is also mentioned in the context of Fortitude: "con un león entrará a hacer desafío con más fortaleza, o brío, que Lisimaco, o Sansón."[16] The latter reference is to the Old Testament hero Samson, who destroyed the Philistines by pulling down the pillars of their banquet hall, collapsing the roof onto their heads. Another Old Testament figure makes an entrance as the patriarch Jacob who wrestled with God. This personage appears onstage in Lope de Vega's biblically based *El robo de Dina*,[17] where another character reminds him: "Porque si con Dios tuviste, Jacob, tanta fortaleza, más la tendrás con los hombres."[18] Mere men could not frighten him after he had wrestled with the Deity.

The contours emerge here of a Virtue associated with soldiers, valour, and heroism. This picture of Fortitude participates in a larger characterization of Virtue as warlike strength: "sobre el Planeta de la quinta Esfera la virtud militar triunfos aumente."[19] This conception of military

Virtue traces its roots to classical Rome: "Roma ... premiaba la virtud militar de sus soldados."[20] This practice of praising and rewarding good soldiers is referred to simply as sound military strategy: "Alabar la virtud de los soldados fue siempre de excelentes Capitanes."[21] One of Fortitude's equivalencies is valour, as in "allá se sabe que obró el Valor, y la Fortaleza, y aquí se experimentan iguales Virtudes."[22] It is intimately connected to honour, as in the second part of Lope de Vega's *El príncipe perfecto*: "La fortaleza es virtud que tiene al honor por premio."[23]

Fortitude is the preeminent Virtue of Spain's hero of the Reconquest, El Cid, as we see with multiple references in Guillén de Castro's *Las mocedades del Cid*, in two parts,[24] as well as the same author's *El perfecto caballero*. This perfect knight displays Fortitude as one of his chivalric qualities: "en el campo fortaleza, y en la silla majestad."[25] These same characteristics are exhibited by the Prince of Parma in Lope de Vega's historical drama *El asalto de Mastrique por el Príncipe de Parma*, to whom Don Lope de Figueroa speaks the lines: "excelso señor, lo que manda vuestra Alteza, que esa heróica fortaleza es digna de su valor."[26]

Not just captains, but average soldiers were expected to demonstrate Fortitude, as we see in the following exchange from Lope de Vega's afore-mentioned *Pobreza no es vileza*:

MENDOZA: Pues eres todo heroica fortaleza.
CONDE DE FUENTES: Los soldados quisiera de este modo.[27]

Similarly, in Lope de Vega's *El valiente Céspedes*, based on the life of the military captain Alonso de Céspedes, one of the bravest Spanish soldiers of the sixteenth century who fought against the *moriscos* in the Alpujarras revolt, we find the line: "Yo os confieso que su valor y fortaleza espanta."[28]

This Virtue seems supremely warlike, linked with specific imaginary statistics such as killing 5,000 men: "en la guerra, matando cinco mil hombres con tan alta fortaleza."[29] We should remember here that war itself was called virtuous, going back at least as far as medieval texts: "¡O virtüosa, magnífica guerra!"[30] Paradoxically, this so-called Virtue was associated with acts of carnage, as in "cortaré la cabeza, que la mayor fortaleza consiste en saber huir."[31] These words are spoken in Lope de Vega's *El Perseo* by the titular character, Perseus, to Medusa as he threatens to chop her head off and then run away quickly before she turns him to stone. Sometimes the greatest Fortitude consists in running like a jack rabbit away from danger.

Do these examples seem odd to us, or at least not what we were expecting to find in the way of straightforward, unambiguous depictions of Virtue? How could so much bloodshed – and cowardice – be held up for Spaniards to emulate?

Here it might be useful to remember that in early modern Spain, down-and-dirty warfare was not incompatible with spiritualized readings for these moral categories; just because we think we understand the Virtues in a certain preconceived way, this does not mean that our preconceptions necessarily line up with theirs. The perfect example of a spiritualized reading which nonetheless integrates a blatantly bellicose model for Fortitude would be the numerous depictions we find onstage of the archangel Gabriel.[32] The archangels were believed to be the quintessential models of Fortitude because they had overthrown Satan in heavenly battle. The Devil himself acknowledges this in one of the sacramental dramas: "menester valerme de Militares aprestos; fue Gabriel, que se interpreta fortaleza, el que primero vino a batirme la Estrada, la Tierra."[33] Appearing as an allegorical figure in a different play by the same author, the archangel Gabriel explains why he is the one chosen to represent this Virtue: "Guarda del Pueblo de Dios, que Gabriel no en vano Fortaleza me interpreto."[34] In other words, he is the designated guardian angel for God's people. We find references to Fortitude in connection to the other two archangels as well, as in "aquel Ángel, o vienes en su virtud a ser otro Rafael"[35] or "Cuando en virtud de la Pasión de Cristo venció Miguel la guerra."[36] These allusions are to the archangels Raphael and Michael, respectively (see Figure 13). The fact that there is confusion in these plays over which archangel represents Fortitude may contribute to this Virtue's literary ambiguity.

This quasi-militaristic Virtue bore special relevance for plays based on saints' lives as well. In hagiographical dramas we find lines such as "viva la virtud heroica de Capistrano" – this from Antonio Zamora's *El custodio de la Ungría, San Juan Capistrano*.[37] Known to history as the "Soldier Saint," this Franciscan friar at age seventy(!) led a military campaign against the Turks, who in 1456 invaded Hungary. In similar fashion, in Lope de Vega's *Juan de Dios y Antón Martín*, the Demon asks, "¿Qué es esto[,] cielos? ¿que no puedo vencer la fortaleza de este varón de Dios?"[38] In this play, the Portuguese-born Saint John of God (1495–1550) begins his adult life as a soldier, but then establishes a hospital in Granada where he treats prostitutes who have contracted syphilis. His story shows with what remarkable ease a Virtue like Fortitude can be transposed from the terrestrial to the heavenly realm.

Figure 13. Archangel Michael (symbol of Fortitude) dressed for battle, defeating Satan: Juan Fernández Navarrete ("El Mudo"), *San Miguel* (1565), Parish church of Briones, Rioja, Spain (photo courtesy of Art Resource).

These convenient distinctions – i.e., terrestrial vs heavenly – were frequently blurred in an era when holy war was vividly remembered in the form of Crusades and subsequent struggles against practitioners of Islam. Great Fortitude was needed to fight heresy, as in "el santo zelo, la militar fortaleza."[39] These lines come from Lope de Vega's *Las cuentas del Gran Capitán*, written about Gonzalo Fernández de Córdoba (1453–1515), a Spanish general who invented trench warfare. He fought a holy war against the Muslims as part of Spain's Reconquest. In more abstract terms, the allegorical figure representing the sacrament of Confirmation says in Calderón de la Barca's *No hay instante sin milagro*, "le da mi Fortaleza al que en la Fe se confirma contra sus Contrarios."[40] Here the sacraments are seen to fortify believers (literally, infuse them with Fortitude) as they sally forth to do battle against enemies of the faith. But perhaps the best example of holy warfare in the context of Fortitude occurs in Lope de Vega's *La Santa Liga*, written about the Holy League organized by Pope Pius V to include most of the Catholic maritime powers of the Mediterranean. It was under the auspices of this union that the Spaniards fought the Battle of Lepanto against the Turks on 7 October 1571 (a battle in which Cervantes lost the use of his hand, thereby earning the nickname "el Manco de Lepanto"). In Lope's historical drama about this event one character appeals to God, asking Him to grant the specific Virtue of Fortitude for the purpose of fighting the Turkish heresy: "humana mi flaqueza, si vuestra virtud concede a mi brazo fortaleza."[41] This prayer and others like it must have worked, as the Spaniards were successful in routing the Turks, thereby preventing their expansion along the European side of the Mediterranean Sea.

For many Spaniards, Lepanto was merely an extension of their centuries-old struggle against the Muslims, who had inhabited the Iberian Peninsula for nearly 800 years. The Reconquest still proved exciting to early modern Spanish audiences and provided fodder for historical dramatists wishing to exploit racial prejudice. In these plays we find allusions which early modern audiences would have understood to specific battles over particular cities, such as Alfonso VI of León's reconquest of Toledo in 1085: "pudo a Toledo otro Alfonso conquistar / con ser tal su fortaleza."[42] This Christian king was not only courageous, but wily: after pitting several Muslim leaders against each other, he successfully defeated a coalition comprised by the *taifas* of Badajoz, Zaragoza, and Seville.

The Muslims were not Spain's only military enemies during this period; to the north, they also had to worry about the French. Patriotic propaganda was always a crowd-pleaser at the theatre. We hear typically nationalistic chest-beating in Juan de la Cueva's *La libertad de España por Bernardo del Carpio* in the vociferous harangue: "¿Dónde está el valor? ¿dónde está la fortaleza? ¿dónde el belicoso ardid? ¿dónde el invencible Ardor de España?" Here the titular character, Bernardo, exhorts Suero Velázquez not to cede the kingdom of Castile – left without a successor to its throne – to France. In the same play we find the lines, "Veré como resiste su fiereza, / Del valiente Roldán la fortaleza,"[43] in reference to Bernardo's legendary defeat of Roland and the French at the Battle of Roncesvalles.

But at the time when these plays were written, Spain was no longer in defensive mode; instead, at the peak of world dominance, it was looking to expand control over an empire that spanned two continents. The connection between Fortitude and empire is made explicit in these plays, as in "Ya, señor, indicios das de tu imperial fortaleza." The next line brutally refers to chopping off heads.[44] Spain saw itself as the natural heir to Rome's empire, and as such, displayed a fascination with historical dramas like Juan de la Cueva's *La libertad de Roma por Mucio Cevola*, the title of which refers to a figure we met earlier in this chapter. In this play, Bruto speaks to Tarquinio of "tu esfuerzo ... y fortaleza, / Que tiene al Mundo de temor sujeto."[45]

This notion of Fortitude connected to empire extends even to the sacramental plays. In Calderón de la Barca's *El nuevo hospicio de pobres* the allegorical figure of Fortitude appears as an angel whose dual function is to serve as the King's (God's) *valido* as well as his messenger: "Mensajero del Rey, que en dos Mundos reina, a quien Fortaleza ha dado nombre."[46] We should note that this allegory works on two levels: on the one hand, the "two worlds" mentioned here refer clearly to Earth and Heaven; but in early modern Spain, this heavily resonant phrase would also have evoked "New" World conquest.

As it happens, Fortitude was a Virtue self-consciously employed by the actual conquistadores themselves. For example, Hernán Cortés in his second letter to the king of Spain engages in this remarkable bit of self-fashioning, recounting how at moments during the conquest of Mexico when they were most fearful, he urged his fellow Spaniards to be brave:

> Yo los animaba diciéndoles que jamás en los españoles en ninguna parte hubo falta, y que estábamos en disposición de ganar para Vuestra Majestad los mayores reinos y señoríos que había en el mundo y que demás de

hacer lo que a cristianos éramos obligados en puñar contra los enemigos de nuestra fe, y por ello en el otro mundo ganábamos la gloria y en éste conseguíamos el mayor prez y honra que hasta nuestros tiempos ninguna generación ganó; y que mirasen que teníamos a Dios de nuestra parte y que a él ninguna cosa es imposible, y que lo viesen por las victorias que habíamos habido, donde tanta gente de los enemigos eran muertos y de los nuestros ningunos.[47]

In reference to this text, William Childers writes: "In his celebrated *Second Letter*, he [Hernán Cortés] invented a fictional character named Hernán Cortés, the embodiment of the Christian hero who brings together the virtues of service to God and king, prudence, and courage."[48] The disjunction of this ideal with reality[49] only makes his rather strained effort at self-fashioning all the more rhetorically dazzling.

As we see with Hernán Cortés, Fortitude can be confused with Pride,[50] especially when pious words are not given substance with virtuous actions. This ambiguity shows up in the *comedias* as well. In Juan de la Cueva's *La libertad de España por Bernardo del Carpio* the Frenchman Don Reinalte charges the Spaniard Bernardo with overweening Pride: "Orgulloso Español, la fortaleza / No está en echar al viento esos blasones."[51] It is fascinating to watch this Spanish author place criticism of Spaniards in the mouths of their enemies. There seems to be some self-awareness here, and this author is not alone in expressing it. Spain's national playwright Lope de Vega feels the need to criticize, if not Spaniards on this score, then at least their Roman predecessors: "La Romana fortaleza fue soberbio pensamiento."[52] If we listen carefully, we hear a warning that this Virtue may contain, buried within it, a Vice: "tiene del león la soberbia, y fortaleza."[53] We start to wonder: is Fortitude necessarily accompanied by Pride?

The ambiguity we find in these dramas in their treatment of this Virtue is striking. At best, Fortitude is often equated with Stoic suffering: "Pues prevén sufrimiento, y fortaleza, que otro pesar es."[54] This negative characterization starts to make this Virtue less attractive. Fortitude is of little profit: "aunque piadosa, sin ningún provecho pide el gobierno heróica fortaleza."[55] These lines may show disillusionment with the government at a time when Spain's star was starting to wane. Even when it is profitable, Fortitude can turn evil when applied inappropriately, as when strength takes advantage of weakness. This is the scenario we find in Juan de la Cueva's classicizing tragedy *La muerte de Ayax Telamón sobre las armas de Aquiles*: "tu ánimo, y fortaleza, en mi flaqueza lo pruebas."[56] These lines are spoken by Andromeca (wife of Hector) to Pirrho, who has taken her captive and wants to kill her.

The perversion of Fortitude becomes even more haunting when we hear this Virtue being twisted in the sadistic words of a rapist. In Juan de la Cueva's *El degollado*, the Muslim Chichivali taunts the damsel Celia, "No porfíes, que es locura. ¿No ves que a mi fortaleza se rinde ya tu flaqueza?"[57] At this moment, Arnaldo draws his sword and kills Chichivali before he can rape the woman. The dubious nature of his extreme solution is reinforced within the text when the king sentences him to having his throat slit (hence the title of the play). He only manages to escape this severe punishment when another condemned prisoner's body is substituted for his. If nothing else, at least the *comedias* are clear on this point: if not mixed with wisdom, Fortitude becomes insanity: "Fortaleza ... que no acompaña a la cordura, no es fortaleza, llámese locura."[58]

Still further ambiguity is introduced in the depiction of this Virtue when the supposedly Christian quality of Fortitude is attributed to a villain. This happens in Juan Ruiz de Alarcón's *El Anticristo* when the titular character boasts: "dios Maozin ha de ser mi nombre, cuya grandeza significa fortaleza, majestad, gloria, y poder. Mi estatua el sagrado asiento ocupará." Significantly, another character makes the distinction between this false Fortitude and the Christian kind, reminding him, "Remedios pruebas en vano en Cristiana fortaleza."[59] Maybe the potential for confusion on the part of the audience was too great, so the playwright felt the need to clarify things a bit. As Comte-Sponville notes perceptively, "the most suspect thing about courage is its indiscrimination."[60]

Even when Fortitude is not perverted in so extreme a fashion, it can still be conflated all too easily with other Virtues. It seems interchangeable with Temperance, as in "que cuando valor tenemos, los apetitos sabemos refrenar con fortaleza."[61] This sounds exactly like the definition of Temperance, not Fortitude. Fortitude also appears to be allied with Charity or generosity, as when King Minos of Crete says to Theseus in Lope's *El laberinto de Creta*, "Teseo, la fortaleza de tu generoso pecho no pudo dar mayor muestra."[62] Normally generosity is mentioned in the same breath with Charity, not courage. In a beautiful but also potentially confusing image, Calderón de la Barca describes a constellation of Virtues working in concert together like the interconnected parts of a sword carried by a warrior: "Pomo, la Fortaleza, y si se aúnan en ser la Templanza el Puño, y la Vaina la Cordura."[63] Here Temperance is the sword's hilt, good judgment its sheath, and Fortitude the knob on the hilt which keeps the whole weapon balanced. The catch is that the difference between a sword's hilt and its knob would seem to be minimal at best. The image works, the lines sound great, but there does not really seem to be much of a difference between these Virtues after all.

The way out of this dilemma, of course, is to recognize that ideally these Virtues should be combined, just as Plato recommended with his pronouncements on the unity of the Virtues. In the way that a good pharmacist mixes a compound drug with just the right proportions of its various ingredients, so a playwright recommends "en un Reino, o ciudad la junta maravillosa de la fortaleza, y de la templanza."[64] The goal is to achieve tenderness mixed with heroism: "un prudente Salomón que aconseja mi terneza, y una heróica fortaleza que conserva mi opinión."[65] Here the Prudence of Solomon appears as a third Virtue we should bring into the mix, along with Fortitude and Temperance. The baby Jesus actually embodies the right mixture of meekness with Fortitude, as we see in Guillén de Castro's *El mejor esposo*, written about Saint Joseph (Mary's husband). Speaking to her future son, the Virgin Mary says: "manso niño, de Dios Omnipotente, de Señor soberano tendréis la fortaleza, tan levantado, heróico, y eminente, que con valiente mano entre glorias, y asombros, vuestro Reino afirméis en vuestros hombros."[66] Here her meek child is also envisioned as a brave hero who will carry the weight of a heavenly kingdom upon his shoulders. A final verbal picture of the Golden Mean as applied to Fortitude appears in the *loa* for Calderón de la Barca's sacramental drama *El Santo Rey Don Fernando, primera parte*: "si consideras Miel en Boca de León, que Dulzura, y Fortaleza uniendo, Símbolo es del Sacramento."[67] Here the Eucharist itself is held up as the ultimate union of sweetness with strength. An example from the natural world is incorporated too, namely honey in the mouth of a lion. The Baroque age loved paradox, and here we experience a visual (and gustatory) one in all its splendour.

In the dramas we find not only paeans to the Golden Mean, but cautionary tales for what will happen if this fragile equilibrium is not respected. With unusual candor, Lope de Vega states rather bluntly in the prefatory matter to his *La discreta venganza*: "El temor y la temeridad son los extremos de la fortaleza."[68] Fear and temerity: these are the pitfalls every brave hero must avoid. As Bouvet wrote in his *Tree of Battles*:

> in each of the extremes lies vice; for in rashness appear over-boldness and excess, and in fear appear weakness and excess of fear ... But the

mean is that strength of fortitude which knows how to wait and to attack opportunely and virtuously, and how to wait and to flee wisely and fittingly.[69]

Fortitude does not always mean attack – under the right circumstances, it can also mean retreat. Ultimately, the greatest Fortitude of all is to conquer one's self: "el vencerse a sí mismo es divina fortaleza."[70]

Now, the reader will recall that at the start of this chapter I promised to address the gendered aspect of this Virtue. This is the time to do so. The ancients saw courage as a mark of virility (the word *andreia*, which means courage in Greek, and the word *virtus* in Latin come from *anêr* and *vir*, respectively, root words that denote man, not in the general sense but as opposed to woman).[71] So at first glance, Fortitude would appear to be exclusively the province of men.[72] *Comedia* characters even say so, as in the line, "a las flores pertenece la blandura, y a los hombres la heroica fortaleza."[73] The conjunction of femininity with Fortitude would seem incongruous, as we gather from the following exchange in Lope de Vega's *La batalla del honor*:

TEODORO: Retírate, gran señor.
ALMIRANTE DE FRANCIA: ¿Adónde?
TEODORO: A la fortaleza de Blanca.
ALMIRANTE DE FRANCIA: ¿Mujer y fuerte?[74]

To his credit, Teodoro replies, "¿Por qué no, cuando es buena?" Likewise, a female character asks in a different play whether beauty is incongruous with Fortitude: "¿que mi hermosura es extraña en mi fortaleza?"[75] This commonly held prejudice still resonates centuries later within our culture today.

In one especially misogynistic exchange, two of Lope de Vega's characters conclude that it is impossible for women to possess this Virtue:

REY: No hay en mujer fortaleza.
ALBANO: Fuertes en flaquezas son.[76]

Other, similar exchanges emphasize women's alleged weakness as well as fearfulness.[77] Alternatively, women's only strength derives from men: "que el hombre como cabeza dio a la mujer fortaleza, y recibió enfermedad."[78] This line may refer either to the Fall in the Garden of Eden or else, more contemporaneously for Golden Age viewers, to venereal disease.[79]

But Lope de Vega was apparently more progressive than these misogynistic lines make him sound. In his significantly titled *El valor de las mujeres*, he makes a character declare of women: "la más flaca, la más vil, puede ser vasa de jaspe en fortaleza y virtud: hoy de su alabanza sale el triunfo, Mujeres."[80] Indeed, a woman's Fortitude paradoxically may consist of weakness. In another play by the same author with another significant title – *La vengadora de las mujeres* – we find a similarly puzzling line: "la mayor fortaleza de la mujer es flaqueza."[81] Clearly there is room here for alternative or paradoxical definitions of Fortitude. Lope de Vega's mountain woman in *La serrana de Tormes* refers to this as a specifically masculine Virtue but nonetheless appropriates it for herself: "Y más ahora que intento con varonil fortaleza cubrir esta vil flaqueza de tan loco atrevimiento."[82] It is interesting to note that here we see a reference to the veneer of Virtue (a topic for our conclusion later), in which Fortitude is described as a covering for weakness. The question then becomes: how genuine is it? Are women allowed to possess their own version of Fortitude, or must they merely borrow it from men?

A key play for this topic is Calderón de la Barca's *¿Quién hallará mujer fuerte?* a sacramental drama about the Judge Deborah which also mentions other illustrious women from the Old Testament.[83] For example, this play praises Jael, who impaled Sisera with a tent peg: "sacó de esclavitud a Israel, en cuya prosecución de Templanza, y Fortaleza Jael asistida, mató a Sisara."[84] (But note that her Fortitude is tempered, as it were, by Temperance – or at least we are told this in the play; if stabbing with a tent peg is the temperate version, one would hate to see the intemperate one.) This praise of women's courage echoes Cervantes' compliment to *La gran Sultana*: "Es gloria de su nación, y de su fortaleza ejemplo."[85] The heroine described in such eloquent terms, Doña Catalina de Oviedo, according to legend was a Spanish Catholic who married a sultan and sat on the throne of the Ottoman Empire. Calderón de la Barca, likewise, in *La gran Cenobia* about the Queen of Palmyra (ancient Syria) makes reference to the protagonist's "varonil valentía."[86] Other examples abound; one need only glance at the titles of plays such as Lope de Vega's *La varona castellana*, about the legendary woman who defeated Alfonso I of Aragon in single combat, or Diego and José de

Figueroa y Córdoba's seventeenth-century *La dama capitán* to see that in the area of gender, Golden Age dramatists were more than willing to think outside the box.[87]

This was especially true in the area of female saints. The titular character in Agustín Moreto's *Santa Rosa del Perú* refers to Fortitude as one of her spiritual weapons: "siendo espada mi valor, y escudo mi fortaleza."[88] Likewise, the angel speaking to Saint Teresa in Juan Bautista Diamante's *Santa Teresa de Jesús* proclaims the efficacy of this Virtue for this holy woman: "a tus temores cobardes traigo en él la fortaleza para resistir las dudas."[89] He then pierces her heart with an arrow, which is the same moment pictured in Bernini's famous sculpture *Ecstasy of Saint Teresa*.[90]

Debates over whether women could possess Fortitude often centred on whether this Virtue held a predominantly physical or rather spiritual component. Chapter XI of Part Four of Bouvet's *Tree of Battles*, "Is Fortitude a Moral Virtue?" presents various arguments on both sides of this quandary:

> Now we must consider in this part a rather subtle question, to wit, whether fortitude is a moral virtue. And I prove that it is not, for fortitude is a disposition of the body. But it is clear that every moral virtue has to do with the soul, so that fortitude is by no means a moral virtue.

Later he resolves this apparent impasse by way of a subtle distinction: "fortitude of body is not a moral virtue, but strength of soul truly is."[91] Juan de Mena takes a similar path in stanza CCXI of his fifteenth-century *Laberinto de Fortuna*:

> Fuerça se llama, mas non fortaleza,
> la de los miembros, o grand valentía;
> la grand fortaleza en el alma se cría
> que viste los cuerpos de rica nobleza,
> de cuerda osadía, de grand gentileza,
> de mucha costancia, de fe y lealdat:
> a tales esfuerça su autoridad
> que débiles fizo la naturaleza.[92]

This passage highlights the difference between *fuerza* and *fortaleza* (force and Fortitude). In the *comedias*, likewise, we find that Fortitude is not necessarily tied to large stature: "El hombre cuando pequeño tiene valor espantable, porque la virtud unida puede más que si se ensanche."[93] In other words, even physically weak men (or women!) can exhibit strength of character – here we might think of Napoleon, who was notoriously short. The bottom line would seem to be that "courage commands respect";[94] and by this measure, Fortitude could prove equally applicable to either gender.

The androgynous nature of this Virtue is only one of its many ambiguities. We shall examine the intersections of Virtue with gender more fully in the chapter "Class Trumps Sex: (En)gendering Virtue." Let us now move on to two more typically "feminine" Virtues, Charity and Chastity, to see whether they prove to be similarly ambiguous.

3 Charity as Greed

Es la liberalidad una virtud atractiva, quien da venza, quien da viva.

– Lope de Vega[1]

Charity is said to be the root from which love towards others springs forth like fruit: "del Árbol en la Raíz ya simbolizada queda la Caridad, y es mi Amor al Próximo el Fruto de ella."[2] Of the three Theological Virtues (Faith, Hope, and Love), Charity stands out as the only one that is in heaven:

Caridad santa, virtud,
que de las tres Teologales
sola tú estás en el cielo,
el mismo cielo te alabe,
pues unir puedes al hombre
con Dios en lazo admirable
de amor, con tan alto nudo,
y coyunda tan suave,
que él está en Dios, Dios en él.[3]

Coyunda is the harness around an ox's neck attaching him to the yoke used to plow a field. The reciprocity expressed here stems from the fact that typically there were two oxen hitched to the same yoke, reflecting the notion of balance or equilibrium. Furthermore, Charity is a "sovereign" Virtue which stimulates gratitude: "Tanta liberalidad, no merece ingratitud, qué soberana virtud la magnánima piedad."[4] By its very nature – Charity is sometimes translated simply as Love – this Virtue highlights the role of the affects in morality. In one sacramental drama Charity presents herself as, "Yo, que soy la Caridad, primera Virtud, en quien ejercitaste el afecto, de convertir, y atraer tanta parte del Hebreo Bando, a la Católica Ley."[5] In other words, generous Love is more effective at persuading "heretics" (i.e., Jews) to convert than brute force.[6] In this scene, Charity rides onto the stage in a *carro* with the other two Theological Virtues, Faith and Hope.

But Charity on the early modern Spanish stage does not stay within the airy realm of affects. Instead, it translates into action, specifically works of mercy directed towards one's fellow man. This Virtue is especially prominent in biblical and hagiographical dramas, such as Lope de Vega's *La Historia de Tobías*, where these lines are spoken about the Tobias of the play's title: "Quien las virtudes contara, hijos de aquel santo viejo, su prudencia, su consejo, la caridad con que ampara / al pobre, y sepulta al muerto."[7] Two specific works of mercy mentioned here are giving aid to the poor and burying the dead. In a similar play by another author about the same biblical character, namely Francisco de Rojas Zorrilla's *Los trabajos de Tobías*, we witness the following exchange regarding different works of mercy between the saintly Tobias and his wife Ana:

ANA: Yo he estado
visitando el hospital.
TOBÍAS: ¡No vi caridad igual!
ANA: Y la sepultura he dado
a algunos muertos que vi ...
y a mil Hebreos, y más
limosna en tu nombre di.[8]

The holy Tobias's pious actions are practised by his wife (but still in her husband's name) as well. Another saintly character even carries the poor on his back: "pudiera hacer las cosas, que se saben de su gran caridad: habrá seis noches, que le vieron llevar un pobre a cuestas."[9] These lines are spoken about Saint John of God in Lope de Vega's *Juan de Dios y Antón Martín*. In addition, these virtuous figures routinely obey Christ's implied command to care for the sick (Matthew 25:36). As one ill character who is a recipient of Charity declares, "soy muy malo, es verdad, pero si es enfermedad, la caridad no se espanta."[10] Here true Charity is not scared off by disease – which, we should note, is the explanation given for evil, in yet another clear conflation of moral with medical metaphors.

A different situation in which Charity was practised both in Golden Age culture and onstage was kindness or hospitality being offered to pilgrims. This might happen as a chance encounter on the road, as we see in this narrative account buried inside the third act of Tirso's *Santo y sastre*:

> Salió una vez de Cremona
> con las alforjas a pie,
> y en la mitad del camino
> vio cansado a un Peregrino,
> con él platicando fue,
> supo su necesidad,
> hízole que se asentase,
> rogóle que merendase,
> es larga su caridad:
> diole de lo que llevaba,
> con el vino satisfizo
> su sed.[11]

The location of Cremona in Lombardy insinuates that this pilgrim was probably going to Rome. Charitable people also gave money to pilgrims who went begging from door to door. We find this scenario in Lope de Vega's *San Nicolás de Tolentino*:

> SAN NICOLÁS: Pobres están a la puerta,
> ¡o quién tuviera que dar!
> PEREGRINO: Pues aquí queréis entrar,
> la caridad será cierta,
> dadme limosna.
> SAN NICOLÁS: ¿Quién es?
> PEREGRINO: Un Peregrino que pasa
> a Roma.
> SAN NICOLÁS: Esta santa casa
> os la puede hacer después,
> que saldrá gente piadosa
> de este ejercicio. Entre tanto,
> peregrino, os daré cuanto
> traigo con mano amorosa.
> Cien monedas me habían dado
> de una rentilla que tengo,
> aquí va.

In addition, he offers the pilgrim his own cloak: "Muy pobre de ropa estáis, mi capa os ha de cubrir." The pilgrim protests in disbelief, "¿También me queréis vestir?" To which Saint Nicholas replies,

Mas antes vos me la dáis,
que por ésta que en el suelo
os doy Peregrino a vos,
dará el Pontífice Dios
capa de coro en el cielo.[12]

We shall examine the special significance of cloaks and other garments for Charity later in this chapter.

But even more desperate than pilgrims were the actual beggars who lined the streets of Spain's largest cities during the Baroque period. These figures also find their way into the theatre. I have studied the proliferation of beggars, bandits, gypsies, and other social undesirables in Golden Age drama in the Greed chapter of my *Sins of the Fathers* book.[13] If specific figures quoted in the dramas are to be believed – and in this case, specific monetary amounts may add to the scenes' realism – the going rate for alms given to these personages was set at a decent price:

CABALLERO: De limosna os mando veinte escudos.
PISANO: Págueos el cielo caridad tan grande.[14]

The titular character of Lope's *Juan de Dios y Antón Martín* is known for his habit of going out on the streets with money to distribute to the needy:

MARQUÉS DE TARIFA: ¿Pero que es tan liberal?
DON LUIS: No hay caridad que le iguale.
MARQUÉS DE TARIFA: Él con el dinero sale ...

A poor, needy character who knows about this habit of the saint comes to him, asking for alms: "que a pedirle por Dios llego. Muestre en mí su caridad, que muero de hambre." In reply, Saint John of God gives him 100 *escudos*:

A la fe,
que me pesa, pero esté
cierto, que su Majestad

a ninguno desampara.
Allá el hermano Marqués
de Tarifa, como es
tan bueno, y al pobre ampara,
en esta bolsa me dio
cien escudos, tome, y coma.

The beggar exclaims with gratitude, "¡ay caridad semejante, ay hombre tan compasivo!"[15] These are relatively straightforward theatrical examples of the Virtue of Charity in action.

A more extreme case even than beggars depicted onstage would be giving alms to madmen. We find these lines in Lope de Vega's *Los locos de Valencia*, written about a madhouse:

MARTÍN: ¿Hay quien nos dé limosna, hay quien nos haga
alguna caridad a aquestos pobres?
BELARDO: ¿Hay quien les dé limosna a aquestos locos?[16]

Michel Foucault's *Madness and Civilization* studies the birth of the insane asylum in France, but no exactly equivalent theoretical treatment exists for Spain.[17] Interestingly, in this literary depiction we see that the walls of the madhouse are porous enough to allow alms to be distributed in person to its inhabitants, who were also permitted to leave the institution periodically to go out begging.[18]

A similar situation may be found in the case of literary portrayals of war veterans. Referred to in modern times as the "walking wounded," former soldiers from imperial Spain's multiple foreign wars might also have suffered from PTSD and other mental health problems, but did not enjoy the benefit of institutions such as veterans' hospitals to provide them with shelter. Instead they wandered the streets, stopping in at monasteries or convents known to distribute assistance to the needy. Monasteries distributed food to former soldiers such as one named Fisberto in Lope de Vega's *San Nicolás de Tolentino*, in an instance where literature reflects (rather than refracts) historical reality:

FISBERTO: A este Convento ha venido
gente pobre, si la hay más
que de estos rotos soldados,
señal que en este Convento
deben de darles sustento;

digan señores honrados,
¿hay por aquí caridad?
MUJER: Aquí en este Monasterio
nos dan algún refrigerio,
llegad, señor, y llamad.[19]

The Saint Nicholas of the play's title is able to distribute bread from this monastery even during a time of war by praying over it so that it multiplies.

The very need for this miracle shows us that increasingly in this society, comestible resources were scarce. Saint Nicholas had to multiply bread because there was not enough. Even animals were hungry, such as the chickens: "hasta el hermano pollino siente ver a los muchachos sin caridad, y él, y ellos andan a coz, y bocado."[20] The colloquial expression *andar a coz y bocado* means to play roughly. In this dog-eat-dog world where children were not charitable, the normal scraps one would expect to fall from the table were practically snatched in mid-air. The most saintly characters we meet give food to the animals, perhaps in imitation of Saint Francis, who is famously depicted with birds sitting on his shoulder and eating out of his hand. Lope de Vega's Saint Isidore is described this way: "quien vio caridad igual, a las aves da a comer."[21] Spain's food shortage meant that animals too depended on Charity.

There is no escaping the impression that there simply was not enough food (or money to buy food) to go around. In Francisco de Rojas Zorrilla's *Santa Isabel, reina de Portugal*, the *gracioso* Tarabilla speaks to the lady Isabel, the saintly figure of the title:

Señora, ya están aquí
los cincuenta escudos, pienso,
que aguardan en la antesala
dos mil pobres, y si cuento
irlandeses y chiquillos,
no hay número para ellos,
que éstas son tan pedidoras,
que cuando no hallan dineros,
piden, que de caridad
les hagan un niño de estos.

This passage describes a fictitious situation in which 50 *escudos* could not possibly cover the need of 2,000 beggars. We see here a thinly disguised racism in the reference to Irish immigrants as scruffy indigents. Further almsgiving is portrayed in this play when Saint Isabel commands Ramiro, "llevad esta cadena, y gastadla en limosnas a los pobres."[22] (Note that here, as is often the case in these plays, the figure exhibiting Charity is a woman). Saint Isabel was the queen of Portugal, which is how she managed to lay her hands on gold chains to be sold in order to raise money for the poor. Most Golden Age subjects outside of the theatre, even ones who might be charitably inclined, did not have her vast resources to work with.

Those who still wanted to help, but might not necessarily have money to offer, could instead provide food directly to the hungry. As I described in my Gluttony chapter in *Sins of the Fathers*, depictions of hunger abound on the early modern Spanish stage.[23] For example, in Luis Quiñones de Benavente's interlude *La verdad*, a little girl sings,

Den a esta mísera pobre,
una humilde caridad,
que ha mil días que en su boca,
no ve un mendrugo de pan.[24]

Here she claims that in 1,000 days she has not eaten so much as a stale crust of bread. In a similar instance, the *gracioso* Morrión makes an entrance onstage, limping on crutches and with a leg wrapped in bandages: "Déle a este pobre un remedio ... pues son las doce, y no se ha comido pan y medio. Den su caridad, y amor a este pobre."[25] It is already noon, but still he has had no breakfast. This hunger is so acute that characters faint from lack of sustenance, as we see in this exchange from Tirso de Molina's *Santo y sastre*:

HOMO BONO [SANTO]: Ay Pendón,
a mis puertas desmayado
está un pobre, yo habré dado
a su desgracia ocasión.
PENDÓN [GRACIOSO]: Tú, ¿por qué?
HOMO BONO [SANTO]: Porque vendría
con hambre, y necesidad,
faltóle mi caridad.[26]

Charity fails here, as even the well-intentioned giver does not act quickly enough to get there in time.

Food offered to beggars by monasteries or other sources might typically be very basic, such as a little bread eaten with cheese: "dan en esta hermita del santo que celebra España tanto caridad de queso, y pan,"[27] although Jodi Campbell in *At the First Table* demonstrates convincingly that food offered charitably was often more healthful than the sumptuous fare enjoyed by the rich. Sometimes the monks themselves would make these food products out of the milk their own cows produced. In a detail reflecting a substantial cultural difference from our world today, occasionally beggars would be offered their meal with a little wine, as in "a cuantos fueren les doy caridad de pan, y vino."[28] Now the conventional wisdom is that beggars are all drunkards and giving them wine would merely exacerbate their alcoholism.

But far and away the most common food donation was simple bread, which in Castile in the mid-seventeenth century was in increasingly short supply.[29] Bread was notable not just for its scarcity but also for the symbolic connections it bore. In many of the *autos sacramentales* Charity is in fact symbolized by a loaf of bread, which may or may not have appeared onstage in the form of an actual prop. In an important play for this Virtue, Calderón de la Barca's *El nuevo hospicio de pobres*, the character of Charity states unequivocally, "el Pan es la Caridad."[30] Jesus also called himself the Bread of Life (John 6:35). Bread was especially significant during the feast of Corpus Christi, which was the occasion for many *autos sacramentales*.[31] In another *auto* Joy declares, "el Pan de la Caridad nos quita el hambre."[32] We should recall that God sent bread from heaven to Moses in the form of manna: "Dios que dio a Moisés nuestro primer caudillo, la caridad más nueva que vieron nuestros siglos."[33] Here the manna is referred to as a new form of Charity. Likewise, Tirso de Molina's *La mejor espigadera* recalls Christ's ancestor Ruth who gleaned sheaves of wheat left over in the field of Boaz, her kinsman-redeemer. These biblical examples of God providing for his people, with the command that they in turn should provide charitably for others, found particular resonance in early modern Spanish culture.

In response to Spain's increasingly acute social and economic crisis, there was a rise of social organizations to perform works of mercy. Anne Cruz has studied these phenomena both historically and as depicted in picaresque literature in *Discourses of Poverty: Social Reform and the Picaresque Novel in Early Modern Spain*.[34] Antón Martín in Lope's *Juan de Dios y Antón Martín* laments the lack of such poor houses: "Dios le valga: ¿Ésa es la caridad? Ya que no tenga dónde albergar los pobres."[35] These lines suggest that these were pressing social problems which were much discussed, as reflected by their appearance on the *comedia* stage. This was an era when hospitals like the one in the title of Calderón de la Barca's *El nuevo hospicio de pobres*, formally called the Hospicio de la Congregación del Dulce Nombre de María (1668), were being built and patronized by confraternities.[36] Lope de Vega makes reference to one of these: "tan dulce puerto, como el de la caridad, que este hospital ejercita."[37]

Other charitable organizations included military orders.[38] We see this instrument of social welfare in Calderón de la Barca's auto *Las órdenes militares*, the full title of which is *Las órdenes militares, en metáfora de la piadosa Hermandad del Refugio, discurriendo por calles, y templos de Madrid*.[39] In this play we find the allegorical figure of Charity offering help to travellers: "en Madrid, que es la Corte del Siglo, la gran Caridad os ofrece su auxilio." Later a needy character begs, "Ten de mí piedad," to which Charity responds, "Aquese es mi oficio." A specific work of mercy performed by Charity in this play and its *loa* is burying convicted criminals who have been executed ("enterrar Ajusticiados").[40] A separate reference to this pious fraternal organization, the Hermandad del Refugio, may be found in a secular play by the same author: "deben de ser gente del Refugio, que anda quitando por caridad a las mujeres."[41] This is a humorous reference in context, spoken by a man who is tired of listening to his wife and hopes the Hermandad will come pick her up. Nonetheless, the literary reference shows us that this confraternity, like many others, was active in the rehabilitation of wayward women. This specifically gendered vocation as exercised by the confraternities has been studied recently by Margaret Boyle in *Unruly Women: Performance, Penitence, and Punishment in Early Modern Spain*.[42]

In fact, Charity became so closely identified with the *hermandades* that in the plays we see Charity as an actual garment worn by characters which had been donated by the Confraternity of the Santa Caridad.[43] This is logical, considering that another specific work of mercy was clothing the naked. In the *loa* for Calderón de la Barca's *Psiquis y Cupido, que escribió para la ciudad de Toledo*, Charity perfoms this specific task, simultaneously identifying herself with the jewellers' guild: "El Gremio de Joyas, que significo la Caridad, que es mi intento, vestir al desnudo."[44] The patron saint for this work of mercy would be Saint Martin, who divided his cloak in two with his sword to give to someone in need. We hear his name referenced in Lope's *Juan de Dios, y Antón Martín* when another character says to the titular figure, "pues tanto le parecéis, que el sobrenombre Martín por la caridad os viene tan bien, que el pobre en vos tiene capa que le cubre."[45] This characteristic garment of a cloak or cape became so symbolic of Charity that the allegorical figure for this Virtue appeared onstage in a cloak, shrouding poor people under it. The stage directions indicate, "Váyase el demonio, y descúbrase una cortina, y véase la Caridad con un manto extendido, debajo de él estén algunos pobres, y niños."[46] Dramaturgically speaking, Charity must have been a larger-than-life figure to accommodate so many people under her skirt.

But a discordant note is introduced into the theatrical depiction of this Virtue by the fact that Charity was also sometimes a garment worn by condemned criminals. The *alcalde* informs one of the prisoners in Lope de Vega's interlude *La cárcel de Sevilla*, "Hermano, esto va muy derrota, el escribano me ha notificado, que os suba a la enfermería, y que os ponga el hábito de la Caridad."[47] This unwelcome news implies that he is about to be hanged. The prisoner objects vigorously: "que no se me ponga el hábito de la Caridad, que sacó el ahorcado del otro día, que estaba viejo, y apolillado."[48] Here the prisoner complains not about his impending execution but about the fact that this garment is so moth-eaten and shabby as to offend his dignity.

At other times a similar garment was worn by nobility to disguise themselves when in the act of giving alms. For example, the titular figure in Lope de Vega's *La vida de San Pedro Nolasco* is described thus: "soldado y Caballero en hábitos pobres anda. En obras de caridad se entretiene."[49] These lines begin to unlock the supremely theatrical potential of a Virtue which is also a garment, which can also double as a disguise.

Once a Virtue can be used to play dress-up, disturbing implications arise. How can one tell if Charity is real or false? This dilemma is compounded by lines contrasting True Charity to its false double, such as "se dilata la Caridad verdadera."[50] What is the difference? Motivation counts, as true Charity must be animated with the fire of faith: "es bien que a la Caridad pase el amoroso incendio de Oración, y Fe."[51] This goes back to the role of the affects, specifically Love, that we mentioned at the chapter's outset. As we read in 1 Corinthians 13:1, whose words are repeated by Spanish dramatists, works of mercy without love are like a noisy gong or clashing cymbal: "el que obra sin Caridad, en el sonido se queda, como Campana." Later in the same *loa* we hear confirmed, "obras sin Caridad, también serán obras muertas."[52] It is curious to note that here Calderón de la Barca tweaked another scripture verse, "faith without works is dead," perhaps to avoid accusations of Protestantism.[53]

But let us for a moment cast these doubts about Charity's authenticity aside. When exercised in good faith, Charity is the lifesaver tossed into the dark cave of poverty: "su voluntad tu larga mano responda, que es soga la caridad para aquella cueva honda."[54] Here Charity is seen as a "long hand" outstretched to save the needy. Charity is, further, the light that illuminates the picaresque world: "es luz de aquestas tinieblas la encendida caridad."[55]

We must pause to note that some of the most genuine examples of Charity in the Golden Age theatre are women, to the point that women are more commonly associated with Charity than men. This is not immediately obvious, since some lines point in the opposite direction, indicating that men are more generous, while women are characteristically prone to Greed.[56] But throughout Europe in the popular genre of the *querelle des femmes*, we begin to see the opposing viewpoint prevail: "nella carità, quale come dice l'apostolo è de l'altre virtù maggiore, la donna è vincitrice." In case we missed it the first time, Italian ambassador Galeazzo Flavio Capra compares women's generosity to men's and finds it superior.[57]

Of course, women are often the needy ones, not the sources of beneficence. In one scene, Nise scolds Porcia: "no has andado discreta en desestimar del Duque la generosa largueza: viendo que por tantas partes la necesidad te cerca."[58] As in all times and cultures, needy women will be forced to stay dependent on men. But such jarring social realities do not escape the fact that pious Charity is primarily characterized as feminine on the early modern Spanish stage. For example, witness the following exchange:

> CELIA: Qué piadosa, Julia, eres.
> JULIA: Es virtud de las mujeres, y es atributo de Dios.[59]

Charity is the Virtue of women. It is also an attribute of God. Does this make God feminine? That is one possible implication of this line, much explored currently by feminist theologians,[60] which was deliberately left unpacked by Renaissance Spanish playwrights.

There was believed to be a direct connection between a woman's Virtue and her dowry, as in Lope's appropriately titled *La niña de plata*, where Enrique vows: "Daré veinte mil ducados de dote a aquesta doncella, aunque en las virtudes de ella van más de cien mil guardados."[61] There is an obvious allusion to Chastity here, which we shall explore in the next chapter. Women were legally entitled to keep control over their dowries during this time period, as Stephanie Fink De Backer has shown, which means they had more resources to draw upon in the exercise of Charity.[62] Lope de Vega confirms that pious generosity is the highest Virtue to which a woman may aspire: "mujer valiente y generosa, que la virtud más alta y celebrada de la mujer, fue siempre el ser piadosa."[63] This line comes from a play with a significant title for the gendering of Virtue, *El valor de las mujeres*.

But in what we shall soon see as a larger pattern for women and Virtue more generally, class trumps gender when it comes to Charity. Charity appears first and foremost in the *comedias* as an obligation of the nobility, expressed in the cultural imperative of *noblesse oblige*. Much like with the gold chain in the *Celestina*,[64] this generosity is specifically paid in jewels.[65] Here we see that *largesse* is the defining factor for a noble disposition. Noble families, including royal ones, were expected to endow convents or monasteries, as we note in the following exchange from Tirso's *La santa Juana*:

EMPERADOR CARLOS: Avisadme Tesorero,
para que limosna haga
a esta casa.
ARZOBISPO: Yo la doy
por ser su pobreza tanta,
el Beneficio de Cubas.
ABADESA: Tu largueza nos ampara.
CAPITÁN: Yo la doy quinientos mil maravedís.
ABADESA: Esos bastan,
para que un cuarto labremos.

In this literary depiction, the Abbess of the monastery quantifies the exact cost of adding on a room.[66] Unbelievable as it seems, some wealthy clergy actually had to be reminded to practice Charity (a fascinating dig at their peers, when we consider that most of these Spanish Golden Age playwrights were also priests), as in "enseñando a los Prelados con este ejemplo la caridad que deben ejercitar con los pobres."[67] Wealthy households were also expected to practise Charity close to home, namely in the form of how they treated domestic servants. One character hopes this generosity will cover for other faults.[68] Ultimately Charity became a societal expectation which reflected one's status as a nobleman or *hidalgo*, as in "Estimo vuestra largueza, y gran liberalidad, esa hidalga voluntad, y conocida nobleza."[69] It is easier to be virtuous if you are rich.

But the study of social attitudes towards Charity should not efface its spiritual aspect. For countless devout believers in the early modern period, Charity was the Renaissance equivalent of Led Zeppelin's "Stairway to Heaven." We find many lines such as "Que caridad más justa, o virtud de que el cielo tanto gusta."[70] Charity is described as a vine climbing right up to the sky: "la caridad, que es hiedra / que a Dios alcanzan sus ramas."[71] The modern reader may have a hard time, while reading this passage, suppressing the mental picture of the children's fairy tale *Jack and the Bean Stalk*. Finally, Charity is called godlike, as when Antón exclaims, "O caridad endiosada, quien te tiene, ¿qué no tiene, pues tiene a Dios, que le inflama?"[72] In other words, whoever shows Charity will lack for nothing, because he (or she) has God.

By extension, the poor too were considered sacred and were thought to be permitted by God to exist in their condition in order to give the rich an opportunity to redeem themselves: "cobre al rico que ladre al pobre, esa es poca caridad, que el pobre en la calidad, es oro."[73] The poor man is golden, while the rich man's quality is only that of a baser metal, namely copper. In the play that bears his name, Saint John of God complains that a beggar stole from him, thereby robbing him not just of his money, but of the chance to give charitably.[74] An extended exchange in Tirso de Molina's *Segunda parte de Santa Juana* illuminates for us the complex and often conflicting attitudes within this society regarding the poor and what, if any, constituted one's obligation to help them. The context is that an arrogant nobleman, Don Jorge, is threatening to appropriate a stash of bread normally reserved for charitable distribution to his needy vassals:

DON JORGE: ¿Qué depósito tiene aquí el Consejo?
MINGO: Cien fanegas de pan, que da cada año
a pobres del lugar.
DON JORGE: Lindo aparejo
para holgazanes.
MINGO: No teme ese daño,
porque sólo se da al enfermo viejo,
y a la mísera viuda.

DON JORGE: Ése es engaño:
aplícolo a mi renta.
BERRUECO: Pues ¿los pobres?
¿Qué han de comer cuando su pan los cobres?
DON JORGE: Remedio habrá para ellos.
BERRUECO: ¿De qué suerte?
DON JORGE: A los pobres enfermos desterrarlos.
CRESPO: Que eres Cristiano, y que lo son advierte.
DON JORGE: En Illescas podrán mejor curarlos.
BERRUECO: ¿Y a los viejos?
DON JORGE: ¿Los viejos? Darlos muerte:
pues no hay limosna igual como sacarlos
de este mal mundo.
MINGO: ¿Y ése es buen consejo?
DON JORGE: ¿Para qué ha de vivir, si es pobre un viejo?
MINGO: Plegue a Dios, que no llegues a esos días.
DON JORGE: Las viudas hilen, si de edad no fueren
para casarse.
BERRUECO: Bien tu intento guías.
DON JORGE: No ha de haber pobres, los que aquí lo fueren
hacedlos desterrar, que son harpías,
que a nuestras mesas sustentarse quieren,
y un poderoso, que los desterraba,
ratones de los ricos los llamaba.
CRESPO: Mejor nombre les da el cristiano zelo;
de quien en este mar los llama naves,
en que la Caridad despacha al cielo,
riquezas de que tiene Dios las llaves.
El mundo es mar, y en cierto recelo,
de sus Caribdis, y sus Syrtes graves,
en su golfo pierde el que navega,
sola la Caridad al Cielo llega.

In this long, wordy exchange, classical imagery such as quicksand and a sea monster become the metaphors for temptations exerted upon rich people so they will not practise Charity. Don Jorge – who advocates killing elderly people instead of feeding them – characteristically becomes outraged at this accusation, to which Mingo wisely replies, "Si limosnero, señor, fueras, tus vicios con ser tantos encubrieras."[75] In these words, Charity is characterized as the veneer of Virtue (a topic we shall explore later) which has the ambiguous capacity to cover over Vice. But the main message of Crespo's final speech is clear: alms are like ships sent off by Charity into the eternal great unknown. This image would have found particular resonance in a culture where merchants financed ships' voyages to the "New" World without any assurance of a return on their investment.[76] As Crespo rightly insinuates, these boats will reach a safe port only in heaven, where God is the harbour master.

Perhaps the best example of the "stairway to heaven" approach to Charity occurs in Lope de Vega's *Don Juan de Castro, primera parte* when a ghost named Tibaldo comes back from the dead to preach the message of Charity to the living Roberto. He thanks him for the good deeds performed to help him while he was alive and assures him that none of this effort has been lost, as it is all being stored up for him in heaven:

> Oye atento.
> De tu virtud los bienes excesivos,
> la caridad, y generoso intento
> contra mis deudos míseros y esquivos
> que usaste con mi cuerpo y alma, ahora
> en los cambios del cielo se atesora.

He later confirms, "y mira que el favor que se hace a un muerto / de Dios el premio aun en la tierra alcanza."[77] So the rewards for Charity are not just eternal, but also terrestrial. Charity starts to look like one gigantic insurance policy.

As Carlos Eire has shown in *From Madrid to Purgatory: The Art and Craft of Dying in Sixteenth-Century Spain*, this constellation of beliefs became so prevalent that some families went bankrupt in this life in an effort to pave their way clear for the next:

> Guided by the dictum "charity begins at home," Castilian legal codes in the Middle Ages attempted to protect the families of testators, especially the children and grandchildren, from those who would willingly hand over entire estates to charity in exchange for an assurance of salvation.[78]

We see these attitudes likewise reflected in the popular theatre. In Cervantes' picaresque *Pedro de Urdemalas*, Belica says to a poor widow and her companion, trying to convince them to accept her assistance: "tómame esa caridad, no hagáis si no hacer alarde de vuestra necesidad."

Here she actually begs them to accept her Charity! In the subsequent dialogue, roguish characters make fun of her desperate attempts to use money to earn her salvation:

Veisla Pedro, pues es fama
que tiene diez mil ducados
junto a los pies de su cama
en dos cofres barreados,
a quien sus Ángeles llama.

Requiébrase así con ellos,
que pone su gloria en ellos,
y así en verlos se desalma,
que han de ser para su alma
lo que a Absalón sus cabellos,

sólo a un ciego da un real
cada mes, porque le reza
las mañanas a su umbral
oraciones que endereza
al eterno tribunal.

Por si acaso sus parientes
su marido, y ascendientes
están en el purgatorio
haga el santo Consistorio
de su gloria merecientes.

Y con sola esta obra piensa
irse al cielo de rondón
sin desmán, y sin ofensa.[79]

Although simultaneously placing trust in 10,000 ducats, calling them her "Angels," Belica fears her treasure will be her downfall, just as the Old Testament prince Absalom's long hair became the means by which he died (it caught in a tree as he rode along under it, leaving him hanging there until soldiers from an opposing army pierced his heart with a spear).[80] To ease her conscience, she gives a blind man one *real* each month for praying at her doorstep, in the fervent hope that his prayers will be enough to win for her God's mercy.

What we have here is a total perversion of this Virtue within this imaginary economy of sins and souls. In this figuration, Charity is really only disguised self-interest:

> The charitable bequests of many testators betrayed a certain dimension of self-interest. As had been the case throughout the Middle Ages in Castile, much of charitable giving was aimed at gaining spiritual favors or at communicating a message to the poor about their own dependence and lack of self-worth. Many of the bequests made by sixteenth-century *Madrileños* openly asked for prayers and intercession in return from the poor or sought in some way to confirm and display the social status of the benefactor. *Madrileños* believed in the salvific power of almsgiving, but in death as in life they assigned a very broad meaning to the term "charity," and sought to derive as much personal gain as possible – in this world as well as the next – from each *real* bequeathed as *limosna* in their wills.[81]

Given this atmosphere, it was almost inevitable that Charity, along with its companion Virtues, would suffer irrevocable distortion.

Such a Protean transformation for this Virtue becomes evident likewise in the theatre. For example, in Tirso de Molina's ironically titled *Marta la piadosa* we find an exchange which appears at first to be a straightforward dialogue between a poor, sick student begging and a woman giving alms:

DON FELIPE [*dressed as a poor student*]:
A de casa, ¿hay quien se acuerde
de remediar la pobreza
de un estudiante que empieza
cánones, y el tiempo pierde
por la fiera enfermedad
que mis cursos no consiente?
Dad limosna noble gente,
si es caridad, calidad.
DOÑA MARTA: Padre y señor, ¿ve ese pobre?
Pues no sé qué compasión
las telas del corazón
me mueve para que cobre
remedio: si un hospital
el cielo hacerme permite,
déjeme que me ejercite

en éste, y cure su mal.
DON GÓMEZ: Dale un cuarto, y váyase
que en la Corte hay pobres hartos.
DOÑA MARTA: Si limosna haces cuartos,
verdugo tu zelo fue,
¿echar al pobre es razón?
Al rico avariento imitas:
daréle, pues me le quitas,
los brazos, y el corazón.
¡Ay pobre de mis entrañas!
Llega al alma que te doy.[82]

This apparently heartwarming scene turns to burlesque when the "poor student" is unmasked as the not-so-pious Marta's suitor Don Felipe, much to her father Don Gómez's surprise. If we read closely, we find that this exchange occurs within the larger context of a rather cynical discussion about how true devotion is a thing of the past, "en nuestros días la devoción va expirando." Instead of pearls, rosaries are now made out of coconuts, or – even worse – dead men's teeth:

DOÑA MARTA: Dejo intentos locos
y en mi rosario de cocos,
cuentas paso por contar.
PASTRANA: ¿Rosario de cocos?
DOÑA MARTA: ¿Pues?
Así se llaman, ¿qué quieres?
¿Si hacen cocos las mujeres,
porque anda el mundo al revés?
¿A lo bueno? *En nuestros días*
la devoción va expirando,
pues si rezan ya, es cocando
hasta a las Ave Marías ...
Profánanse ya las suertes,
ya la devoción es gala,
traigan todas noramala [en hora mala]
unos rosarios de muertes,
que sirvan de centinelas,
que yo desde hoy pienso hacerlo.
PASTRANA: ¿Muertes en rosario al cuello?
Parecerán sacamuelas.[83]

Pious women will thus look like dentists collecting teeth they have extracted. Here a pun is made on the dual meaning of the noun *coco*, meaning coconut or – by extension – any nut or seed from the "New" World used to make rosaries, and the colloquial verb *cocar*, which means to flatter or seduce someone. We also find in this passage an explicit reference to the classic Baroque topos of the upside-down world. Devotion here has turned to ornament. Nothing is what it seems. True religion has been profaned. The dead men's teeth used as rosary beads and worn around young women's necks comprise a particularly grotesque permutation of the traditional *memento mori*. It is hard to imagine, for this Virtue, what might constitute a greater perversion.

As a corollary to this patent fraud, in the same way that we must ask whether Charity is real, we must also ask whether the beggars we see onstage are "real" either. What we find here is a double falsehood: charlatans disguised as beggars often set out to deceive the wealthy, but then actors onstage were tasked with playing the part of beggars who were already fraudulent. False beggars always proliferate in the context of need, as when a wealthy character reports of a supplicant: "contóme sus desgracias y pobreza, a que acudió piadosa mi largueza."[84] Próspero (whose name undoubtedly denotes prosperity) speaks here of lending aid to Bruno, who tricked him with a sob story into giving him money. In similar fashion, in Calderón de la Barca's *El gran mercado del mundo*, Culpa or Fault tries to fool Buen Genio into giving her alms by dressing up as a poor beggar and pretending to be blind. Just prior to this, she has tried the same trick with Mal Genio and been turned down:

CULPA: Dad una limosna, ya
  que nada compráis.
MAL GENIO: No quiero,
  que Mendigos, Holgazanes
  lo sean con mi dinero.
CULPA [APARTE]: Si supieráis quién yo soy,
  harto me dabas en eso.
[AL BUEN GENIO]: Caballero,
  pues Vos sois
  tan Piadoso, Justo, y Cuerdo,
  que en el Mercado del Mundo
  hacéis del Oro desprecio,
  y compráis pobres alhajas,
  dad limosna a un pobre Ciego.

BUEN GENIO: En mí hay caridad; tomad.
CULPA: No negaréis por lo menos
 que ya no me has dado parte
 del Talento.
BUEN GENIO: Sí haré, puesto
 que no te le he dado a ti.
CULPA: ¿Pues a quién?
BUEN GENIO: Al sentimiento
 de verte necesitado,
 que es Dios tan Piadoso, y Recto,
 que aun lo que se da a la Culpa
 del hombre, que va pidiendo
 sin necesidad, *lo pone*
 a cuenta suya, diciendo,
 que es por quien se da, y no en quien
 consiste el merecimiento.[85]

Here Culpa makes reference to Christ's parable of the talents (Matthew 25:14–30) to extend this conversation into a larger debate about stewardship of resources. The upshot is that even if Buen Genio has been tricked into giving Charity to Culpa, who is only disguised as a blind beggar, God will give credit to him for actions performed in good faith ("lo pone a cuenta suya"). This mathematical language of accounts echoes the Old Testament's assertion that Abraham believed God, and it was credited to him as righteousness.[86] God appears here as the great Accountant in the sky adding up columns of figures in a ledger and keeping an eye on the running total. One could almost say that Charity becomes a matter of waging successful bets.

So who comes out ahead in this exercise in divine mathematics? Charity is suddenly evacuated of positive meaning when it becomes merely an exercise in self-preservation. Over and over again in the *autos sacramentales* we find the explicit warning that Charity should begin with oneself, as in "ser piadoso conmigo mismo, que la buena Caridad de sí empieza."[87] This passage foretells the potential pitfall of taking care of everyone else at the expense of one's own needs. A similar example may be found in the *loa* for Calderón de la Barca's *Psiquis y Cupido*: "que nadie en perjuicio proprio haga el bien, que no deseo, pues la caridad perfecta es comenzar de sí mismo."[88]

This truism is repeated in the secular plays as well. In Juan Ruiz de Alarcón's play titled *Examen de maridos* (*Test of Spouses*), Doña Inés proclaims, "que de sí misma comienza la caridad ordenada."[89] Young, noble and wealthy, she sets up a sort of contest or examination to survey prospective husbands. Yet she announces from the outset her intention to "look out for Number One" – i.e., herself. This saying about Charity beginning with oneself was apparently a favourite of this playwright, for whom it was as relevant in the context of friendship as in the context of marriage. In his *Ganar amigos*, the *gracioso* Encinas offers the nugget of wisdom: "La caridad, señor, de sí misma empieza."[90] This line is echoed word for word in Lope de Vega's *Amor, pleito y desafío*.[91]

Now, although these ideas might have found traction and gained currency, they did not meet with universal, unquestioning acceptance. Some characters debate whether this rule is applicable in every case:

ROBERTO: Que has hecho como Christiano,
Don Juan, confesarte quiero:
pero dar todo el dinero
ha sido un hecho inhumano.
¿De sí mismo no comienza la caridad?
JUAN: Es verdad,
pero la necesidad
te desenoje y te venza.[92]

These last lines are spoken by the noble titular character in Lope de Vega's *Don Juan de Castro, primera parte*. But although it is occasionally questioned, this principle of "Charity begins with oneself" is roundly affirmed, with some playwrights even criticizing the excessive Charity of otherwise saintly characters who fail to attend to their own needs:

TOBÍAS VIEJO: Que bien guardara la ley
de Dios con entrañas frías.
Ana, aquel caritativo
fuego en el alma encubierto,
sale sepultando al muerto,
y favoreciendo al vivo.
Por Dios es poco poder
la hacienda sola.
ANA: Es verdad, mas la propia caridad
su lugar ha de tener.[93]

Here Tobias's wife Ana seems to counsel him not to give away his entire inheritance, thereby turning himself into one of the very beggars he is trying to assist. Generosity is one thing, but giving too liberally is frowned upon: "generosidad será, mas generosidad necia; y tanto, que casi frisa en género de bajeza."[94] Excessive *largesse* leads to madness: "es tal, y tan larga, que según su mucha largueza, es un Alejandro irracional."[95] The reference here is to the alleged madness and irrationality of a hero so universally accepted as Alexander the Great.[96] These qualifiers amount to a distinction between "good" and "bad" Charity. For example, in Lope de Vega's *El molino* a count says to a prince, "no es buena caridad daros mi propia virtud."[97] Charity is not genuine if it gives all the goodies away.

In the end, it would appear that if this Virtue is to remain relevant at all, then it must act in combination with other Virtues to mitigate its tendency towards self-destruction. In this vein, Charity appears in connection to Justice: "ser franco, ser liberal, que sobre buen natural viene esta virtud al justo."[98] We may recall that like this "good" kind of Charity, distributive Justice gives to every person his due – which is emphatically *not* the same thing as giving away the whole pie.

Another Virtue seen to act in combination with Charity is Prudence. Prudence mitigates Charity, as in "Esta bondad con prudencia, que celebraba Platón, y le imitó Menandro, resplandece en V[uestra] M[erced]."[99] We find this citation of classical philosophers (evidence of Renaissance awareness of Virtues construed as pagan ethics) in the prefatory matter to Lope de Vega's *El honrado hermano*. What seems most desirable, in summary, is some type of balance in giving to others while asking others' help for one's self, as in "es la mejor diligencia ir mezclando con prudencia siempre el pedir con el dar."[100] This would entail a search for that ever-elusive quotient we have referred to consistently as the Golden Mean.

In this chapter we have seen the multiple ways in which Charity appears as an ambiguous antidote, or *pharmakon*, as well as how it was primarily (but not exclusively) the province of women. The next chapter will engage in a similar exercise with Chastity. Along with other ambiguities, even the seemingly straightforward gendering of this predominantly sexual – as opposed to legal, military, or economic – Virtue was not unproblematic.

4 Loose Chastity

¿Quién puede negar, Señor, que el Virginio estado es al conjugal preferido? Pues siempre la basa fue de las virtudes mayores.

– Guillén de Castro[1]

The speaker of these words is none other than the Virgin Mary, appearing onstage as a fictional character in Guillén de Castro's *El mejor esposo*. She goes on to explain why Chastity is the base of the column supporting the weight of the "greater" Virtues:

Consagrando al cielo en él
no sólo puras las almas,
pero los cuerpos también,
sin que entre el sumo Criador,
y las criaturas esté
el corazón dividido,
sino entero, limpio, y fiel.[2]

Here we see that purity of body is the logical counterpart to purity of soul. If Chastity is not exercised, the result will be a "divided heart" essentially at war with itself. This is without doubt the Virtue that appears in the *comedias* accompanied by the gravest warnings of what will happen if its precepts are not upheld.

Other playwrights confirm the conventional wisdom of the time that Chastity is the foundation for the greater Virtues, or *virtudes mayores*. In Lope de Vega's description of a *doncella*, or unmarried woman, in his appropriately named *La doncella Teodor*, the ideal young female "ha de ser generosa, y en las virtudes mayores, que es ser casta, y vergonzosa, merecer eternos loores."[3] As we have encountered before in so many conflicting examples, here we find a rank-ordering or hierarchy of Virtues in which Chastity is placed above even generosity or Charity – a detail which is curious, considering that Charity is one of the three Theological Virtues, and is in fact the greatest of the three, according to Saint Paul.[4]

In further superlative statements made in the plays, a woman's Chastity is said to be her greatest dowry: "[¿]dote de una mujer? [¿]lo qué más debe traer, que castidad, e hidalguía?"[5] Note here the way in which Chastity is equated to (at least minor) nobility. This Virtue protects its practitioner by building strong walls, like an impregnable fortress: "invencible, incontrastable, que la hacen inexpugnable los muros de su virtud."[6] Invoking ancient and medieval allegorical tropes, Chastity is pictured as a closed garden or monastic cloister: "pues haciendo claustro de sus hojas mismas, encierra en su castidad el oro de su pureza."[7] The *pureza* cited here was a concept freighted with cultural baggage in a society obsessed with blood purity, or *limpieza de sangre*,[8] as was the reference to gold during a time when Spain's thirst for "New" World bullion led it into an increasingly precarious economic situation.[9] As the saying goes, not all that glitters is gold; and in like fashion, this Virtue came to seem increasingly tarnished.

In its most basic definition, Chastity was equated to virginity, as we see from the title of Pedro Galindo's *Excelencias de la castidad y virginidad* (1681). Going back at least as far as Spain's medieval period, Chastity was defined in negative terms as the lack of sexual activity: "Es abstinencia de vil llegamiento / la tal castedat."[10] Perpetual virgins are described in a play by Lope as never seeing marriage, thus deserving the palm leaf – a symbol of Chastity – as well as a seat with the angels in heaven, who were believed not to be sexual beings.[11] In fact, virginity is identified so closely with Chastity in these plays that it actually takes Chastity's place in discussions onstage of the Virtues; for example, in Francisco de Rojas Zorrilla's *Los trabajos de Tobías* we find the lines, "El recato es un remedo de la virtud más perfecta, pues es la virginidad: y si en Dios caber pudiera una virtud, que sea más que esas otras virtudes; ésta más preeminente virtud que esas otras virtudes fuera."[12] This author is not willing to acknowledge that all Virtues are not equal, but hypothetically claims that if there were a hierarchy, virginity would come out on top. This seeming obsession with sexuality, or avoidance of same, is telling in its refusal to contemplate fulfilment of desire.

Needless to say, with its fixation on abstinence / virginity, this form of Chastity was viewed as an issue mainly for women. As that (in some respects) great defender of women, Galeazzo Flavio Capra, pointed out a generation earlier in his *Della eccellenza e dignità delle donne* (1525), this Virtue had been considered the special province of females since the time of the Romans: "volendo i Romani consecrare uno tempio alla pudicizia, elesseno una femina e non uomo che lo consecrasse."[13] In other words, the ancient Romans consecrated a temple to Modesty and chose a female to perform the consecration ceremony. Here Capra refers to Chastity by one of its other synonyms, Pudicizia (modesty), a concept invoked in similar fashion by the medieval Spanish writer Juan de Mena as "la grand pudiçiçia, / virtud nesçesaria de ser en la fembra."[14] He goes so far as to call modesty a "necessary Virtue" in women. In other places in his same text, the *Laberinto de Fortuna* (1444), synonyms for Chastity continue to proliferate, in a different instance morphing into something so general-sounding as "honesty":

ha de virtudes aquella noticia
que en fembra demanda la honestidat.[15]

Here once again we see this Virtue – no matter which name it goes by – depicted not as a mere desideratum, but instead as an implacable demand.

Why was this Virtue, perhaps more than others, perceived as so urgently necessary? Chastity was needed in large doses to quench the raging fires of Lust.[16] In Calderón de la Barca's sacramental drama *El año santo de Roma*, the allegorical figure of Chastity declares it her mission to eradicate Lust: "Porque aqueste es mi Oficio, que siendo la Castidad, es mi mortal Enemigo la Lascivia." In this same play the figures of Chastity and Honour together drag Lust across the stage.[17] In similar fashion, in the same playwright's *El año santo en Madrid*, Chastity is said to extinguish the fires of Lust: "a la Pureza la Lascivia ofrece luego, por la Castidad, que es quien siempre apagó sus incendios, el Estandarte."[18] This scene alludes to outright war, replete with battle flags, in the very best *bellum virtutum et vitiorum* tradition (see once again Figure 1, in which the female warrior-figure Chastity impales Lust with a sword). This trope is repeated in numerous other plays by this same author; for example:

la Castidad, que es la suma
Pureza, que vence a un tiempo,

para los Triunfos del Alma,
las Rebeliones del Cuerpo.[19]

The body is a mutinous faction whose rebellion must be brutally supressed.

Not surprisingly, given the apparent gendering of this Virtue, most of the exemplary figures mentioned in relation to it are female. In addition to the Virgin Mary, one of the biblical figures mentioned is Asenath, wife of the Old Testament patriarch Joseph: "Assenét, que es de Castidad ejemplo."[20] Noble and well-educated, daughter to a priest of the Egyptian sun god Ra, the historical Asenath later gave birth to Manasseh and Ephraim. Her marriage to Joseph was arranged by the pharaoh to reward Joseph for interpreting his dreams. There is no biblical evidence of her being particularly chaste or unchaste; rather, any association of her with this Virtue based exclusively on scripture would seem to stem from an implied contrast with Potiphar's wife, who had previously attempted to seduce Joseph, thereby landing him in jail. Presumably this comparison could have been constructed to show that not all Egyptian women were lascivious. If we look at other ancient sources, however, namely the apocryphal *Joseph and Aseneth*, we find a prehistory of her life before marrying Joseph.[21] In this text, Asenath is a virgin who rejects many other potential bridegrooms before finally agreeing to marry a Hebrew. Her instinct towards Chastity even within her native pagan culture enhances her qualifications to become the mother of two of the twelve future tribes of Israel. In Calderón de la Barca's auto *Sueños hay que verdad son* she has become so completely identified with this Virtue that the allegorical figure of Chastity appears to Joseph in a dream, assuming the human form of Asenath.

In addition to biblical characters, figures from classical Roman mythology also make their appearance. The foremost of these is Diana ("Diana, Diosa de la castidad"),[22] a virgin goddess who swore she would never marry. Ironically, she became the patroness of hunters after transforming the hunter Acteon into a stag and setting his own hunting dogs to kill him. She did this because he saw her bathing naked in the forest. Such a fierce defence of Chastity could only selectively inspire emulation. Another figure from Roman legendary history who is mentioned frequently in these plays in the context of Chastity is Lucretia (as in "la castidad de Lucrecia").[23] These references portray Lucrecia and women like her as scornful of men, such as "en castidad Lucrecia, que como a gusarapa te desprecia."[24] The Real Academia Española defines *gusarapa* as a water worm: "animalejo, en forma de gusano, que se cría en un líquido."[25] Not exactly a compliment to a man! What happened to

Lucretia to make her hate men so much? While there are many variants on the legend, most versions agree on the basic facts of her situation: she was a married Roman matron raped by Prince Sextus Tarquinius who then committed suicide by stabbing herself with a dagger rather than live with dishonour. Her bloody corpse was paraded through the Roman Forum around the year 510 BC, thereby inciting a revolt against Rome's tyrannical king, Sextus's father, and heralding the birth of the Republic. But do women have to be raped and commit suicide to demonstrate their Chastity?[26] This exemplary figure seems highly ambiguous in terms of potential life applications by Golden Age Spanish women.

Lucretia's name is repeated in one of Lope de Vega's many plays about gender and Virtue, *Virtud, pobreza y mujer*, this time in the company of two other women of renown: "su casta fortaleza Sulpicia, Lucrecia, y Drias."[27] Note here the conflation with the Cardinal Virtue of Fortitude. The interesting thing to notice about this characterization is that there are two possible Sulpicias to which this line could refer, and neither of them was especially chaste. Lope here almost certainly makes reference to a Roman woman by the name of Sulpicia who lived during the reign of Emperor Domitian. She was married to a Roman man, Calenus. Some very sparse verses of poetry attributed to her describe the joys of erotic love within the context of marriage. While it is clear she was not promiscuous, her explicit description of naked lovemaking is difficult to square with received notions of Chastity. The other possible attribution is even more problematic. The other Roman poet Sulpicia lived under Emperor Augustus and penned a half-dozen elegiac poems to her lover Cerinthus. At least one classics scholar, Thomas Hubbard, believes that the poems' content is too risqué to have come from the pen of a high-born Roman woman.[28] The third classical figure mentioned by Lope in conjunction with Lucretia, namely Drias (alternatively spelled Dryas), according to Greek mythology was the daughter of Faunas and a sister of Acis. She hated men so much that she never even appeared in public. This legendary woman and her behaviour seem to fit better with an extreme paradigm for Chastity such as the one promoted by the stereotype of the *mujer esquiva*.[29]

Some further exemplary figures mentioned in the *comedias* in connection with Chastity stem from Arabic sources as well as Anglo-Saxon history. Antonio says of the female titular character in Lope de Vega's *El mayordomo de la Duquesa de Amalfi*, "en castidad ha igualado / A Zenobia, y a Etelfrida."[30] In the third century AD Zenobia was queen of Palmyra in Syria before leading a revolt against the Roman Empire. Perhaps the original *mujer varonil,* whom we have already met in the context of Fortitude, she led her soldiers personally into battle and even at one point conquered Egypt. She was famous for her Chastity until her marriage to Septimius Odaenathus, king of Palmyra, who was later assassinated. She herself was eventually taken hostage by the Roman general Aurelian, who paraded her through Rome wearing chains made of gold. From there her fate is unknown, although at least some sources place her in Rome as the result of a second marriage to a high-born Roman, perhaps a senator or even a governor. Thus the reference to her in the context of Chastity only makes sense in terms of her earlier life as an unassailable warrior queen.

Once again, Lope seems to pair a problematic example of Chastity with a more logical one, perhaps hoping that his audience will somehow take an average of the two. According to Antonio de Yepes's *Corónica general de la Orden de San Benito* (1609), Etelfrida was a saintly Anglo-Saxon nun of the seventh century, daughter of King Osubio of Northumbria and sister of Elfleda, who became an abbess of the monastery of Santa Hilda. Princess Etelfrida herself lived in another monastery, this one run by an abbess named Congilda, whose holy life she imitated.[31] This exemplary figure, for a change, at least seems to have practised the Virtue she was designated to exemplify.

Still further examples of Chastity in the *comedias* are derived from the courtly love tradition,[32] beginning with one of its foremost practitioners, Francesco Petrarca. Specific reference is made by Lope de Vega to Petrarch's allegorical *Trionfo della Pudicizia* (1351–1374), the protagonist of which is his elusive beloved, Laura: "el Petrarca, en los triunfos que escribió de la castidad."[33] This example is potentially ambiguous because in this text, although it is often interpreted as a straightforward paean to modesty, Laura leads illustrious women of legend such as Dido (mistress of Virgil's Aeneas) to take a ride in the chariot of Love. They end up at the Temple of Modesty, it is true; but taking a ride in Love's chariot would seem to lead them in the wrong direction, at least so far as Chastity is concerned. Further examples derive from the world of chivalric romance. In Lope de Vega's afore-mentioned *Virtud, pobreza y mujer* we hear the following exchange in reference to Ludovico Ariosto's *Orlando furioso*:

HIPÓLITO: Valdrá en Sevilla mi hacienda
sin las naves que la India
navegan, y que Dios vuelva

cien mil ducados y más.
DON JUAN: Pues conquistaréis con ellas
a los bárbaros de Chile,
y no a la casta Isabela.
Que aunque se llama Isabel,
porque Ariosto celebra
una casta de este nombre,
de quien mil virtudes cuenta,
la llama Toledo así.[34]

The heroine Isabella who appears in Ariosto's text is a thinly disguised allusion to none other than the historical noblewoman Isabella d'Este, who was one of his patrons at the courts of Ferrara and Mantua. As her characterization has been interpreted by modern scholars, Ariosto calls her "chaste" in an attempt to flatter her and secure further patronage.[35] Her namesake Isabel (or Isabela) in Lope's play lives up to her name because money cannot persuade her to give in to men's advances. But considering the fact that money was exactly what Ariosto wanted when he penned his praise of Isabella d'Este, at least through modern lenses, this example too becomes problematic.

Another Italian noblewoman mentioned in the *comedias* in the context of Chastity is Grimalda: "Gentil es Grimalda, pues con tal noble guirnalda de castidad la cubrís."[36] Wordplay aside (*Grimalda / guirnalda*), this line is probably a reference to Benedettina Grimaldi, a patroness of the Ospedale di Pammatone who personally nursed patients there who were suffering from the plague and leprosy. She may or may not have been chaste, but she certainly was generous; here we see a conflation of the Virtue of Chastity with the Virtue of Charity, typical of the collapsing together of "distinct" Virtues which we have seen in this and other chapters.

As multifarious as these historical and legendary examples are, they all have one thing in common: the exemplary figures mentioned in the context of Chastity in the *comedias* are primarily women. Chastity was not typical for men on the *comedia* stage; and when they were chaste, they seemed to worry that their Chastity could be confused with lack of virile potency. As King Alfonso declares in Lope de Vega's *Las famosas asturianas*: "maguer que Casto me llaman. Que el Casto fue por virtud, no porque el brío me falta."[37] He seems obsessed with clarifying that for him, Chastity was a choice, not a default setting. Even playwrights such as Calderón de la Barca, who advocate Chastity for men, are forced to concede, in line with Saint Paul, that men have a stronger sex drive and thus it is better for them to marry than to burn with Lust; he ventures the judgment, "Mejor es la castidad, que el matrimonio" but tempers this idea with the acknowledgment that Chastity – however preferable – is not mandated for all believers: "el matrimonio es bueno, y permitido, porque su contrario la castidad, que es mejor, no es mandado."[38] This line echoes 1 Corinthians 7:8–9,

> But I say to the unmarried and to the widows: It is good for them if they so continue, even as I. But if they do not contain themselves, let them marry. For it is better to marry than to be burnt.

This dictate from scripture would seem to breach no argument. But a small percentage of Catholic Christians through the centuries have interpreted things differently, choosing instead to give up voluntarily all sexual contact. Some early examples of these unusual individuals have been examined by Peter Brown in *The Body and Society*, a study of permanent sexual renunciation (continence, celibacy, and life-long virginity) among both men and women in Christian circles from around 50 AD to 430 AD. The most fascinating part of Brown's book is its discussion of male attitudes towards sexuality and how, in one ancient mindset, Chastity could equal virility for a man, not its polar opposite:

> A powerful "fantasy of the loss of vital spirit" lay at the root of many late classical attitudes to the male body. It is one of the many notions that gave male continence a firm foothold in the folk wisdom of the world in which Christian celibacy would soon be preached. The most virile man was the man who kept most of his vital spirit – the one, that is, who lost little or no seed.[39]

Stemming, according to Brown, from the voluntarily castrated Origen's "peculiarly majestic ideal of virginity,"[40] this iteration of Chastity as a Virtue paradoxically also came to mean fear of becoming sexually depleted through too much sexual activity. In this "complex and resilient ecology of moral notions," writes Professor Brown, "[i]t was never enough to be male: a man had to strive to remain 'virile.'"[41] He clarifies regarding the typical Roman man that, as we have seen previously in the chapter on Fortitude, "scenes of battle and the submission of barbarians represented his *virtus*."[42] This conflation of two of the Virtues at a deeper level – namely Fortitude with Chastity – shows just how inextricably notions of Virtue were intertwined. Eventually they became muddled up until they were impossible to separate or see as distinct entities.

It turns out that in Spanish literature also, Chastity is a virtue for men too. Juan de Mena devotes the entirety of stanza LXXXIII to this point in his *Laberinto de Fortuna* (1444):

> Aprendan los grandes bevir castamente,
> non vençan en viçios los brutos salvajes,
> en vilipendio de muchos linages,
> viles deleites non viçien la gente.
> Mas los que presumen del mundo presente
> fuigan de donde los dapños renascen;
> si lindos cobdiçian ser fechos, abraçen
> la vida más casta con la continente.[43]

Here a medieval Spanish author seems to uphold Chastity as a higher Virtue to which truly great men, *los grandes*, may aspire. He opposes the exercise of this Virtue to the behaviour of brute beasts ("brutos salvajes") who damage that most precious commodity of pure family lineage ("En vilipendio de muchos linages"). Note here that the ever-present fear of miscegenation, which we have already seen to be a hallmark of early modern Spanish culture, haunts this as well as other texts, lurking never very far in the background.[44]

These complex attitudes towards male sexuality are carried over, likewise, to the Renaissance Spanish stage. Among male examples for Chastity appears Saint Joseph, husband to the Virgin Mary, who says to her in Juan Bautista Diamante's zarzuela *El nacimiento de Cristo*: "no, Esposa, olvidaré mi amor por mi castidad, vive con seguridad."[45] Here he promises her that because of his Chastity, she will not have to worry about him making sexual advances, but this does not mean he does not love her. This was an interpretation of the nature of Mary and Joseph's marriage which ultimately derived from Saint Jerome:

> Christian understanding of the relationship between Joseph and Mary had undergone a dramatic development since the second and third centuries. Some early writers of the church, such as Tertullian, had argued that Mary and Joseph had had normal sexual relations after the birth of Jesus, bringing forth the brothers of Jesus – namely James, Joseph, Simon, and Judas (cf. Matt. 13:55 and Mark 6:3) ... Jerome, however, dismissed these claims and defended Mary's perpetual virginity. Once having done so,

> however, he was compelled to consider the nature of the relationship Mary and Joseph enjoyed. Could they be seen as married partners if they never had consummated a union? ... Jerome sees Joseph as Mary's companion and protector more than her husband, and he seems to hold that Joseph could have left Mary at any time in order to marry another woman ... Nevertheless, Joseph chose Mary, loved her, and preserved along with her his perpetual virginity in a union that forms an analogy to Christ's union with the church.[46]

In "Marriage in Medieval Culture: Consent Theory and the Case of Joseph and Mary," Irven Resnick has shown how the Holy Family's chaste marriage became a paradigm for medieval couples, some of whom self-consciously chose to imitate Joseph's renunciation of what would have been the normal sexual hierarchy.[47]

As we might expect, decisions in favour of Chastity on the part of male or female figures in these plays usually appear as the result of a solemn religious vow. In Agustín Moreto's hagiographical drama *Santa Rosa del Perú*, the titular character predictably declares, "Yo en fin, dedicar a Dios mi castidad he resuelto."[48] The Virgin Mary makes it clear that in her case, she takes this vow on a purely voluntary basis: "que debo hacer por mí misma, siendo yo la que castidad voté, apeteciendo el morir con la palma del nacer."[49] Here she equates Chastity with a kind of death, or at least the death of her natural desires as a red-blooded woman. Nonetheless, it is a death that whets her appetite.

It seems important for characters who take this vow to clear up for their audience any possible confusion regarding their actions; while permanent Chastity may not technically be required of all good Christians, it exists as an option reserved for the select few who choose to accept this lifelong challenge. As the High Priest explains of ancient Hebrew culture, "el permanente estado de Castidad, nunca ha sido en nosotros recibido, ni en nuestra costumbre."[50] This line comes from Guillén de Castro's *El mejor esposo*, another play about Jesus's stepfather Joseph, who allegedly maintained the sanctity of Mary's womb while she carried the Christ Child by not indulging in sexual relations with her. Mary defends their choice: "el hacer voto de castidad, no es romper los fueros de la costumbre."[51] In other words, both halves of this couple are aware that their decisions are unorthodox, to the point of running counter to prevailing cultural norms; but as Mary's divinely selected husband, Joseph too is being held to a higher standard. We can see in this choice of subject matter a fascination on the part of Golden Age playwrights with extreme or liminal cases which scholars have consistently highlighted as characteristic of Baroque manneristic hyperbole.[52]

Vows of Chastity were sometimes taken by both spouses within a marriage, and not just in the extreme case of the Holy Family. We find this scenario in Lope de Vega's *Los locos por el cielo* in the line "[l]a castidad ya jurada por el voto de los dos."[53] This example is consummately ambiguous in the sense that the very title of the play calls these saintly figures crazy. The validation of madness in a holy setting, including Erasmus's praise of folly and the wisdom of fools in his *Moriae Encomium*, is beyond the scope of our discussion here, although I have touched upon it elsewhere.[54]

Sometimes in practice marital celibacy meant both spouses would retire to a convent. This is what happens with a saintly couple in Calderón de la Barca's *El purgatorio de San Patricio*. Their son describes his parents:

> Mis piadosos padres, luego
> que pagaron esta deuda
> común, que el hombre casado
> debió a la naturaleza,
> se retiraron a dos Conventos, donde en pureza
> de castidad conservaron
> su vida, hasta la postrera
> línea fatal, que rindieron
> con mil Católicas muestras
> el espíritu a los cielos,
> y el cadáver a la tierra.[55]

Here we see a formerly married couple – living separately in twin convents, no less – preserving their mutual vow of Chastity until they die.

But an even more unusual example of Chastity within marriage occurs when both spouses pledge to remain celibate while living together outside of a convent, although they are technically still married. This medieval practice has been studied for Germany by Claudia Bornholdt in *Saintly Spouses: Chaste Marriage in Sacred and Secular Narrative from Medieval Germany (12th and 13th Centuries)*, an examination of select very extreme cases of saints who agreed to remain celibate within marriage because they considered all sexuality to be sinful. Spanish Golden Age plays make it clear that this kind of Chastity is not so high up as monastic celibacy in the hierarchy of Virtues. As Saint Rose of Peru declares, "La castidad conjugal es virtud de menos precio que la virginal." This line rather bluntly places a comparative price on Virtue. At this, a different character objects: "Eso niego, que siempre es más consumada virtud la del casamiento."[56] Here the dramatist Agustín Moreto plays humorously even in a serious drama upon the word *consumada*, which can mean both *consummate* and *consummated*.

Perhaps the classic case of Chastity within marriage occurs somewhat involuntarily and in a way that is only temporary in the apocryphal Old Testament story of Tobias and Sarah. In this tale, the beautiful Sarah marries several men in rapid succession, all of whom die before the marriage can be consummated. After praying to God for a merciful death, finally she marries Tobias the younger (his father also bears the same name) and they decide to wait strategically for three nights before attempting to consummate their union. They spend those three nights in prayer. In Francisco de Rojas Zorrilla's version of the Tobias story from the Catholic Bible, the demon Asmodeo appears to Tobias and thunders the reproach, "[¿]Cómo de la castidad violaste el templo?"[57] (Here we should note that the discourse of the Virtues is available for appropriation even by demons.) Following some advice from the archangel Raphael, Tobias is able to perform an exorcism of sorts and rid his poor bride of the demonic presence which had killed all seven previous husbands. This temporary, strategic Chastity within marriage is the kind alluded to by Lope de Vega in his own version of this legend, *La Historia de Tobías*, in which he refers to the "limpieza matrimonial en los dos Tobías."[58] Somehow or other – as often happens with legends – the exaggerated, larger-than-life qualities of their heroes multiply and expand to fill the space available, so that now Tobias the elder is also connected to Chastity within marriage. There seems to be no basis for this association in the Catholic Bible. But the book of Tobias offers some general words regarding Chastity and motivation for sexual union within marriage that generations of Catholics have taken to heart and even read aloud at wedding ceremonies. The angel Raphael speaks to Tobias:

> Hear me, and I will shew thee who they are, over whom the devil can prevail. For they who in such manner receive matrimony, as to shut out God from themselves, and from their mind, and to give themselves to their lust, as the horse and mule, which have not understanding: over them the devil hath power.[59]

This passage may well have given rise to early modern Spanish confessors' apparent fixation on sex positions and the "sinfulness" of marital pleasure.[60] This apocryphal text – considered to be canonical by early modern Catholics, and still accepted as Holy Writ by the Catholic Church today – clearly identifies procreation as the only acceptable goal of sex within marriage. As Tobias says to his young new wife Sarah, "for these three nights we are joined to God ... For we are the children of saints, and we must not be joined together like heathens that know not God." In his prayer he then specifies an acceptable motivation for sex: "And now, Lord, thou knowest, that not for fleshly lust do I take my sister to wife, but only for the love of posterity, in which Thy name may be blessed for ever and ever."[61] From this text was derived a curious idea so often repeated in Renaissance confessional manuals, namely that the proper goal of sex within marriage was not pleasure, but procreation; and therefore that the Deadly Sin of Lust within marriage was still sinful.[62]

Was this an impossible standard? Did Chastity "work" as it was conceived in early modern Spanish culture and portrayed upon the early modern Spanish stage? I would argue that it did not, and that in true proto-Derridean form, the presence of Chastity was most notable in early modern Spanish culture by its absence. Countless lines from *comedias* reiterate this cynical view of Virtue, as in "se rindió a la hermosura, que no hay castidad segura en santos que comen bien."[63] Here a man gives in to Lust, inspired by a woman's beauty, and Chastity is proven to be uncertain without monastic austerity to serve as a suitable framework. It is interesting to note here the conflation of Lust with Gluttony, and on the flip side Chastity with Temperance, as saints who eat well are pictured as giving in to other bodily pleasures too. We shall see further examples of this type of conflation of two or more Virtues later.

For now, let it suffice to say that in these plays, Chastity is literally dispensable. For the sake of convenience, even a vow of Chastity can be nullified with a papal dispensation, as in Tirso de Molina's *Marta la piadosa*:

> DOÑA MARTA: ¿Y el voto de castidad?
> CAPITÁN URBINA: Con una dispensación, pues fue simple tu afición.[64]

Here the mere "simplicity" of a girl's state of mind when she made her vow can argue in favour of her breaking it later. Of course, Marta is not really so pious as Tirso's facetious title would at first make her sound, as we saw in her extended appearance in our chapter on Charity. Even a priestly male playwright such as Tirso de Molina had to admit the inverisimilitude of asking women to be chaste right up until the point when they were married, then brazen sluts in the bedroom after the wedding in order to please their spouses: "en todo el mundo celebrada por Vesta en castidad cuando doncella, ¿lasciva Venus es, cuando casada? Mil imposibilidades tiene ..."[65] Here he invokes the Vestal virgins, ancient guardians of the domestic hearth goddess Vesta's shrine, in contrast to lascivious Venus, goddess of love.

On the rare occasions when Chastity does work, it is called rare, as in "Estimo por cosa rara su defensa, y castidad."[66] A chaste woman is ambivalently described as a rose surrounded by thorns.[67] In other words, Chastity protects a woman from grabbing hands but it also inflicts bloody wounds upon herself as well as her lover. Even when Chastity appears in full force, it can be expended more like social capital than an actual Virtue, as when a woman says, "tú verás como le doy con mi castidad castigo."[68] Here she cleverly plays upon the alliterative word pair *castidad / castigo* and uses (false) Chastity like a weapon to punish her would-be suitor.

Although Chastity may not always be subverted for other purposes, but instead exercised occasionally in good faith, doubts will still linger as to its authenticity. One thing is reputation, the other the reality: "Mas esta castidad que maravilla consiste más que en conservar la fama."[69] A person's Chastity is likened in these plays to the purity of gold, which (particularly in the age of alchemy) could allegedly be faked or fabricated from baser metals:[70] "y oro un metal que tanto puede dude de la castidad y de la sangre que tiene."[71] Upon further inspection, this Virtue might only be skin-deep, as in "por dar a mi castidad estos esmaltes famosos."[72] We will explore later in our conclusion the ramifications for this veneer of Virtue.

The tantalizing vestiges of ambiguity surrounding it lead to a discourse in which – like we saw with Charity – some kinds of Chastity are deemed "good" and others "bad." In Lope de Vega's *La vengadora de las mujeres*, we read that women should not imitate Dido, not because she was unchaste in her love affair with Aeneas, but because she committed suicide: "Dido quiso matarse, por guardar su castidad, que no la gozase nadie."[73] There was much confusion among late medieval and early Renaissance writers about whether Dido had been chaste or not. Giovanni Boccaccio apparently changed his mind about her legacy as a result of his contact with Francesco Petrarca. In his writings subsequent to this contact, the myth of a chaste Dido prevails. The alternative tradition of a chaste Dido, constructed in counterpoint to Virgil's poetic version in the *Aeneid* of a lascivious one, was rooted in an account by the ancient historian Justinus:

> The alternative tradition of the historical Dido, however, gave Boccaccio an even better way to bring his criticism of the Dido story into line with the principles of epideictic criticism. By rejecting Virgil's account in favor of that found in Justinus and the *veteres historiographi*, as he does in *De claris mulieribus* ... Boccaccio can put forth the image of a chaste and constant Dido, an image that is clearly worthy of praise and that he clearly prefers.[74]

Lope shows an awareness of the multiple ambiguities surrounding the legend of Dido in the next few lines by presenting an alternative version of these same events: "luego hay hombre que diga, / que se mató por vengarse / de los agravios de Eneas, / con quien fue huéspeda fácil." In another of Lope's plays, women are told implicitly, "Don't be like Dido": in the playwright's words, "no sea su castidad la de Elisa."[75] Why not? Is it because in Virgil's version, she was not so chaste, after all? Or because in either of the two main possible variants of her story, this "Virtue" only led to heartache and death?

Perhaps not surprisingly, given the inherent dramatic appeal, these dramas are full of "chaste" heroines who prefer death to dishonour. As Teodosia says in Juan de la Cueva's *Tragedia del príncipe tirano*, "yo moriré en la firmeza, que debo a mi castidad." She reiterates later,

> Sabrás, Rey excelente, que intentando
> tu hijo hacer ofensa a mi marido,
> mi honesta y pura castidad robando,
> quise antes que ver mi honor perdido,
> que a mis manos muriese el monstruo infando.[76]

The situation here is one of murder, but with mitigating circumstances: the tyrannical prince of the play's title has first buried Teodosia's husband alive and then had her sent to his bedroom where he means to violate her Chastity. In revenge, she murders him with her own hands. In this case it is the would-be rapist who dies instead of his victim; but even so, blood is shed at the altar of Chastity.

Almost any way you cut it, this Virtue requires human sacrifice. We hear in the chivalric legend of the enchantress Alcina, derived from Ariosto's *Orlando furioso* and repeated in Calderón de la Barca's sacramental drama *El pastor fido*, that a nymph who was wrongfully

convencida de adulterio,
a muerte fue condenada,
sacrificada en el Templo
de la Castidad, a no
dar Víctima humana, en precio
del Rescate de su Vida.[77]

In Ariosto's version, Alcina also takes captive a Saracen named Ruggiero, who then must be freed from her magical island. More innocent victims are slaughtered on Chastity's altar.

But allegorical and mythical treatments aside, the real victims on the early modern Spanish stage are wives legally murdered by their husbands on merely the suspicion that they might have been unfaithful. Matthew Stroud urges caution when it comes to interpreting the many Golden Age theatrical representations of uxoricide, or wife-murder, as indicative of real-life events:

> Archival research into the historical accuracy and legal validity of the wife-murder plots reveals both that there were occasional cases in which a husband killed his wife or had her killed, and that there were laws that allowed a man to defend the sanctity of his marriage by violence, at least under certain conditions. It is also true, however, that the actual number of cases of wife murder was very small.[78]

But even if we take such salubrious caveats into account, we are still left with at least thirty-one plays[79] depicting wife-murder as (at very minimum) a cultural fantasy too prevalent to be ignored.

Given the bloody massacre these plays collectively represent, how could Chastity ever succeed? The plays and their packaging seem to indicate that some exemplary figures did succeed in this mission, at least according to the way Dido is praised in the prefatory matter to Lope de Vega's *Las almenas de Toro*:

Fenisa Dido, que en el mar Sidonio
las rocas excediste conquistada,
y en limpia castidad, jamás violada,
conservaste la fe del matrimonio.[80]

But these words cannot fail to sound ironic, coming from the pen of Lope de Vega, that notoriously promiscuous womanizer whose series of affairs has been dramatized most recently in the historical fiction film *Lope*.[81] And in fact, if we read further, we discover that El Fénix was playing with us all along: his tongue-in-cheek "praise" of Dido was only meant to poke fun at her lack of Chastity. Referring to Guillén de Castro's play about her, *Dido y Eneas*, he offers the following sarcastic jibe:

> Que más gana tu fama con su pluma,
> que pierde en ser burlada tu firmeza.

One wonders how he would have felt about being the butt of such jokes.

Are we witnessing the famous double standard here, in which certain norms of morality were unevenly applied to women as opposed to men?[82] Or is this a case of *un aprovechado sin vergüenza*, a man who flaunted shamelessly the very moral standards he (as a priest, no less!)[83] was charged to uphold?

The double standard was a recognizable problem within Golden Age culture. For the real trouble with Chastity as a Virtue was that (whether this behaviour was warranted or not) real-life wives were constantly being scrutinized by their husbands. In terms posed by Michel Foucault, in the Panopticon that was early modern Spain, women were the object of almost perpetual *surveillance*, including internalized forms of self-vigilance which operated even more effectively in the shadows than the (also-present) more bluntly obvious methods of control.[84] In her *Perfect Wives, Other Women: Adultery and Inquisition in Early Modern Spain*, Georgina Dopico Black has offered the most persuasive account in recent years of the plight of women misogynistically assumed to be teetering on the brink of moral catastrophe.[85] The men who accuse them populate these dramas. For example, in Francisco de Rojas Zorrilla's ominously titled *La traición busca el castigo*, a husband says, "juez de mi causa misma, examino las virtudes de mi esposa."[86] Virtue here becomes an object for examination, where the language of the courtroom is specifically invoked to show the husband paradoxically acting as the judge of his own lawsuit. In similar fashion, Guillén de Castro's drama *El curioso impertinente*, fashioned after the model of Cervantes' intercalated tale by the same name, contains a preliminary assessment of the wife's faithfulness: "Es en el mundo un retrato de la misma castidad, un Sol de la honestidad, y un ejemplo del recato."[87] But we all know how that story ends: the curious man of the title puts his wife's Chastity to the test by asking his best friend to woo her and see if he gets anywhere. In the play, as in the novel from which it is derived, the wife's Chastity is not so infallible / unspotted as her husband thinks. He commits suicide upon discovering his error in judgment, realizing that he alone is to blame for leading her into temptation.

In historical fact as opposed to the theatre's artificially constructed laboratory for the study of moral behaviour, the litmus test is whether a wife will remain faithful in her husband's absence. This concept, as explored in Lope de Vega's *La viuda casada y doncella*, was known as "castidad en ausencia."[88] Allyson Poska has studied actual Inquisition trials of women accused of bigamy because they remarried after waiting a certain amount of time past the point when their husbands had disappeared.[89] If they happened to be the wives of soldiers or conquistadores, these abandoned women were considered – by their communities, at least – to be widows after a certain amount of time. But if their husbands surfaced later, whether released from jail, returned from a battle front, or suddenly reappearing after making a fortune in the "New" World, then these women could be charged formally with crimes ranging from bigamy to adultery. The ironically named Lucrecia worries over this danger in Lope's *Los Porceles de Murcia*: "no diga mi esposo ausente, que fui adúltera, y me maten."[90]

An extension of this Chastity in absentia theme would be the widow's comportment after her husband's death. Several *comedias* allude to the societal expectation that widows will behave chastely, as when the Countess claims in Tirso de Molina's *El castigo del penséque*, "en la constancia imito a la viuda de Sicheo, en fortaleza la igualo."[91] Note here once again the conflation of Chastity with Fortitude. The source of a woman's strength is said unequivocally to be her husband's love, as in "da el amor del marido a la mujer fortaleza."[92] With alliterative splendour, one female character rather humorously claims that she is so strong, she has actually become a mountain of asperity: "con las nueve efes de Francisca, fe, fineza, firmeza, y fortaleza, soy toda junta un monte de aspereza."[93] She can perhaps be forgiven for poking fun mildly at her society's unattainable expectations for her.

I would like to end this chapter a little unexpectedly, in a way that reflects the (for me) tantalizing findings presented in the course of this discussion. By way of conclusion, I want to focus the reader's attention on an image that can also be admitted as evidence, given that it is a cultural artefact not too distant in terms of either time or place from the stage plays we have been studying. The image in question is a sculpture, namely Antonio Corradini's allegorical statue of Pudicizia, or Modesty, in the Sansevero Chapel of what was historically the Spanish kingdom of Naples (Figure 14) (at the time of the sculpture's creation,

Figure 14. Antonio Corradini's allegorical statue of *Pudicizia*, or modesty, in the Sansevero Chapel of what was historically the Spanish kingdom of Naples (1751) (photo courtesy of Art Resource).

1751, Naples was no longer part of Aragon and the Spanish Empire but instead a sovereign state operating under a branch of the Spanish Bourbon monarchical dynasty). This image is an arrestingly sensual depiction of a woman who is supposed to be a figure of Modesty, but definitely is not. A gauzy veil clinging to her firm, upright nipples – for she is very clearly experiencing a heightened state of arousal – this woman holds a garland of roses draped seductively across her pelvis. Her slightly parted lips and barely slanted eyes communicate a "come hither" message rather than its opposite. If this is modesty, I would hate to see wanton abandon! It may be argued that this late Baroque flowering of moral ambiguity in the visual arts serves as a suitable counterpoint to the multiple instances of indeterminacy, not to mention downright confusion, we have seen in this chapter regarding the Virtue of Chastity. Like the other Virtues we have studied, this one is simply not so easy to define or pin down as we might have thought.

Finally, after having explored two allegedly "masculine" and two supposedly "feminine" Virtues, we come to Prudence, which can only be termed fully androgynous. This Virtue's consummate indecidability ranges from gender, to power, and back. With this catch-all category – in Spanish, a *cabe lo todo* – we will hope to wrap up our discussion of specific Virtues so that we can move on to asking ourselves what it all means. But first, let us witness Prudence's spectacularly anticlimactic finale.

5 Prudence: Panacea or Placebo?

Todas las virtudes se guisan con la prudencia.

(All the Virtues are cooked with Prudence.)

– Lope de Vega[1]

The reader may notice that each chapter of this book has begun with one or more quotations in which the Virtue in question is deemed superlative. Prudence receives more accolades than most. In line with Thomistic theology, it is the Virtue that governs all the other Virtues: "Prudencia ... de quien las demás virtudes son gobernadas."[2] The well-ordered soul is governed by "ordinary" Virtues, with Prudence as the general who keeps them all marching in line.[3] Prudence is the Virtue that kills evil desires and destroys Vice:

> Es la prudençia çiençia que mata
> los torpes desseos de la voluntad,
> sabia en lo bueno, sabida en maldad,
> mas siempre las vías mejores acata;
> destroça los viçios, el mal desbarata,
> a los que la quieren ella se combida;
> da buenos fines, seyendo infinida,
> e para el ingenio más neto que plata.[4]

Juan de Mena calls this Virtue a "science," functioning as a precision instrument, almost like a modern-day drone strike. Once Prudence has completed its mission, the Vices are destroyed.

The Romans translated the Greek *phronēsis* or practical wisdom as *prudentia*. As such, it appears in the *comedias* in the context of consultation, as in "espero consultar con la Prudencia, Virtud de que me guarnezco, la Religión por que aguardo."[5] This consultation should precede action, as when one character chases after his comrades to make sure they do not act rashly: "Tras ellos voy, porque no obren sin prudencia, o sin consejo."[6] The desired response to Prudence's decrees is one of submission to authority; for example, "a vuestro parecer yo me sujeto, que de vuestra prudencia soy testigo; sin duda es ése el celestial decreto."[7] But while I have treated elsewhere the scenario of *comedia* characters asking one another for advice onstage,[8] that is not always precisely the case here. Instead, Prudence constitutes the main interlocutor for internal debate as opposed to asking advice of someone else; for example, "déme la prudencia aviso"[9] or "entré en consejo con mi prudencia, que soy muy prudente, cuando puedo."[10] Note that here the speaker admits limitations to this Virtue, only acting prudently insofar as possible.

So what, precisely, is all this advice about? Topics for which Prudence was especially needed include affairs of the heart, business or commercial interests, and especially government. The love intrigue which is at the literal and figurative heart of most *comedias* requires Prudence in the extreme, as when Don Pedro beseeches Don Juan in Juan de Matos Fragoso's *Con amor no hay amistad*: "Yo, Don Juan, vengo a pediros que dé fin vuestra prudencia a tan locos galanteos, y a pretensiones tan necias."[11] He needs to quit flirting, which leads to foolish pretence. In a different play by the same author, we find the line, "Señor, no sé más que la prudencia, nunca confía su dama al mayor amigo."[12] As we saw in the chapter on Chastity with *El curioso impertinente*, Prudence dictates not entrusting one's lady to one's best friend.

Prudence is the Virtue to which one entrusts grave business, however (as in, "fió a su prudencia negocio tan importante"),[13] with the most serious business of all being that pertaining to good governance. A prudent person deserves to rule: "El gobierno por su valor, y prudencia, le ha dado el Reino."[14] Prudence is quite literally the Virtue needed to herd sheep, or by extension, rule wayward subjects: "la prudencia es virtud con que se rige el ganado."[15] This Virtue takes pride of place in Tirso's ironic meditation on the principles of good government, *La república al revés*, where a character commands: "Tenle bien siendo prudente, que con la prudencia sola gobernarás bien tu gente."[16] Here Prudence appears as the sole qualification for rule. More specifically, Prudence is a Virtue for the Byzantine Senate, which appears in this same play as a mirror of Prudence: "Senado, que es en tu Imperio el espejo, de la prudencia y consejo."[17] This connection is repeated in other plays regarding senators, such as "imaginaba yo con la prudencia, que se mostraba Senador perfecto."[18] Often the Senate will use its authority to delegate leadership, as when Carlos says of Pompeyo in Agustín Moreto's *El licenciado Vidriera*, "quien el Senado encarga del gobierno de este Estado, por su prudencia, y sus canas, su discreción, y su sangre, la justicia."[19] Note here the conflation with another of the Virtues, namely Justice.

Prudence is a quality befitting a king,[20] as when Peransules predicts "Querrálo el Rey remediar con su prudencia y cordura" in the first part of Guillén de Castro's *Las mocedades del Cid*.[21] It is associated with royalty ("tan Docta Prudencia de Reales Consejos")[22] and stately decorum ("o cuál incendio os ampara, un Príncipe y un Infante: así a los decoros faltan, el uno de su prudencia; y el otro de su constancia").[23] Here Casandra invokes two Virtues together – Prudence and constancy, or faithfulness – to protest that neither her husband nor his brother is behaving in a way suitable for his station. This Virtue is further associated with the monarch in the 1628 edition of Juan Ruiz de Alarcón's *La cueva de Salamanca* in the prefatory matter addressed to Ramiro Felipe de Guzmán, Duke of Medina de las Torres in reference to his service as *sumiller de corps* (head of the privy chamber) for King Philip IV: "concedo, cuanto debo y puedo, a la prudencia y divino dictamen de su Majestad."[24] Prudence is particularly noteworthy when it comes to deciding matters of state: "porque es prudencia, y en materia de estado esto se advierte."[25]

Much like Justice, a Virtue to which it is close cousin, Prudence bears an intimate connection to law, as in the accusation that someone is "discurriendo sin tino, ley, ni prudencia."[26] More specifically, it is equated to natural law, particularly the absence thereof.[27] Its role is likened to that of a particular officer of the law, the *fiscal*, who personally represented the monarch in legal matters: "que me fiscalize la prudencia humana el juicio."[28] Richard Kagan explains the role of the *fiscales*: "Lawyers by training, *fiscales* intervened as an interested party in every criminal suit to make certain that malefactors were punished according to the king's law."[29] Given this connection to criminal lawsuits, it should not surprise us to find references to Prudence in relation to the court system: "Israelitas, venid a la Audiencia, a donde hallaréis Justicia, y Prudencia."[30] Here the Old Testament Judge Deborah and her tribunal are invoked as models of Prudence (but also of Justice). Another character speaks to her in the same play (Calderón de la Barca's *¿Quién hallará mujer fuerte?*) of "la Prudencia de tu piadosa Sentencia."[31] Deborah is proof that women too can be prudent.

In fact, references to prudent women abound in these plays. Queens are called prudent, as in "la prudencia de la Reina" and "prudente Reina."[32] So are noble women, as in "será dama fío, de honor, prudencia, y recato"[33] as well as mothers: "la prudencia prevenida de mi madre."[34] Sometimes characters urge women to exercise Prudence, proving that they are judged to be capable of it, as in "Señora, tu prudencia has de mostrar aquí."[35] The play most illustrative of feminine Prudence is Tirso de Molina's *La prudencia en la mujer*. In this play a character refers to the apparent incongruity of this notion: "en nuestro siglo apacible, lo que parece imposible, que es prudencia en la mujer."[36] In a play by Lope, *El sembrar en buena tierra*, Doña Prudencia appears not as an allegorical figure but as a character whose name is symbolic: "Doña Prudencia os llamáis, y es tanta vuestra prudencia, que toda estudiada ciencia, afrentáis, y aventajáis."[37] Sometimes, however, this Virtue in women becomes distorted, as in "es prudencia en la mujer mostrar al hombre alegría."[38] In this case Virtue is confused with pretending to be happy around men to make them feel better. But taken as a whole, references to women as prudent in these plays indicate that this Virtue is fully androgynous.

Again bearing certain similarities to Justice, Prudence is further invoked in an economic context of debts and accounting. For example, in this passage the prudent man is advised not to collect on a debt:

De lo poco, y de lo mucho,
siempre liberal te muestra,
pronto en prestar al amigo;
pero no en cobrar la deuda;
antes ponerlo en olvido,
porque el hombre de prudencia,
ha de hacer cuenta, que es dado
lo que a sus amigos presta.[39]

These lines further associate Prudence with liberality or Charity. Much like distributive Justice, Prudence treats rich and poor the same: "Pobres, y Ricos mide iguales, bien la Bengala a la Prudencia le toca."[40] In this context the *bengala* was a visual military symbol used to lead troops into battle; on the stage this would translate to the use of a physical prop such as a flag, sceptre, or baton. The implication is that Prudence is no respecter of persons and would not send either rich or poor soldiers into battle first, but instead an army made up of troops of every socio-economic status together. Prudence is thus objective and neutral, weighing all sides, as we see in this description of Prince Enrique, who takes everything he hears with a grain of salt: "Confiriendo atentamente el suceso, su prudencia ni del todo le acredita, ni del todo le desprecia."[41] Prudence is rational and orderly, measuring everything with right reason ("mida la prudencia, y la razón")[42] along with superb organizational ability ("y así con mucha prudencia ordenarlo pienso").[43]

As it is specifically exercised by monarchs or nobility, Prudence may consist of conceding favours or granting a boon, as when a supplicant requests, "a una merced que os suplico me dad prudente respuesta."[44] A particular area of good governance where Prudence is especially required is that of meting out punishment. Interestingly, when judged by the standard of Prudence (as opposed to Justice), a violent punishment was considered usually to be a bad idea, as it was often exacted in Anger and led to actions one would later regret.[45] Here Temperance is equated to Prudence, both of which serve as a sheath to Anger's sword. The important thing is to ensure that a punishment is proportional, i.e., that it is a suitable fit for the crime.[46] An excessive punishment irritates and tries one's patience, even if it might be warranted by the facts of the case. This is an interesting instance, potentially, of two Virtues in conflict with one another, as Justice often connotes harsh rigour and exemplary punishment. Prudence may be invoked in a plea to a monarch to act more fairly than he is currently doing, as when Doriclea exclaims in Juan de la Cueva's *Tragedia del príncipe tirano*,

O Rey, qué pasión tan fuerte,
señorea tu prudencia,
que a mi padre dés sentencia
de prisión fiera, o cruel muerte.
¿Qué razón hay que te rija?
¿No ves tú que es sin razón,
dar muerte al padre, o prisión,
si la culpa está en la hija?[47]

In subsequent lines she offers to die in her father's place rather than see him imprisoned or even executed.

Prudence prefers pardons, as in "el amor les da disculpa, y la prudencia perdón."[48] This Virtue teaches people to forgive, even if that is not their natural inclination:

REY: Sed, Conde, de Iñigo, y Ordoño
juez de vuestra misma causa,
y pronunciad su sentencia.
CONDE: Si tú con prudencia tanta
me enseñas a perdonar,
de ti he de aprender.[49]

Here the king gives the count an opportunity to act as his own arbiter, perhaps guessing that the nobleman will not take unfair advantage of the situation.

Prudence has the ability to multiply itself or produce a ripple effect. (Perhaps this Virtue is contagious.) In another example where Prudence literally has the ability to prevent death, the Prince of Fabriano declares: "Mucha prudencia he tenido, pues muerte no les he dado."[50] In the preceding moments he was tempted to run his sword through some peasants, but thought better of this idea. Prudence prefers to avoid death by seeking some other, less drastic solution. The Duke says to his sister of his decision not to kill Don Juan: "fuera linaje de tiranía matarle, con más prudencia me he de portar ... Hacerle matar no es cosa que está bien a mi grandeza."[51] We shall discuss the link between nobility and Virtue more generally in the next section. For now let it suffice to say that Prudence is often appealed to in cases involving honour, a perennial preoccupation of the Spanish aristocracy.

Prudence is said to defend and repair honour, as in "Defendida la honra con los reparos de la prudencia."[52] Don Diego asks heaven to grant him Prudence in an aside: "El cielo me dé prudencia, cuando anegan la paciencia tempestades del honor."[53] Prudence calms the storm produced by honour crises. It does this by challenging Jealousy to a duel: "el celoso rigor, que la prudencia suele sacar al campo en desafío."[54] Prudence mitigates the obsession with Chastity which leads to wife-murder, or uxoricide. Prudence is preferable to the sword: "que trances de honor, el cuerdo los venga con su prudencia, antes que con el acero."[55] This is especially true before evidence in a case has been verified, as in Lope de Vega's *Los peligros de la ausencia*, a play whose title announces its subject matter of suspected adultery. In this *comedia* we find a warning to husbands and would-be wife-murderers: "hasta confirmar indicios es suspender los juicios prudencia de los casados."[56]

By illuminating such cases, Prudence brings light to a dark night, as in "trajera a la oscura noche de Aragón Sol su prudencia."[57] Light as opposed to dark, soft as opposed to hard: this Virtue enjoys a wealth of metaphors to illustrate its attractiveness. Prudence can be counted upon to employ soft (as opposed to harsh) means of getting the job done.[58] Prudence brokers peace: "su prudencia aseguraría las paces."[59] It calms people down: "ve luego de lealtad, y de prudencia armado, a procurar el general sosiego."[60] It prevents danger[61] as well as damage.[62] It does this by placating violence, as we see in lines spoken by the Prince to Beraldo in Juan de la Cueva's *Comedia del príncipe tirano*: "Vengo a ti Beraldo amigo, confiando en tu prudencia, que aplacará la violencia de mi padre, y mi enemigo."[63] Sadly, things have spun so far out of control in this play that he feels the need to call his father an enemy.

Prudence can placate violence in the macrocosm as well, including for entire armies, if need be. We see this happen in the lines "La Reina llegó, y bastó su santidad y prudencia a refrenar la violencia, que en los ejércitos vio."[64] This historical drama by Lope de Vega, purposefully titled *La inocente sangre*, takes place within the context of the civil war between King Fernando IV of Castile and his uncle Juan. The Queen referenced here is the king's mother, María de Molina, who in real life did pacify the realm and prevent her son from being dethroned. She is another excellent example of a prudent woman. In these instances one of the most common ways to avoid bloodshed is to refuse to escalate or engage in a game of retribution and revenge. We see these aims and objectives in the command, "haz prudencia la razón, y no la venganza apoyes."[65] Unlike Justice, Prudence is not easily confused with revenge.

Now that we have seen – at least in its general outlines – what Prudence looks like, it is time to ask who most often practises it. By and large, this Virtue is seen to be the province of old men, whose grey hairs are its seat or its station: "las canas, asiento de la prudencia."[66] Green or inexperienced youth is deliberately contrasted to old age, as in Juan de Matos Fragoso's *El hijo de la piedra* when a character is described eloquently as "verde en aplausos, en prudencia cana."[67] Some passages would even seem to indicate that old age is necessary for Prudence, as in the following exchange from Juan Ruiz de Alarcón's *Los favores del mundo*:

GARCÍA: Aconséjame.
JULIA: El consejo edad y prudencia quiere.
GARCÍA: Mi honor en tus manos dejo,
que al más sabio, y al más viejo
tu claro ingenio prefiere.[68]

Tellingly, a young woman's intelligence here rises above the wisdom of her elders. But normally, aged Prudence provides an antidote to youthful obstinacy.[69]

As we saw in the dialogue between García and Julia, there will always be exceptional cases of "old souls" who are wise before their time, as when Licurgo says to the young king approvingly in Alarcón's *El dueño de las estrellas*: "En tan verde adolescencia vuestra madura prudencia excede a la admiración."[70] As the following exchange demonstrates, King Solomon was also young when he delivered his famous verdict of ordering the baby to be cut in half in order to see who its real mother was:

GRANDE 1 [GRANDEE OF ENGLAND]: ¿No es muy mozo?
ENRIQUE: ¿Qué importa a la prudencia? Más mozo Salomón dio igual sentencia.[71]

Here Prince Henry in Lope de Vega's *Los pleitos de Inglaterra* desires to emulate the wisdom of King Solomon by displaying Prudence at a very young age. But once again, according to the conventional wisdom of the time, it is exceedingly unlikely that Prudence will be found in young men: "que no viene sin canas la prudencia, ¿cómo vendrá sin barbas?"[72] To seem legitimate, Prudence must at least be able to grow a beard.

King Solomon is the most often-cited figure exemplifying Prudence, and references to him in the context of this Virtue are numerous.[73] Another personality from the Old Testament deemed prudent was the patriarch Joseph ("de Joseph su prudencia"),[74] who saved the lives of his brothers that had left him to die in a water well by giving them grain during Egypt's famine.[75]

In addition to biblical personages, classical heroes likewise excel at the Virtue of Prudence. This quality is attributed to wily Odysseus ("la prudencia de Ulises"),[76] who engineered the Trojan horse, thereby allowing the Greeks to invade Troy. Another classical figure – this time historical – mentioned in the context of Prudence is Cato ("la prudencia de Catón").[77] This is a reference to Marcus Porcius Cato during the Punic Wars, who argued for the destruction of Carthage before the Roman Senate, with Publius Scipio providing a rebuttal. The *arbitrista* Pedro de Valencia's proposed iconographical program for the ceiling of the palace of El Pardo called for Cato to be painted as a symbol of Prudence (but he called for Scipio to be pictured too, along with two-faced Janus, so Cato was only half of the equation).[78] It is somewhat disturbing to see that in visual art as well as theatre of this time period, this Virtue could be attributed to an advocate of genocide.[79]

Along with biblical, legendary, and historical figures, early modern Spaniards also attributed Prudence to some of their contemporaries. Venetians were esteemed to be prudent ("prudencia Veneciana"),[80] in addition to exemplifying many of the other canonical Virtues, as Craig Kallendorf has explained in *Virgil and the Myth of Venice*.[81] Spain's relationships with other countries or republics were to be governed by Prudence, a quality much sought-after in an ambassador ("las partes, a Embajador requisitas, soy en extremo discreto, con prudencia, y cortesía").[82] Humility was presumably not one of the Virtues he practised. Some of these same Virtues directed outward towards foreigners are exalted by Don Juan in the Corregidor of *La ilustre fregona*: "Huesped, el Corregidor con su prudencia, y valor siempre honró [a] los forasteros."[83] Note that previously Prudence was paired with discretion and courtesy, whereas now she is accompanied by valour.

In their zeal to marshal relevant examples, playwrights could not neglect to praise Spain's own denizens of Virtue, most notably King Philip II. Such laudatory rhetoric is most evident in Juan Pérez de Montalbán's panegyrical *Segunda parte del Séneca de España, Don Felipe Segundo,* where he declares that the current monarch "en virtud, en cordura, y en prudencia excede a sus pasados."[84] Such rhetoric was standard issue boiler-plate filler, but telling in its knee-jerk patriotism nonetheless. In historical terms, this same king's life is currently being reassessed in light of this Virtue by scholars. The title of Geoffrey Parker's recent book *Imprudent King: A New Life of Philip II* is deliberately ironic because this monarch was referred to during his lifetime as *el Rey prudente*.

Prudence was felt to carry over from the king himself to his *privados*. For example, Don Fernando says to the Marqués in Juan Ruiz de Alarcón's *Ganar amigos,* "Ejemplo sois de valor y de prudencia, y no en vano ocupáis en la privanza del Rey."[85] In similar fashion, in the same author's *La amistad castigada,* Policiano refers to Dion, "quien goza por su prudencia privanza tan merecida."[86] These words would have resonated loudly by contrast for contemporaneous viewers weary of the machinations of Philip IV's *privado,* Gaspar de Guzmán, the Count-Duke of Olivares.[87]

Two final contemporaneous practitioners of Prudence were Spain's famed *arbitristas* as well as the administrators of its far-flung colonial empire. The word *arbitrista* etymologically meant a sort of judge or referee, what George W. Bush would have called a *decider,* as in "a ser árbitro entre entrambas, fiando de su prudencia, su autoridad, y sus canas, conseguir el componerlas."[88] The *árbitros* pronounced *arbitrios,* which

Spanish subjects were admonished to respect: "advierte con prudencia, estos arbitrios en tu bien trazados."[89] The post of *arbitrista* required an enormous knowledge base, which is why they were also often humanists; we find a recognition of this superior training in the line, "la ciencia es madre de la prudencia."[90] Virtue does not just spring up naturally; it requires education and must be cultivated. Another name for *arbitristas* was *letrados*, or men of letters. The *letrados* are specifically mentioned in the context of Prudence with the phrase "el consejo de tan famoso Letrado Vuestro esfuerzo, y su prudencia junta."[91]

Finally, Prudence was required for the administrators of Spain's vast empire. In the case of Netherlandish territories which provide the geographical setting for Lope de Vega's *Los españoles en Flandes*, we find this line spoken of King Philip II: "Mira el mundo que sostiene con prudencia, Religión, y justicia."[92] These words are spoken at the moment of the king's apotheosis in a tableau scene in which he appears seated, surrounded by three maidens who suspend a globe over his head. In similar fashion, in the same author's historical drama *Bamba* we find these instructions from Paulo the Greek to Alicán, the Muslim king: "este Reino bélico avasallas, has de tener cordura y gran prudencia, que sólo en la prudencia está la gloria, que sin ella se halló jamás victoria."[93] Prudence keeps the people of conquered realms pacified and content.[94] Prudence further helps them to obey the law. The Virtues are remarkably useful to imperial ambition: "los Príncipes sagrados, en cuyos hombros el Imperio pesa, destierran la codicia, y abrazan la prudencia, y la justicia."[95] Freud would have had a field day with this specific denial of conquistadores' Greed.

By now the reader will have anticipated that this Virtue, like its counterparts, cannot fail to have presented itself in some way as ambiguous. Like all the others, this Virtue arrives cloaked as an antidote; but the question is, to which illness? The odd answer is that this Virtue is a pinch-hitter; apparently, it works as a panacea or cure-all of sorts for many Vices simultaneously. Prudence competes with Pride or arrogance, which is thereby implied to be its opposite.[96] It is also said to be an antidote to cruelty, in the same way that Temperance is an antidote to Anger.[97] But Prudence itself is also an antidote to Anger, as in "mas gobierne la prudencia; porque la cólera es mucha."[98] A similar line contains an apostrophe to this Virtue: "Gobernadme vos prudencia, no deis lugar a la ira, que cuando con pasión mira hace al engaño evidencia."[99] This antidote proves largely successful when applied properly, as when a character reports, "ferié toda la cólera a prudencia."[100]

Not only does Prudence serve as an antidote to many Vices, but also it is conflated with many Virtues. It can be combined with Fortitude or valour, as in the phrases "si es el valor prudencia"[101] and "Déme mi valor prudencia."[102] Valour actually produces Prudence in the sense that a strong person has strength, but may also have the self-restraint not to use it. In Juan Bautista Diamante's *El cerco de Zamora*, the Cid orders Don Arias to show Prudence in the exercise of valour or Fortitude – "muestre prudencia vuestro valor" – to which Don Arias replies, "Buen consejo."[103] When fortified with Fortitude, as it were, Prudence shows itself to be of the martial or military variety, as in Lope de Vega's *La nueva victoria del Marqués de Santa Cruz*, where the General of Malta says of Don García de Toledo, "he conocido su Marcial prudencia."[104] In similar fashion Tiberio in Lope de Vega's *Los pleitos de Inglaterra* boasts of himself, "pasarme quiero con Borbón a Francia, que estimará la militar prudencia de un hombre como yo."[105] He may have shown Prudence in military matters, but not so much in areas of diplomacy. This military Prudence tempers valour, as in the case of "Simeón, a quien el tierno pecho ocupa dignamente prudencia, y valor eterno, en la conquista valiente, y prudente en el gobierno."[106] Valiant conquest must be followed by wise governance.

But Prudence may just as easily be conflated with Temperance. These twin Virtues are uttered in the same breath in lines such as "ha de ser con prudencia y con templanza."[107] Prudence and Temperance together are called divine counsellors to the human republic.[108] Prudence can prove to be coterminous with Temperance, even when not conflated with it, as in "Pero la grave prudencia del Conde, hallará templanza."[109] Situational applications of Prudence in textbook cases requiring Temperance involve Gluttony, Lust, money, and control of the bodily senses. Gluttony and Lust are invoked tangentially through the resonant word *apetito*, which (as I have shown in *Sins of the Fathers*) could be applied in either the context of hunger or the framework of sex.[110] This word appears in the plural in Guillén de Castro's *Las mocedades del Cid, Comedia primera* in the line "Un vasallo ha menester que tan leal, como sabio, enfrene sus apetitos con prudencia, y con recato."[111] This desideratum is expressed by King Fernando after the death of Gonzalo Bermúdez, who had been the tutor of Prince Sancho, as he describes the qualities he seeks in a replacement tutor or *ayo* (ultimately he chooses Diego

Laínez). To help contain or rein in the appetites, Prudence marshals the bodily senses, which pay homage as vassals to this Virtue, who is their feudal lord: "Siempre los sentidos fueron vasallos de la prudencia."[112] Yet another Vice that normally opposes Temperance is thrown into the mix with allusions to Prudence in the context of money, as in "so pena de obediencia, que gastes tus dineros con prudencia."[113] The Vice in question here is not so much Avarice as prodigality, the original spendthrift being the biblical prodigal son.[114]

What should be clear by now is that Prudence is the most Protean of Virtues. At one point we even find it conflated with two other Virtues, Fortitude and Temperance, at the same time: "muestra tu valor aquí, de templanza, y de prudencia."[115] Huh?? So which is it? Some, none, or all of the above? Things get even more confusing when Prudence starts to condone objectionable actions, as in "tal vez en la prudencia del Ministro es tolerancia lo que parece violencia."[116] How to define a given action? Is it tolerance or violence? In a brilliant stroke of perspectivism, what looks like valour to one person (i.e., to be poor and in love) may seem imprudent to another: "pobreza, y amor, o dicen mucho valor, o dicen poca prudencia."[117] Patience might resemble Prudence, but it can also lead quickly to dishonour.[118] How can one be sure? Prudence might be confused with love, as in the words "reparar en los daños, no es amor, sino prudencia."[119] For this confusion to exist, there must be a fine line between the two. Prudence can even be found in combination with madness, as in "Pero de ti me asegura ver prudencia en tu locura."[120] Don Quijote and the Licenciado Vidriera are prime examples of madmen who nonetheless manifest "prudent" lucid intervals.[121]

It will come as no surprise whatsoever to the reader to discover that the answer to this – as to so many other similar dilemmas – lies in the ever-elusive Golden Mean. One Virtue tempers another until they balance each other out: "tal vez debe la prudencia moderar a la justicia."[122] In other words, Prudence possesses the ability to make Justice more moderate by avoiding the two extremes of either cruelty or laxity. The same thing happens with Prudence and Fortitude, as in the lines, "Muy cortés, muy advertido, valor y prudencia mide, lo que presta no lo pide."[123] Here valour and Prudence are weighed or measured in order to strike an acceptable balance between the two.

That most theological of Golden Age playwrights, Calderón de la Barca, offers a succinct definition of this Virtue: "Prudencia es escoger de dos daños el menor."[124] This sounds good enough – after all, who would object to choosing the lesser of two evils? – but this line admits that both options constitute *daños*, i.e., that neither option is good, which is not exactly the scenario we might expect for the definition of a Virtue. The same idea of *pharmakon* or ambiguous antidote is conveyed with a slight variant in other lines by the same playwright, this time from his *Gustos y disgustos son no más que imaginación*: "en dos peligros forzosos, cordura, y prudencia ha sido con el peligro menor, vencer el mayor peligro."[125] This language reminds us of the reasoning process behind the decision to receive a vaccine: by accepting a slight risk of fever, chills, or other passing symptoms, we avoid the greater danger of coming down with a bad case of the flu.

In this acknowledgment of danger and damage in the discourse of the Virtues, the end result is an inevitable mixing of Virtue with Vice. Conflicting perspectives war within the same breast,[126] while polar opposites combine to form odd oxymorons such as "En la locura prudencia, en la soberbia humildad."[127] These strangely ill-fitting combinations melt together to form a monster, as when Muhammad in Francisco de Rojas Zorrilla's *El profeta falso Mahoma* reveals that "en lo interior te digo que soy cruel con prudencia, soy con recato lascivo, desenfrenado con miedo, a las maldades me inclino."[128] Golden Age prejudice against Islam[129] saw no problems with turning its founder into the ultimate arch-villain, but the surprising thing is that he too appropriates the discourse of the Virtues.

But wait a second ... surely true Prudence could not be mixed with cruelty! Placed in the mouth of Muhammad, these Christian words have been emptied out until they are almost devoid of meaning. Perhaps even worse than the vile brew he mixes would be the Virtues competing not just with their opposites, but instead with each other in a spectacular free-for-all. We are faced here with a nightmarish scenario in which Virtues compete with each other instead of teaming up to war against Vice. Virtues such as Prudence and faithfulness or constancy may compete in two different people, as in "Ya no puede mi prudencia competir con tu constancia,"[130] or within the same person, as we see in the line "compite en su proceder el valor con la prudencia."[131] These Virtues are not always compatible.[132] What valour might dictate would not meet the criteria for Prudence, and vice versa. There is some question as to which Virtue will win out, as in "no sé si pudiera más el valor, que la prudencia."[133] Valour or Fortitude can reverse in an instant what Prudence has slowly and steadily built for ten years: "venciendo el ánimo gallardo diez años de prudencia."[134] What follows is an agonistic picture of Virtues fighting against each other instead of collaborating against the Seven Deadly Sins.[135] One Virtue topples another, which ends up quivering in a wounded mass at the first one's feet.

To rectify this dystopic vision, we must weigh on the other side at least as many instances found in the plays of rank-ordering the Virtues in a fairly standard hierarchy which most playwrights came to accept. On the question of which Virtue is higher, valour or Prudence, the *comedia* corpus as a whole answers this question definitively: "más veces la Prudencia suele vencer, que las Armas."[136] *Comedia* characters encourage one another to trade weddings for weapons, which suits the comic endings typical of the genre as a whole.[137] Even better, valour and Prudence should work together.[138] Guillén de Castro repeats this motif, but in reverse order: "quise juntar con la prudencia el valor."[139] These two Virtues should be joined like brothers: "es menester hermanar la prudencia, y el valor."[140] This combination is not just wholesome, but also politically shrewd.[141]

These combinations and permutations of the Virtues are not the same thing as the conflations we saw earlier, where one Virtue gets collapsed into another. Instead, in these examples we see how it becomes possible for the Virtues to work in concert. In our first chapter, we already saw how Prudence works in synchrony with Justice,[142] in an image where Justice trods upon the path that Prudence has already blazed. Prudence works hand-in-hand with Temperance in the realm of emotions.[143] The secret to this equation is balance, like finding the precise proportion of ingredients when an apothecary mixes a drug. Guillén de Castro explicitly invokes the principle of moderation,[144] whereas Francisco de Rojas Zorrilla incorporates the specific image of a scale: "Si tu prudencia previenes carga en balanzas iguales, tanta alegría a los males."[145] The prudent person balances or weighs competing obligations.[146] The result will be that on either side, a weak man will not be forced to carry too heavy a load.[147]

The bottom line: Prudence is fully synonymous with the Golden Mean. It appears in these specific terms in Lope de Vega's dramatic meditation on kingship, *El príncipe perfecto*: "De suerte que es la prudencia, de los extremos el medio, en mercedes y castigos."[148] Presumably, Prudence is located precisely at some midpoint between the two extremes of boons and punishments. There is some confusion as to where we should plot the different points on this continuum of Virtues, as in the objection that "el valor es hijo de la prudencia, no de la temeridad."[149] But such speeches merely show the pitfalls of graphing morality in a process parallel to mathematical interpolation.

At this juncture, are we hopelessly lost? Does Prudence compete with other Virtues, or cooperate with them? Is it conflated with other Virtues so often that its identity is no longer distinct? Perhaps all we lack is Prudence to sort through these conflicting descriptions. After all, Prudence is the Virtue that guides one through the morass, posing alternately as the ship's captain, the north star, or even the boat's mast. In the stormy sea of fortune, Prudence is the pilot.[150] Conversely, Prudence is the north star guiding the ship's captain: "Y quítale a la violencia la aceleridad, teniendo a la prudencia por norte, y por ayudante al tiempo."[151] This line appears in a *comedia* written about the Virtues with a suitably oxymoronic title, Guillén de Castro's *La justicia en la piedad*. Prudence is the mast of the ship to which Odysseus lashes himself in order to resist the Sirens' wiles.[152] In effect, Prudence will keep us on track, even if it has to tie us up in order to do so.

In non-marine metaphors, Prudence is a man's strong shoulders which might serve to lift high someone's innocence like a little child. Thus a character looks for a hero to vindicate him, "quien saque a luz mi inocencia en hombros de tu prudencia."[153] Prudence is a special kind of eyesight and ability to see things others cannot.[154] In fact, emblematic of Prudence is the eye, the organ most frequently associated with sight. Thus we find "el ojo de la prudencia, que es del alma el mayor bien."[155]

Prudence is associated with sight, but curiously not with speech. In fact, the most prudent course of action seems to be, in most cases, to hold one's tongue. Thus in Juan Ruiz de Alarcón's *La manganilla de Melilla* the Muslim Alima commands, "Toma, y ve con advertencia, que debes a mi prudencia el callar yo de esta suerte."[156] This line may be connected to the Muslim practice of *taqiyya*, by which believers were allowed to dissimulate in matters of faith if they would thereby avoid persecution.[157] Quiet Prudence is said to be the cure for sorrow, as in "amortigüe a ese dolor tu recato, y tu prudencia, pon de tu parte el silencio."[158] *Comedia* characters seemingly never tire of telling one another to shut up.[159] In fact, Prudence should literally tie one's tongue.[160] This is especially true in the context of gossip, which is the theme of Lope de Vega's didactic *Loa en vituperio de la mala lengua*.[161] On the contrary, lack of Prudence means blurting things out, as when the Marqués Octavio confesses to the king, "alabo vuestra prudencia, sin ella hablé."[162] Lope de Vega quotes Euripides as saying that if talking constantly were Prudence, then swallows would be more prudent than men: "Euripides decía, que si el hablar continuamente era prudencia, que mayor la tenían las golondrinas que los hombres."[163] This line has interesting ramifications for the possible attribution of Virtue to animals, which we shall discuss presently.

If Prudence does not talk, then how does it communicate?[164] It resorts instead to writing in code, as in "Basta el haberlas cifrado con prudencia y discreción."[165] Prudence places a premium on the utmost secrecy.[166] Trustworthiness comes only through long experience: "sé por experiencia tu secreto y tu prudencia, bien te lo puedo fiar."[167] In situations of romantic dalliance, Prudence is of the highest import.[168] Paradoxically Prudence can even lead to stealthy, surreptitious actions such as following one's beloved home or spying on him or her: "Seguí hasta su casa con prudencia, y de su estado me informé en secreto."[169] Here the knight Lisardo describes the covert *surveillance* operation he performs in the process of his courtship of Flora. Prudence in love may require sending emissaries back and forth, as in "Embajador secreto, y aún discreto, que trate tus deseos con prudencia,"[170] in what is clearly a word play on *secreto / discreto*. Prudence is the Virtue of palace intrigue, as when Don Juan confides to Tristán in Alarcón's *La prueba de las promesas*: "pues tengo tan conocido tu secreto, y tu prudencia; vos sois ya mi Camarero."[171]

The down side of Prudence's silence is that it may all too easily be confused with weakness. It can be interpreted simply as fear[172] or cowardice[173] to the point of death by not defending oneself: "fallecer de cobarde, más es miedo, que prudencia."[174] We might recall here the Golden Age picaresque novelist Mateo Alemán's self-portrait containing an emblem which shows a spider about to pounce on a sleeping snake (symbol of Prudence), with the intention of killing it by injecting it with venom. Alemán explains the meaning of this picture with the comment that no Prudence is powerful enough to resist deceit.[175]

Even if it manages to survive, Prudence is sometimes ineffectual or incapable of producing results. One counsellor dismisses his advisee in disgust: "deja los consejos, pues que has visto tan incapaz mi prudencia."[176] Sometimes Prudence is not enough, as when Don Gómez swears: "Ya la prudencia no basta, Jesús."[177] Prudence is actually controlled by a different, non-canonical Virtue, namely counsel, which does not appear on any standard list.[178] The implication is that Prudence needs a different Virtue to prop itself up.

On the one hand, Prudence is consummately patient, as in "siendo en todos los males la prudencia remedio, a quien jamás faltó paciencia."[179] Prudence proceeds with caution, especially when the green-eyed monster of jealousy rears its ugly head.[180] Prudence moves very slowly, employing tactics of delay.[181] Special cases require investigation (e.g., "Este caso ha menester prudencia y reportación"),[182] and Prudence can only be learned with time.[183] Its function within the drama is often to produce a deferral of the resolution, as in a passage I commented upon in *Conscience on Stage*: "la dilación no nace de resistencia, mas de buscar con prudencia el tiempo a la ejecución."[184] A similar example would be the line, "dilación al tiempo, información a la fama, y a la prudencia consejo, trataremoslas de espacio."[185] The effect of all these stalling tactics is to capture the attention of the audience and extend the time frame for the play's performance.

This is all well and good, until one runs out of time. Prudence ultimately places shackles on one's feet, making motion impossible.[186] Like the song "Killing Me Softly," Prudence dictates killing little by little instead of draining the blood all at once: "dicen que han de ser sangrías a pausas, porque es prudencia no sacar toda la sangre de un golpe."[187] Bleeding a person to death was of course a spectacular strategy employed in Golden Age theatre, most notably Calderón de la Barca's horrific *El médico de su honra*. Prudence can be lethargic, distilling a sleep-inducing poison, as when a character rants: "¿qué causa, qué letargo, o qué beleño de vuestra prudencia hoy forma las tinieblas en que os veo?"[188] Note here that this Virtue is literally called a poison, in what may be one of the best examples of what we now recognize as *pharmakon* logic at work. A lethargy-producing narcotic, Prudence moves so slowly as to appear cumbersome, like the machinery of state.

In fact, Prudence seems to be frozen in time. The result is an ossified Virtue that most closely resembles an immoveable mask. Like the cape or cloak (another "hiding" garment) that was Charity, this performative Virtue constitutes a disguise to hide one's true feelings, as in "disimulado el dolor con máscara de prudencia."[189] It is crafty enough to cover a tarnished reputation with gold.[190] As Jeremy Robbins has demonstrated using non-dramatic Golden Age sources in his chapter "Prudence and the Compass of Deceit," this "Virtue" is equated with dissimulation, pretending, and lies.[191] In Lope de Vega's casuistically titled *Del mal lo menos*, the king declares, "Él sabrá disimular, mucho su prudencia estimo."[192] Prudence is starting to look like merely the veneer of Virtue, a topic we shall cover in our conclusion.

It does not hesitate to use artifice, as in the explicit instructions we hear in Juan de Matos Fragoso's *Callar siempre es lo mejor*: "el Rey os manda, que aqueste asombro temido le cautele la prudencia, y prevenga el artificio, que ha resuelto tu cuidado."[193] Here a monarch deliberately employs the discourse of Virtue to hide a scandal. Prudence can prove tantamount to pretending: "iréis con tal prevención, que vuestra prudencia finja la ocasión."[194] It can even advocate lies.[195] In a humorous example, Prudence is said to involve hiding an ornery disposition: "algún día, señor, conocerías, cuanto mejor te fuera, con prudencia, disimular tu condición esquiva."[196] A character may not be able to change his personality, but he can at least learn to hide his mood swings.

In the context of Prudence we find a specific reference to the Jesuitical doctrine of equivocation, which I discussed in both *Sins of the Fathers* and *Conscience on Stage*: "Tú por donde te está bien, el equívoco sentido, el literal has querido, porque es prudencia también."[197] Knowing how to dissimulate prudently is an inborn gift, which means that human beings are innately sneaky: "saber disimular con la prudencia nació."[198] The ability to deceive, in turn, has been identified (though not unproblematically) by philosophers and psychoanalysts from Aristotle to Lacan and Derrida as a defining feature of human as opposed to animal life. As Derrida carries on merely one thread of this debate,

> The fox is the animal that knows how to lie. What in the eyes of some people (for example, Lacan) is supposedly, like cruelty, proper to man, what the animal supposedly cannot do: lie or efface its tracks.[199]

At the root of this ongoing discussion is an attempt to deconstruct the human / animal dichotomy. But the ability to tell a good lie and get away with it is seldom praised in traditional accounts of Virtue. Here the dark, poisonous side of the *pharmakon* takes precedence.

~

So where does this leave us? Is Prudence ultimately a Virtue at all? Once it has been stretched enough to accommodate everything and the kitchen sink, has it by then lost all identificatory specificity? Is this androgynous Virtue an indeterminate hermaphrodite?[200]

Before we try to answer these questions – which could apply, in greater or lesser measure, to the other Virtues as well – we shall take a brief detour to discuss a possible gendering of the very notion of Virtue. Then we will be well-positioned to take a step back and ask how we reached the point where Virtues could be evacuated. That journey will lead us from Virgil, to Machiavelli, to Erasmus, and beyond. But it is only through such a tortuous and painstaking fleshed-out genealogy that we can establish the historical contours of moral categories. For thinking people who care about what they believe and why, for serious students of Spanish Golden Age culture, for historians of ethics or religion, or simply for those who like to indulge in idle curiosity, that remains a worthwhile and constructive endeavour.

6 Class Trumps Sex: The (En)gendering of Virtue

Our bodies are our gardens, to the which our wills are gardeners; so that if we will plant nettles or sow lettuce, set hyssop and weed up tine, *supply it with one gender of herbs or distract it with many*, either to have it sterile with idleness or manur'd with industry – why, the power and corrigible authority of this lies in our wills.

– William Shakespeare[1]

This passage from Shakespeare's *Othello* is remarkable for several reasons, not least of which is the fact that it is spoken by the evil Iago (hardly our go-to guy for moral advice). Another is the relatively unusual deployment of the word *gender*, derived from the Latin word *genus*, which can refer generically, as it were, to type. The word's modern definition places it squarely in the realm of sexuality, as we know, and I would submit that the bard's use of the term here is far from innocent. In fact, as Renaissance botanists understood,[2] plants do exhibit certain traits which are still now being categorized as *gender*[3] – fascinatingly enough, these include both "sexual strategies"[4] and the ability to change sexual identification.[5] A specific example of plants being "gendered" is the case of rosemary, considered male, whose companion herb was supposed to be lavender: "His wife or else the female to him is Lavender."[6] Needless to say, a knowledge of these botanical qualities proved exceedingly useful to a pharmacist or *boticario* as he mixed drugs or antidotes for male versus female patients. Some plants were even judged to be hermaphrodites, in which case they were believed to produce different effects in men versus women. Lope de Vega refers to this idea in his autobiographical *La Dorotea*.[7] Whether or not we accept categories like gender as relevant today,[8] we would do well not to neglect them entirely as we attempt to account for early modern mindsets.

Plants and herbal antidotes were gendered in the Renaissance, and so was Virtue. The very notion of Virtue itself was connected etymologically to masculinity and men.[9] The root of the noun *Virtud* in Spanish, derived from the Latin *Virtus*, was of course *vir*, or man (the source also for the Spanish word *varón*).[10] This web of associations goes back at least as far as ancient Rome, where Virtues were qualities attributed exclusively to male emperors in the process of their deification as gods.[11] In the words of Cicero,

> Atquin uide ne, cum omnes rectae animi adfectiones uirtutes appelentur, non sit hoc proprium nomen omnium, sed ab ea una, quae una ceteris excellebat, omnes nominatae, sint. Appellata est enim ex uiro uirtus: uiri autem propria maxime est fortitudo, cuius munera duo sunt maxima mortis dolorisque contemptio.
>
> [And yet, perhaps, though all right-minded states are called virtue, the term is not appropriate to all virtues, but all have got the name from the single virtue which was found to outshine the rest, *for it is from the word for "man" that the word virtue is derived*; but man's peculiar virtue is fortitude, of which there are two main functions, namely scorn of death and scorn of pain.][12]

Here Cicero confirms the gender-specific etymology of the word *Virtue* and mentions Fortitude as man's particular province. Thus we see that in the classical period, the Virtues as such were by definition exclusively male attributes, and that the Spanish word *Virtud* bears within it the Derridean trace[13] of this fuller genealogy.

~

At first glance, Spanish Golden Age *comedias* would seem to echo this assignation of Virtue to the masculine realm, as when Diego flatters the Marqués don Fadrique in Alarcón's *Ganar amigos* with the words, "os contemplo de prudencia, de nobleza, de justicia y fortaleza muro fuerte, y vivo."[14] Virtue is equated with valour, from which women are excluded, as when Pompeyo protests: "Pero estaba confiado de tu virtud, ni sabía, que en tanto valor cabía pensamiento afeminado."[15] Instead, women are depicted as weak and sinful:

si del corazón del hombre
fueran las mujeres hechas,
o que tuvieran, don Juan,
de virtud y fortaleza:
son flacas, son temerosas,
que si tuvieran más fuerza
nos dieran mil azotes.[16]

This humorous forecast by the *gracioso* Panduro (whose name means *hard bread*) predicts that if women were stronger, they would give men 1,000 lashes with a whip. In like fashion, Calderón de la Barca takes a typically misogynistic stance in his character Tristán's approval of the mission to "enseñar a las Mujeres tres Virtudes tan excelsas, callar, dar, y no tomar" (teach to women three lofty Virtues: shut up, give, and don't drink).[17] Case closed, apparently ... or perhaps not.

On several occasions, theatrical characters – and their authors – are willing to acknowledge exceptions to the rule, both for women more generally and for Spanish women in particular. As Elisio says to Silvio in the pastoral mode in an eclogue appearing as part of the prefatory matter to Lope's *El Amor enamorado*, "La virtud, y el valor de las mujeres conozco," although he concludes with the disclaimer, "si Porcias, si Lucrecias me refieres."[18] Portia was Cato's daughter, the wife of Caesar's assassin Brutus;[19] Lucretia's problematic exemplarity has been discussed already in our chapter on Chastity. Tirso de Molina's previously referenced *La prudencia en la mujer*, which we mentioned in the chapter on Prudence as illustrative of the fact that women could possess this Virtue, contains a line that is partial to Spanish women in this regard: "hay mujeres en España con valor, y con prudencia."[20] Here Spanish women are specifically linked to the Virtues of Prudence and Fortitude. Some characters and / or their creators are even willing to leave room for lots of exceptions to the general rule that women are not virtuous: "No ofendiendo la virtud, de tantas mujeres buenas, de que están mil casas llenas."[21] Here 1,000 houses are judged to be full of virtuous women – perhaps a counterpoint to the same playwright's 1,000 whip lashes from before? Although we should note that all of these thousand virtuous women are pictured sitting at home, not out in the street ... We may infer that in some literary depictions, at least, their proper place is the domestic sphere.

When feminine Virtue *is* acknowledged in these plays, men seem surprised to find it. As Saint Jerome exclaims in Lope de Vega's hagiographical biopic *El cardenal de Belén*, "o soberano Dios, ¡que en las mujeres haya tanto valor, virtud tan grande!"[22] These lines are spoken about the godly women Saints Paula and Eustoquia, with whom Jerome is pictured in a contemporaneous painting by Francisco de Zurbarán (figure 15). Jerome's words are unusual because they attribute to women the quality of valour or bravery, a Virtue often reserved for men, except – as we have noted in the chapter on Fortitude – in cases of the *mujer varonil*.

Normally praise of women is limited to more "feminine" Virtues like Chastity, as in the proposition, "Si está la virtud en ser doncella, casta, y hermosa."[23] Note the prominent place given here to the state of being a *doncella*, or virgin, as well as physically beautiful (*hermosa*). Other Virtues, such as pity or mercy, are also attributed more to women in contrast to men, as when Lope's Don Carlos urges Blanca in *La locura por la honra*, "no te alteres, que es la piedad en efecto, propia virtud de mujeres."[24] Effectively he tells her not to show weakness by crying, indicating at the same time that some Virtues are "proper" to women. In *Renaissance Feminism*, Constance Jordan confirms that these and other of the "softer" Virtues were perceived as feminine: "Attributes of the governor which allowed him or her to be temperate, merciful, and especially secure in the arts of making peace were deliberately and emphatically gendered as feminine."[25] Women are deemed virtuous in their role as matrons – "las muchas matronas que por su virtud se alaban"[26] – this coming from Lope de Vega's *El ejemplo de casadas*. For young girls, Virtue may be used to catch a husband ("Bien se casa la mujer a fama de su virtud")[27] – but notice that ironically, this line appears in Lope's *La mal casada*.

Once a woman is married, her Virtue may be used to enhance her husband's prestige, for a wife "con virtud y discreción es corona en el varón."[28] This line comes once again from Lope de Vega's *El ejemplo de casadas y prueba de la paciencia*, a play about a peasant girl named Lucinda who marries Count Enrico, only to have him put her to a cruel test (the *prueba* of the play's title). She suffers a series of humiliations, including separation from her spouse and even her children's death, all ostensibly designed to prove her loyalty as a wife. The play shows not so much a woman's Virtue as her husband's Vice.

Which leads us to an interesting question: are there other instances in the plays which seem to indicate that women might actually be *more* virtuous than men? In Lope de Vega's *El mejor mozo de España* the Duke

Figure 15. Francisco de Zurbarán, *Saint Jerome in the Company of Saint Paula and Saint Eustoquia*, National Gallery of Art, Washington, DC (ca. 1640–50).

of Nájera declares, "Cuando en la virtud aprueban, son portento y maravilla las mujeres, Caballeros."[29] Now admittedly, this could be a backhanded compliment: the implication is that women are so infrequently virtuous that when it actually happens, the result is a portent and a marvel. But the same playwright has one of his male characters, Nuño, note that both Virtue and Vice were routinely depicted in iconographical sources as female: "Con nombre, y forma de mujer pintaron el vicio y la virtud antiguamente."[30] In the case of Virtue, such depictions go all the way back to the classical period, when Virtus was a female goddess with her own cult:

> The goddess Virtus was worshipped by the Romans from the earliest times and the cult is referred to in Cicero's *De Natura Deorum;* in the first centuries of the Christian era this concept underwent a gradual metamorphosis. The goddess Virtus appears in the *De Nuptiis* of Martianus Capella where she advises Mercury to marry.[31]

The goddess Virtus appeared on the coins issued to commemorate many of the Roman emperors (Figure 16).[32] She later graced the Virginia four-dollar note issued by the US Continental Congress in 1777 (Figure 17), and is still emblazoned on Virginia's state flag (Figure 18).

But Lope de Vega does not limit his allowance for feminine Virtue to goddesses only. Citing Ovid's *Heroides*, he recalls actual flesh-and-blood women deemed illustrious by the ancients for their Virtue and wisdom: "Heroidas llamaban los antiguos a las mujeres ilustres por virtud, y entendimiento."[33] Ironically, in Ovid's text these women are arguably not exemplary at all; his epistolary genre centres on the trope of famous women sending letters to their absent lovers. But as Marina Brownlee explains, medieval exegetes performed a tour-de-force of transformative ethical interpretation on this text, with the result being that somehow these wayward women became paragons of Virtue:

> If Ovid programmatically dismantles the exemplary, paradigmatic function that had initially accorded his heroines their legendary status by showing them to be all too humanly vulnerable, the Middle Ages effected a reversal of this hermeneutical procedure ... Wishing to leave nothing to chance, medieval exegetes make explicit what for them constitutes the extradiegetic, ethical exemplarity of the *Heroides*.

Figure 16. Goddess Virtus appearing on a gold coin minted in Spain in 68 AD to commemorate the Roman emperor Galba, who was governor of Hispania Tarraconensis (Tarragona, Spain) (photo © The Trustees of the British Museum).

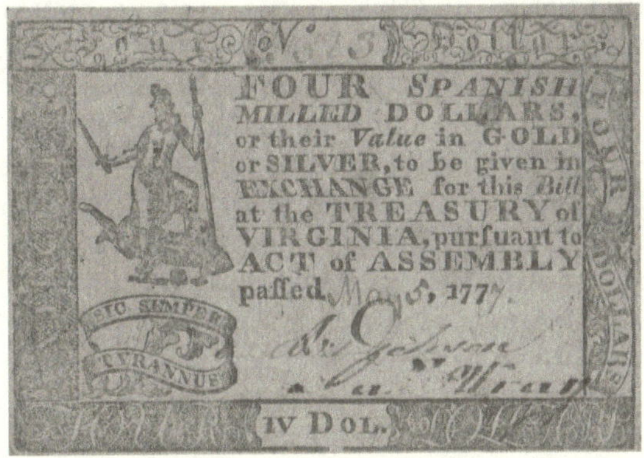

Figure 17. Goddess Virtus on Virginia treasury bill issued by the US Continental Congress in 1777, worth "four Spanish milled dollars" (The Colonial Williamsburg Foundation, Gift of the Lasser family).

Figure 18. Goddess Virtus on Virginia's state flag.

She goes on to examine the moralizing reception of Ovid's *Heroides* in Spain, noting that King Alfonso X was in large part responsible for Ovid's heroines' ethical recuperation there:

> Alfonso looks to the same heroines as objective "proofs," universal examples of his extraliterary (decidedly imperial) public values. In so doing, he seeks, in effect, to return the legendary women to the heroic, external, public world of male values from which Ovid had liberated them.[34]

Were early modern Spanish women deemed worthy heirs to this imagined tradition? At the very least, such references tell us that in the minds of these dramatists, Virtue is possible (theoretically) for women.

It is true that in early modern Spanish stage plays we do not find many defences of women that would go to the opposite extreme of privileging women's Virtue over men's. This absence forms a contrast to such over-the-top Renaissance defences of women as Galeazzo Flavio Capra's *Della eccellenza e dignità delle donne* (1525), written in Italy a generation or two earlier. For Capra, feminine Virtue is greater than the masculine variety, "per esser le donne de più privilegi e virtù dotate."[35] But then again, this is the same guy for whom sex positions have moral connotations:

> Per ragion dil luoco dicevano ancora l'uomo essere più degno, perciò che la donna è sottoposta e l'uomo sta sopra in luoco più nobile. Ma chi con diritto occhio riguarda, conoscerà che la donna negli ultimi diletti d'amore sta in luoco più nobile giacendo supina e con gli occhi al cielo, a guisa che debbono far gli animali dotati di ragione e l'uomo stassi come fanno le bestie col volto e con gli occhi verso la terra.[36]

With this bizarre assignment of moral superiority to the supine (eyes facing heaven) versus the missionary position for sexual intercourse (eyes facing the earth), he takes the traditional *querelle des femmes* to new depths of absurdity. If women must be defended this way, I dare say many of them would rather stay defenceless.

To sum up, then, the *comedias* and *autos sacramentales* do not offer any unified consensus on the question, "Is Virtue available to women?" This is a suitably ambiguous answer for a particularly thorny problem, given all we know about Spain's legendary *machismo*. The dramas do seem to offer some limited defences of women, but they often restrict words of praise to classical figures or conventional topoi such as the *mujer varonil*. A notable exception to this rule is the hagiographical play, in which saintly women are praised to the heavens, and here dramatists do not hesitate to pull out all the stops.[37] Another sphere where women are more unequivocally praised is the domestic arena – particularly when, as in Lope de Vega's *Ejemplo de casadas*, the female character serves as a foil to point out the foibles of a man. We would do well here to recall Constance Jordan's assessment of how even Renaissance texts which allegedly offer defences of women prove contradictory:

> Despite the polemical nature of the debate on women, many texts cannot be characterized as simply for or against women. Treatises ostensibly defending women are sometimes ambiguous because their intention is in fact twofold and to a degree contradictory. They are designed both to praise and to blame women, to allow them a dignified and honored place in society while at the same time demonstrating that this place is beneath that of men, and to make attractive to women their (new) role as social subordinates by stressing its basis in divine and natural law. In a more general way, this literature is intended to guarantee that the authority of men is unquestioned by anticipating and coming to terms with certain kinds of disaffection among both men and women. It attempts to make acceptable the traditional (and probably reemphasized) subordination of women, both by extolling the virtues required by household government (likening them to the civic virtues needed by men) and by severely circumscribing the actual activities in which these virtues are to be brought into play.[38]

It is in this circumscribed realm that we shall leave early modern Spanish women – for now. But the question arises: if these playwrights were not intent on exploring the gender question, what instead were some of their other overarching concerns? Elizabeth Rhodes has demonstrated convincingly in *Dressed to Kill: Death and Meaning in Zayas's* Desengaños that even in the case of a female author such as María de Zayas, class trumps gender when it comes to defining what is at stake in this society as viewed through its literary representations:

> The *Desengaños* are not a defence of women; they are a defence of noblewomen. Because the signifying class of the seventeenth-century Spanish novella is the nobility, the fictional meaning is invested in their interests, and in Zayas's book, a female character has more meaning and power by virtue of her high birth than by virtue of being female. Logically, then, the author empowers noblewomen by stressing their uncontestable right to respect as nobility rather than their problematic, conditioned

> rights as women, who lived under prescribed subservience to upper-class men. In other words, class trumps gender in the *Desengaños*.[39]

I would submit that we encounter a similar phenomenon in the dramas. We find many more lines in these plays assigning Virtue to individuals based on their class than based on their gender. Let us now turn to some of these examples to see where the evidence leads.

In Juan de Matos Fragoso's *El hijo de la piedra* the Duke makes it clear that his Virtue of Prudence places him above the "malicious" villagers: "¡Hay semejante osadía! Mucho debo a mi prudencia en sufrir de estos villanos la maliciosa simpleza."[40] Aristocratic prejudice regarding Virtue is likewise painfully evident in the words of the female character Estela to Duke Arnaldo as she asks rhetorically, "Pues ¿qué virtud puede haber en tus vasallos?"[41] Vassals and *villanos* themselves seem aware of this limitation on what type of Virtue they could even have access to. For example, the *villano* Belardo asks a similarly rhetorical question: "¿Qué puede a tanta prudencia decir mi ruda ignorancia?"[42] Here he contrasts his own rude ignorance to the Prudence of Duke Octavio.

There are, of course, exceptions to this rule, as Marxist critic Noël Salomon has demonstrated in an insightful chapter titled "Virtudes económicas y bienes del villano":

> Al oponerse a los gastos inútiles en ropa, en platería, o en coches, al criticar al juego y a la ociosidad, el villano teatral exalta en contrapartida valores aldeanos que son, al mismo tiempo que valores morales, virtudes económicas y nacionales: la sencillez patriarcal de antaño, el ahorro, el trabajo, la riqueza agraria.[43]

Aristocractic characters in the *comedias* also recognize the possibility that peasants might be virtuous, as in "El Duque que adora de un villano la virtud."[44] However, the reaction to rustic Virtue is often surprise, or the assumption that such cases are so rare, they would warrant monuments built to their memory: "Estatuas merece eternas tal prudencia en ofendido, y en villano tal nobleza."[45] A (to our eyes, humorous) ramification of this overt bias against the lower class is the implication that a virtuous villager, in order to be so clever, must really be a Muslim. Talk about a backhanded compliment! We see this perverse logic in Calderón de la Barca's *El alcalde de Zalamea* with the exclamation, "¡Qué ladino es el villano! ¡O cómo tiene prudencia!"[46] *Ladino* is defined by Covarrubias as someone who is very discreet and refined in the use of the Latin language, and acknowledges that this term is often applied to *moriscos* and other foreigners:

> La gente bárbara en España deprendió mal la pureza de la lengua romana, y a los que la trabajaban y eran elegantes en ella los llamaron ladinos. Éstos eran tenidos por discretos y hombres de mucha razón y cuenta, de donde resultó dar este nombre a los que son diestros y solertes en cualquier negocio; al morisco y al extranjero que aprendió nuestra lengua, con tanto cuidado que apenas le diferenciamos de nosotros, también le llamamos ladino.[47]

As we have seen in our chapter on Prudence, the Virtue of Prudence was associated with education, and Muslims were traditionally linked to vast learning.[48] Thus we find a situation where race provides an important loophole, morally speaking.

Now, it should be clarified that certain Virtues were actually imputed to the lower class, such as Charity; for example, "si riqueza tiene, haga a lo labrador alarde de su largueza."[49] The assumption here is that lower-class people do not know how to save their money (they do not understand the important principle for nobles we learned in the chapter devoted to this Virtue, namely that true Charity starts with oneself). Other Virtues such as Chastity could be practised by rich and poor alike: "Aldeanas; porque solamente llevan por dote la honestidad, y la virtud por riqueza."[50] Village girls have no other dowry besides their Virtue. Curiously, the allegorical figure Moral in Calderón de la Barca's sacramental drama *La humildad coronada de las plantas* refers to "la moral prudencia mía, rústicamente cortés."[51] So evidently Prudence is sometimes permitted for rustics. Virtue can even lurk hidden behind a lowly exterior, as in "virtud esconde en la corteza rústica y villana."[52] We shall see more instances of this tendency in our conclusion with the apothecaries' boxes known as *Sileni*. Time and again we hear characters who pertain to a lower social class vindicate their right to claim the terrain of Virtue; for example, "decir que soy villano, sin ver que adquiere hidalguía la virtud con el ingenio."[53] This character literally charts out an alternative path to nobility with the formula

> Virtue + ingenuity = *hidalguía* (minor noble status).

Such a calculus makes Virtue into a commodity that can be quantified.

This formulation is even accepted, at least to some degree, by the nobility, who recognize that the lower class may exceed their lineage: "lo que falta en sangre suplen virtud, y belleza."[54] This recognition is expressed in the words of the Duke about Friar Félix in Juan de Matos Fragoso's *El hijo de la piedra*:

> Yo, Padre, apruebo
> su virtud, no su linaje;
> y de humildes nacimientos
> se originan en el mundo
> tal vez blasones supremos.
> Y la nobleza adquirida,
> que la heredada, no es menos.[55]

The Duke makes a distinction here between acquired versus inherited nobility. This prompts us to ask: what is the relationship of Virtue to nobility? Are they coterminous, or in some way equivalent? Or is there instead a massive disconnect?

In *El caballero de Illescas*, Lope de Vega's lower-class character Juan Tomás, a *labrador*, states succinctly, "La nobleza es la virtud."[56] Nobility consists of Virtues ("la nobleza consta de virtudes"),[57] which are further associated with honour and lineage ("honras, virtudes, linajes").[58] Virtue is nobility's emblem, flag, or coat of arms.[59] Virtue is associated with education and upbringing, as in "conforme a su calidad, conocida nobleza, letras, virtudes, y amables partes."[60] It accompanies Spain's oldest families, of immortal renown. Thus the prefatory matter to an early printed edition of Calderón de la Barca's *El alcalde de Zalamea* makes reference to "lo antiguo de sus Casas, lo heroico de sus virtudes, haciendo inmortales sus nombres."[61] These words penned by playwrights reinforce "a commonplace of humanist thinking ... that true nobility must be virtuous," as described by Anthony Cascardi in "Civil Society, Virtue, and the Pursuit of Happiness."[62] Anita K. Stoll confirms these ideas for the context of stage plays: "Nobility is therefore an inborn virtue, measured by attention to friendship, the honor of ladies, and by courage and loyalty to king."[63] Nobility must be virtuous, nobility is an inborn virtue – how do we square these statements with the worthy *villanos* we met before?

One possibility is that nobility and Virtue are separate, but coterminous, as with the characters Fulgencio and Marcia, who are "nobles por sangre y virtudes."[64] They could be noble for two different reasons:

by way of blood, as well as virtuous action. In fact, Virtue and nobility may coexist in equal proportions: "igual se mira en los dos la virtud, y la nobleza."[65] Blood is inherited, but Virtue is one's own, as we see with the king's chamberlain: "El Camarero mayor del Rey, por sangre heredada y virtud propia, aunque tiene también de quién heredarla."[66] The ambiguity here is that he did not inherit his Virtue, although presumably he could have (this would imply that Virtue is a legacy which it is possible to inherit). Nobility may even serve as a precursor to Virtue, as in "De nobleza venís llena, y lo estaréis de virtud."[67] Presumably this character's Virtue is still a work in progress.

Another possibility is that nobility and Virtue are separate, but high birth makes Virtue more effective: "la virtud es más, si es bien nacida."[68] Nobility is the beginning of Virtue, but not its *terminus*.[69] But this still does not answer the question of whether Virtue is imbibed with a mother's milk, or cultivated by each generation all over again. There is some evidence for the "inherited Virtue" position, as in Lope de Vega's *El postrer godo de España*, where a character pronounces the verdict, "Rodrigo hereda las virtudes de su abuelo."[70] But presumably these Virtues could not have been very real or lasting, considering the fact that through the Lust of this king, Spain was lost – his affair with La Cava precipitated the Muslim invasion and occupation which lasted for nearly 800 years.[71] Virtue is further equated with blood in the claim, "a don Diego nadie le prefiere en la virtud, y sangre que ha heredado."[72] Specific Virtues such as valour or Fortitude and Prudence may be inherited along with a noble family tree.[73] We even find Virtue providing a *hacienda*, or landed estate, for women who might otherwise remain propertyless:

> DON VASCO DE ARAGÓN: ¿Qué hacienda?
> ISABEL: Mucha virtud, heredada de mis padres.[74]

These lines come from Lope de Vega's *Virtud, pobreza y mujer*, a play with important implications for both the class and gendered connotations of Virtue we have been exploring in this chapter. In this drama, the rich Carlos marries the poor Isabel and then abandons her when he becomes interested in other women. After killing a man, he is exiled and taken captive in Algiers. Isabel collects enough money for his ransom, begging in the streets of Madrid but refusing to resort to prostitution. She ultimately sells herself into slavery.[75] Hipólito, her master, helps her to effect Carlos's ransom. She is the perfect example of a girl from a poor family who proves more virtuous than her wealthy husband.

But a reaction to all these "Virtue is inherited" arguments is the occasional suspicion that even if it were possible to inherit a moral intangible such as Virtue, this particular means of acquiring it might not be such a good thing. We see this doubt expressed, for example, in the line "la virtud heredada fue de paternal herencia, y no adquirida y comprada."[76] One implication here is that inherited Virtue is worth little compared to the kind that is bought or acquired by the sweat of one's own brow. It would also not prove possible to inherit Virtue if one's parents were not virtuous. Such appears to be the case in a character's confession that "no heredé de mis padres virtud, sino sangre hidalga."[77] These lines express a disjunction: blood and Virtue do not go together. In the *comedias* we also find lines where the opposite view is expressed, namely "Mi virtud es mi fortuna, que la virtud no se hereda."[78] Here we have an emphatic declaration that Virtue *cannot* be passed down from one generation to the next. In the absence of such a categorical denial, often we find nagging doubts confessed as to the correlation between Virtue and nobility. Characters vow to wait "hasta ver si corresponde su virtud con su nobleza."[79] This leaves open the likelihood that one's Virtue will not measure up.

At best, these two entities – nobility and Virtue – would seem to coexist in uneasy tension with one another. Theoretically, they are supposed to embrace ("Que la nobleza, y la virtud se abracen"),[80] but we might note that *se abracen* is only one letter removed from *se abrasen*, which would mean instead *to burn one another up*. Blood might be gold, but Virtue is the enamel that covers it: "el oro divino de tu sangre diese esmalte con la virtud de tus obras."[81] Note here the emphasis on *obras*, which are works or concrete actions (we shall study the concept of enamel or *esmalte* in our conclusion). Between Virtue and nobility, there is definitely a hierarchy in place: "es la virtud el primero y la nobleza el segundo."[82] If anything, these dramas seem to manifest an obsession with nailing down such distinctions. Virtuous ancestors can give one models to follow, as in "la fama, a que me provoca, y llama la virtud de mis abuelos,"[83] but true nobility is based on Virtue alone.[84]

It is hard to escape the pseudo-democratizing message of these plays that Virtue is more important than lineage: "la virtud natural es la mayor hidalguía."[85] One character states bluntly, "mi virtud es mi linaje."[86] Another makes reference to an *ejecutoria*, or written proof of noble origins: "aunque no lo dice nadie, tiene en la virtud que tiene su ejecutoria, su sangre."[87] Personal Virtue is championed as more of an indicator than genealogy. True nobility is said to reside more in one's own Virtue than in one's nature, or family.[88] One character is even urged to leave behind her maiden name, for the symbolic reason that soon her family will be known for her Virtue, not the other way around ("Tú, y cuantos de ti desciendan dejen de su casa antigua el apellido, pues hoy tu virtud los apellida").[89] This message sounds all the more subversive when we consider the importance of retaining multiple family names in Hispanic cultures.[90]

Considering the Catholic (specifically, Jesuit) education of many Golden Age playwrights,[91] we seem to hear them pose the question: which type of nobility counts more in heaven? The stage character Pope Pius V addresses this point specifically in Juan de Matos Fragoso's *El hijo de la piedra*: "Para el Cielo la virtud es la nobleza esencial."[92] Persons of quality may best be identified by scrutinizing their souls, for "el alma es quien da nobleza, la virtud es calidad."[93] Arguably, Virtue is even more laudable when found in the lower class, as when Pope Pius says in a separate play by a different author, "Más luce, hijo, la virtud de un hombre cuanto de más humilde, y pobre sangre."[94] The spiritual *hijo* to whom he speaks is Pope Sixtus V, born in 1521 to a humble family living in the rural mountains. Tirso de Molina's *La elección por la virtud* recounts the prophecy of an astrologer that one day this child would be pope, to which he responded with years of secret study to prepare himself for his higher destiny. This play ridicules the privileging of background over behaviour, as when Pope Pius confirms: "precia de su sangre el necio, más noble es la virtud de que me precio."[95] Straight from the horse's mouth – or at least from the lips of the pope himself.

These tantalizing tidbits of social prejudice regarding Virtue we find popping up in early modern Spanish stage plays were obviously not new ideas. Indeed, the debate about the nature of true nobility was derived directly from the discourse of Renaissance Italian humanists.[96] Buonaccorso da Montemagno, Jr (1391?–1429) wrote a popular Latin treatise on nobility in which he claimed that (as summarized by Charles Trinkhaus),

> Wealth also confers nobility because it makes possible liberality and the practice of virtues which the impoverished person is in no position

> to exercise. Through wealth one's virtue becomes known; in poverty it remains obscure.[97]

However, in the same treatise Buonaccorso presents the opposing view, namely that

> Virtue and nobility come only by one's own labor, since the soul, the seat of virtue, is not inherited and is superior to the body ... [A]ll virtues can be practiced without the aid of wealth.[98]

This would seem to answer definitively the question, "Can poor people be (equally) virtuous?"

But Italian Renaissance humanists apparently never tired of debating this issue. They were not satisfied with simply leaving the matter there. Poggio Bracciolini's Latin treatise *On Nobility*[99] injects into the voice of the Florentine potentate Lorenzo de' Medici, who appears as a character in his dialogue, the view that "virtue cannot be practiced without wealth" and "poverty leads to the corruption of virtue." Still another facet to this argument was voiced by Francesco Filelfo, who pointed out that when the Spartans were poor and virtuous, they were also great and free.[100]

These examples could be multiplied. Suffice it to say that the correlation of Virtue to social class was a preoccupation of Renaissance humanists, and that interest in this question carried over to early modern Spanish playwrights. More direct links between these diverse literary and philosophical traditions may be sought in such specific texts as Mosén Diego de Valera's *Espejo de verdadera nobleza* and a treatise called *Nobleza virtuosa* by the Countess of Aranda, Doña Luisa de Padilla,[101] who was a friend of Baltasar Gracián. She wrote this book in the form of advice to her own eldest daughter. It may be argued that the debate about what constitutes true nobility was already a concern in Renaissance Italy, but became a veritable conflict several generations later during the early modern period in Spain. It would be interesting to speculate about whether this theme took on special resonance at a time when, legally and economically speaking, the artistocracy was in crisis.[102]

Within early modern Spanish culture, the drama was not the only place where these issues were being debated. We would do well to recall here Don Quijote's discourse on the Virtues necessary for civic life: Prudence, Temperance, Courage, and Justice (i.e., the four Cardinal Virtues).[103] The knight errant's advice to Sancho as governor of the Ínsula Barataria focuses on the question of public versus private Virtue: "La sangre se hereda, y la virtud se aquista, y la virtud vale por sí sola lo que la sangre no vale."[104] Cascardi finds in this speech by Don Quijote "a profound and critical deflation of the aristocratic presumption that virtue is aligned with social status." In the chapter "Politics Brought down to Earth," he describes

> a process by which the social markers of honour and rank had become increasingly detached from any necessary connection to the virtues, and were associated instead with the categories of social class, where privilege attaches principally to wealth. If Cervantes outlines an ethical frame in which virtue might indeed be valued over rank, this is in part so as to point up what has been called the problem of "status inconsistency" among the nobility, i.e., the discrepancy between social rank and nobility of character.[105]

This is the same set of problems we find explored in the *comedias*. It might be pointed out that in one particularly ambiguous formulation which we find current in the early modern period, Virtue as an alternative path to nobility could be translated into social capital. This is an especially cynical view of Virtue which we may or may not choose to espouse.

In summary, then, what can we conclude about social class and gender as connected to Virtue in early modern Spanish dramas? I would suggest that the *comedias* offer some space for moral meritocracy, but less than the novel. In general, the *comedia* is more a genre that reinforces hierarchy.[106] But I have argued elsewhere for reading the dramas "novelistically" and seeing stage plays as a nascent space for at least some limited moral and artistic freedom.[107] The key to this alternative poetics of the *comedia* as a genre is the individual agency afforded through casuistical debate.

If we think about it for a moment, Virtue must remain attainable at least in theory by women and *villanos* on the stage for the simple reason that it keeps the action moving. If Virtue is impossible or always out of reach, that is like sticking a giant pin in the balloon of the *comedias'* ever-expanding, infinitely accommodating moral universe. Then there would be no ethical suspense to drive the action. The plot would be too predictable. On the other hand, the more messy, complex, and ambiguous Virtue is, the better. Its uneven texture only adds to its theatricality.

In this chapter we have added two additional layers of complexity, the second one admittedly thicker than the first. Virtue per se is accessible to women on the stage, but only in a limited and theoretical way. (Notable in this regard is the veritable abyss between what playwrights say about women's participation in activities associated with specific Virtues, which are relatively numerous – as we have seen in the preceding chapters – versus their comments about the possibility of female Virtue more generally. This fissure shows, ironically, that women were deemed less virtuous in theory than in practice.) The reality is that these playwrights had more pressing concerns. Their chief obsession seems to be with exploring issues of social class, which might be seen as opening a theatrical space for upward mobility, but more likely as reinforcing the existing hierarchy or status quo. As Noël Salomon writes regarding the favourable depiction onstage of "virtuous" peasants,

> La comedia, que por boca de sus villanos ejemplares, hace encomio del trabajo y condena la ociosidad urbana, ¿va pues a contracorriente? Apurando el análisis, no, porque el trabajo al que glorifica es precisamente el de los campesinos, en otros términos, la labor de los vasallos sobre la cual descansa toda la sociedad monarquicoseñorial y sin la cual no sería ya posible la existencia de los señores y terratenientes que viven en la ciudad (y que asisten a los espectáculos); sólo en apariencia, y superficialmente, va a contracorriente el campesino ejemplar por su trabajo.[108]

Peasants, by their labour, uphold the seigneurial system. Thus we see that even lines praising *villanos'* alleged "Virtues" must, in some sense, be taken with a grain of salt.

Playwrights' urgent need to establish through dialogue whether a correlation existed between nobility and Virtue may be traced to Italian Renaissance humanists, but does not stop there. If we want to speculate a little, we might entertain the notion that early modern Spanish playwrights – most of whom were also priests[109] – in this area decided to use their bully pulpit by preaching to a captive audience, with the democratizing message that Virtue is accessible to all and moral destiny is not determined by birth. More likely, I believe (although this is the more cynical view), individual dramatists such as Lope de Vega, who themselves were not noble,[110] wanted to claim for themselves and their contemporaries as much Virtue – defined in this case as an alternative form of nobility (and hence, mobility), which translates into social capital – as they could possibly get away with. To this desperate grab for power, combined with a more-or-less altruistic didacticism, we may attribute the uneasy tension we encounter in these plays regarding the question of how Virtue is (en)gendered.

Conclusion

What sin you do to save a brother's life,
Nature dispenses with the deed so far
That it becomes a virtue.

– William Shakespeare[1]

I (Not Just) the Veneer of Virtue

Saints or priests are referred to in the *comedias* as glasses or vessels of Virtue, as in "gran Gregorio Nazianzeno, vaso de virtudes lleno"[2] or "justos, santos, Sacerdotes, vasos de virtudes llenos."[3] But is the glass half full, or half empty? Virtue was supposed to be a clear mirror, as in "de virtud heroica espejo"[4] or "el espejo de mi virtud"[5] (this last line in reference to a woman, from Lope de Vega's *Virtud, pobreza y mujer*). But often the mirror becomes cloudy. Sometimes Virtue appears in unlikely trappings, as in "Debaxo de ese gabán muchas virtudes están"[6] or "la virtud prodigiosa que ocultaba entre la jerga,"[7] with *jerga* bearing the dual signification of rough cloth worn by peasants or those who were practising penitence (the biblical equivalent would be sackcloth), and also a variety of rough or colloquial speech employed by subalterns living at the fringes of society. These metaphors share one thing in common: the idea that when it comes to Virtue, all may not be as it seems.

There is such a thing as false Virtue ("Miren si es su virtud falsa")[8], as we see in Juan Bautista Diamante's *El negro más prodigioso*. A ubiquitous potential for hypocrisy, or fake pretence to Virtue, appears in the wish that the face of a person match his actions.[9] Sometimes Virtue is merely apparent, lacking substance, as in the accusation that "humildades afectadas, más que virtud, son industria."[10] Affected or pretended

Virtue is not genuine, but instead the result of industry or fabrication. This false Virtue is referred to onstage as "hipócrita virtud," "virtud mentida," or "virtud fingida."[11] Specific reference is made in this context to the *beatas* who feigned stigmata and other mystical marks of divine favour: "ésa es virtud de almohadillas, y milagro de mujer."[12] The ultimate feigned Virtue was the Antichrist's. In Juan Ruiz de Alarcón's *El Anticristo* the titular character declares at the outset "que simulada luz de virtud pura desde este punto ostento y acredito."[13] According to the eschatalogical prophecies of Revelation, the Antichrist's Virtue will be feigned so convincingly that many people are deceived into thinking he is actually the Christ (Revelation 13).

But looking at the corpus of Golden Age drama taken as a whole, false *beatas* and Antichrists are the least of our worries. In fact, theirs are the easiest cases to understand. Once we begin to look closely at the discourse surrounding Virtue, we realize there are literally layers of complexity we must navigate before we can begin to comprehend what is going on. There is an entire subcategory of discourse in which Virtue appears as a veneer or enamel, sometimes used to coat good actions and make them shine more brightly, but other times invoked to disguise bad ones. A person might be "en todas acciones esmaltado con sus virtudes"[14] (enamelled with Virtues) in a linguistic register employed by multiple playwrights. For instance, in Tirso de Molina's *Santo y sastre* one character asks regarding another, "¿no es todo él un pino de oro? Pues la virtud es su esmalte."[15] Piety in turn provides another layer to cover Virtue: "Esmaltar la virtud de sus hazañas con tan rara piedad."[16] Getting at the "core" of these saints begins to feel (to borrow from *Shrek*) like peeling an onion. In a negative example of this discourse, Virtue may be worn like a cape to cover fear.[17] We start digging deeper, and encounter the ugliness of something which first looked beautiful when viewed from outside.

This linguistic register about covering ugliness with a gorgeous façade blended perfectly in Golden Age society with an existing discourse decrying the use of cosmetics by women. Opposing sides of this debate are represented by Alonso Carranza, *Discurso contra los malos trajes y adornos lascivos*, and Arias Gonzalo, *Memorial en defensa de las mujeres de España y de los trajes y adornos de que usan*, both originally published in 1636.[18] In Tirso's *Marta la piadosa*, a play about a woman who pretends to be pious but really isn't, we find a description of this hypocritical figure who "se deleita, y algunas veces se afeita, y así es virtud afeitada."[19] This cynical take on Virtue serves the simultaneous purpose of reinforcing patriarchal misogyny. Even when the abuse of Virtue is not so blatant, the possibility for deceit lurks just beneath the surface:

> MARCELA: ¿No me abona mi virtud?
> OTAVIA: No sé si esconde Engaño.[20]

Here we begin to glimpse radical doubt regarding Virtue's authenticity. There is the suspicion that a liar will sell Virtue like a commodity, as with the accusation in Tirso's *Santo y sastre* that the titular character Homo is "con hipócritas mentiras, santo solo en las palabras: aquel que virtudes vende."[21] Things even reach the point where Virtue is labelled a counterfeit currency, as in "tu virtud, y opinión, por buena moneda pasa" – these lines from a play about deception, Lope de Vega's *Los embustes de Zelauro*.[22] In fact, characters speak openly about Virtue deployed to achieve dishonest ends:

> NUÑO: Gran virtud la honestidad.
> FERNANDO: Para engañar hay virtud.
> NUÑO: Así Dios me dé salud.[23]

This reference to health or *salud* in the context of Virtue reinforces the medical metaphor of Virtue as antidote, but twists it sarcastically in the words of a character acting in bad faith.

Even when it is not directed towards pernicious ends, Virtue can still deceive when it hides behind an ugly outer shell. This was the case for Socrates, described by Erasmus as a great philosopher who in terms of physical appearance was notoriously ugly. The Christian humanist compared the ancient Greek sage to apothecaries' boxes called *Sileni*, which were carved with harpies, satyrs, and horned geese. The boxes were so ugly that no one could believe a wondrous remedy might be contained inside. The comparison of Socrates to French apothecary boxes is made in Erasmus's adage *Sileni Alcibiades* (1508, expanded 1515).[24] This striking ekphrastic image is appropriated likewise by François Rabelais – who was a medical doctor – in his prologue to the first book of *Gargantua*:

> Sileni, in the days of yore, were small boxes such as you may see nowadays at your apothecary's. They were named for Silenus, foster father to Bacchus. The outside of these boxes bore gay, fantastically painted figures of harpies, satyrs, bridled geese, hares with gigantic horns, saddled ducks,

> winged goats in flight, harts in harness and many other droll fancies ... But inside these Sileni, people kept priceless drugs such as balsam of Mecca, ambergris from the sperm whale, amomum from the cardamon, musk from the deer and civet from the civet's arsehole – not to mention various sorts of precious stones, used for medical purposes.[25]

This metaphor for Virtue appears likewise in Golden Age dramas, as with the description of "los que están más feos por de fuera, porque guardan la virtud en sus secretos, sin vanidad exterior."[26] Indeed, sometimes hidden Virtue works in secret until the outside and the inside slowly come to match.[27] But at other times, as a survival strategy (like we have seen with theatrical costumes such as capes and masks), Virtue must be sneaky enough to cloak itself in such as way as to resemble Vice. This is true in Calderón de la Barca's rewriting of Heliodorus, *Los hijos de la Fortuna Teágenes y Cariclea*, where we read the exculpatory lines, "por desvelar malicias, me fue preciso, que la virtud se valiese de las cautelas del vicio."[28] Potential for deceit leads characters onstage to question metatheatrically whether a mask is being worn: "¿hayan puesto a la virtud la máscara del delito?"[29] Virtue and Vice figure in this calculus as masks we try on, then discard.

II *Virtus* or Virus?

The only way this game works is if Virtue and Vice resemble one another enough for each to impersonate the other one. This is in fact the impression we get from reading numerous lines in these dramas. Vice and Virtue can be confused, as in the rather cutesy rhyme, "haciendo en su prejuicio, que la misma virtud parezca vicio."[30] This is especially true in the case of lies.[31] Federico in Agustín Moreto's *Primero es la honra* calls courtly music an "ejercicio, que con señales de vicio suele a veces ser virtud." This leads to a humorous exchange with the *gracioso* Torrezno:

> TORREZNO: Si esto es virtud, y agasajo,
> y a tu dama se le aplica,
> será una virtud que pica.
> FEDERICO: ¿Cuál es esa?
> TORREZNO: La del ajo.[32]

Here Virtue is compared unflatteringly to the pungency of garlic which is supposed to promote health in spite of its vile odour. It is hard to escape the impression that in this theatrical castle we have somehow wandered out of the chapel and into the kitchen.

But this confusion goes deeper than playful jokes or simple perspectivism. These authors of stage plays go to great lengths to show the boundaries between Vice and Virtue becoming increasingly blurred. Throughout the *comedias* and the *autos sacramentales* we find lines such as, "hay Amor que es Virtud, y Amor que es vicio."[33] So who gets to decide? Apparently a given action is approved by heaven for some people, but not others: "yo tuve del cielo aviso para hacer en mí virtud, lo que en otro fuera vicio."[34] This line comes from none other than Juan Pérez de Montalbán's *El valiente Nazareno*, about the Old Testament hero Samson, who here defends his choice to marry the pagan Delilah with God's permission. Later in the play's spectacular finale he will use his supernatural strength to bring down the roof of a banquet hall onto the Philistines' heads – another sin, namely mass murder, which he commits with heavenly licence. Scruples of conscience may also fall into this category of things that might be Virtues for some people but Vices for others: "soy desdichado, y el escrúpulo en mí será pecado, si es virtud el delito en el dichoso."[35] So scruples of conscience might actually be sinful? And crimes can actually be virtuous, as long as you are happy (or lucky)? We encounter subtle distinctions worthy of casuists' hairsplitting; for example, "esta ofensa ... es vicio que se piensa, más que virtud que se sabe."[36] The offence referenced is the hiding of a man in one's house, which could damage the owner's honour or reputation. The implication seems to be that although it might have the appearance of Vice, this action actually becomes virtuous once all the circumstances are taken into account.[37] Other examples include, like Robin Hood, stealing in order to give money to someone in need. The verdict pronounced regarding this action is that theft is still a Vice, not a Virtue.[38] Playwrights seem more ambivalent about a dubious stance such as hating marriage, on which the following commentary is offered: "desde sus primeros años, o fuese virtud, o vicio, aborreció el casamiento."[39] This type of Chastity was not necessarily virtuous: "es casta, ni sabe si eso es vicio, o es virtud"[40] (i.e., a chaste married woman might be guilty of not meeting her husband's sexual needs). Telling a lie is once more called virtuous, as in the words, "Que esta mentira virtud, y no culpa sea," although we should note that the Demon is the one talking.[41] In the light of this radical ambiguity, even murder is called a Virtue: "hallarte con un muerto, y muerto de aquesta suerte más es virtud que delito."[42]

When reading these plays, it is hard to avoid the conclusion that in this extreme version of perspectivism, a dubious action may be viewed alternatively either as a Virtue or a Vice. This would apply not just to actions, but also to attitudes, as in "humildad que a no haber sido en su naturaleza virtud, hubiera sido en su desconfianza digna de reprehensión."[43] Is it humility or lack of confidence? How can we tell the difference? Calderón de la Barca offers us one possible criterion in the following exchange:

> NATURALEZA: No es delito; mas no sé que sea Virtud.
> CULPA: Cuando va a digno fin, Virtud es.[44]

Here Virtue is merely a means to an end.

In fact, once we know what to look for, we begin to see that Virtue and Vice almost always show up in tandem in these plays. They are inseparable, like Siamese twins. Witness these lines from Lope de Vega's *La noche de San Juan*:

> Criado, y señor parecen,
> juntos siempre, el bien y el mal.
> Nunca el bien delante viene,
> sin venir el mal detrás.[45]

Good never comes without Evil following close behind. Vice and Virtue may be present in the same person at the same time: "en mí tendré juntos hoy los vicios, y las virtudes."[46] But they don't just come together – they are interchangeable, as in the possibility "si el ejemplo que se ve de vicio, virtudes fuera."[47] They morph into one another, as in "leyes de su albedrío, previniéndose a los riesgos, puede hacer virtud del vicio."[48] The transformation goes both ways: "hecho delito lo que fuera virtud."[49]

This is partly the logical inversion which occurs any time the devil takes something good and perverts it. As an allegorical figure says to the devil in Calderón de la Barca's sacramental drama *El árbol del mejor fruto*, "no hay Virtud que en Dios resplandezca, que no sea vicio en ti."[50] However, for the most part what we see in these plays is a more radical ambiguity than that. Vice and Virtue actually swing back and forth: "Si de un vicio la inquietud, de una virtud el indicio, vuelve la virtud en vicio, antes que el vicio en virtud."[51] Calderón de la Barca is playing with us here, hoping to provoke a furrow in our brow. When these concepts dissolve, an intensification takes place: "fuera, el que ahora es defecto, virtud, y virtud tan alta que dorara vuestros yerros."[52] But that is only the best case scenario. More typically of human propensity for error, Virtue diminishes, while Vices multiply: "sacando en ti, y tu retrato, de una virtud dos delitos."[53] This at first glance strikes us as funny math: two sins for every one Virtue. If we think about it, however, that is the logical conclusion for the Golden Mean scenario: if every Virtue appears as the midpoint between two Vices, then that means there are twice as many Vices as there are Virtues.

This makes morality a happy hunting ground for cynics like the fiddling Emperor Nero in Lope de Vega's *Roma abrasada*, who savagely boasts: "Hago del vicio virtud, y de los daños mercedes. Así gozaré a Popea"[54] (when Poppea first became Nero's mistress, she was still the wife of his boyhood friend Otho – awkward). Even less opportunistic characters such as Tobias in Lope's *La historia de Tobías* recognize the potential ease of this transformation. He admonishes his wife, "Ana, callad, que es mal hecho, no hagáis vicio la virtud."[55] His admonition bears within it the recognition that this segue is possible. On the flip side, these metamorphoses are the very stuff of conversion narratives,[56] in the sense that the more vicious the sinner was, the more virtuous the saint will be once (s)he is transformed. This is true, for example, of Mary Magdalene,[57] or of Cristóbal del Lugo (who later becomes Cristóbal de la Cruz) in Cervantes' *El rufián dichoso*. According to the doctrine of free will,[58] it is always in one's power to make the switch, as when a character decides: "Y así pienso trocar de aquí adelante la inquietud en virtud."[59] Especially in hagiographical dramas, a dramatic reversal or *peripeteia* is needed. Thus characters speak of the desire to "hacer virtud lo que entonces fue flaqueza" or else command one another, "haz virtud lo que en ti es vicio."[60]

But this proliferation of examples begs the question: why is this transition so smooth? The dramas themselves offer us some tentative answers in terms of shared origins. Virtue and Vice stem from the same source: "Y pues virtudes, y vicios de una causa se producen."[61] The two concepts seem mutually interdependent. They need each other: "que no haya la virtud el que no comete el vicio."[62] It could even be said that the experience of Vice is necessary in order to arrive at Virtue. "I cannot praise a ... cloistered Virtue," wrote John Milton in *Aeropagitica* (1644).[63] An equivalent idea may be found in Calderón de la Barca's *El médico de su honra* in the line, "pues no hay virtud sin experiencia, perfecto está el oro en el crisol."[64] Virtue is like gold refined by the fire of Vice. The *comedia* characters themselves stop to question the irony of this: "¿Y es buena la disculpa, de una virtud fundada en una culpa?"[65] How can Virtue find its very foundations in fault?

Virtue appears as Protean in these plays, making it hard to escape the overwhelming sensation that Virtue means different things to different people. For example, in Calderón de la Barca's *La cena de Baltasar* Pensamiento declares, "soy en el Rico, justicia, la culpa, en el Delinquente, virtud, en el Pretendiente, y en el Próvido, malicia."[66] How can the same entity, Thought, possibly mean all these different things in all these different contexts? It turns out that the exact identical action may be judged a Virtue or a Vice, depending on the circumstance – for example, speaking or staying silent (i.e., refraining from speech), as in Calderón de la Barca's pedagogical *No hay cosa como callar*: "que hablar en tiempo es virtud, si es vicio el hablar sin tiempo."[67] The same desires might be sinful or virtuous, depending on their object.[68] In this fluid economy, Vices and Virtues morph into one another and switch attribution. They can change suddenly.[69] In one fell swoop, honour can turn to crime, just as Virtue can turn to infamy. Recognition (in the sense of complimenting someone else for a positive quality) only participates in Virtue if it is not affected or fake.[70] These reversals shift in both directions: "tiernos amantes, seremos grandes amigos, y en los dos sería virtud lo que hasta ahora fue vicio"[71] (this from Guillén de Castro's *El vicio en los extremos*, a play we have already mentioned as epitomizing the Golden Mean). These texts are haunted by the spectre of the *pharmakon*, the remedy which is also a poison. A venom is also its cure. In a Baroque age addicted to paradox, dramatists seemed to enjoy teasing out this ambiguity.

III Historical / Literary Roots

In the instances where it is stated most baldly in the *comedias*, we encounter the raw formulation: "el vicio será virtud."[72] This is the *pharmakon* in its most purified, distilled essence. But where does it come from? From what source or influence are supposedly orthodox Catholic playwrights (let us not forget, many of whom were also priests) getting this notion?

We do not need to look any further than the ancient Roman poet Virgil, whose first *Georgics* contain the words, "Quippe ubi fas uersum atque nefas" [Here right and wrong are reversed].[73] These lines first caught the attention of renowned classics scholar Bernard Knox when he was a young man stationed in Italy during the Second World War in the OSS (Office of Strategic Services). He liked to tell the story of how he found an old copy of Virgil in an abandoned villa. He picked up the book, read these words, and felt the line reflected the situation of the war. This was the inciting incident for his decision to become a scholar of the classics.[74]

As Don Cruickshank points out, these words were later refashioned by Luis de Camões, the "Portuguese Virgil," in the *Rimas* (1595): "Vi o bem suceder mal, / e o mal, muito pior" [I saw the good converted into evil, and evil into much worse].[75] Spanish playwright Pedro Calderón de la Barca repeats them in *El Laurel de Apolo*:

> Que como quien
> teme un veneno violento,
> suele hacer de él alimento,
> porque cuando se le den
> el mal se convierta en bien.[76]

These ideas from Virgil, Camões, and Calderón de la Barca in turn inspired multiple play titles in various countries in Europe throughout the seventeenth century, including Calderón de la Barca's *Peor está que estaba* and *Mejor está que estaba*, De Brosse's *Les Innocens coupables* (1645),[77] and Le Métel de Boisrobert's *Les Apparences trompeuses* (1656),[78] in addition to a lost English adaptation described by Cruickshank:

> On 20 July 1664 (OS [Old Style]) Samuel Pepys saw *Worse and Worse*, a lost adaptation made from a Spanish play by George Digby, Earl of Bristol, whose father, Sir John, had been the ambassador in Spain at the time of the Spanish Match. *Peor está* is the best candidate for the source, particularly since the same writer also produced *Tis Better than it Was* (?by 1665, printed London, 1708) from *Mejor está que estaba*.[79]

So radical moral ambiguity – what by now we might recognize as "the *pharmakon* syndrome" – struck a chord widely at this time.

A missing link to this chain may be found in the Spanish medieval poet Juan de Mena, whose *Laberinto de Fortuna* incorporates some of these ideas. A concrete example of this slippage or ambiguity occurs in Stanza C [Roman numeral for 100] of his poem:

> Venidos a Venus, vi en grado especial
> los que en el fuego de su joventud

fazen el vicio ser santa virtud
por el sacramento matrimonial.[80]

Another example occurs earlier in Stanza XCIII in an apostrophe to worldly fear, whom the poet blames for making us reverse moral categories such as Vice and Virtue, right and wrong:

¡O miedo mundano, que tú nos compeles
grandes plazeres fingir por pesares,
que muchos Enteles fagamos ya Dares,
e muchos de Dares fagamos Enteles!
Fazemos de pocos muy grandes tropeles,
buenos nos fazes llamar los viciosos,
notar los crüeles por muy pïadosos
e los pïadosos por mucho crüeles.[81]

Golden Age dramatist Pedro Calderón de la Barca, in turn, borrows from Mena directly in *La devoción de la Cruz*:

a un tiempo vienen
envueltas iras piadosas
entre piedades crueles.[82]

By now we have established that this discourse of moral ambiguity was not merely extant, but actually prevalent. But were these playwrights way out in left field with their emphasis on this conception of ethics? This was certainly not the sanctioned, orthodox Catholic view. It might help for us to reconstruct their mental scaffolding so we can at least see how they climbed the early modern intellectual equivalent of skyscrapers in order to balance precariously on this tightrope. The journey will take us through Italy and to the Low Countries before finally ending up back in Spain.

IV Machiavellian *Virtù*

Any effort to fill the enormous gap between Plato, Aristotle, Horace, Virgil, and early modern Spanish drama in terms of intellectual history as it relates to morality would have to take into account several key figures. One of them is undoubtedly Juan de Mena, whose *Laberinto de Fortuna* (1444) is crucial to understanding the Virtues and their history in Spain. I have deliberately sprinkled quotations from this medieval work throughout the current study in an effort to acknowledge that these ideas did not arise in a vacuum. But Mena was frankly not big enough, not influential enough, to account for the dramatic currency of these somewhat unorthodox conceptions of Virtue.

The most radically original thinker in this area for perhaps the whole of the Renaissance would be, by most accounts, the Florentine political strategist Niccolò Machiavelli (1469–1527). A contemporary of the powerful Medici family, he has been called the founder of modern political science. His two main works are the supremely inflammatory *The Prince* and his *Discourses on Livy*, intended to be used as a mirror for princes. Let us survey these works and their reception briefly in an effort to understand Machiavelli's concept of *Virtù* as it may or may not relate to the paradigms we have been looking at so far in this book.

So how does Machiavelli understand Virtue, exactly? *Virtù* is a clearly masculine concept in Machiavelli, but not necessarily anti-religious:

> Y aunque parece que se ha afeminado el mundo y desarmado el cielo, esto procede sin duda de la vilez de los hombres, que han interpretado nuestra religión según el ocio, y no según la virtud.[83]

Misogynist though he might be, his thought contains the germ of the sort of radical ambiguity we have called characteristic of Virtue as *pharmakon*:

> For if you look at matters carefully, you will see that something resembling virtue, if you follow it, may be your ruin, while something else resembling vice will lead, if you follow it, to your security and well-being.[84]

As modern scholar Juan Manuel Forte summarizes Machiavelli's position on this question, "en el espacio de la política los vicios pueden ser virtudes y las virtudes vicios."[85]

Specific examples of Virtues becoming Vices and vice versa, as it were, in Machiavelli include the sliding scale on which generosity or liberality bleeds over into stinginess:

> For if you exercise your generosity in a really virtuous way [*virtuosamente*], as you should, nobody will know of it, and *you cannot escape the odium of the opposite vice.*[86]

Likewise, he describes the spectrum ranging from overconfidence to overtimidity in a passage in which he uncharacteristically seems to advocate the Golden Mean:

> Yet a prince ... ought to proceed cautiously, moderating his conduct with prudence and humanity, allowing neither overconfidence to make him careless, nor overtimidity to make him intolerable.[87]

But there are many other instances in his writing when he actually recommends sliding all the way over on the spectrum between two opposing Vices to choose one of those two extremes instead of the "Virtue" in the middle. This is the case, for instance, with humility and arrogance:

> There are to be found numerous cases in which humility is not only no help, but is a hindrance, especially when used to dealing with arrogant men who, either out of envy or for some other cause, have come to hate you.[88]

Here he recommends the Deadly Sin of Pride or arrogance as opposed to humility in what is an explicit reversal between a Virtue and its opposing Vice.

These ideas may seem to resonate, to some extent, with some of the plays we have been studying, but a different question is: was Machiavelli known in Spain? The author himself was certainly aware of Spanish politics and even invokes the example of Fernando el Católico in *The Prince*.[89] As Cascardi describes his conflicted attitude towards the Catholic Monarch, "Fernando is at once the object of Machiavelli's admiration and of his displeasure."[90] Machiavelli's works were not prohibited in Spain until 1584, two decades after they were forbidden in Italy (1559).[91] Before that a translation by Juan Lorenzo Otevante dedicated to none other than Philip II had appeared in Medina del Campo in 1552, a censored copy of which may be found at the Escorial (see Figure 19).[92] In the seventeenth century, Machiavelli's works still circulated in Spain, albeit in manuscript.[93] In her essay "Maquiavelo y maquiavelismo en España," Helena Puigdomenech states unequivocally that Machiavelli was known in Spain in both the sixteenth and seventeenth centuries. She affirms, "obras de Maquiavelo circulaban a pesar de estar prohibidas."[94]

This scholar and others have proven that Machiavelli's ideas were available in Spain, but what was his reception there? Diego Saavedra Fajardo refers in several places in his *Empresas políticas* to "la escuela de

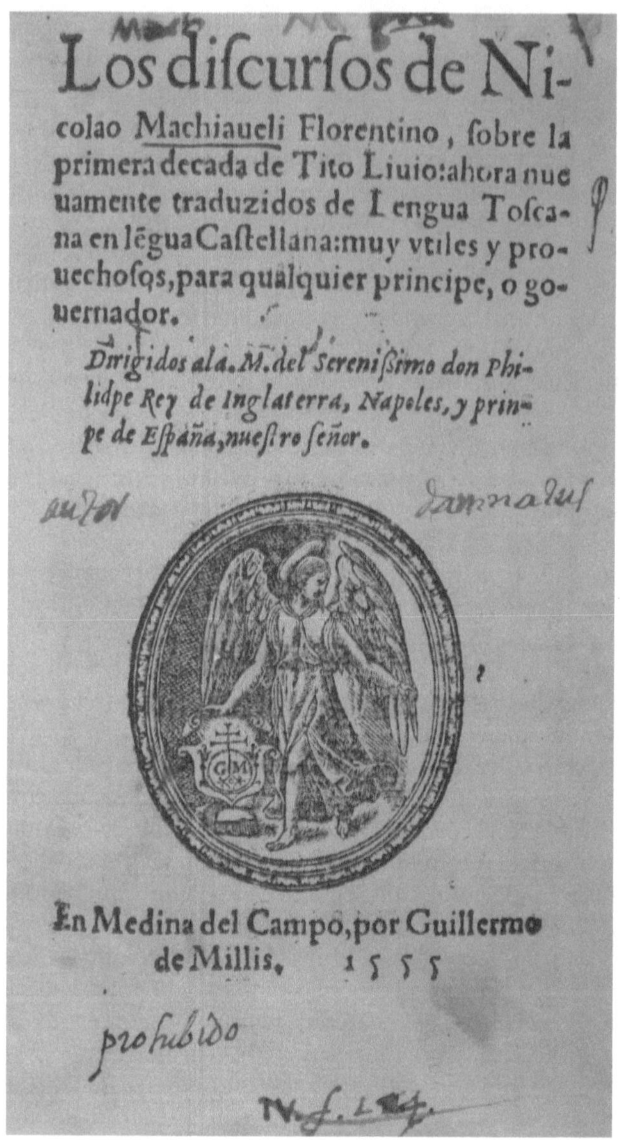

Los diſcurſos de Nicolao Machiaueli Florentino, ſobre la primera decada de Tito Liuio: ahora nueuamente traduzidos de Lengua Toſcana en lēgua Caſtellana: muy vtiles y prouechoſos, para qualquier principe, o gouernador.

Dirigidos a la. M. del Sereniſſimo don Philidpe Rey de Inglaterra, Napoles, y principe de Eſpaña, nueſtro ſeñor.

autor damnatus

En Medina del Campo, por Guillermo de Millis. 1555

prohibido

Figure 19. A translation of Machiavelli's *Discourses on Livy* by Juan Lorenzo Otevante dedicated to Philip II (1555), this censored copy of which may be found at the Escorial (© Patrimonio Nacional).

Maquiavelo"[95] and notes that Machiavelli only advocates the appearance of virtue:

> Quisiera Maquiavelo a su Príncipe ... que estuviese en las puntas de su cetro la piedad e impiedad para volverle, y hacer cabeza de la parte que más conviniese a la conservación o aumento de sus Estados. Y con este *fin no le parece que las virtudes son necesarias en él, sino que basta el dar a entender que las tiene ... Impío e imprudente consejo, que no quiere arraigadas, sino positivas, las virtudes.*[96]

Here Saavedra Fajardo critiques Machiavelli but nonetheless shows a detailed awareness of his theories. Elsewhere he further criticizes Machiavelli's characterization of humility and meekness as "virtudes, que crían ánimos abatidos."[97] Similarly, in 1616 the Portuguese author Alvia de Castro calls Machiavelli impious and ignorant, refuting his political philosophy thus: "*que de tal manera tenga el Principe Christiano las virtudes, que sepa y pueda mudarse, y hacer al contrario dellas;* y que por conservar su Reyno estará obligado a obrar contra la fe, caridad, humanidad, y religión, lo que le convenga."[98] The most obvious case of anti-Machiavellianism in Spain, which also nonetheless shows a detailed knowledge of his ideas, is Pedro Ribadeneyra's refutation of Machiavelli's *The Prince*, titled *Tratado de la Religion y Virtudes que deue tener el Principe Christiano para gouernar y conseruar sus Estados: contra lo que Nicolas Machiauelo y los Politicos deste tiempo enseñan* (1595). Ribadeneyra criticizes Machiavelli for providing his prince a hypocritical mask of Virtue, "una máscara de virtudes."[99] Another important work written during this time period in Spain to refute the Florentine was Claudio Clemente's *El maquiavelismo degollado por la cristiana sabiduría de España y de Austria. Discurso cristiano-político a la católica majestad de Felipe IV, rey de las Españas* (1637). These texts and other elements of Spain's anti-Machiavellian tradition have been analysed persuasively by Jeremy Robbins as falling within the broader context of prudence, scepticism, epistemology, and neo-Stoic political philosophy.[100]

Juan Ginés de Sepúlveda, better known for his well-publicized debate with Bartolomé de las Casas over whether "New" World natives had souls, also argued against Machiavelli's contention that Christianity made men weak:

> [U]n imperio justo ... no se mantiene con engaños ni malas artes, sino con religión, justicia, humildad y magnanimidad, y finalmente con *el ejercicio*

> *de todas las virtudes*; mucho más que haciendo muestra y apariencia de ellas como éstos quieren que se haga, porque la vana opinión muy pronto cae, y, mudada en lo contrario, trae aborrecimiento, lo cual ocasiona una muy cierta destrucción de los tiranos.[101]

Here he refutes the proposition that tyrants can hold onto power successfully by the mere appearance (vs actual substance) of Virtue. But the influential theorist of the Baroque, José Antonio Maravall, believed Sepúlveda's conception of Virtue to be quite close to Machiavelli's, a formulation he attributes to their shared Aristotelianism:

> El concepto de ésta [*virtù*] nos lo da un escritor español que estudió en Bolonia y recibió intensamente la influencia de medios intelectuales próximos a los que influyeron sobre Maquiavelo: estos medios fueron los del aristotelismo paduano. Según el escritor al que nos referimos, Ginés de Sepúlveda, Virtud se llama "el poder o facultad inherente a una persona para conseguir un fin cualquiera propuesto": "*Vis enim seu facultas insita ad finem qualemcumque propositum perveniendi, virtus solet appellari.*"[102]

Sepúlveda's Aristotelian concept of Virtue as described by Maravall extends further to the Golden Mean as expounded in the *Nicomachean Ethics*: "[la virtud] es el hábito de escoger puesto en el medio."[103] He goes on to elaborate what sounds almost like a mechanical definition of political virtue:

> En los gobiernos rectos, sobre todo en las aristocracias, *la "virtud" que constituye a alguien en buen ciudadano y en buena persona es la misma: a saber, la prudencia, justicia, fortaleza y templanza y las demás virtudes que se asocian a estos como goznes sobre los que gira todo el programa de vida y sus, por así decir, mecanismos.*[104]

Here he calls the Virtues the hinges or mechanisms upon which a good citizen's life program should turn. This concept makes Virtue sound strikingly utilitarian, in the sense of being useful like a door hinge (a lowly object, to be sure, but without which one can nevertheless not open a door).[105] This metaphor echoes St Thomas Aquinas, the main Christian thinker who called the Virtues "Cardinal" because they were the hinges of a moral life.

All of this makes it sound perhaps as if Machiavelli was roundly rejected in Spain, caveats about shared Aristotelianism aside. But

Machiavelli was not without early modern Spanish proponents and even followers. Baroque poet Francisco de Quevedo would at first appear to figure among Machiavelli's detractors. As Walter Ghia explains, "El nombre de Maquiavelo aparece en la *Hora de todos*, en *Lince de Italia u Zahorí español* y en las *Migajas*. Quevedo expresa siempre execración, guarda distancias, o refuta doctrinas."[106] But Ghia argues from textual resonances that Quevedo had read Machiavelli's *The Prince* with some care.[107] Finally, Ghia concludes that Quevedo was actually not anti-Machiavellian and may well have embraced some of his ideas:

> En definitiva, sólo los lectores que navegan por la superficie de las palabras pueden situar a Quevedo entre las tropas de los antimaquiavélicos. Quevedo no es en absoluto crítico con Maquiavelo por lo que concierne a la relación entre medios y fines, y el tema de la eficacia de la acción ocupa el primer plano de su reflexión. Es diferente su postura por lo que atañe al orden político, pero las diferencias no proceden de preocupaciones éticas.[108]

In similar fashion, Saverio Ansaldi sees the great Baroque theorist of *conceptismo*, Baltasar Gracián, as Machiavellian,[109] although this seems like a stretch, given the seeming authenticity of the Jesuit's faith. Indeed, in Gracián's *Oráculo manual*, he expounds upon the beauties and excellencies of Virtue:

> *Es la virtud cadena de todas las perfecciones*, centro de las felicidades; ella hace un sujeto prudente, atento, sagaz, cuerdo, sabio, valeroso, reportado, entero, feliz, plausible, verdadero y universal héroe ... *La virtud es el sol del mundo menor* y tiene por hemisferio la buena conciencia; es tan hermosa, que se lleva la gracia de Dios y de las gentes. *No hay cosa amable sino la virtud*, ni aborrecible sino el vicio. *La virtud es cosa de veras*, todo lo demás de burlas. La capacidad y grandeza se ha de medir por la virtud, no por la fortuna: ella sola se basta a sí misma.[110]

But we should note that some of Virtue's advantages, according to Gracián, are things like happiness and plausibility, which are not necessarily ethical principles. Like Donald Trump's so-called theology of power, they sound more like pragmatic advantages for living well and getting what you want.[111]

Political theorist Fadrique Furió Ceriol, writing towards the middle of the sixteenth century, was quite possibly influenced by Machiavelli.

He defined the prince as a political professional and asserted that he did not necessarily have to be good, but merely an able performer. He likened him to a professional musician who knew how to play his part.[112] Around the same time, Diego de Salazar's *Tratado de Re Militari* appeared as a translation / adaptation of Machiavelli's *Dell'arte della guerra* (1521).[113] This text likewise could have proven important for disseminating Machiavelli's pagan / military concept of *Virtù*.

In summary, then, "Machiavelli's texts were officially banned in Spain, but his ideas were known, and 'substitute' texts were found; indeed, Tacitus became a stand-in for Machiavellian pragmatism in a context where Machiavelli could not be invoked."[114] There would seem to be no insurmountable obstacle to retaining him as a viable option if we are looking for influential proponents of alternative systems of morality in early modern Spain.

But our gut instinct tells us that for at least most of the plays in question, this lead turns out to be a dead end. Machiavelli seemed like the most logical place to start, since his is unquestionably the most cynical read on Virtue of any thinker anywhere during the early modern period. However, in addition to the problem of his works being prohibited in Spain, the references to Virtue in these plays do not seem to me as cynical as Machiavelli's. These playwrights were priests, and as such, concerned about actually being good, not merely seeming so. In addition, Machiavelli's model might work for political theory but does not transfer so easily to non-political contexts. Machiavelli is too limited to political discourse, whereas this moral flexibility or ambiguity we have found in the realm of drama applies more evenly to all the (political as well as not so overtly political) Virtues. A further consideration is that if we consult our Index of *Comedias* at the back of this book, a disproportionate share of the plays cited here were authored by Pedro Calderón de la Barca – no surprise, given the subject matter of this study, and the fact that he is generally acknowledged to be the most overtly theological of all mainstream Spanish dramatists. His work specifically has been scrutinized for Machiavellian sentiment by Stephen Rupp, who concludes that Calderón de la Barca was actually anti-Machiavellian:

> Gracián's realism represents one extreme in the spectrum of Spanish political thought. At the other end lies an obdurate conservatism of the kind that Quevedo attributes to the court of the grand Turk in *La hora de todos* (1650) ... In relation to these contrasting positions Calderón occupies

> the middle ground. He denies that human foresight and intelligence can empower the prince to meet all contingencies, and advocates instead a moral respect for providence and the hierarchy of laws. *His stance is conservative in its fidelity to the traditional virtues* and limits of kingship, but it is not hostile to all forms of change in government. Calderón follows the shifting relations of the Crown, the councils, and the office of the favorite, and he values the political balance that arose among these institutions during the mature reign of Philip IV. The creation of a theater that sustains the anti-Machiavellian argument for Christian statecraft and limited sovereignty, and adapts that argument to the changing conditions of politics in seventeenth-century Spain, is a striking achievement in his long dramatic career.[115]

If Rupp is right, then it would be hard to make the case that Machiavellian notions of Virtue were embraced so heartily by Calderón de la Barca and his fellow playwrights[116] as to become prevalent on the early modern Spanish stage.

So if not Machiavelli, where does this more flexible notion of Virtue which we have been tracing come from, at least as a more proximate cause than the classical authors from whom these ideas ultimately derive? The great Christian humanist Erasmus of Rotterdam was also prohibited in Spain, but not at first, and that left significant time for his ideas to take root there. It is to this thinker, therefore, that we must now turn in order to understand how more "elastic" notions of Virtue were introduced into (or revived in) Spain and how they became so popular.

V Erasmus at the Theatre

The primary work by Erasmus which is relevant for our purposes here is his *Enchiridion militis christiani* (Handbook of a Christian Knight) written in 1501. In this text, he specifically defines sin in medical terms as an illness and a poison:

> *el pecado es una espantable pestilencia y una enfermedad abominable y contagiosa* assí del ánima como del cuerpo ... *[E]s una ponçoña mortal.*[117]

This is far from an isolated instance of a crossover in Erasmus's thinking between moral and medical discourse. Earlier in this same text, the humanist refers to "las tales aficiones" – his pet phrase to refer to the Vices – as "*enfermedades del ánimo.*"[118]

Virtue, by contrast, is defined as a fast-working medicine for the soul: "pone en el ánima enferma *una medicina de virtud*."[119] But where does this medicine come from? In what is really a remarkable instance of *pharmakon* logic, Erasmus explains that the Vices themselves may be used as a spur to Virtue:

> Los peripatéticos, por el contrario, enseñan que **las tales aficiones** avemos siempre de procurar de refrenarlas; pero que no se han de desraygar del todo, ca piensan aver en ellas algún provecho, porque éstas **nos fueron dadas naturalmente por espuelas y incitamientos para la virtud**. Como veemos que **la yra,** *aunque es passión, pero no siendo desmedida,* **es despertadora de la virtud de la fortaleza; y la embidia,** *siendo liviana,* **despierta a la industria y diligencia**; y otras por el semejante.[120]

In fact, it would appear that there is no Vice so evil that it cannot be transformed into a Virtue: "no ay ninguna destas aficiones tan rezia ni tan forçosa que no se pueda refrenar o traerse a que sea virtud."[121] Similarly, his Regla XII of the same text is that "de la mesma tentación podemos tomar ocasión para la virtud."[122] He elaborates upon this concept:

> Y de esta manera verás que cada una de las tentaciones se te convertirá en hazerte renovar tu santo propósito y en darte más bivos desseos de passar adelante con otro aliento, y *será como una aguzadera en que se tome un filo más delgado* y para crecer en las cosas de Dios con mayor aprovechamiento.[123]

Temptations should be embraced by the Christian soldier as tools for sharpening Virtue's knife.

Ultimately Erasmus arrives at the exact same *pharmakon* metaphor we have been exploring throughout this book, namely the ambiguous antidote which works as both poison and cure: "*luego hagamos de nuestros males remedio y melezina para ellos mesmos, como quien con una ponçoña alcança otra.*"[124] He further takes this reasoning process forward to its logical conclusion, which is that Virtue and Vice become virtually, as it were, indistiguishable as a result of their close proximity:

> *ay otras passiones viciosas que son vezinas de las virtudes, y tan semejantes a ellas, que si no tenemos mucho aviso, apenas podemos hazer diferencia entre ellas* sin ser engañados. Estas tales se deven corregir, endereçándolas y aplicándolas a aquella virtud a quien son más vezinas y semejantes.[125]

Once again, this passage is not an aberration in his thought; two hundred pages later, he affirms the same message: "los ... vicios, por ventura se podrían compadecer o tener alguna compañía a ratos con algunas de las virtudes."[126]

But now, as with our other favourite candidate for transmission of these ideas, Machiavelli, it will be necessary not merely to demonstrate the presence of moral ambiguity in Erasmus's thought, but also to demonstrate the availability of those ideas in Spain. It turns out that for the second time, we are in luck. Erasmus's reception in Spain has been summarized recently by Barry Taylor and Alejandro Coroleu in *Humanism and Christian Letters in Early Modern Iberia*:

> As with other parts of Europe, Erasmus's doctrine reached Iberia. With the arrival of the Flemish court of the first Habsburg king of Spain, the future Emperor Charles V, in 1516, Erasmianism was to have a transformative impact on Spanish society. In the early years of Charles's reign the most devoted disciples of Erasmus were men deeply involved with the imperial machine. Particularly receptive to Erasmian ideas was the influential lobby of humanists gathered around the emperor and led by Juan de Valdés and his brother Alfonso, secretary for Latin correspondence at the imperial court and *erasmicior Erasmo*. In addition, in the 1520s many of Erasmus's works – issued chiefly under the imprint of Miguel de Eguía at Alcalá de Henares – were translated into the vernacular, thus contributing to the popularity of his ideas. In 1526 Alfonso Fernández de Madrid, the archdeacon of Alcor, who had undertaken the translation of the *Enchiridion militis Christiani* two years earlier, wrote triumphantly to Erasmus that, whereas formerly the text had been read by the few who were skilled in Latin, "there is now hardly anyone who does not have in hand the Spanish version in the imperial court, in cities, in churches, in monasteries, and even in inns."[127]

Alejandro Coroleu says of the University of Alcalá, established in 1499, that Erasmus's first enthusiastic supporters in Spain could be found there, among the ranks of both professors and students.[128] But Taylor and Coroleu conclude that "enthusiasm for Erasmus and for his reformist kind of humanism began to wane in the later 1530s."[129] Francisco Sánchez de las Brozas, better known as El Brocense, was professor of rhetoric and Greek at the University of Salamanca between 1554 and some terminal point before he died in 1601. His rather late-flourishing Erasmianism got him into trouble with the Inquisition.[130]

The classic treatment of the specific reception in Spain of the text we have been examining, Erasmus's *Enchiridion*, may still be found in Marcel Bataillon's magisterial *Erasmo y España*. He did not exaggerate when he wrote of Erasmus's work: "Este libro ... va a realizar en España una verdadera revolución espiritual."[131] As we have learned already, a Spanish translation of the *Enchiridion* was composed in 1524 by Alonso Fernández de Madrid, the Archdeacon of Alcor. Bataillon estimates that "ese buen éxito fue tal, que ningún libro religioso lo había tenido semejante desde la introducción de la imprenta en España."[132] The book's most ardent advocate was Luis Coronel, secretary to Inquisitor General Alonso Manrique. It was published with Inquisitorial approval in 1526, with the Inquisitor General's coat of arms actually appearing in the printed edition of the book (see Figure 20 for the frontispiece to the 1528 Joffre edition, which shows the word *Virtus* emblazoned on the knight's horse's garment).[133]

The press run sold out immediately. In the summer of that same year a second edition was released. Thousands of copies were printed, but the market was still not saturated.[134] The Illuminists adopted this book as one of their founding documents, and this decision on their part actually contributed to the internationalization of their movement.[135] We have proof that none other than St Ignatius Loyola read this book,[136] which might surprise some, given that later both Erasmus's and Juan Luis Vives's books were prohibited by the Jesuits.[137] As Bataillon notes, St Ignatius was mistaken for an *alumbrado* early on in his career.[138] Here is a radical thought: could some of the Jesuits' famous trademark casuistry and equivocation have derived ultimately from their founder's having been influenced by the ambiguity regarding Virtue and Vice to be found in Erasmus's *Enchiridion*, which he is known to have read?[139]

Later, Erasmus's reception in Spain became more problematic. Bataillon describes the landscape: "Erasmo es rey de las escuelas, rey por la voluntad unánime de los estudiosos."[140] But his enemies at this time were the Scholastics, whom Bataillon calls "enemigos jurados de Erasmo, sus detractores infatigables."[141] A third group, "la masa popular," were his fervent supporters. A fourth group were the friars, although Bataillon subdivides this bunch into Erasmian supporters and Erasmian detractors.[142] Monastic institutions were threatened by Erasmus's attack on monks in his famous dictum, "*Monachatus non est pietas*."[143] The two main monastic orders that decided to counterattack were the Benedictines and the Franciscans.[144]

Figure 20. Valencia, 1528 edition of the Spanish translation of Erasmus' *Enquiridion, o manual del caballero cristiano*, printed by Juan Joffre; the word *Virtus* adorns the knight's horse's garment at the far left in the engraving (77.Dd.24 PS, Österreichische Nationalbibliothek, Vienna).

Even then the prohibitions backfired, making Erasmus more appealing in light of the persecution he suffered: "Ciertamente, España erasmizaba cada vez más."[145] Bataillon mentions that by now Archbishop Bartolomé Carranza had converted entirely to Erasmus's ideas.[146] Quickly the battle lines were drawn:

> Al acercarse el otoño de 1526, el éxito del *Enquiridion* desencadena en el interior de España una especie de guerra espiritual que enfrenta a la mayoría de los frailes con una gran minoría erasmizante seguida por el público de los semiletrados. El movimiento, además de tener una amplitud mucho mayor que la fermentación iluminista que motivó el Edicto de 1525, cuenta con la aprobación oficial de la Inquisición. Los acontecimientos se agravan y su ritmo se acelera. Antes de que pase un año, la Inquisición se verá obligada a someter el conflicto a un arbitraje.[147]

Here he refers to the Edict of 1525 against the *alumbrados*.

The upshot was a very moderate position adopted by the Inquisition in the interval between its enthusiastic endorsement of Erasmus and his subsequent prohibition. Bataillon describes this middle-of-the-road stance:

> El Consejo de la Inquisición no se deja intimidar ni por los discursos ni por las griterías de unos cuantos violentos ... y mantiene firmemente su prejuicio favorable a Erasmo. Este autor no está condenado como herético ... La lectura de los libros de Erasmo debe tolerarse mientras no se haya demostrado su peligro.[148]

The book's translator into Spanish, Alonso Fernández de Madrid, famously congratulated himself on the book's splendid success.[149] Bataillon cites the impartial testimony of a contemporary, the ambassador Johannes Dantiscus (Juan Dantisco), who wrote in the course of his diplomatic correspondence, the totality of which dates from 1519 to 1530: "El *Enchiridion militis christiani* ... traducido al español sin oposición de los obispos e impreso en España, es leído por todos y en todas partes."[150]

But in the 1530s the tide began to turn. In January of 1536 an Aragonese man named Miguel Mezquita (whose last name, meaning *mosque*, makes him sound like he might be of *morisco* origin) was processed by the Inquisition in Valencia for, among other things, reading the *Enchiridion* of Erasmus. According to surviving records, a friar saw him reading the book in the castle of Alcañiz and told him that if he thought that book was good, then he must not be a Christian.[151] Then the *Enchiridion*, along with other works by Erasmus, began to appear on the Indices of prohibited books:

1554 Index of Venice (*Enchiridion* prohibited)[152]
1559 Index of Valdés (*Enchiridion* prohibited in both Spanish and Latin)[153]
1571 Amberes *Index expurgatorius librorum qui hoc saeculo prodierunt* (expurgated the *Enchiridion* in four places)
1583 and 1584 Index of Quiroga (*Enchiridion* prohibited)

In 1564 the merchant Alonso de Castilla was processed by the Inquisition in Mexico for having bought and sold prohibited books, among them six copies of Erasmus's *Enchiridion* translated into Spanish.[154] Eventually the Inquisition started confiscating any book that bore the title *Enchiridion*, even if it was not written by Erasmus.[155]

If anything, Bataillon considers the book's later suppression so paradoxical as to approach historical anomaly:

> Es una paradoja histórica la floración de traducciones de Erasmo en el país de la Inquisición, en esa España donde la censura de los libros sería, unas cuantas décadas después, más severa que en ningún otro lugar. Para comprender esto hay que tener en cuenta seguramente las coyunturas que, hacia 1527, aseguraron a las ideas erasmianas la protección oficial de los poderosos de la corte de Carlos V, del Primado y de varios obispos españoles, y por último, la del Inquisidor General en persona.[156]

So to conclude, Erasmus's ideas circulated widely in Spain before they were suppressed, and this text of his in particular seems to have resonated in a special way with Spanish readers.

Alban Forcione has long argued for the primacy of Erasmian thought in the novels and *novellas* of Cervantes[157] (the last of which was composed near the time of his death as late as 1616); but despite the theatrical dialogue form in which Erasmus's *Colloquies* were written, few critics have studied the possible impact of Erasmianism on Spain's popular drama.[158] If the genealogy we have been tracing here is accurate, and we are hearing Erasmian echoes in the *comedias* and *autos sacramentales* a century or more after Erasmus's works were prohibited, then his ideas remained prevalent in Spain (and in different circles) for much longer than we had previously thought. Erasmus is widely acknowledged to have impacted the other great popular genre besides the novel and the *comedia* to have been pioneered in Golden Age Spain, namely the picaresque.[159] If we think about it, it would actually be more surprising if Erasmian concepts had *not* found their way into the drama as well. To his opponents, Erasmus's ideas were like the hydra heads of heresy which only grew back stronger each time they were tentatively lopped off. The Inquisition tried to close this Pandora's box, to stuff this genie back in the bottle, but it was too late – ambiguous antidotes had already been released into the world.

A resurgence of Erasmianism in popular theatrical production becomes more plausible once we take into account Erasmus's own famous comment about the theatre, in which he speaks directly about moral ambiguities and reversals at the very same moment as he repeats the *pharmakon* topos of the apothecary's box (*Silenus*) to which he devoted the adage mentioned earlier:

> **For first 'tis evident that all human things**, like Alcibiades' Sileni or rural gods, **carry a double face**, but not the least alike; so that **what at first sight seems to be death, if you view it narrowly may prove to be life**; and so the contrary. **What appears beautiful may chance to be deformed**; what wealthy, a very beggar; **what infamous, praiseworthy**; what learned, a dunce; what lusty, feeble; what jocund, sad; **what noble, base**; what lucky, unfortunate; what friendly, an enemy; and **what healthful, noisome**. In short, view the inside of these Sileni, and you'll find them quite other than what they appear ... If anyone seeing a player acting his part on a stage should go about to strip him of his disguise and show him to the people in his true native form, would he not, think you, not only spoil the whole design of the play, but deserve himself to be pelted off with stones as a phantastical fool and one out of his wits? But **nothing is more common with them than such changes; the same person one while impersonating a woman, and another while a man**; now a youngster and by and by a grim seignior; now a king, and presently a peasant; now a god, and in a trice again an ordinary fellow. **But to discover it were to spoil all**, it being the only thing that entertains the eyes of the spectators. **And what is this life but a kind of comedy**, wherein men walk up and down in one another's disguises and act their respective parts, till the property-man brings them back to the attiring house. And yet he often orders a different dress, and makes him that came but just now off in the robes of a king put on the rags of a beggar. **Thus are all things represented by counterfeit**, and yet without this there was no living.[160]

Here Erasmus convincingly makes the case that moral ambiguity is inherently theatrical. He even mentions the ambiguity of gender, or androgyny. Where else would antithetical moral positions be better debated than on the stage, as dialogue between particular characters bears the capacity to voice different viewpoints?[161] The "all the world's a stage" or *theatrum mundi* commonplace is of course not unique to Erasmus, but became tremendously popular during this time period[162] and was employed by artists and thinkers from Shakespeare to Calderón de la Barca.[163] The fact that Erasmus rehearses this trope within the by-now-familiar framework of the apothecaries' boxes, in the process making explicit reference to health resembling disease, merely solidifies the connection we have been tracing between moral ambiguity and medicine in the context of Golden Age drama.

Epilogue: Virtual Virtue

So what might we conclude about early modern Spanish culture in the wake of this painstakingly reconstructed genealogy? We are not the first to have noticed that Virtue was in crisis during the early modern period in Spain. In "Baroque Quixote: New World Writing and the Collapse of the Heroic Ideal," William Childers has argued for a radical paradigm shift with respect to morality which he relates to a larger trend of cynical Baroque *desengaño*, or disillusionment:

> Under these conditions, which reflect the mirror structure of Baroque representation, heroism is never anything more than a heroic pose, a grandiose gesture; the "authentic" virtue of one who is reputed a hero is simply unknowable ... The outcome is a permanent play of mirrors in which each participant tries to gain a reputation for virtue and use it to enhance his status.[1]

Childers traces this paradigm shift from Cervantes to Gracián, quoting first a description of the ideal hero from a speech by the Canon of Toledo near the end of *Don Quijote*, Part I:

> Puede mostrar las astucias de Ulixes, la piedad de Eneas, la valentía de Aquiles, las desgracias de Héctor, las traiciones de Sinón, la amistad de Eurialio, la liberalidad de Alejandro, el valor de César, la clemencia y verdad de Trajano, la fidelidad de Zopiro, la prudencia de Catón, y, finalmente, todas aquellas acciones que pueden hacer perfecto a un varón ilustre.[2]

Childers sees this passage as standing in marked contrast to Gracián's *El héroe* (1637), no one passage of which is necessarily representative, but which he feels instead should be evaluated in the conglomerate:

> Unlike the Canon's virtues, however, in Gracián's baroque conception of the hero, these qualities are not fixed traits of moral character but strategies for creating an impressive public image. For Gracián, heroism is a simulacrum; being a hero is knowing how to get people to think of you as one. There is no "inner" or "authentic" meaning, no ethical "truth" on which a concept of heroism could be based, only the necessity of pleasing one's public in accordance with popular taste, to which the successful hero must be attuned.[3]

This stance might be summarized as "collapsing exemplarity into strategic positioning" or a "performative concept of heroism."[4] Childers concludes, "[I]n Gracián, the representation of heroism has been entirely emptied of ethical content ... Gracián's Baroque reduced Renaissance idealism to one more element in the simulacrum of power."[5] Is this the same downward trajectory we have seen for Virtue in the popular dramas examined in this study?

I would argue that it is not, for one important reason. Childers's comments might be true of the drama if their only model were Machiavelli, but instead there is also Erasmus. Erasmus genuinely wanted his Christian soldier to be spurred on to Virtue – he was just realistic enough to acknowledge that he might have to use the experience of Vice as a *pharmakon* in order to get there. Childers's argument may be fine as far as it goes, but it does not go far enough. A more radical deconstruction of the very notion of Virtue is necessary.

If Virtue appears as ambiguous in these dramas, it is not because some previous heroic ideal has crumbled, but because the edifice of Virtue was never sturdy to begin with. It was built from the outset upon the shifting sand of polyvalent concepts inherited by Christian humanists like Erasmus from classical antiquity, which were often impossible to translate in an adequate manner – the mismatch of Latin *Virtus* with Greek *arete* being a prime example. This disjunction is so egregious that D.C. Earl famously claimed that the word *Virtus*, in turn, is untranslatable.[6] In other words, even at the start of the Renaissance – and actually much, much earlier – Virtue was already problematic.

In fact, new research published only within the last decade or so has demonstrated concretely what classicists had long intuited, which is that going back to the classical world, the meaning of the word *Virtus* evolved along with forms of government, culture, and political structure: "the meaning of *virtus* ... changed over the course of centuries."[7] This is thought to have been the result of the increasing Hellenization of Roman culture:

> Greek ideas about ideal manliness, and in particular the place that ethical considerations played in them, affected and altered Roman attitudes over the course of the last two centuries of the Republic ... In the last half-century of the Republic's existence, a period of marked social, political, and ideological discontinuity, divergent ideals of manliness, one drawing openly on an Hellenic model, the other claiming to represent traditional values, were publicly debated, and ... the contested meaning of Roman manliness played a critical ideological role in the crisis that shook and finally ended the Roman Republic.[8]

First used exclusively to denote martial valour,[9] it was only gradually that the word *Virtus* came to bear any ethical connotations at all:

> In the same way that the Roman gods aided not the ethically good but the ritually correct, and that Roman law assisted the person who followed correct legal procedure over one who might have had the better claim, so too in judging the behavior of public men ethical conduct was secondary to martial prowess. This is not to say that Romans regarded ethical behavior as unimportant, but that *in regard to ideal manly behavior issues of right or wrong were not paramount* ... As the traditionally warlike society of mid-Republican Rome was adapting to a more ethically sophisticated Greek culture, it was natural that the meaning of central concepts would also expand their primary field of reference ... Since *virtus* certainly took on a variety of new meanings ... it is likely that the decidedly ethical connotations ... also affected the Latin word.[10]

According to linguists, this type of semantic *calque* or loan-shift occurs most frequently in bilingual populations, such as that of cosmopolitan Rome inhabited by Greek speakers during the late third century.[11]

Indeed, the thesis of Myles McDonnell's extraordinary book *Roman Manliness: "Virtus" and the Roman Republic* is that "*Virtus* was a far more complex value than modern scholarship has supposed, and how it came to be used in various and contradictory ways requires explanation."[12] In nearly four hundred erudite pages, he traces a genealogy of this word's use from Ennius to Caesar to Cicero:

> Although there can be conceptual overlap between courageous and ethical *virtus* ... the confluence of these two senses of *virtus* – ethical and courageous – was never total, and ... ethical qualities and conduct could be opposed to martial *virtus*. Viewed synchronically, the overtly non-ethical use of *virtus* by Ennius and Caesar, and the regular use of *virtus* in a strictly ethical sense by Cicero and others, is a puzzling linguistic phenomenon. Diachronically considered, however, it makes sense. The contradictory usages suggest that the narrowly ethical sense in which *virtus* is found in Roman comedy and in later Latin was not a traditional or indigenous usage, but one that developed as both a literary and cultural borrowing. Such a development, moreover, corresponds to what is known about the values of Rome of the middle Republic. *The contradiction in the usage of* virtus *reflects a distinction observed in many cultures between societal norms and mores on the one hand and a more strictly ethical consideration of right and wrong on the other.* In some cultures, the two more or less correspond, but in ancient Rome native moral concepts seem to have been predominantly social as opposed to private, and they centered around the ideas of function and success rather than abstract ethical notions of right and wrong.

In fact, McDonnell makes the bold assertion that "in a society as militaristic as that of middle republican Rome ... issues of right or wrong were apparently not paramount, and an individual's ethical failing might be overlooked if he excelled as a soldier."[13] This commentary begs the further question of who gets to define right and wrong, particularly with regard to individual "Virtues." For example, Charity was simply not practised at all in Roman culture, although it had been exercised by the Greeks: "The obligation to help impecunious peers ... was quite foreign to Romans of the middle Republic, and had no connection to *virtus*."[14]

What catalyst sparked the change, aside from gradual linguistic borrowing? Events as seemingly mundane as a law passed in 129 BC which excluded senators from the state cavalry may have had an impact on notions of *Virtus*, as did the removal by censors in 158 BC of unauthorized equestrian statues.[15] As McDonnell demonstrates convincingly using the images emblazoned on Roman coins, "numismatic evidence shows beyond a doubt that the mounted warrior was the preeminent symbol of *virtus* for the ancient Romans."[16] So if equestrian statues were emblematic of *virtus*, why were they removed? By this time the statues were also associated with arrogance, which McDonnell sees as symptomatic of Roman ambivalence towards *virtus* itself.[17] The statues had originally purported to be lifelike representations of single combat, or *monomachy*, the skill for which was gradually being lost with each subsequent generation:

> Because they had no stirrups, and until the late Republic, no proper saddles, maintaining their mount cannot have been easy. In combat the difficulty would have been extreme. This is the reason why we hear so much about Roman horsemen taking serious, sometimes fatal, falls.[18]

The stories of single combat had been preserved in families for generations through banquet songs, choral dirges, and funeral eulogies, but by now – if these stories survived at all – they were the tales of remote ancestors who had lost their relevance for the more urbane new Roman youth. Soon the practice of single combat itself (not just its artistic representation) was restricted by law:

> The great glory gained by victory in single combat was a potential threat to *libertas* and the Republic. The ethos of republican elite warfare, therefore, required that this highest manifestation of *virtus* be performed only with the permission of a magistrate, and only by men too young to gain immediate political benefit from the achievement. Displays of aristocratic *virtus* were restricted in order to insure the preservation of the Republic.[19]

Along with this dampening of enthusiasm for single combat arose a concomitant dampening of enthusiasm for the quality it was believed to represent, i.e., *virtus*. Such chronicles illustrate the rise and fall of values which are culturally constructed (as all values are, by definition).

In our chapter on class and gender we mentioned that in ancient Rome, *Virtus* was also a goddess replete with a temple dedicated to her along with *Honos*, or honour. But what may not have emerged clearly from that discussion was that "divine Virtus was from first to last a deity of war."[20] As such, she was frequently invoked by socially ambitious Romans, but her cult remained very much elitist in nature: "politically ambitious and militarily successful Romans associated themselves with divine Virtus."[21] The *transvectio equitum*, or collective parade on horseback, was literally "ancient Rome's most important regular military spectacle, its purpose being to reaffirm the martial role of the upper classes, its collective *virtus*."[22] So the decree to take away the senators' publicly financed horses "constituted a public humiliation and was a form of political attack."[23] This was about the same time when ten years' military service ceased to be a requirement for holding public office.[24] It is to this divisive atmosphere that we must trace Virtue's origins, to a classical culture that was itself conflicted over the cultural baggage attached to *virtus*, its definition, its artistic representation, and the goddess who allegedly bestowed it. Or did she?

It turns out that even the overtly religious aspect of ancient *Virtus* is problematic. The state-sanctioned cult to the goddess Virtus may be dated to 205 BC. She was understood to be a deity who bestowed power on individuals.[25] But a dissenting voice may be found in the later Latin grammarian Aulus Gellius (130–80 AD), who pronounced crisply, "The gods ought to approve virtue, not bestow it."[26] As Gellius was educated in Athens, his was an even more directly Hellenized view, in which *virtus* had morphed back into *arete*, defined as the innate excellence of a human being (as opposed to a deity).[27] This was the classical equivalent of preaching the doctrine of secular humanism.

Yet another chapter in the history of Virtue's classical ambiguity unfolds with Julius Caesar, who in *De bello Gallico* attributes *virtus* both to his own soldiers and to the enemy. As McDonnell explains this shrewd rhetorical move,

> Attributing *virtus* to the enemy served a number of purposes ... By exalting the valor of his opponents Caesar not only magnified his own victories, but also provided justification for his aggressive actions.[28]

This strategy may well have worked to Caesar's advantage rhetorically. But its practical effect was to enhance the ambiguity of a word that was already straining to bear the weight of all its baggage. Suddenly there were no clear-cut distinctions between the good guys and the bad guys any more.

A further layer of ambiguity was added by the orator and politician Marcus Tullius Cicero, who attempted to "reshape *virtus* into his own political slogan." The word occurs an astounding three times in the tiny fragments that survive from *De consulato suo*, his lost epic poem about his own consulship.[29] Cicero was the first Roman to be granted a *supplicatio* (state sacrifices to the gods offered in thanks for a military victory) without ever having defeated an army on a battlefield.[30] It is significant that in other extant writings, Cicero describes his consulship as a war between Vices and ethical Virtues of the sort we have been looking at in this study, among them *aequitas, temperantia, fortitudo,* and *prudentia.*[31] In the cynical view, at least, with this stroke of genius, Cicero managed to hijack and hybridize *virtus*, thereby harnessing its cultural power to serve his own political ends:

> When the opportunity presented itself, Cicero would seek to gain for himself the highest prestige traditionally reserved for the man of military *virtus*. He would do this by clouding the distinction between the martial and non-martial references of the term ... Cicero's strategy ... [was] appropriating to his merit for investigating, exposing, and arresting the Catilinarian conspirators in the city of Rome, the glory that heretofore had been reserved for Roman military victories.[32]

It is no exaggeration to claim that with this move, Cicero changed forever the meaning of the term.

The scope of McDonnell's study only extends until the end of Rome's Republic, but it is an easy matter to continue the thread of his chronicle through Rome's decline. Steve Tuck fills in part of this story in "The Origins of Roman Imperial Hunting Imagery: Domitian and the Redefinition of *Virtus* under the Principate":

> Attempts to redefine *virtus* begin under the principate with Gaius. His efforts develop from the circumstances of his succession. He came to power when very young and without military experience so sought to demonstrate his personal qualities and abilities in an arena (literally) beyond that of the traditional battlefield. Instead of relying on traditional models of Roman military behaviour, he instead referred to Greek antecedents, expecially the model of Alexander the Great. Areas of achievement closed to upper-class Romans such as gladiatorial combat and chariot racing were major components of his efforts ... [T]he concept of redefining *virtus* does not die with Gaius and continues almost immediately with Nero.[33]

Given the Emperor Nero's infamous reputation – he is supposed to have played the fiddle while watching Rome burn – it is not hard to see how Virtue would suffer irrevocable distortion at his hands.

But most classical philologists agree that it was the late poet Lucan – born in Spain, no less, and chronicler of Rome's civil war, part of which was fought in Spain – who nailed the lid on Virtue's coffin.[34] In *The Taste for Nothingness: A Study of* Virtus *and Related Themes in Lucan's* Bellum Civile, Robert Sklenář traces the fortunes of this concept as it jumps off the cliff into nihilism:

> Few things more vividly exemplify Lucan's jumbled cosmos than the semantic misadventures that befall *virtus* during the course of his epic. For him, *virtus* is a paradigm of disorder ... In his treatment of the *virtus* of martial epic, Lucan does not betray the impoverishment of the tradition within which he writes; rather, he asserts the unique prerogative of the literary *epigone*. Like the wastrel heir who seeks out the most frivolous pursuits on which to squander his patrimony, Lucan bestows his inheritance on the most undeserving recipients that he can possibly contrive.[35]

These undeserving recipients include the half-giant Antaeus as well as the ethically and physically small Curio, an "amoral *homunculus* who incarnates civilization in the final stages of decay, when all behavioral norms have broken down."[36] Ultimately, in this world view, right and wrong are reversed to the extent that "*virtus* itself is presented as criminal in the context of a civil war ... *[V]irtus* becomes emblematic of ... moral nullity."[37] In Sklenář's perceptive view, this reversal is accomplished in Lucan's poetry by his deliberate wordplay on conflicting definitions of the term:

> In Lucan's scheme, the personal conflict between Pompey and Caesar pits *virtus* against *virtus* in the same way that civil war represents a single political entity at war with itself ... These lines depict not merely the *virtus* of one man striving against another but *an internal conflict within the term* virtus *itself* ... *Nescia stare loco* thus foreshadows an instability of definition for Caesarean *virtus* and for *virtus* in the entire epic. *The very word, like the Roman civic entity, is divided into factions, self-destructive and irreconcilable.*

This scholar finishes with a candid assessment of Lucan's "knowing manipulation of the term's rhetorical power" and "the capacity of *virtus* to designate its own opposite":

> The poem closes with the absolute negation of the term itself, *non virtus* – *virtus* pulverized and ultimately nullified by a lexical marker whose only function is to negate.[38]

And so we see that there was no single "classical tradition" of Virtue for Renaissance humanists to recover. *Pace* Childers, there never was a unified heroic ideal to lose.

Should such considerations lead us to existential despair? *Nec cessat naufraga virtus.* [*Nor does virtue cease, though shipwrecked.*][39] The Spanish Latin poet Lucan, writing at the time of Rome's civil war, while recognizing Virtue's complexity, did not declare it extinct. In a post-modern world of virtual Virtue, or Virtue as simulacrum,[40] in which various systems of Virtue-based ethics are being proposed for programming robots,[41] now more than ever we need to embrace the messiness of struggling to find that sweet spot between two Vices which is the Golden Mean. The knowledge that Vices surround us, by definition, in any position on this spectrum should not deter us from seeking to achieve that elusive balance. It might just be a matter of getting to know our "neighbours."

Notes

Prologue

1 "The return to ethics in literature and philosophy during the last two decades encompasses numerous themes and methodologies ranging from feminist, ethnic, and queer criticism grounded in ethico-political commitments to the examination of moral themes in literature to the Levinasian call of responsibility to the other" (Langis, "Virtuous Viragos," 399).
2 Childers, "Hispanic Casuistry Studies."
3 See Finkelberg, "Virtue and Circumstances."
4 See Romano, "The Ancient Stadium-Athletes and *Arete*"; and Miller, Arete: *Greek Sports from Ancient Sources.*
5 On Latin's shortage of words, see McDonnell, "Roman Men and Greek Virtue," 236.
6 See McDonnell, *Roman Manliness.*
7 Recent work on Prudentius includes Mastrangelo, *The Roman Self in Late Antiquity*; and Smith, *Prudentius'* Psychomachia. Important previous work includes Haworth, *Deified Virtues, Demonic Vices, and Descriptive Allegory in Prudentius'* Psychomachia; and Malamud, "Making a Virtue of Perversity."
8 In Plato's words, "I think that this quality which makes it possible for the three we have already considered, *wisdom, courage, and temperance,* to take their place in the commonwealth, and so long as it remains present secures their continuance, must be the remaining one. And we said that, when three of the four were found, the one left over would be *justice*" (Plato, *Republic,* Book IV, 432, p. 127, emphasis mine). In this context "wisdom" is the equivalent of "prudence." In Plato's *Protagoras* these four Virtues

appear alongside a fifth one, namely holiness or piety (Plato, *Protagoras*, in *Plato in Twelve Volumes*, 3:349b–c).

9 For Saint Augustine's contribution to Christianized notions of Virtue see Johnson, "Virtus." Saint Thomas Aquinas's work on the Virtues is available in English translation as Aquinas, *Treatise on the Virtues*. Useful commentary may be found in Houser, *The Cardinal Virtues*.

10 For a discussion of the Cardinal Virtues and their history, see Pieper, *The Four Cardinal Virtues*.

11 A portion of Suárez's work is available in English translation as Suárez, "A Work on the Three Theological Virtues." On the Cardinal Virtues in Juan de Mena, see Beltrán, "The Poet, the King and the Cardinal Virtues in Juan de Mena's *Laberinto*."

12 Lope de Vega, *Arte nuevo de hacer comedias*, ll. 327–30, p. 149, emphasis mine.

13 Calderón, *¿Quién hallará mujer fuerte?* auto sacramental.

14 Calderón, *La vida es sueño*, auto sacramental. Here *pomo* refers not to an apple or other fruit, but to the hilt of a sword.

15 Kallendorf, "Foreword: A Note on Method," in *Sins of the Fathers*, ix–xii.

16 "Even atheistic scholars can benefit from considering sins as nodes of cultural anxiety" (Kallendorf, "Foreword," xi).

Introduction

1 *Macbeth*, V.iii, 43–5. Macbeth asks this question of the Doctor regarding Lady Macbeth.

2 *A Small Treatise on the Great Virtues*, 5.

3 This tradition seems to have been particularly influential in the sacramental drama before Calderón de la Barca. See Louise Fothergill-Payne's study of Francisco Palomino's Spanish translation of Prudentius's *Psychomachia* and its impact in "La *Psychomachía* de Prudencio y el teatro alegórico pre-calderoniano."

4 Calderón de la Barca, *La inmunidad del sagrado*, loa for *auto sacramental*.

5 Calderón de la Barca, *Amar y ser amado, y divina Philotea*, auto sacramental.

6 Jaeger, "Aristotle's Use of Medicine," 54. This association is repeated by Aquinas, who cites Aristotle as his source (Aquinas, *Treatise on the Virtues*, question 50, article 1, p. 12).

7 See Huguet-Termes, "Madrid Hospitals and Welfare."

8 An abundance of scholarship is available on intersections of medicine with Golden Age theatre, but none of these complete the triangulation to include also a connection to Virtue. María Luz López Terrada claims a high

degree of specific medical knowledge for Golden Age playwrights: "The great majority of the medical knowledge in the *comedia* comes directly from medical texts" ("'Sallow-Faced Girl,'" 170). On representations of medicine in the *comedias*, see Albarracín Teulón, *La medicina en el teatro de Lope de Vega*; Pérez Bautista, "La medicina y los médicos en el teatro de Calderón de la Barca"; and Sancho de San Román, *La medicina y los médicos en la obra de Tirso de Molina*. On medicine in the *entremeses*, see Slater and López-Terrada, "Scenes of Mediation." For depictions of medicine in Spanish literature more generally during this time period, see David-Peyre, *Le Personnage du médecin*; and Chevalier, "Le médecin dans la littérature du Siècle d'Or."

9 Arellano, *Historia del teatro español del siglo XVII*, 64–6.

10 John Slater and María Luz López Terrada describe a parallel development for the *entremeses* which they call the "medicalisation of theater": "Both at market and on stage, the lines demarcating medicine and drama seem to approach, almost vertiginously, a vanishing point" ("Scenes of Mediation," 234).

11 Lope de Vega, *El genovés liberal*, Acto 1.

12 Calderón de la Barca, *Los misterios de la Misa*, auto sacramental.

13 Lope de Vega, *El ruiseñor de Sevilla*, Acto 2. On real-life counterparts to these literary healers, see Tausiet, "Healing Virtue."

14 Lope de Vega, *Juan de Dios y Antón Martín*, Acto 2.

15 Lope de Vega, *Juan de Dios y Antón Martín*, Acto 3.

16 Matos Fragoso, *El genízaro de Hungría*, Jornada 2.

17 Tirso de Molina, *El amor médico*, Acto 2. This detail about Madrid's bout with the plague appears in Cruickshank, *Don Pedro Calderón*, 298.

18 Lope de Vega, *Los melindres de Belisa*, Acto 3.

19 Lope de Vega, *El niño inocente de la Guardia*, Acto 2.

20 On the lovers' ruse, see Kallendorf, "Romance, the Interlude, and the Restoration of Order," in *Exorcism and Its Texts*, 99–103.

21 A modern edition of this treatise is available as *"Here men may se the vertues off herbes."*

22 Tirso de Molina, *Amazonas en las Indias*, Acto 2.

23 Lope de Vega, *La fe rompida*, Acto 3.

24 Lope de Vega, *Los Ponces de Barcelona*, Acto 3.

25 Lope de Vega, *El acero de Madrid, primera parte*, Acto 2. On *curanderas* during this and a slightly earlier time period, see Cabré, "Women or Healers?"

26 Calderón de la Barca, *Fuego de Dios en el querer bien*, Jornada 3.

27 Zamora, *El hechizado por fuerza*, Jornada 3.

28 Calderón de la Barca, *La torre de Babilonia*, auto sacramental.
29 Lope de Vega, *El padrino desposado*, Jornada 3.
30 Calderón de la Barca, *La vida es sueño*, Jornada 2.
31 Quiñones de Benavente, *Entremés famoso del abadegillo*, preliminares. These lines appear as part of a sonnet.
32 On the world's first lay medical school, see Valdéz García, "Salerno: la primera escuela de medicina."
33 Harvey, "Medieval Plantsmanship in England." To arrive at his conclusions, Harvey compared the following manuscripts: Trinity College, Cambridge, MS O.I.13, ff. 77v–82v; British Museum, Sloane MS 7, ff. 40–1; Bodleian Library, Oxford, MS Ashmole 1438, ff. 107–9; and British Museum, Sloane MS 962, ff. 79–82.
34 Keiser, "Rosemary: Not Just for Remembrance," 182. The broadside he cites is RSTC 24844.7. See Appendix A to his article (198–201) for a manuscript list of rosemary treatises and Appendix B (201–4) for sample text drawn from some of them. See also Larkin, "The Virtues of Rosemary."
35 López, *The Text and Concordance of Biblioteca Universitaria, Salamanca, MS 2262*.
36 Calderón, *La exaltación de la Cruz*, Jornada 2.
37 *Conciliorum oecumenorum decreta*, ed. Giuseppe Alberigo (Bologna: Istituto per le Scienze Religiose, 1972), 244–5; quoted in English translation in Walter Stephens, *Demon Lovers: Witchcraft, Sex, and the Crisis of Belief* (Chicago: University of Chicago Press, 2002), 274.
38 Cascardi, *Cervantes, Literature, and the Discourse of Politics*, 24.
39 Kallendorf, "Exorcizing the Body Politic," in *Exorcism and Its Texts*, 56–66.
40 Lope de Vega, *La necedad del discreto*, Jornada 1.
41 Calderón de la Barca, *El alcalde de Zalamea*, preliminares to 1683 edition.
42 Lope de Vega, *El Perseo*, Acto 2.
43 Rojas Zorrilla, *El más impropio verdugo por la más justa venganza*, Jornada 3.
44 Calderón de la Barca, *La primer flor del Carmelo*, auto sacramental.
45 Calderón de la Barca, *El pintor de su deshonra*, loa for auto sacramental.
46 Tirso de Molina, *La lealtad contra la envidia*, Acto 3.
47 Agustín Farfán, *Tratado breve de Medicina* (1579), quoted in Folch Jou, "Las drogas en la obra de Fray Agustín Farfán," 169.
48 Ángel Martínez explains the origin of the term *concordia* as it was used to designate these books:

> Las primeras Farmacopeas conocidas en España son las editadas en el siglo XVI en la región catalanoaragonesa, cuyo título empieza en todas con la palabra "Concordia," nombre por el que son generalmente

conocidos, y se cree significa conformidad o aceptación sin discusión del contenido, tanto por médicos como por farmacéuticos. En dicho siglo se publicaron, que se sepa, cinco Concordias: tres en Barcelona (1511, 1535 y 1587) y dos en Zaragoza (1546 y 1553). ("Estudio comparativo," 344)

He also mentions a later example from Barcelona, a *Pharmacopea Cathalana* (1686), which he declares to be more properly designated an *antidotario* ("Estudio comparativo," 344).

49 Martínez calls this book "la que puede considerarse cronológicamente como primera Farmacopea española y segunda mundial" ("Estudio comparativo," 344).

50 Martínez, "Estudio comparativo," 341.

51 Martínez, "Estudio comparativo," 341. He gives the following examples: Bernardus de Pujol, "Receptari de Manresa" (1347), "Receptari de Micer Johan" (1466), Arnaldo de Vilanova, "Antidotarium y cánones," and Nicolás Salerniano, "Antidotario" (341, n. 4).

52 Martínez, "Estudio comparativo," 341–2.

53 We know this from the protest lodged in Francisco Valles's *Tratado de las aguas destiladas, pesos, y medidas de que los boticarios deven usar, por nueva ordenanza y mandato de su Magestad y su Real Consejo* (Madrid: Luis Sánchez, 1592).

54 Martínez, "Estudio comparativo," 342.

55 Martínez, "Estudio comparativo," 342.

56 Cost was a factor particularly in cases where patients bought medicine on credit instead of paying for it up front: "Keeping a pharmacy well stocked with up-to-date medicines was a costly endeavor. Many clients bought medicines on credit, including the crown. Successfully recuperating those costs was typically a lengthy process and sometimes came after a drawn-out and costly legal battle. Having the financial means to weather such fiscal hazards meant the apothecary would not be tempted to sell old, corrupted medicines or commit fraud by substituting one ingredient for another" (Clouse, "The Apothecary's Profession," 128).

57 The Spanish government attempted to crack down on such alterations and substitutions of ingredients in an effort to protect unsuspecting consumers: "Any substitution of one substance for another, such as making syrups with sugar instead of honey, was an act of fraud and punishable as such. This type of fraud was taken quite seriously by municipal authorities. The city of Seville set the punishment for this crime as follows: a first offense cost the apothecary his shop; a second offense was a fine equal to double

the value of his shop; a third offense resulted in 100 lashes" (Clouse, "The Apothecary's Profession," 117).

58 Michele Clouse confirms that this chicanery was punishable as homicide, even if attributable to negligence: "The crown had fixed penalties for criminal cases of misuse or outright poisoning. Any apothecary giving a life-threatening drug such as scammony to a man or woman without the proper prescription could be charged with homicide. Should a physician or apothecary knowingly provide someone with a poisonous substance for malignant purposes, they too would be guilty of murder and subject to a dishonorable death" ("The Apothecary's Profession," 115). Such anxieties about pharmaceutical fraud or malpractice led to the appointment by King Philip II of a medical doctor to the post of *protomédico* (for example, in the kingdom of Valencia), a job which entailed the inspection of pharmacists' shops and control over the medicines they dispensed. On this royal appointment, see López Terrada, "Medical Pluralism in the Iberian Kingdoms," 21.

59 It was deemed necessary to scrutinize the ancestry of pharmacists because Christians were paranoid that Jews or Muslims might try to harm them if they had access to the poisons contained in a *botica*:

> In 1501, the Catholic monarchs restricted those of Moorish or Jewish ancestry, those unable to pass the test for blood purity, or limpieza de sangre, from practicing the apothecary's profession. In 1564, Philip II ratified the guild statutes of apothecaries in Valencia, which insisted that "for the well-being of the city" no members could be of Jewish descent ... The cities of Zaragoza and Seville enacted similar restrictions. These restrictions, in part, stemmed from fear stirred up by the discovery of "conspiracies" in which Moriscos and Coversos used the medicinal arts to harm Christians in Spain. The Bishop of Plasencia felt he had uncovered such a conspiracy and brought it to the crown's attention in 1580. His proof was a letter in which the Jews planned "to teach their sons the science of medicine and the art of the apothecary" as a means of killing off a number of Old Christians. Similar conspiracy theories surfaced regarding Moriscos. During the Cortes of 1607, the representatives discussed an incident involving a Morisco physician called El Vengador (the Avenger). The Morisco had been taken into custody by city officials in Madrid and had confessed to poisoning more than 3,048 Old Christians. (Clouse, "The Apothecary's Profession," 120–1)

60 Rodríguez González, "Información," 28.

61 Cruickshank, *Don Pedro Calderón*, 138.

62 Rodríguez González, "Información," 29. These records date from 1763 but describe his activities prior to that time. Teresa Huguet-Termes notes that the brother apothecary at the two apothecary "shops" in the General

Hospital and Antón Martín in Madrid around 1589–90 did not actually have any professional training as a pharmacist. These pharmacies were run by a qualified apothecary, but one who was subject to the brother apothecary's supervision (Huguet-Termes, "Madrid Hospitals and Welfare," 79).

63 Rodríguez González, "Información," 37.

64 Clouse confirms that apothecaries were not legally required to obtain a university education prior to establishing their practice ("The Apothecary's Profession," 112).

65 Andrés de Laguna himself had participated in the collection of herbs while in Italy, specifically in the mountains in the northeast known as the Dolomites (Andretta, "The Medical Cultures of 'the Spaniards of Italy,'" 143).

66 Peset Llorca, "A Note on the Spanish Version of Dioscorides' *Materia medica*," 52, n. 3. Mar Rey Bueno describes the profitable pharmaceutical use which was made from the plants that were grown in this garden:

> The distillation house of Aranjuez specialized in distilled waters from plant material: rosewater, wormwood, oxlip, fennel, chicory, marjoram and salsify were among the favourites of the royal family. Regular deliveries served the requirements of the court, and, in addition, various monasteries and convents also occasionally received provisions. For example, by 1573, approximately 300 litres a year were being sent out from Aranjuez. Its laboratory was the first step in a project to provide all the royal houses with attractive gardens whose plants could be used to distil essences. The distillers employed by the monarch were experts in these arts ... they took a practice that was basically alchemical and adapted it to therapeutic purposes. ("*La Mayson pour Distiller des Eaües* at El Escorial," 32)

See also Valverde López, Carmen Téllez, and González Gómez, *La botica del real sitio de Aranjuez.*

67 "In early spring 1573, Philip II handed 4,000 *reales* to his personal apothecary, Rafael de Arigón, with instructions to travel to Medina del Campo (Valladolid) in order to acquire all the plant simples necessary to set up a new pharmacy. What were these simples destined for? The royal decree is clear. They were to be used in the pharmacy of the monastery of San Lorenzo, in the town of El Escorial" (Rey Bueno, "*La Mayson pour Distiller des Eaües*," 36).

68 Peset Llorca, "A Note on the Spanish Version," 55.

69 Peset Llorca, "A Note on the Spanish Version," 55–6.

70 Lope de Vega, *Pobreza no es vileza*, Acto 1.

71 *El hospital de los podridos*, in Cotarelo y Mori, *Colección de entremeses*, 1:97.

72 Torquemada, *Los Coloquios satíricos con un Coloquio pastoril* (1553), ed. Lina Rodríguez Cacho (Madrid: Universidad Autónoma de Madrid, 1990), 127–58.

73 Clouse, "The Apothecary's Profession," 115. She cites Miguel Eugenio Muñoz, *Recopilación de las leyes, pragmáticas reales, decretos y acuerdos del Real Protomedicato* (Valencia: Viuda de Antonio Bordazar, 1751), 184.
74 Clouse, "The Apothecary's Profession," 134, 137–9.
75 The relevant Cortes de Castilla mandate from 1567 reads as follows: "mandamos que los nuestros Corregidores, y Justicias ordinarios, con dos Regidores, y un Médico aprobado del tal lugar, haga el examen de las dichas Boticas" (Actas de las Cortes de Castilla, Cortes de Madrid, cited in Clouse, "The Apothecary's Profession," 126, n. 63). Clouse describes the visitation of an apothecary shop owned by a certain Amador Pérez in Zamora in 1595 which deemed his pharmacy to be deficient. Similar cases are studied in Aler Ibarz, Camps Clemente, and Camps Surroca, "Las farmacias de Zaragoza."
76 Clouse, "The Apothecary's Profession," 126–7.
77 Clouse, "The Apothecary's Profession," 118.
78 Clouse, "The Apothecary's Profession," 123, n. 51. She cites Biblioteca Nacional de España, Pragmática Real, Lib. III, Tit. 16, Ley 11.
79 Biblioteca Nacional de España, Capítulos de Las Cortes de Madrid, Capítulo 85, fol. 30; cited in Clouse, "The Apothecary's Profession," 130, n. 77.
80 Cortes de los antiguos reinos de León y Castilla, Cortes de Valladolid; cited in Clouse, "The Apothecary's Profession," 134, n. 97.
81 Derrida, "Plato's Pharmacy," 70.
82 Derrida, "Plato's Pharmacy," 126.
83 Derrida, "Plato's Pharmacy," 71.
84 Derrida, "Plato's Pharmacy," 99, emphasis mine.
85 This idea, or some version of it, appears in diverse contexts in later centuries, including the fourteenth-century *Tree of Battles* by Honoré Bouvet. This writer employs the antidote analogy to claim that war is virtuous, but – like any remedy – it brings collateral damage: "For the truth is that war is not an evil thing, but is good and virtuous ... indeed, war is to be compared to a medicine. We can see how illness comes to the human body through excess of humours, and to reduce this excess the doctor gives the remedy. Very often, however, the drug affects the good humours along with the bad, for in such degree are they mingled and intermixed that it cannot be otherwise: and this is because they are so near and neighbouring, one to the other" (Bouvet, *Arbre des Batailles* [1387] trans. Coopland as *The Tree of Battles*, 125). This passage appears in chapter I of Part Four, "From What Law Does War Come?" Bouvet goes on to give the example of God wiping out Sodom and Gomorrah where some innocents may have died, but these casualties were necessary to wipe out the other inhabitants' sin. God here appears as a physician who applies war as a type of medicine to remedy illness.

86 In *Violence and the Sacred* René Girard employs the closely related concept of *pharmakos* to elaborate his theory of the scapegoat (94–8). In the course of his argument, he touches upon the same confusion surrounding *pharmakon* that concerns us here: "It is not surprising that the word *pharmakon* in classical Greek means both poison and the antidote for poison, both sickness and cure – in short, any substance capable of perpetrating a very good or very bad action, according to the circumstances and the dosage. The *pharmakon* is thus a magic drug or volatile elixir, whose administration had best be left by ordinary men in the hands of those who enjoy special knowledge and exceptional powers – priests, magicians, shamans, doctors, and so on" (95).

87 "Writing, pedagogy, masturbation, and the *pharmakon* share the property of being – with respect to speech, nature, intercourse, and living memory – at once something secondary, external, and compensatory, and something that substitutes, violates, and usurps" (Derrida, "Plato's Pharmacy," 110, n. 46).

88 An equivalent term might be "dangerous remedy." Witness Calderón de la Barca's *El purgatorio de San Patricio*: "Médicos doctos/a peligrosas heridas/dan remedios peligrosos" (*El purgatorio de San Patricio*, Jornada 3).

89 A recent academic study demonstrating beyond any possibility for argument the currency of Plato's ideas, along with those of his fifteenth-century Italian interpreters, in Renaissance Spain is Susan Byrne, *Ficino in Spain*. See in particular the fifth chapter, "Ficino as Plato," 165–87.

90 Pérez Bautista, "La medicina y los médicos," 190.

91 "Item fac stupham ex eo et seruabit iuuentutem tuam et renouabitur ut aquile virtus tua et comfortabit omnia membra tua" (MS Sloane 3545, fols 4r–5v; cited in Keiser, "Rosemary," 203).

92 "Item ex lignis et folijs eius fac fieri fumum iuxta foramen serpentis et statim morietur vel recedet aliunde" (MS Sloane 3545, fols 4r–5v; cited in Keiser, "Rosemary," 204).

93 "Item si dictam herbam in hostio domus tue posueris non timebis scorpiones nec serpentes" (MS Sloane 3545, fols 4r–5v; cited in Keiser, "Rosemary," 203).

94 Cited in Granjel, *La medicina española renacentista*, 254.

95 Shakespeare, *Romeo and Juliet*, I.iii.23–30.

96 "*Pharmakos* (wizard, magician, poisoner), a synonym of *pharmakeus* (which Plato uses), but with the unique feature of having been overdetermined, overlaid by Greek culture with another function. Another role, and a formidable one. The character of the *pharmakos* has been compared to a scapegoat. The *evil* and the *outside*, the expulsion of the evil, its exclusion out of the body (and out) of the city – these are the two major senses of the character and of the ritual" (Derrida, "Plato's Pharmacy," 130).

97 Calderón de la Barca, *Eco y Narciso*, Acto 3.
98 Calderón de la Barca, *Las tres justicias en una*, Acto 1.
99 Calderón, *El galán fantasma*, Acto 2. I owe this reference to Cruickshank, *Don Pedro Calderón*, 159.
100 Calderón de la Barca, *El maestrazgo del Toyson*, loa for auto sacramental.
101 Calderón de la Barca, *La siembra del señor*, auto sacramental, emphasis mine.
102 Cruickshank, *Don Pedro Calderón*, 232.
103 Lope de Vega, *La francesilla*, Acto 3.
104 Tirso de Molina, *La lealtad contra la envidia*, Acto 1.
105 Such incidents quickly became the stuff of literature, for example Tirso de Molina's *La prudencia en la mujer*, in which the queen María de Molina, widow of King Sancho IV, saves her son Fernando IV from being poisoned by a Jewish doctor at the behest of Sancho's brother Don Juan. When she discovers the plot, she makes the doctor commit suicide by taking the poison himself.
106 Cruickshank, *Don Pedro Calderón*, 139–40.
107 Tirso de Molina, *El mayor desengaño*, Acto 2.
108 Lope de Vega, *La fuerza lastimosa*, Jornada 1.
109 Pérez de Montalbán, *La deshonra honrosa*, Jornada 1.
110 Calderón de la Barca, *Mañanas de abril y mayo*, Acto 1.
111 Lope de Vega, *La hermosa Esther*, Acto 2.
112 Calderón de la Barca et al., *El monstruo de la fortuna*, lines 1289a–b; cited in Cruickshank, *Don Pedro Calderón*, 141.
113 Collard, *Le Crime de poison au moyen âge*, 92.
114 Derrida, "Plato's Pharmacy," 125.
115 See Presberg, *Adventures in Paradox*.
116 Numbers 21:4–9.
117 There is debate about what the symbol commonly used to represent the medical profession actually represents. Most scholars trace its origins to the Greek god of medicine, Asclepius. For further resonances of this symbol, see Antoniou et al., "The Rod and the Serpent," and Ramoutsaki et al., "The Snake as the Symbol of Medicine."
118 Calderón de la Barca, *Los encantos de la Culpa*, auto sacramental.
119 Calderón de la Barca, *Las tres justicias en una*, Acto 1.
120 Calderón de la Barca, *La gran Cenobia*, Jornada 3.
121 Calderón de la Barca, *Agradecer y no amar*, Jornada 1. *Epitictima* may be a vulgarized version of the Latin *epithema*, which is a poultice applied to a wound as a remedy.
122 Calderón de la Barca, *La hija del aire, segunda parte*, Jornada 2.
123 Calderón de la Barca, *Peor está que estaba*, Jornada 2.

124 See Webster, "Golden-Mean Form in Music"; Kappraff, "The Relationship between Mathematics and Mysticism of the Golden Mean through History"; Dickson, "The 'Golden Mean' in Journalism"; Ostwald, "Under Siege"; Davis and Altevogt, "Golden Mean of the Human Body"; Burton, "The Quest for the Golden Mean"; Cunningham, "Getting it Right"; and Linn, *The Golden Mean*.

125 Aristotle, *Nicomachean Ethics*, II.6–7, 2.1104a12–26. This text, which was the standard moral philosophy textbook assigned to university classes during the Renaissance, experienced wide diffusion in Spain, as we see from Pagden, "The Diffusion of Aristotle's Moral Philosophy in Spain." Queen Isabel *la Católica* alone possessed five manuscript copies of it, while the Count-Duke of Olivares's copy may still be found at the Escorial, along with Diego Hurtado de Mendoza's (he was Emperor Charles V's representative to the Council of Trent) (Pagden, "The Diffusion," 295–7). See also Kraye, "Renaissance Commentaries on the *Nicomachean Ethics*"; and more specifically the Coimbra Commentators, "Commentary on the 'Nicomachean Ethics.'" This so-called Coimbra Commentary was written by Emmanuel de Goes and published by the Jesuit College of Coimbra in 1593.

126 Horace is not the only other classical author to address these issues, but his formulation may be the most famous. For another classical definition of Virtue as a mean between excess and deficiency, see Seneca, *De beneficiis* (On Benefits), in *Epistulae morales* (*Moral Essays*), 2.16.2. Seneca was born in Spain. This definition is repeated by the Renaissance neo-Stoic Justus Lipsius – who was a correspondent of Francisco de Quevedo – in his *De Constantia*, 79.

127 Horace, *Odes and Epodes*, 114–17.

128 On some of the controversy surrounding this term, see Ionescu et al., "Apologia de Mediocritate," and Marroni et al., "The Average and the Excellent."

129 Plato, *Protagoras*, 349b–c. On this aspect of Plato's thought, see Devereux, "The Unity of the Virtues in Plato's *Protagoras* and *Laches*." On the unity of the Virtues as this concept appears also in Aristotle, see Gottlieb, "Aristotle on Dividing the Soul and Uniting the Virtues." On the unity of the Virtues in general see Penner, "The Unity of Virtue."

130 Cascardi, *Cervantes, Literature, and the Discourse of Politics*, 217.

131 Saavedra Fajardo, *Empresas políticas*, 509.

132 Francisco de Quevedo, *Sueño del alguacil endemoniado*, in *Sueños y discursos*, ed. James O. Crosby (Madrid: Castalia, 1993), 149–84, at 173.

133 Baltasar Gracián, "Discurso VIII: De las ponderaciones de contrariedad," in *Agudeza y arte de ingenio*, ed. Evaristo Correa Calderón (Madrid: Castalia, 2001), 2 vols, 1:105–14, at 109, 105.
134 Robbins, *Arts of Perception*, 207, n. 18. He refers to Gracián, *El Criticón*, I.5, p. 65.
135 Núñez de Cepeda, *Idea de el buen pastor*, *Empresa* XI, 205, emphasis mine.
136 Lope de Vega, *Arte nuevo de hacer comedias*, vv. 153–6, emphasis mine.
137 Lope de Vega, *El perro del hortelano*, Acto 2; Lope de Vega, *El verdadero amante*, Acto 3.
138 Tirso de Molina, *Tanto es lo demás como lo de menos*, Acto 3; Tirso de Molina, *Santo y sastre*, Acto 2.
139 Lope de Vega, *Lo cierto por lo dudoso*, Acto 1.
140 Lope de Vega, *La niña de plata*, Acto 1.
141 Guillén de Castro, *La justicia en la piedad*, Jornada 3.
142 Lope de Vega, *El ingrato arrepentido*, Acto 1; Lope de Vega, *El poder vencido y amor premiado*, Acto 1.
143 Lope de Vega, *El casamiento en la muerte*, Jornada 1.
144 Lope de Vega, *El sembrar en buena tierra*, Acto 1.
145 Lope de Vega, *La obediencia laureada, y primer Carlos de Ungría*, Acto 1.
146 Lope de Vega, *La octava maravilla*, Acto 3.
147 Lope de Vega, *Los Ramírez de Arellano*, Acto 2.
148 Lope de Vega, *El mejor mozo de España*, preliminares to 1625 edition.
149 Shakespeare, *Othello*, I.iii.326–9.
150 See Peraita, "Arte del disimulo y paradoja."
151 Rojas Zorrilla, *Entre bobos anda el juego*, Jornada 2.
152 Rojas Zorrilla, *El más impropio verdugo por la más justa venganza*, Jornada 3.
153 Lope de Vega, *El capellán de la Virgen*, Acto 1.
154 Moreto, *De fuera vendrá*, Jornada 1.
155 Rojas Zorrilla, *Los áspides de Cleopatra*, Jornada 2.
156 Rojas Zorrilla, *La traición busca el castigo*, Jornada 3.
157 Alarcón, *El Anticristo*, Acto 2.
158 All three quotations are from Guillén de Castro, *El vicio en los extremos*, Jornada 2.
159 Guillén de Castro, *El vicio en los extremos*, Jornada 1.
160 Lope de Vega, *Servir a señor discreto*, Acto 2.
161 See Kallendorf, "Dressed to the Sevens," and Arellano, "Emblems at the Golden Age Theater."
162 Calderón de la Barca, *¿Quién hallará mujer fuerte?* auto sacramental.
163 Lope de Vega, *El anzuelo de Fenisa*, Acto 3.
164 Lope de Vega, *La corona merecida*, Acto 3.

165 Calderón de la Barca, *El diablo mudo*, loa for auto sacramental.
166 Calderón de la Barca, *El diablo mudo*, loa for auto sacramental.

1 Blind Justice

1 Comte-Sponville, *A Small Treatise on the Great Virtues*, 61.
2 Scarry, *On Beauty and Being Just*, 93–4. She quotes John Rawls, *A Theory of Justice* (Cambridge, MA: Harvard University Press, 1971), 83–7.
3 Comte-Sponville, *A Small Treatise on the Great Virtues*, 74, 77. He quotes Benedict de Spinoza, *A Theologico-Political Treatise*, in *The Chief Works*, trans. R.H.M. Elwes (New York: Dover, 1951),1:208.
4 Capra, *Della eccellenza e dignità delle donne* (1525), 71. Capra served as ambassador from Verona to Venice (Ricciardi, "Galeazzo Capra").
5 Comte-Sponville, *A Small Treatise on the Great Virtues*, 62–3.
6 Cruickshank, "'Pongo mi mano en sangre bañada a la puerta,'" 60, n. 16.
7 Cueva, *La muerte del Rey don Sancho*, Acto 4.
8 Calderón de la Barca, *Agradecer y no amar*, preliminares to 1682 edition.
9 Rojas Zorrilla, *Lo que quería ver el Marqués de Villena*, Jornada 1.
10 Tirso de Molina, *La vida de Herodes*, Acto 2.
11 Lope de Vega, *El alcalde mayor*, Acto 2. On the system of primogeniture, see Clavero, "*Favor Maioratus, Usus Hispaniae*."
12 Lope de Vega, *La corona merecida*, Acto 3.
13 Calderón de la Barca, *Las espigas de Ruth*, loa for auto sacramental.
14 Lope de Vega, *La imperial de Otón*, Acto 3.
15 Calderón de la Barca, *Los alimentos del hombre*, auto sacramental.
16 Calderón de la Barca, *La estatua de Prometeo*, Jornada 3.
17 Diamante, *Ir por el riesgo a la dicha*, Jornada 3.
18 Cervantes, *Pedro de Urdemalas*, Jornada 1.
19 Lope de Vega, *El piadoso veneciano*, Acto 2.
20 Lope de Vega, *La resistencia honrada y Condesa Matilde*, Jornada 1; Lope de Vega, *El testigo contra sí*, Acto 1. On the Chancillería Real in Valladolid, see Kagan, *Lawsuits and Litigants in Castile*, 110–11.
21 Calderón de la Barca, *A Dios por razón de estado*, loa for auto sacramental.
22 Calderón de la Barca, *Lo que va del hombre a Dios*, auto sacramental.
23 Tirso de Molina, *Próspera fortuna de Don Álvaro de Luna, primera parte*, Jornada 2.
24 Lope de Vega, *La fortuna merecida*, Acto 3.
25 Lope de Vega, *El labrador venturoso*, Jornada 3. Specific amounts are also listed: "para gastos de justicia le condené, que pagase cuarenta cruzados" (Lope de Vega, *El príncipe perfecto, parte segunda*, Acto 1). The *cruzado* was

a coin established in Castile by King Enrique II in 1269. These might have been lawyers' fees or else other costs associated with prisoners' upkeep. Richard Kagan notes that "Case-by-case figures for the cost of litigation in the sixteenth century are not available, but in one of its lawsuits the city of Seville paid 3,200 mrs. [*maravedíes*] in fees to the court receiver, over 2,000 mrs. for the *carta ejecutoria* or final writ, and at least 1,100 mrs. to the court reporter" (Kagan, *Lawsuits and Litigants*, 39; for this information Kagan cites Archivo Municipal de Sevilla: Secc. II, carpeta 201). Kagan explains the rationale behind these charges: "In most cities, the administration of justice was plagued by a bewildering array of lesser courts and tribunals, the jurisdictions of which were often poorly defined. Magistrates vied with one another for power and prestige, and matters were more complicated by the fact that the livelihood of the scribes, notaries, and other officials attached to these tribunals depended largely upon fees paid directly to them by litigants. Competition for control of the local judicial market was therefore intense, encouraging litigants to shop among the various tribunals for the best deal" (35).

26 Lope de Vega, *Del mal lo menos*, Acto 1.

27 Tirso de Molina, *La peña de Francia*, Acto 3.

28 Lope de Vega, *La viuda casada y doncella*, Acto 1.

29 Lope de Vega, *Los pleitos de Inglaterra*, Acto 3.

30 For a description of the judge's role historically, see Kagan, *Lawsuits and Litigants*, 181–2.

31 Pérez de Montalbán, *Amor, lealtad y amistad*, Jornada 3. The *justicia mayor* was not just any judge, however; this term may refer to the *adelantados mayores*, who were first appointed as itinerant judges by the Catholic Monarchs "with the authority to decide, both in the first instance and on appeal, the civil cases of vassals living on seigneurial estates ... These magistrates ... were the most important of the king's *corregidores* and among the best paid" (Kagan, *Lawsuits and Litigants*, 229). In another example, in a different play the King proclaims, "O Fortunio de Rojas, desde ahora, mi Justicia mayor os constituyo, y Canciller mayor de España os hago" (Lope de Vega, *El servir con mala estrella*, Acto 1). In this instance, given the reference to the royal Chancillería of Valladolid, the term probably alludes to a higher post still.

32 Calderón de la Barca, *No hay instante sin milagro*, auto sacramental.

33 Tirso de Molina, *Por el sótano y el torno*, Jornada 2.

34 Lope de Vega, *Carlos quinto en Francia*, Acto 3.

35 Lope de Vega, *Los cautivos de Argel*, Jornada 3.

36 Lope de Vega, *La mayor victoria de Alemania de Don Gonzalo de Córdoba*, preliminares to 1637 edition.

37 Calderón de la Barca, *Los cabellos de Absalón*, Jornada 2. Real-life counterparts to these *espejo de príncipes* admonitions have been collected in Truman, *Spanish Treatises on Government*.
38 Lope de Vega, *El Marqués de Mantua*, Acto 3.
39 Calderón de la Barca, *Los cabellos de Absalón*, Jornada 2. King David privileges mercy over justice in the source play, not wishing to punish his son for committing incest.
40 Cueva, *Comedia del príncipe tirano*, Acto 2.
41 Alarcón, *Ganar amigos*, Acto 3. These lines also appear in Lope de Vega's *Amor, pleito y desafío*, Jornada 3. On these two playwrights' apparent borrowings from one another, see Peña, "Los varios tonos de la relación Lope de Vega-Juan Ruiz de Alarcón."
42 Lope de Vega, *La boba para los otros, y discreta para sí*, Acto 2.
43 Calderón de la Barca de la Barca, *La cisma de Inglaterra*, Jornada 3.
44 Lope de Vega, *Barlán y Josafa*, Acto 2.
45 Rojas Zorrilla, *La traición busca el castigo*, Jornada 3.
46 Lope de Vega, *La inocente sangre*, Acto 3.
47 Calderón de la Barca, *El alcalde de sí mismo*, Jornada 3.
48 Lope de Vega, *El Marqués de Mantua*, Acto 1.
49 Cueva, *La muerte del Rey don Sancho*, Acto 1. Farfán repeats this sentiment in the line, "Justicia, cielos, contra un Rey" (Guillén de Castro, *La justicia en la piedad*, Jornada 1).
50 This term may only somewhat problematically be applied to *Fuenteovejuna*, although it could work for other tyrannicide plays. Bárbara Mujica believes that Lope's play has been misunderstood by modern critics who mistakenly apply anachronistic categories: "Although many critics and directors have seen a revolutionary message in *Fuenteovejuna*, Lope was not actually advocating civil disobedience. Lope was a monarchist at a time when monarchy was considered normal and natural. The peasants of Fuenteovejuna do not demand to govern themselves, but to be governed by a just lord ... However ... it would also be a mistake to see *Fuenteovejuna* as propaganda for the monarchy" (Mujica, *A New Anthology of Early Modern Spanish Theater*, 70). For a sophisticated, nuanced reading of *Fuenteovejuna* as a staging of "conceptual resistance" to the secret foundations of sovereignty, see Lorenz, "Resistance: Waiting for Power in *Fuenteovejuna*," in *The Tears of Sovereignty*.
51 Tirso de Molina, *La prudencia en la mujer*, Jornada 1; Lope de Vega, *El mejor maestro, el tiempo*, Acto 3.
52 Calderón de la Barca, *Ni Amor se libra de Amor*, Acto 1.
53 Kallendorf, *Conscience on Stage*, 192–8.
54 Calderón de la Barca, *Darlo todo, y no dar nada*, Jornada 3.

55 Lope de Vega, *El Marqués de Mantua*, Acto 3.
56 Lope de Vega, *Amor, pleito y desafío*, Jornada 3.
57 Calderón de la Barca, *Psiquis y Cupido, que escribió para la ciudad de Toledo*, loa for auto sacramental.
58 Calderón de la Barca, *El pintor de su deshonra*, auto sacramental.
59 Moreto, *El mejor amigo, el rey*, Jornada 3.
60 Calderón de la Barca, *El Santo Rey Don Fernando, primera parte*, auto sacramental.
61 Lope de Vega, *El mayorazgo dudoso*, Jornada 2.
62 Calderón de la Barca, *El pintor de su deshonra*, loa for auto sacramental.
63 Calderón de la Barca, *A tu prójimo como a ti*, loa for auto sacramental.
64 Calderón de la Barca, *El amor, honor y poder*, Jornada 3.
65 Calderón de la Barca, *Los cabellos de Absalón*, Jornada 2.
66 Rojas Zorrilla, *Los áspides de Cleopatra*, Jornada 1.
67 Kagan, *Lawsuits and Litigants*, 37. Kagan cites Bibliothèque Nationale Paris, Manuscrits espagnols 261, fol. 69.
68 Calderón de la Barca de la Barca, *La cura y la enfermedad*, loa for auto sacramental.
69 Lope de Vega, *El animal de Hungría*, Acto 3. The article *el* in this line denotes a male judge or police-type figure as opposed to the allegorical figure of Justice in the sacramental dramas, universally designated *la Justicia*.
70 Tirso de Molina, *Segunda parte de Santa Juana*, Acto 3.
71 Calderón de la Barca, *Los alimentos del hombre*, auto sacramental.
72 Calderón de la Barca, *El postrer duelo de España*, Jornada 3.
73 Mena, *Laberinto de Fortuna* (1444), stanza CCXXXI, lines 1841–8, p. 226.
74 Lope de Vega, *El príncipe perfecto, parte segunda*, Acto 2.
75 Agamben, *Il Regno e la Gloria*, 266.
76 Calderón de la Barca, *Los alimentos del hombre*, auto sacramental.
77 Calderón de la Barca, *Los alimentos del hombre*, auto sacramental.
78 Calderón de la Barca, *La inmunidad del sagrado*, loa for auto sacramental.
79 Lope de Vega, *El genovés liberal*, Acto 2.
80 Calderón de la Barca, *El día mayor de los días*, loa for auto sacramental.
81 Calderón de la Barca, *El nuevo hospicio de pobres*, auto sacramental.
82 Calderón de la Barca, *El año santo de Roma*, auto sacramental.
83 Calderón de la Barca, *No hay más fortuna que Dios*, auto sacramental.
84 Calderón de la Barca, *El laberinto del mundo*, auto sacramental.
85 For example, the allegorical figure of Justice says, "Yo, que siendo la Justicia, y la Justicia de Dios, Truenos, y Rayos la di" (Calderón de la Barca, *¿Quién hallará mujer fuerte?* auto sacramental). Similarly, we find references to "Divina Justicia ... que fulminase rayos vengativos contra él" (Pérez de Montalbán, *El divino portugués, San Antonio de Padua*, Jornada 3).

86 Tirso de Molina, *La santa Juana*, Acto 1.
87 Lope de Vega, *El Nuevo Mundo descubierto por Cristóbal Colón*, Acto 3.
88 Calderón de la Barca, *El Viático Cordero*, auto sacramental.
89 "no ya vara de piedad la vara sí de justicia, levanta Moisés airado que en mansiones las divida al mar" (Tirso de Molina, *La huerta de Juan Fernández*, Jornada 1).
90 Rojas Zorrilla, *Los áspides de Cleopatra*, Jornada 1.
91 Calderón de la Barca, *Andrómeda y Perseo*, auto sacramental.
92 Justice and Mercy are said to be the twin poles of monarchy ("Justicia, y Misericordia, Polos de la Monarquía" [Calderón de la Barca, *El indulto general*, auto sacramental]), and this unique mixture is said to make kings approach divine status: "que con justicia y piedad se hacen Dioses los Reyes" (Lope de Vega, *Los pleitos de Inglaterra*, Acto 2). On the divine right of kings in Lope de Vega, see Exum, "Lope's King Pedro."
93 Guillén de Castro, *La justicia en la piedad*, Jornada 3.
94 Alarcón, *El tejedor de Segovia*, Acto 3.
95 Lope de Vega, *La imperial de Otón*, Acto 3; Calderón de la Barca, *Mujer, llora y vencerás*, Jornada 1.
96 Lope de Vega, *Contra valor no hay desdicha*, Acto 3.
97 For period understandings of this concept, see De la Cámara, "La mémoire de Bartolomé de Las Casas chez Quevedo."
98 Guillén de Castro, *Las mocedades del Cid, Comedia segunda*, Acto 2; Lope de Vega, *El asalto de Mastrique por el Príncipe de Parma*, Acto 3.
99 Pérez de Montalbán, *Segunda parte del Séneca de España, don Felipe Segundo*, Jornada 1.
100 See, for example, Diego del Castillo de Villasante (1515–51), *Doctrinal de confesores en casos de restitución*, a sixteenth-century manuscript held by the Biblioteca Nacional in Madrid (MSS/102).
101 Calderón de la Barca, *La hija del aire, segunda parte*, Jornada 3.
102 Calderón de la Barca, *El origen, pérdida y restauración de la Virgen del Sagrario*, Jornada 3.
103 Calderón de la Barca, *El Rey Don Pedro en Madrid*, Jornada 3.
104 Calderón de la Barca, *La gran Cenobia*, Jornada 3.
105 Calderón de la Barca, *El segundo Scipión*, Jornada 3.
106 "al tribunal de León llegó una oveja a pedir justicia de un carnicero lobo, que un hijo le había muerto" (Alarcón, *La amistad castigada*, Acto 2).
107 "hazme justicia, señor, don Juan de Córdoba ha muerto a mi esposo" (Lope de Vega, *Las cuentas del Gran Capitán*, Acto 3).
108 "el nido pensó robar del pájaro que en vano pide justicia al aire enternecido" (Lope de Vega, *La primera información*, Jornada 2).

109 Calderón de la Barca, *¿Quién hallará mujer fuerte?* auto sacramental.
110 He continues his lament: "A mi Rebaño llegaron, /y porque se le defiendo, /me han tratado como ves, /y es harto no haberme muerto."
111 Calderón de la Barca, *Darlo todo, y no dar nada,* Jornada 3.
112 "Justicia pide, bien como la Sangre de Abel" (Calderón de la Barca, *La humildad coronada de las plantas,* auto sacramental); "mató a Camilo, cuya sangre en estas piedras está pidiendo justicia" (Lope de Vega, *El alcalde mayor,* Acto 3).
113 Lope de Vega, *El amigo por fuerza,* Acto 2.
114 Calderón de la Barca, *Amar después de la muerte,* Jornada 3.
115 Lope de Vega, *Las grandezas de Alejandro,* Acto 1.
116 Calderón de la Barca, *No hay más fortuna que Dios,* auto sacramental.
117 Lope de Vega, *El rey sin reino,* Acto 1.
118 "el vil esclavo, y el que guarda bueyes alcanza la justicia que perdiera por su pobreza, cuando ley no hubiera" (Lope de Vega, *La sortija del olvido,* Acto 2).
119 Calderón de la Barca, *La primer flor del Carmelo,* auto sacramental.
120 Fink De Backer, *Widowhood in Early Modern Spain,* 268.
121 Calderón de la Barca, *No hay instante sin milagro,* auto sacramental. This phrase appears likewise in Calderón de la Barca's secular *comedias,* not just his religious *autos sacramentales*: "Él procedió cuerdo, y sabio, pues ejerció la justicia, castigando una malicia" (Calderón de la Barca, *Las armas de la hermosura,* Jornada 2).
122 Calderón de la Barca, *El indulto general,* auto sacramental.
123 Calderón de la Barca, *La fiera, el rayo y la piedra,* Jornada 3.
124 Moreto, *El valiente justiciero,* Jornada 3.
125 "puedo hacer justicia, cortándole la cabeza a Tello, venga el verdugo" (Lope de Vega, *El mejor alcalde, el rey,* Acto 3).
126 Calderón de la Barca, *La gran Cenobia,* Jornada 3.
127 Cueva, *El Infamador,* Acto 4.
128 Lope de Vega, *Las ferias de Madrid,* Jornada 3.
129 "destierra, echa a galeras, y a justicia, a diestro y a siniestro, sin reparo" (Tirso de Molina, *Todo es dar en una cosa,* Acto 1). Note that the playwright Lope de Vega was exiled for slander of Elena Osorio.
130 Lope de Vega, *El animal de Hungría,* Acto 2.
131 Calderón de la Barca, *Las tres justicias en una,* Jornada 3.
132 Lope de Vega, *Arauco domado por el excelentísimo señor don García Hurtado de Mendoza,* Acto 3.
133 Cueva, *La muerte de Virginia y Appio Claudio,* Acto 2.

134 Exemplary Romans: "tan pocos años me impedirán que no imite en la justicia a Trajano" (Tirso de Molina, *La prudencia en la mujer*, Jornada 3); or "invicto señor, que a Catón, que a Augusto excedes en justicia y equidad" (Lope de Vega, *El Duque de Viseo*, Acto 2). Pagan gods: "Pues numen de la justicia, soberana Themis, eres, piedad, divina Themis" (Zamora, *Amar es saber vencer, y el arte contra el poder*, Acto 1).

135 Lope de Vega, *La fuerza lastimosa*, Jornada 1.

136 Calderón de la Barca, *El Rey Don Pedro en Madrid, e infanzón de Illescas*, Jornada 3. This play has at times been attributed to Calderón de la Barca, but its authorship is problematic (Kirby, "Theater and the Quest for Anointment in *El rey don Pedro en Madrid*," 157 n. 2).

137 Alban Forcione writes eloquently of the "epithets that crown with an ambiguous halo the sinister figure who himself looms enigmatically over the darkest period in Spain's bloody history: Peter I of Castile ... Is he Peter the Cruel or Peter the Just? Perhaps Peter the Cruel *and* Peter the Just?" Of this specific drama, to which he devotes the second half of his latest remarkable book, Forcione asserts that "Certainly the most powerful effect of this grotesque, violent, and disturbing play is its strange vision of the inseparability of justice and cruelty, order and brutality, law and violence" (*Majesty and Humanity*, 101–2).

138 Alarcón, *Ganar amigos*, Acto 2. These lines are echoed in Lope de Vega's *Amor, pleito y desafío* (Jornada 2).

139 Calderón de la Barca, *Fineza contra fineza*, Jornada 3.

140 "mi justicia, de su corazón ingrato arranque aleves raíces de delitos recatados" (Diamante, *Cuánto mienten los indicios, y el ganapán de desdichas*, Jornada 1).

141 Lope de Vega, *El hombre por su palabra*, Acto 3.

142 Lope de Rueda, *Eufemia*, Scena 1.

143 Lope de Rueda, *Prendas de amor*, Acto 1.

144 This scenario occurs in Calderón de la Barca's *El médico de su honra* (Acto 1) and has been explicated by Watson in "Peter the Cruel or Peter the Just?" 332.

145 Tirso de Molina, *Escarmientos para el cuerdo*, Acto 3.

146 Guillén de Castro, *El Conde Alarcos*, Jornada 2.

147 Calderón de la Barca, *Las armas de la hermosura*, Jornada 3.

148 Calderón de la Barca, *Agradecer y no amar*, preliminares to 1682 edition.

149 Rojas Zorrilla, *Los áspides de Cleopatra*, Jornada 1.

150 Calderón de la Barca, *El Rey Don Pedro en Madrid*, Jornada 3.

151 Calderón de la Barca, *Saber del mal, y el bien*, Jornada 3.

152 "fuego arrojo por la boca: bueno es que el hacer justicia llama Castilla crueldad" (Lope de Vega, *Los Ramírez de Arellano*, Acto 3).
153 Moreto, *El valiente justiciero*, Jornada 1.
154 "aunque pide venganza mi sentimiento, entre venganza, y justicia a la justicia prefiero" (Diamante, *Cuánto mienten los indicios, y el ganapán de desdichas*, Jornada 2; Jornada 3).
155 Moreto, *Los jueces de Castilla*, Jornada 1.
156 Rojas Zorrilla, *No hay ser padre siendo rey*, Jornada 3.
157 For example, Don Diego says, "Esto es justicia, y por ella pedimos su cabeza" (Guillén de Castro, *La humildad soberbia*, Acto 3).
158 Guillén de Castro, *La justicia en la piedad*, Jornada 3.
159 Guillén de Castro, *El perfecto caballero*, Acto 3.
160 Guillén de Castro, *Las mocedades del Cid, Comedia segunda*, Acto 2.
161 Guillén de Castro, *La justicia en la piedad*, Jornada 3.
162 Guillén de Castro, *La fuerza de la costumbre*, Jornada 3.
163 Lope de Vega, *La mayor virtud de un rey*, Jornada 3.
164 Calderón de la Barca, *El encanto sin encanto*, Jornada 2.
165 Calderón de la Barca, *El Joseph de las mujeres*, Jornada 3.
166 Guillén de Castro, *Las mocedades del Cid, Comedia primera*, Acto 2.
167 Lope de Vega, *El castigo sin venganza*, Acto 3.
168 Cueva, *La muerte de Ajax Telamón sobre las armas de Aquiles*, Acto 3.
169 "Entre unos paños débiles al filo de mi justicia" (Lope de Vega, *La hermosa Alfreda*, Acto 1).
170 Calderón de la Barca, *La inmunidad del sagrado*, auto sacramental.
171 "el acero sacó; y el rigor severo de la justicia, le da sentencia esquiva de muerte" (Moreto, *El valiente justiciero*, Jornada 3).
172 Calderón de la Barca, *La piel de Gedeón*, auto sacramental.
173 Pérez de Montalbán, *El divino portugués, San Antonio de Padua*, Jornada 2.
174 Calderón de la Barca, *Andrómeda y Perseo*, loa for auto sacramental.
175 Calderón de la Barca, *La cena de Baltasar*, auto sacramental.
176 Lope de Vega, *Las grandezas de Alejandro*, Acto 3.
177 Lope de Vega, *La fuerza lastimosa*, Jornada 3. For another contemporaneous poetic meditation on evolving military technology, see Quevedo's *silva* "Al inventor de la pieza de artillería," in Quevedo, *Silvas*, 155–60.
178 Calderón de la Barca, *Andrómeda y Perseo*, loa for auto sacramental.
179 Calderón de la Barca, *Los misterios de la Misa*, auto sacramental.
180 Calderón de la Barca, *El purgatorio de San Patricio*, Jornada 2.
181 Foucault, *Discipline and Punish*, 283.
182 Calderón de la Barca, *Las tres justicias en una*, Jornada 3.

183 Calderón de la Barca, *El año santo de Roma*, auto sacramental. On these three transactions of Justice enacted simultaneously in this play, see Sullivan, "*Las tres justicias en una* and the Question of Christian Catharsis."
184 Lope de Vega, *Peribáñez y el Comendador de Ocaña*, Acto 3.
185 Calderón de la Barca, *Hado y divisa de Leonido y Marfisa*, Jornada 3.
186 Calderón de la Barca, *Mejor está que estaba*, Jornada 1.
187 Calderón de la Barca, *La vacante general*, auto sacramental.
188 Lope de Vega, *Los enemigos en casa*, Acto 2.
189 This punishment is found frequently in the *comedias*, as for example when the tyrannical King in Juan de la Cueva's *Tragedia del príncipe tirano* threatens one of his subjects: "¿Que tardo en castigar tal osadía? No debo con Justicia Rey llamarme, si no te ahorco en este mismo día" (Acto 3).
190 Lope de Vega, *La fuerza lastimosa*, Jornada 3.
191 Calderón de la Barca, *El laberinto del mundo*, auto sacramental.
192 Moreto, *La confusión de un jardín*, Jornada 1.
193 "La justicia dicen que es como la tela de araña" (Lope de Vega, *Nadie se conoce*, Jornada 3).
194 Calderón de la Barca, *Duelos de amor y lealtad*, Jornada 3.
195 Matos Fragoso, *El genízaro de Hungría*, Jornada 3.
196 Lope de Vega, *El saber por no saber, y vida de San Julián*, Acto 3.
197 Rojas Zorrilla, *Persiles y Sigismunda*, Jornada 3.
198 Moreto, *El valiente justiciero*, Jornada 2.
199 Cervantes, *Pedro de Urdemalas*, Jornada 1.
200 Moreto, *El valiente justiciero*, Jornada 3.
201 Guillén de Castro, *La justicia en la piedad*, Jornada 1.
202 Lope de Vega, *Los embustes de Fabia*, Jornada 3.
203 Cueva, *Comedia del príncipe tirano*, Acto 4.
204 Cueva, *La muerte de Ajax Telamón sobre las armas de Aquiles*, Acto 3.
205 Lope de Vega, *El blasón de los Chaves de Villalba*, Acto 1.
206 Moreto, *La cautela en la amistad*, Jornada 1.
207 "One of the most common adjectives used to describe a malfunctioning, lax, or overly permissive conscience is *wide*" (Kallendorf, *Conscience on Stage*, 164).
208 Lope de Vega, *El príncipe perfecto, parte segunda*, Acto 2.
209 Cueva, *La muerte de Ajax Telamón sobre las armas de Aquiles*, Acto 4.
210 Zamora, *El custodio de la Hungría, San Juan Capistrano*, Jornada 1.
211 Cervantes, *La gran Sultana*, Jornada 1.
212 Tirso de Molina, *La peña de Francia*, Acto 1.
213 Pérez de Montalbán, *El valiente más dichoso, Don Pedro Guiral*, Jornada 1.

214 Tirso de Molina, *La república al revés*, Acto 1. Richard Kagan confirms that this depiction onstage is true to life: "In addition to taking bribes, most court officials engaged in numerous illegal, but lucrative, activities" (Kagan, *Lawsuits and Litigants*, 41).
215 Tirso de Molina, *La villana de la Sagra*, Jornada 1.
216 "no diga después la fama, que abandonó la justicia mi interés" (Calderón de la Barca, *Fineza contra fineza*, Jornada 3).
217 Lope de Vega, *El niño inocente de la Guardia*, Acto 1.
218 Calderón de la Barca, *El alcalde de Zalamea*, Jornada 3.
219 Lope de Vega, *El Perseo*, Acto 3.
220 Alarcón, *Ganar amigos*, Acto 3. These identical lines appear in Lope de Vega's *Amor, pleito y desafío* (Jornada 3). On the vexed relationship between these two playwrights and their works, see once again Peña, "Los varios tonos de la relación Lope de Vega-Juan Ruiz de Alarcón."
221 Lope de Vega, *La boba para los otros, y discreta para sí*, Acto 1.
222 Lope de Vega, *La inocente sangre*, Acto 3. For an iconographical depiction of Occasion with an exaggerated forelock, ready to be seized by the opportunistic, see Figure 12 of my book *Sins of the Fathers*, with discussion on p. 318, n. 116. For an explication of this emblem as it applies to Cervantes, see Plata, "On Love and Occasion."
223 Lope de Vega, *El mejor alcalde, el rey*, Acto 3.
224 Tirso de Molina, *Santo y sastre*, Acto 3.
225 In reference to Spain's slow-moving legal system, Kagan notes that the statutes of the *consulado* of Burgos prohibited merchants from suing their fellow members "because we know that lawsuits among merchants are never finished, largely because of the briefs and papers prepared by lawyers interested in supporting themselves. The lawsuits, consequently, become immortal" (Kagan, *Lawsuits and Litigants*, 18–19; Kagan cites *Los códigos españoles concordados y anotados*, 12 vols [Madrid, 1872–84]).
226 Guillén de Castro, *La justicia en la piedad*, Jornada 1.
227 Cueva, *La muerte de Virginia y Appio Claudio*, Acto 2.
228 Lope de Vega, *El Amor enamorado*, preliminares to 1637 edition.
229 Matos Fragoso, *Amor, lealtad y ventura*, Acto 1.
230 Lope de Vega, *El saber puede dañar*, Acto 3.
231 Tirso de Molina, *Tanto es lo demás como lo de menos*, Acto 1.
232 "las mismas que ciegan a la justicia, lisonja, amor, obligación, y miedo" (Lope de Vega, *Mirad a quién alabáis*, preliminares to 1621 edition).
233 Lope de Vega, *El piadoso aragonés*, Acto 3.
234 "aun siendo el juez recto, y justo, puede faltar la justicia" (Moreto, *Los jueces de Castilla*, Jornada 3).

235 Lope de Vega, *El premio de la hermosura*, Acto 1.
236 Lope de Vega, *Los cautivos de Argel*, Jornada 3.
237 Lope de Vega, *El laberinto de Creta*, Acto 1.
238 "no alcanza en sus arbitrios la justicia igual castigo a tan nefando reo" (Alarcón, *El Anticristo*, Acto 1).
239 Kagan, *Lawsuits and Litigants*, 31–2. Kagan cites Archivo General de Simancas: Diversos de Castilla, legajo 1, part 2, no. 70.
240 Alarcón, *La crueldad por el honor*, Acto 1.
241 Tirso de Molina, *Antona García*, Acto 1. On the principle of "might makes right," see Hourani, "Thrasymachus' Definition of Justice in Plato's *Republic*."
242 Lope de Vega, *La boba para los otros, y discreta para sí*, Acto 3.
243 We see further echoes of this warlike conception of Justice, which is more what we would anticipate from lines describing Fortitude, in Lope de Vega's *La inocente sangre*: "dichoso día de mostrar la valentía de vuestros nobles aceros. Justicia lleváis, soldados, y vuestro Rey defendéis" (Acto 1).
244 Calderón de la Barca, *Amar después de la muerte*, Jornada 1.
245 Matos Fragoso, *Los indicios sin culpa*, Jornada 2.
246 Moreto, *El valiente justiciero*, Jornada 2.
247 Rojas Zorrilla, *Abrir el ojo*, Jornada 2.
248 Lope de Vega, *El acero de Madrid, primera parte*, Acto 3.
249 Lope de Vega, *El saber por no saber, y vida de San Julián*, Acto 3. The work by Anselm of Canterbury that addresses these questions is *De Conceptu Virginali*, translated by Joseph M. Colleran as *Why God Became Man and the Virgin Conception and Original Sin*.
250 Calderón de la Barca, *El año santo en Madrid*, auto sacramental.
251 Matthew 11:29.
252 "estado primitivo de la Original Justicia, de que privados nacimos" (Calderón de la Barca, *El socorro general*, auto sacramental).
253 Calderón de la Barca, *La cura y la enfermedad*, auto sacramental.
254 Calderón de la Barca, *La hidalga del valle*, auto sacramental.
255 Calderón de la Barca, *El orden de Melchisedech*, auto sacramental.
256 Calderón de la Barca, *La segunda esposa, y triunfar muriendo*, auto sacramental.
257 The allegorical figure of Man says, "cauta la Sierpe, incauta la Mujer; en cuya acción perdí la Original Justicia en que nací, infestando tú horror, aun primero la Fruta que la Flor" (Calderón de la Barca, *El diablo mudo*, auto sacramental).
258 Calderón de la Barca, *El gran príncipe de Fez*, Jornada 2.

259 Calderón de la Barca, *Lo que va del hombre a Dios*, auto sacramental.
260 Lope de Vega, *El saber por no saber, y vida de San Julián*, Acto 3.
261 "para las malicias es la justicia, para las fragilidades la indulgencia" (Calderón de la Barca, *Agradecer y no amar*, preliminares to 1682 edition).
262 Pérez de Montalbán, *Segunda parte del Séneca de España, Don Felipe Segundo*, Jornada 1.
263 Calderón de la Barca, *Las órdenes militares*, loa for auto sacramental, emphasis mine.
264 Calderón de la Barca, *La serpiente de metal*, auto sacramental; Lope de Vega, *El molino*, Jornada 1.
265 "no quiero, que parezca el condenarla violenta pasión, sino justicia igual" (Calderón de la Barca, *Fineza contra fineza*, Jornada 3).
266 Guillén de Castro, *Cuánto se estima el honor*, Jornada 2; Jornada 3.
267 Guillén de Castro, *El Conde de Irlos*, Acto 3.
268 Calderón de la Barca, *La gran Cenobia*, Jornada 3.
269 Cueva, *La libertad de Roma por Mucio Cevola*, Acto 2.
270 Moreto, *Industrias contra finezas*, Jornada 1.
271 Guillén de Castro, *La justicia en la piedad*, Jornada 3.
272 Moreto, *El valiente justiciero*, Jornada 3.
273 Calderón de la Barca, *Los alimentos del hombre*, auto sacramental.
274 Calderón de la Barca, *Amar después de la muerte*, Jornada 3.
275 Calderón de la Barca, *Los cabellos de Absalón*, Jornada 3.
276 Calderón de la Barca, *La sibila del Oriente*, Jornada 2.
277 Diamante, *El negro más prodigioso*, Jornada 3.
278 Lope de Vega, *El Hamete de Toledo*, Acto 3.
279 "A público desafío le llamaba; con que usando de la templanza, con que debe en semejantes casos mediar la Justicia, quise componerlos, y ajustarlos, sin sangre" (Zamora, *Mazariegos y Monsalves*, Jornada 2).
280 Calderón de la Barca, *¿Quién hallará mujer fuerte?* auto sacramental.
281 Two of these paintings appear as figures on p. 323 of my article "Cervantes' Democratization of Demonic Possession."
282 Rojas Zorrilla, *El más impropio verdugo por la más justa venganza*, Jornada 3.
283 Comte-Sponville, *A Small Treatise on the Great Virtues*, 74.
284 Guillén de Castro, *La justicia en la piedad*, Jornada 3.
285 Lope de Vega, *El mejor alcalde, el rey*, Acto 2; Acto 3.
286 Calderón de la Barca, *¿Quién hallará mujer fuerte?* auto sacramental.
287 Calderón de la Barca, *El Santo Rey Don Fernando, primera parte*, auto sacramental.
288 Calderón de la Barca, *El Rey Don Pedro en Madrid, e infanzón de Illescas*, Jornada 3.

289 Moreto, *La fuerza de la ley*, Jornada 1.

290 Lope de Vega, *El caballero del Sacramento*, Acto 3. Another example of this pattern appears in the line, "la justicia nueva entra siempre rigurosa" (Lope de Vega, *Contra valor no hay desdicha*, Acto 2).

291 Moreto, *El valiente justiciero*, Jornada 3.

292 Calderón de la Barca, *El indulto general*, auto sacramental.

293 The Angel explains the legal loophole through which Adam becomes eligible for this pardon: "Ya lo imposible le salva, /para que goce el INDULTO, /pues también Ley asentada/es, que nadie a lo imposible / esté obligado" (Calderón de la Barca, *El indulto general*, auto sacramental).

294 Kátherin Valdés Pozueco, "*Los alimentos del hombre*: análisis jurídico del auto sacramental de Don Pedro Calderón," *Anuario Jurídico y Económico Escurialense* 39 (2006): 385–408.

295 Calderón de la Barca, *Los alimentos del hombre*, auto sacramental.

296 Calderón de la Barca, *La inmunidad del sagrado*, auto sacramental.

297 https://inquisition.library.nd.edu/catalog/RBSC-INQ:INQ_106

298 Calderón de la Barca, *La inmunidad del sagrado*, auto sacramental. The trope of Justice and Pity appearing as twin sisters is repeated in other plays by different authors, like, for example, Guillén de Castro's *Dido y Eneas*: "en personas soberanas siempre son de un parto hermanas la justicia, y la piedad" (Jornada 1). The Inquisition is also mentioned in the same breath with Justice in various plays, for example, Tirso's *Don Gil de las calzas verdes*, with specific reference to its function of policing blood purity: "como Inquisición de la Pinciana nobleza, pues cual brazo de justicia, desterrando su inmundicia, califica su limpieza" (Acto 1). The Inquisition's coat of arms is referenced explicitly in other plays by Calderón de la Barca as well, for example, his sacramental dramas *No hay instante sin milagro* and *El indulto general*. We can think what we like about whether the Inquisition attained its stated aim of combining Justice with Mercy, but the iconography and its careful explication in the plays at least help us to understand theoretically the institution's self-concept without imposing anachronistic modern prejudices on early modern beliefs.

299 Moreto, *El valiente justiciero*, Jornada 3. This play affirms this connection towards the end, when Tello says to Perejil, "esto es violencia, pero es justicia también" (Jornada 3).

300 Girard, *Violence and the Sacred*, 19.

301 On the legitimation of violence in stage plays of this period in Spain, see Petro del Barrio, *La legitimación de la violencia en la comedia española del siglo XVII*.

2 Fleeting Fortitude

1 Comte-Sponville, *A Small Treatise on the Great Virtues*, 44.
2 Bouvet, *Arbre des Batailles*, 120. Emphasis mine.
3 Mena, *Laberinto de Fortuna* (1444), stanza CCXIII, lines 1697–1704, pp. 217–18.
4 Comte-Sponville, *A Small Treatise on the Great Virtues*, 48.
5 Lope de Vega, *El conde Fernán González*, Acto 2.
6 Calderón de la Barca, *El pintor de su deshonra*, loa for auto sacramental.
7 "si el magnánimo León significa fortaleza, ved los pies y la cabeza de qué fortaleza son" (Lope de Vega, *El hijo de Reduán*, Jornada 3).
8 Moreto, *Los hermanos encontrados*, Jornada 1.
9 Lope de Vega, *Pobreza no es vileza*, Acto 3.
10 Mena, *Laberinto de Fortuna*, stanza CCX, lines 1679–80, p. 216.
11 Lope de Vega, *Contra valor no hay desdicha*, Acto 1.
12 Lope de Vega, *Las grandezas de Alejandro*, Acto 2.
13 Cueva, *La muerte de Virginia y Appio Claudio*, Acto 4.
14 Lope de Vega, *Los muertos vivos*, Acto 2.
15 Lope de Vega, *La Filisarda*, Acto 2.
16 Lope de Vega, *El ejemplo de casadas y prueba de la paciencia*, Acto 1.
17 This title refers to the rape of the patriarch Jacob's daughter Dinah and how she was avenged by her brothers (Genesis 34).
18 Lope de Vega, *El robo de Dina*, Acto 1.
19 Lope de Vega, *Pobreza no es vileza*, Acto 3.
20 Lope de Vega, *La corona merecida*, preliminares to 1620 edition.
21 Lope de Vega, *Pobreza no es vileza*, Acto 3.
22 Rojas Zorrilla, *Abrir el ojo*, preliminares to 1645 edition. These two complementary Virtues are further equated in the line, "Premiando aquel valor y fortaleza con que me habéis servido, Capitanes" (Lope de Vega, *El hombre por su palabra*, Acto 2).
23 Lope de Vega, *El príncipe perfecto, parte segunda*, Acto 2.
24 "si hay en mí algún valor, y fortaleza" (Guillén de Castro, *Las mocedades del Cid, Comedia primera*, Acto 2); "Sosiega la fortaleza, pues te enseño a costa mía, que venció la valentía" (Guillén de Castro, *Las mocedades del Cid, Comedia segunda*, Acto 3).
25 Guillén de Castro, *El perfecto caballero*, Acto 2.
26 Lope de Vega, *El asalto de Mastrique por el Príncipe de Parma*, Acto 2.
27 Lope de Vega, *Pobreza no es vileza*, Acto 1.
28 Lope de Vega's *El valiente Céspedes*, Acto 2.
29 Lope de Vega, *La madre de la mejor*, Acto 1.
30 Mena, *Laberinto de Fortuna*, stanza CLII, line 1209, p. 184.

31 Lope de Vega, *El Perseo*, Acto 2.
32 These references are actually surprising, given that the archangel Michael is the one depicted wearing full armour in most iconography, including scenes where he triumphs over Satan. The archangel Gabriel, in contrast, when portrayed in the visual arts is most frequently encountered announcing Christ's birth to Mary (the Annunciation).
33 Calderón de la Barca, *Lo que va del hombre a Dios*, auto sacramental.
34 Calderón de la Barca, *Mística y real Babilonia*, auto sacramental.
35 Lope de Vega, *La inocente Laura*, Acto 3.
36 Lope de Vega, *La vida de San Pedro Nolasco*, Acto 1.
37 Zamora, *El custodio de la Hungría, San Juan Capistrano*, Jornada 2.
38 Lope de Vega, *Juan de Dios y Antón Martín*, Acto 3.
39 Lope de Vega, *Las cuentas del Gran Capitán*, Acto 2.
40 Calderón de la Barca, *No hay instante sin milagro*, auto sacramental.
41 Lope de Vega, *La Santa Liga*, Acto 3.
42 Lope de Vega, *La corona merecida*, Acto 3.
43 Cueva, *La libertad de España por Bernardo del Carpio*, Acto 3.
44 "Advertir también podrás que en cortando una cabeza sosegarás las demás" (Lope de Vega, *Los locos por el cielo*, Acto 1).
45 Cueva, *La libertad de Roma por Mucio Cevola*, Acto 1.
46 Calderón de la Barca, *El nuevo hospicio de pobres*, auto sacramental.
47 Cortés, *Cartas de relación*, 182.
48 Childers, "Baroque Quixote," 421. Moving on to Cortes's subsequent missives, Childers continues his analysis: "In his *Fourth Letter*, Cortés represents himself as an ideal lawgiver and judge, the founder of a new society, which he characterizes as a model of justice, peace, and order" (421). Thus it appears that Fortitude was not the only category of Virtue to which Cortés deliberately appealed.
49 The conquistadores are perhaps the last figures whom we in retrospect might associate with Virtue. Modern scholars tend to condemn "the conquistador, embodying the degeneration and perversion of every heroic virtue" (Pastor Bodmer, *The Armature of Conquest*, 186). Nonetheless we should not discount the very real possibility that they were seen as virtuous by their contemporaries.
50 On the ambiguity of this Vice, see my "Pride & Co.," in *Sins of the Fathers*, 15–45.
51 Cueva, *La libertad de España por Bernardo del Carpio*, Acto 4.
52 Lope de Vega, *Ello dirá*, Acto 2.
53 Lope de Vega, *El mayor imposible*, Jornada 1.
54 Zamora, *Todo lo vence el amor*, Jornada 1.
55 Tirso de Molina, *Averígüelo Vargas*, Jornada 1.

56 Cueva, *La muerte de Ayax Telamón, sobre las armas de Aquiles*, Acto 2.
57 Cueva, *El degollado*, Acto 3.
58 Tirso de Molina, *La lealtad contra la envidia*, Acto 2.
59 Alarcón, *El Anticristo*, Acto 3.
60 Comte-Sponville, *A Small Treatise on the Great Virtues*, 45.
61 Lope de Vega, *El hombre por su palabra*, Acto 3.
62 Lope de Vega, *El laberinto de Creta*, Acto 1.
63 Calderón de la Barca, *La vida es sueño*, auto sacramental.
64 Lope de Vega, *El halcón de Federico*, preliminares to 1620 edition.
65 Guillén de Castro, *El mejor esposo*, Jornada 1.
66 Guillén de Castro, *El mejor esposo*, Jornada 1.
67 Calderón de la Barca, *El Santo Rey Don Fernando, primera parte*, loa for auto sacramental.
68 Lope de Vega, *La discreta venganza*, preliminares to 1625 edition.
69 Bouvet, *Arbre des Batailles*, trans. Coopland, 133.
70 Tirso de Molina, *La lealtad contra la envidia*, Acto 3.
71 Comte-Sponville, *A Small Treatise on the Great Virtues*, 49.
72 Recent studies reveal a diachronic aspect to this pattern, for masculinity was identified less and less with "medieval" warlike values as the Golden Age declined into the Baroque period. For a representative sampling, see Middlebrook, *Imperial Lyric*; Donnell, *Feminizing the Enemy*; and Arellano, "Masculinidades ansiosas en tratadistas ibéricos de conducta áulica (Siglo de Oro)."
73 Lope de Vega, *Lo que hay que fiar del mundo*, Acto 2.
74 Lope de Vega, *La batalla del honor*, Acto 3.
75 Diamante, *El Hércules de Ocaña*, Jornada 2.
76 Lope de Vega, *Nadie se conoce*, Jornada 2.
77 "mujeres hechas, o que tuvieran, don Juan, de virtud y fortaleza: son flacas, son temerosas" (Lope de Vega, *Pobreza no es vileza*, Acto 3).
78 Lope de Vega, *San Nicolás de Tolentino*, Acto 1.
79 On depictions of venereal disease in the *comedias*, see "The French Disease or French Pox," a section of López Terrada's "'Sallow-Faced Girl,'" 180–3. For a broader treatment not limited to stage plays, see Berco, *From Body to Community*.
80 Lope de Vega, *El valor de las mujeres*, Acto 2.
81 Lope de Vega, *La vengadora de las mujeres*, Acto 3.
82 Lope de Vega, *La serrana de Tormes*, Acto 1.
83 The play's title also clearly references the woman of Proverbs 31, especially verse 17: "She hath girded her loins with strength, and hath strengthened her arm."

84 Calderón de la Barca, *¿Quién hallará mujer fuerte?* auto sacramental. This story appears in Judges 5:24–32.
85 Cervantes, *La gran Sultana*, Jornada 3.
86 Calderón de la Barca, *La gran Cenobia*, Jornada 2.
87 The classic study is of course Melveena McKendrick's recently reprinted *Woman and Society in the Spanish Drama of the Golden Age*.
88 Moreto, *Santa Rosa del Perú*, Jornada 3.
89 Diamante, *Santa Teresa de Jesús*, Jornada 2.
90 Gian Lorenzo Bernini, *Ecstasy of Saint Teresa* (1647–52), Cornaro Chapel, Santa Maria della Vittoria, Rome.
91 Bouvet, *Arbre des Batailles*, trans. Coopland, 133.
92 Mena, *Laberinto de Fortuna* (1444), stanza CCXI, lines 1681–8, p. 217.
93 Lope de Vega, *Si supieran a qué salgo*, loa.
94 Comte-Sponville, *A Small Treatise on the Great Virtues*, 48.

3 Charity as Greed

1 Lope de Vega, *La discreta venganza*, Acto 3.
2 Calderón de la Barca, *La humildad coronada de las plantas*, loa for auto sacramental.
3 Lope de Vega, *Juan de Dios y Antón Martín*, Acto 3.
4 Lope de Vega, *El piadoso aragonés*, Acto 2.
5 Calderón de la Barca, *El Santo Rey Don Fernando, primera parte*, auto sacramental.
6 This argument was made regarding the *moriscos* by the *arbitrista* Pedro de Valencia. See Valencia, *Tratado acerca de los moriscos de España*.
7 Lope de Vega, *La Historia de Tobías*, Acto 3.
8 Rojas Zorrilla, *Los trabajos de Tobías*, Jornada 1.
9 Lope de Vega, *Juan de Dios y Antón Martín*, Acto 2.
10 Lope de Vega, *Juan de Dios y Antón Martín*, Acto 3.
11 Tirso de Molina, *Santo y sastre*, Acto 3.
12 Lope de Vega, *San Nicolás de Tolentino*, Acto 1.
13 Kallendorf, *Sins of the Fathers*, 68–9. See especially Figure 8, a pen and ink sketch of beggars and cripples by Hieronymus Bosch.
14 Lope de Vega, *Los locos de Valencia*, Acto 3. An *escudo* was a coin made of solid gold, the most valuable metal used to mint currency. As Elvira Vilches explains, "The value of the *escudos* ... was so great because the majority of people never used gold at all" (Vilches, "Doing Things with Money in Early Modern Spain").
15 Lope de Vega, *Juan de Dios y Antón Martín*, Acto 2.

16 Lope de Vega, *Los locos de Valencia*, Acto 3.

17 A useful bibliography for work in this area in Spain, although the analysis in the article remains largely derivative, may be found in Campos Marín and García-Alejo, "Los lugares de la locura." More interesting, but limited to the specific case of Valencia, are Tropé, *Locura y sociedad en la Valencia de los siglos XV al XVII*; Roca Traver, "El Hospital dels folls e ignocents"; and López-Ibor, "La fundación en Valencia del primer hospital psiquiátrico del mundo."

18 As Hélène Tropé explains in the excellent introduction to her edition of Lope de Vega's *Los locos de Valencia* (Madrid: Castalia, 2003), "Si bien es cierto que los locos furiosos estaban encadenados y encerrados en las jaulas o gabias en la época en que Lope estuvo en Valencia, los más pacíficos salían del hospital para realizar colectas los días ordinarios lo mismo que los festivos" (39). These "peaceful" lunatics sent out into the city by hospital administrators were clothed in special dress to alert the populace to their condition: "los locos limosneros llevaban llamativos trajes de cuadros azules y amarillos o azules y verdes" (Tropé, "Introducción," 40).

19 Lope de Vega, *San Nicolás de Tolentino*, Acto 2.

20 Diamante, *El jubileo de Porciúncula*, Jornada 2.

21 Lope de Vega, *San Isidro labrador de Madrid*, Acto 2.

22 Rojas Zorrilla, *Santa Isabel, reina de Portugal*, Jornada 2.

23 Kallendorf, *Sins of the Fathers*, 118–24.

24 Quiñones de Benavente, *La verdad*, entremés cantado.

25 Rojas Zorrilla, *Los trabajos de Tobías*, Jornada 1.

26 Tirso de Molina, *Santo y sastre*, Acto 3.

27 Tirso de Molina, *La villana de la Sagra*, Jornada 1.

28 Lope de Vega, *La serrana de Tormes*, Acto 3.

29 "The most acute suffering from hunger was experienced within Spain in the years between 1645 and 1652, when a series of bad harvests compounded by flooding produced the serious possibility that part of the population might starve to death" (Kallendorf, *Sins of the Fathers*, 117). For more information on bread riots in Spain during this time period, including hunger-related uprisings in Seville, Granada, and Córdoba, see Greer, "Constituting Community," 52–3.

30 Calderón de la Barca, *El nuevo hospicio de pobres*, auto sacramental.

31 For a discussion of bread's many resonances in the context of the Corpus Christi feast, see my *Sins of the Fathers*, 130–2.

32 Calderón de la Barca, *El segundo blasón del Austria*, auto sacramental.

33 Tirso de Molina, *La mejor espigadera*, Jornada 3.

34 Cruz, "The Poor in Spain: Confinement and Control," in *Discourses of Poverty*, 39–74.
35 Lope de Vega, *Juan de Dios y Antón Martín*, Acto 3.
36 The identification of this specific hospital as the one referenced in the play's title is derived from the introduction to Calderón de la Barca, *El nuevo hospicio de pobres*, 9. On confraternities' involvement in charitable activities, see Flynn, *Sacred Charity*.
37 Lope de Vega, *Juan de Dios y Antón Martín*, Acto 2.
38 For example, "es la Orden [de Santiago] hospitalaria, y han sido muchos los hospitales que para enfermos y peregrinos sostenía" (Álvarez de Araujo y Cuéllar, *Las órdenes militares de Santiago*, 26).
39 On the historical Hermandad del Refugio, see Callahan, *La Santa y Real Hermandad del Refugio y Piedad de Madrid, 1618–1832*.
40 Calderón de la Barca, *Las órdenes militares*, loa for auto sacramental. This was an actual activity performed by confraternities, as we see in "To Bury the Dead," a section of Flynn's chapter 2, "The Charitable Activites of Confraternities," in *Sacred Charity*.
41 Calderón de la Barca, *La señora y la criada*, Jornada 2.
42 Boyle, "Reforming Prostitutes: Madrid's Magdalen House," in *Unruly Women*, 25–9.
43 For a discussion of the charitable activities of this specific confraternity, see Cruz, *Discourses of Poverty*: "In 1600, the Confraternity of the Santa Caridad received permission from the diocesan authorities to be the first to beg during Holy Week. In its system of poor relief, which obeyed the biblical directives to visit the sick and the poor in their homes, in jail, or on the streets, the Confraternity of the Santa Caridad exemplified how the majority of *hermandades* treated the poor" (53).
44 Calderón de la Barca, *Psiquis y Cupido, que escribió para la ciudad de Toledo*, loa for auto sacramental. In the same *loa*, we find the explanation that "darte las vestiduras por acción muy justa tengo de Caridad."
45 Lope de Vega, *Juan de Dios y Antón Martín*, Acto 3.
46 Lope de Vega, *Juan de Dios y Antón Martín*, Acto 3.
47 Lope de Vega, *La cárcel de Sevilla*, entremés.
48 Lope de Vega, *La cárcel de Sevilla*, entremés.
49 Lope de Vega, *La vida de San Pedro Nolasco*, Acto 1.
50 Calderón de la Barca, *La humildad coronada de las plantas*, loa for auto sacramental.
51 Calderón de la Barca, *Amar y ser amado, y divina Philotea*, loa for auto sacramental.
52 Calderón de la Barca, *El Santo Rey Don Fernando, primera parte*, loa for auto sacramental.

53 James 2:17. We should recall that Martin Luther's heresy stemmed from his declaration that faith alone (i.e., without works) was necessary for salvation (*sola fide*).
54 Cervantes, *Pedro de Urdemalas*, Jornada 3.
55 Cervantes, *Pedro de Urdemalas*, Jornada 3. These words and the ones from the previous quotation should hardly be taken at face value, however, because in this play Pedro disguises himself as a pilgrim and promises (if she pays him) to pray for the soul of Marina Sánchez's dead niece Quiteria.
56 "propia fue siempre al hombre, como por ejemplo vimos, esta virtud liberal, y de la mujer el vicio de la codicia" (Lope de Vega, *El sembrar en buena tierra*, Acto 2). On women as greedy, see Kallendorf, *Sins of the Fathers*, 52.
57 "vedemo naturalmente le donne più pietose, più misericordiose verso poveri, più volentieri far la elemosina" (Capra, *Della eccellenza e dignità delle donne* [1525], 68).
58 Diamante, *Ir por el riesgo a la dicha*, Jornada 2.
59 Lope de Vega, *El esclavo de Roma*, Acto 2.
60 See, for example, Anderson, *The Feminine Face of God*. A more scholarly man's take on some of the same questions may be compared in Schäfer, *Mirror of His Beauty*.
61 Lope de Vega, *La niña de plata*, Acto 3.
62 "The very fact that the Castilian widow enjoyed rights to half the joint wealth of the estate illustrates how firmly cultural norms insisted that the woman truly owned her dowry: her capital had a calculated worth, recognized as integral to the creation of the couples' wealth. Her receipt of half the joint assets clearly showed the value and importance of her personal financial contribution to the estate. Indeed, free to retake her dowry and her share of the profits it generated, the Castilian widow felt no particular obligation to return to the natal home, nor submit to the demands of her husband's kin" (Fink De Backer, *Widowhood in Early Modern Spain*, 112).
63 Lope de Vega, *El valor de las mujeres*, Acto 3.
64 "pidieron su parte a Celestina de la cadena para remediarse" (Fernando de Rojas, *La Celestina*, ed. Dorothy S. Severin [Madrid: Alianza, 1992], Auto XV, p. 200).
65 "¿Que tal se atreviera a hacer/un hombre a quien acompaña/tan noble disposición? ¿No autorizan su nobleza/las joyas que con largueza/me acaba de dar?" (Tirso de Molina, *La villana de Vallecas*, Acto 2).
66 Tirso de Molina, *La santa Juana*, Acto 3. "Amidst the multiple physical coins in circulation, the *maravedí* conveyed not an object but a measure of value or unit of account" (Vilches, "Doing Things with Money").

67 Lope de Vega, *Las aventuras de Don Juan de Alarcos*, preliminares to 1647 edition.
68 "por todo el mundo me disculpa la generosidad con que yo trato cuantos me sirven" (Lope de Vega, *El servir con mala estrella*, Acto 3).
69 Lope de Vega, *Los amantes sin amor*, Acto 2.
70 Lope de Vega, *Las paces de los reyes, y Judía de Toledo*, Acto 3.
71 Tirso de Molina, *La Dama del Olivar*, Acto 1.
72 Lope de Vega, *Juan de Dios y Antón Martín*, Acto 3.
73 Tirso de Molina, *Segunda parte de Santa Juana*, Acto 3.
74 "Robarme la caridad quiso, y no pedir por Dios" (Lope de Vega, *Juan de Dios y Antón Martín*, Acto 2).
75 Tirso de Molina, *Segunda parte de Santa Juana*, Acto 2.
76 See Francisco de Quevedo's second *silva*, which is a *propemptikon*, or poem written to someone leaving on a voyage, which he directs instead to the ship itself: "Exhortación a una nave nueva al entrar en el agua," in *Silvas*, 93–8.
77 Lope de Vega, *Don Juan de Castro, primera parte*, Acto 2.
78 Eire, *From Madrid to Purgatory*, 235.
79 Cervantes, *Pedro de Urdemalas*, Jornada 1.
80 2 Samuel 18:9–17 (2 Kings 18:9–17 in the Douay version). Absalom was King David's son who had his half-brother Amnon killed for raping their sister Tamar.
81 See Eire, "Aiding the Needy, Aiding Oneself," in *Madrid to Purgatory*, 232–47.
82 Tirso de Molina, *Marta la piadosa*, Acto 2.
83 Tirso de Molina, *Marta la piadosa*, Acto 2, emphasis mine.
84 Tirso de Molina, *El mayor desengaño*, Acto 1.
85 Calderón de la Barca, *El gran mercado del mundo*, auto sacramental, emphasis mine.
86 Genesis 15:6; Romans 4:3.
87 Calderón de la Barca, *No hay instante sin milagro*, auto sacramental.
88 Calderón de la Barca, *Psiquis y Cupido, que escribió para esta villa de Madrid*, loa for auto sacramental.
89 Alarcón, *Examen de maridos*, Acto 1.
90 Alarcón, *Ganar amigos*, Acto 3.
91 Lope de Vega, *Amor, pleito y desafío*, Jornada 3.
92 Lope de Vega, *Don Juan de Castro, primera parte*, Acto 2.
93 Lope de Vega, *La historia de Tobías*, Acto 1.
94 Calderón de la Barca, *Basta callar*, Jornada 2.
95 Solís, *La gitanilla de Madrid*, Jornada 1.
96 Rumours have always persisted regarding Alexander's madness. An important new revisionist assessment, which confirms the view that he

suffered a psychological disorder, is Gabriel, *The Madness of Alexander the Great*.

97 Lope de Vega, *El molino*, Jornada 3.

98 Lope de Vega, *La traición bien acertada*, Jornada 1.

99 Lope de Vega, *El honrado hermano*, preliminares to 1623 edition.

100 Lope de Vega, *La ilustre fregona*, Jornada 2.

4 Loose Chastity

1 Guillén de Castro, *El mejor esposo*, Jornada 1.

2 Guillén de Castro, *El mejor esposo*, Jornada 1.

3 Lope de Vega, *La doncella Teodor*, Acto 3.

4 "And now there remain faith, hope and charity, these three: but the greatest of these is charity" (1 Corinthians 13:13).

5 Lope de Vega, *Los Ponces de Barcelona*, Acto 1.

6 Moreto, *El Cristo de los milagros*, Jornada 3.

7 Moreto, *Santa Rosa del Perú*, Jornada 3. On a woman's body pictured as a forbidden garden of delights, see Ross, *Figuring the Feminine*. Ross traces the history of this concept: "The association of a woman's body with a garden or field can be traced back through the ancient cultures of the Near East and the Mediterranean. In the Greek tradition the *hortus conclusus* or 'enclosed garden' was linked to the representation of such a garden as the metaphorical seat of female sexuality and fertility. This idea was transmitted to Christian medieval Europe through the Song of Songs ... One of the dominant characteristics of this garden ... is its quality of virginity ... [T]he garden is a place of erotic temptation" (111–12).

8 "Spanish racial hysteria focused on covert cultural and religious practices, and on the much more ambiguous register of blood. The widespread consensus ... was that *limpieza de sangre* (blood purity) was almost impossible to determine in any authentic fashion. Absent physical manifestations, how could one tell if any given subject was free of the Semitic or Moorish taint? This ambiguity suggests the possibility of assimilation, passing, and other challenges to the official rhetoric of essentialized difference" (Fuchs, *Exotic Nation*, 118).

9 See Vilches, *New World Gold*.

10 Mena, *Laberinto de Fortuna* (1444), stanza LXXXIV, lines 665–6, p. 139.

11 "que las vírgenes no más, aquellas que el casamiento no vieron, y que la palma de castidad merecieron, con los Ángeles tendrían aquel purísimo asiento" (Lope de Vega, *El capellán de la Virgen*, Acto 1). Angels' supposed lack of sexuality was tied to their lack of a need to reproduce themselves.

This belief is still held by Catholics today. As one modern Catholic apologist explains, "That is why the angels do not marry[,] since they have no need of maintaining their own existence[,] since they do not die" (Taouk, "The Book of Tobias and the Catholic Ideal of Marriage"). The most famous early modern literary depiction of angelic "sexuality" is undoubtedly John Milton's in *Paradise Lost*. See deGruy, "Desiring Angels."

12 Rojas Zorrilla, *Los trabajos de Tobías*, Jornada 1.

13 Capra, *Della eccellenza e dignità delle donne* (1525), 80.

14 Mena, *Laberinto de Fortuna* (1444), stanza CXXXI, lines 1045–6, p. 170.

15 Mena, *Laberinto de Fortuna*, stanza LXXVI, lines 603–4, p. 135.

16 On this topic, see the chapter on Lust in my *Sins of the Fathers*, 74–94.

17 "Ábrese el primer Carro, y se ve la Castidad, y el Honor arrastrando a la Lascivia" (Calderón de la Barca, *El año santo de Roma*, auto sacramental).

18 Calderón de la Barca, *El año santo en Madrid*, auto sacramental.

19 Calderón de la Barca, *Sueños hay que verdad son*, auto sacramental.

20 Calderón de la Barca, *Sueños hay que verdad son*, auto sacramental.

21 See *Joseph & Aseneth*, 473–503.

22 Cueva, *El Infamador*, preliminares to 1588 edition.

23 Lope de Vega, *El perro del hortelano*, Acto 2.

24 Tirso de Molina, *Quien no cae no se levanta*, Acto 2.

25 http://buscon.rae.es

26 The problematical aspects of Lucretia's exemplarity have been explored forcefully in Jed, *Chaste Thinking*.

27 Lope de Vega, *Virtud, pobreza y mujer*, Acto 3.

28 Hubbard, "The Invention of Sulpicia." For a thorough treatment of several centuries of commentaries on these poems, see Skoie, *Reading Sulpicia*. The poems themselves, with English translations, appear in that volume as an appendix.

29 See McKendrick, "The *Mujer Esquiva*."

30 Lope de Vega, *El mayordomo de la Duquesa de Amalfi*, Acto 2.

31 Antonio de Yepes, *Corónica general de la Orden de San Benito*, Tomo II, Centuria II (Universidad de Nuestra Señora la Real de Yrache: Matías Mares, 1609), fol. 367v.

32 For the best analysis of intersections of the *comedia* as an art form with courtly love traditions, see Robert Bayliss, *The Discourse of Courtly Love in Seventeenth-Century Spanish Theater* (Lewisburg, PA: Bucknell University Press, 2008).

33 Lope de Vega, *La necedad del discreto*, Jornada 2.

34 Lope de Vega, *Virtud, pobreza y mujer*, Acto 1.

35 "Ariosto was aware of the power both that the female patron held over him, in economic terms, and of that which he held over her by his control of the public perception of her virtues ... Where for the court lady chastity was the inevitable term of identity, for the court poet that term is flattery, endlessly produced in an effort to improve the author's standing" (Regan, "Ariosto's Threshold Patron," 51).
36 Lope de Vega, *El genovés liberal*, Acto 3.
37 Lope de Vega, *Las famosas asturianas*, Acto 3.
38 Calderón de la Barca, *Agradecer y no amar*, preliminares to 1682 edition.
39 Brown, *The Body and Society*, 19.
40 Brown, *The Body and Society*, xiv. Brown explains of Origen, "Origen was widely believed to have practiced what he preached. It was always said of him that, as a young man of about twenty, around 206, he had discreetly gone to a doctor to have himself castrated" (168).
41 Brown, *The Body and Society*, xvi, 11.
42 Brown, *The Body and Society*, 16.
43 Mena, *Laberinto de Fortuna*, stanza LXXXIII, lines 657–64, p. 139.
44 Patricia Grieve comments on the futility of this obsession: "With generation after generation of intermarriage and sexual intermingling ... in different parts of the Iberian Peninsula at differing times, was it really possible to declare purity of blood in any group of people living there at the time?" (*The Eve of Spain*, 11).
45 Diamante, *El nacimiento de Cristo*, zarzuela, Acto 1.
46 Resnick, "Marriage in Medieval Culture," 354.
47 Resnick, "Marriage in Medieval Culture." See also Dyan Elliott, *Spiritual Marriage*; and Gold, "The Marriage of Mary and Joseph."
48 Moreto, *Santa Rosa del Perú*, Jornada 1.
49 Guillén de Castro, *El mejor esposo*, Jornada 1.
50 Guillén de Castro, *El mejor esposo*, Jornada 1.
51 Guillén de Castro, *El mejor esposo*, Jornada 1.
52 "[L]a casuística áurea, hija de su tiempo y de sus orígenes escolásticos enraizados en la patrística, abusó frecuentemente de la 'agudeza', proponiendo ejemplos difíciles para retar el ingenio teológico, distanciándose así de su función práctica inmediata" (Del Río Parra, *Cartografías de consciencia española en la Edad de Oro*, 40).
53 Lope de Vega, *Los locos por el cielo*, Acto 1.
54 Kallendorf, *Exorcism and Its Texts*, 203.
55 Calderón de la Barca, *El purgatorio de San Patricio*, Acto 1.
56 Moreto, *Santa Rosa del Perú*, Jornada 1.
57 Rojas Zorrilla, *Los trabajos de Tobías*, Jornada 3.

58 Lope de Vega, *La historia de Tobías*, preliminares to 1621 edition.
59 Tobias 6:16–17.
60 For example, witness this passage from Antonio Escobar y Mendoza's *Examen y práctica de confesores y penitentes*: "¿Qué pecados pueden cometerse en el uso del matrimonio? Teniendo cópula contra naturaleza o fuera del vaso natural or derramando fuera. Toda postura extraordinaria hecha por deleite, sin peligro de efusión de semen *extra vas*, es sólo pecado venial; y si se hace por no poder de otra suerte no es pecado. Cuando se llega el uno al otro como si no fuera su mujer o marido, es mortal" (Antonio Escobar y Mendoza, *Examen y práctica de confesores y penitentes, en todas las materias de la teología moral* [Valladolid: María de Quiñones, 1650], 177).
61 Tobias 8:4–5, 9.
62 On Lust within marriage, see Kallendorf, *Sins of the Fathers*, 81.
63 Pérez de Montalbán, *Los templarios*, Jornada 2.
64 Tirso de Molina, *Marta la piadosa*, Acto 2.
65 Tirso de Molina, *La república al revés*, Acto 2.
66 Lope de Vega, *El mejor alcalde, el rey*, Acto 3.
67 "no hay imagen más clara de la castidad hermosa, pues de las manos la rosa con las espinas se ampara" (Lope de Vega, *Mirad a quién alabáis*, Acto 2).
68 Lope de Vega, *El Amor enamorado*, Jornada 3.
69 Lope de Vega, *El Perseo*, Acto 2.
70 On fraud in alchemy, see Nummedal, "The Problem of Fraud in Early Modern Alchemy." On alchemy as it was practised at the court of King Philip II, see Eamon, "Masters of Fire."
71 Lope de Vega, *El Perseo*, Acto 1.
72 Lope de Vega, *Los prados de León*, Acto 2. These lines are spoken by King Alfonso el Casto.
73 Lope de Vega, *La vengadora de las mujeres*, Acto 1.
74 Craig Kallendorf, "Boccaccio's Two Didos," 73. On the reception of the Dido myths in Spain, see Lida de Malkiel, *Dido en la literatura española*.
75 Lope de Vega, *El perseguido*, Jornada 2. Elisa was another name for Dido.
76 Cueva, *Tragedia del príncipe tirano*, Acto 4.
77 Calderón de la Barca, *El pastor fido*, auto sacramental.
78 Stroud, "The Wife-Murder Plays," 93.
79 This is the count offered in Stroud, *Fatal Union*.
80 Lope de Vega, *Las almenas de Toro*, preliminares to 1620 edition.
81 A recent critical treatment of the film *Lope*, which compares it to the movie *Shakespeare in Love*, is Bayliss, "Lope enamorado."

82 On the double standard with regard to gender in England during this time period, see Thomas, "The Double Standard."

83 "After the death of his second wife, Lope became a priest, with the express purpose of correcting the disorders of his life. Unfortunately it cannot be said that the taking of Holy orders led to improvement; his aberrations continued, and he intensified his baseness by playing the part of a poetical panderer for his patron, the Duke of Sessa. Lope was well aware of the vileness of his own behaviour, as his correspondence clearly shows; but he was too weak to reform" (Ford, "Félix de Lope de Vega Carpio"). On the problems occasioned by the clash between Lope's priestly obligations and his love life, see Ricard, "Sacerdocio y literatura en la España del Siglo de Oro: El caso de Lope de Vega," in *Estudios de literatura religiosa española*, 246–58.

84 See Foucault, "Panopticism," in *Discipline and Punish*, 195–308.

85 Georgina Dopico Black, *Perfect Wives, Other Women: Adultery and Inquisition in Early Modern Spain* (Durham: Duke University Press, 2001). Allyson Poska argues persuasively by employing such quantifiable factors as demographics, economics, class stratification, and regional differentiation that in fact there may have been some truth to these suspicious husbands' assumptions. She concludes that at least among non-elites, Chastity was "not a priority for most Spaniards" (Poska, "Elusive Virtue," 135).

86 Rojas Zorrilla, *La traición busca el castigo*, Jornada 1.

87 Guillén de Castro, *El curioso impertinente*, Acto 1.

88 Lope de Vega, *La viuda casada y doncella*, Acto 3. Other plays relevant for the study of this topic are Lope de Vega's *Los peligros de la ausencia* and Cueva y Silva's *La firmeza en la ausencia*.

89 Poska, "When Bigamy is the Charge."

90 Lope de Vega, *Los Porceles de Murcia*, Acto 2.

91 Tirso de Molina, *El castigo del penséque*, Acto 1. The widow of Sicheus is another reference to Dido.

92 Alarcón, *Los favores del mundo*, Acto 3.

93 Lope de Vega, *La esclava de su galán*, Jornada 2.

5 Prudence: Panacea or Placebo?

1 Lope de Vega, *El saber por no saber, y vida de San Julián*, Acto 1.

2 Cueva, *Comedia del príncipe tirano*, preliminares to 1588 edition. This and similar quotations which favour Prudence over other Virtues bear the influence of Saint Thomas Aquinas's *Summa theologica*. For an explication of his position on this and the other Cardinal Virtues, see Nelson, *The Priority of Prudence*.

3 "[el] alma se gobierna por virtudes ordinarias, debe usar de la prudencia, que es quien a todas las manda" (Moreto, *Santa Rosa del Perú*, Jornada 2).
4 Mena, *Laberinto de Fortuna*, stanza CXXXVII, lines 1089–96, p. 173.
5 Calderón de la Barca, *La humildad coronada de las plantas*, auto sacramental.
6 Calderón de la Barca, *La humildad coronada de las plantas*, auto sacramental.
7 Alarcón, *El dueño de las estrellas*, Acto 1.
8 Kallendorf, "Asking for Advice," in *Conscience on Stage*, 108–42.
9 Calderón de la Barca, *Mejor está que estaba*, Jornada 2.
10 Lope de Vega, *El hombre por su palabra*, Acto 1.
11 Matos Fragoso, *Con amor no hay amistad*, Jornada 2.
12 Matos Fragoso, *Los indicios sin culpa*, Acto 1.
13 Matos Fragoso, *Callar siempre es lo mejor*, Jornada 3.
14 Matos Fragoso, *Amor, lealtad y ventura*, Acto 1.
15 Lope de Vega, *El serafín humano*, Acto 1.
16 Tirso de Molina, *La república al revés*, Acto 1.
17 Tirso de Molina, *La república al revés*, Acto 2. As mentioned in the Justice chapter, while the Senate was not a governmental institution existing in Golden Age Spain, the plays nonetheless contain references to this body as it appeared in other times and cultures (in this case, the Byzantine empire).
18 Lope de Vega, *El castigo sin venganza*, Acto 3.
19 Moreto, *El licenciado Vidriera*, Jornada 1.
20 Jeremy Robbins traces the evolution of this Virtue through anti-Machiavellian political thought in Spain and concludes that eventually, "prudence moves centre-stage and becomes the defining virtue of the Christian prince" ("Prudence and the Compass of Deceit," in *Arts of Perception*, 103). With this movement he sees "a shift in the term prudence away from its scholastic definition as the prime moral virtue towards a more specific socio-political usage" (106).
21 Guillén de Castro, *Las mocedades del Cid, Comedia primera*, Acto 1.
22 Calderón de la Barca, *Sueños hay que verdad son*, *loa* for auto sacramental.
23 Rojas Zorrilla, *No hay ser padre siendo rey*, Jornada 2. In this play, Prince Rugero kills his brother, believing him to be in bed with Duchess Violante. Thus the murder qualifies as imprudent (Rugero did not stop to verify the facts of the case first), while the alleged dalliance raises questions about faithfulness and constancy.
24 Alarcón, *La cueva de Salamanca*, preliminares to 1628 edition.
25 Cervantes, *La casa de los celos y selvas de Ardenia*, Jornada 1.
26 Calderón de la Barca, *Llamados y escogidos*, auto sacramental.
27 "a la Prudencia, y a la Ley Natural rompo" (Calderón de la Barca, *La humildad coronada de las plantas*, auto sacramental).

28 Calderón de la Barca, *Amigo, amante y leal*, preliminares to 1682 edition.
29 Kagan, *Lawsuits and Litigants in Castile, 1500–1700*, 11.
30 Calderón de la Barca, *¿Quién hallará mujer fuerte?* auto sacramental.
31 Calderón de la Barca, *¿Quién hallará mujer fuerte?* auto sacramental.
32 Tirso de Molina, *Doña Beatriz de Silva*, Acto 3; Calderón de la Barca, *El Santo Rey Don Fernando, primera parte*, auto sacramental.
33 Rojas Zorrilla, *Donde hay agravios no hay celos*, Jornada 1.
34 Tirso de Molina, *La huerta de Juan Fernández*, Jornada 1.
35 Tirso de Molina, *Los amantes de Teruel*, Jornada 2.
36 Tirso de Molina, *La prudencia en la mujer*, Jornada 2.
37 Lope de Vega, *El sembrar en buena tierra*, Acto 1.
38 Lope de Vega, *El bobo del colegio*, Acto 3.
39 Matos Fragoso, *El hijo de la piedra*, Acto 1.
40 Calderón de la Barca, *¿Quién hallará mujer fuerte?* auto sacramental.
41 Matos Fragoso, *Callar siempre es lo mejor*, Acto 1.
42 Tirso de Molina, *La vida de Herodes*, Acto 2.
43 Rojas Zorrilla, *Progne y Filomena*, Jornada 1.
44 Rojas Zorrilla, *La traición busca el castigo*, Jornada 1.
45 "la espada de la ira guarnece con templanza, y con prudencia, que al castigo violento se sigue el arrepentido sentimiento" (Lope de Vega, *La discreta venganza*, Acto 3).
46 "se vio la prudencia: proporcionado un castigo muchos defectos enmienda, mas un castigo sobrado irrita muchas paciencias" (Calderón de la Barca, *Los dos amantes del cielo*, Jornada 2).
47 Cueva, *Tragedia del príncipe tirano*, Acto 4.
48 Alarcón, *Los pechos privilegiados*, Acto 1.
49 Calderón de la Barca, *Saber del mal, y el bien*, Jornada 3.
50 Tirso de Molina, *La elección por la virtud*, Jornada 3.
51 Pérez de Montalbán, *Cumplir con su obligación*, Jornada 2.
52 Lope de Vega, *El galán de la Membrilla*, Acto 1.
53 Alarcón, *Ganar amigos*, Acto 1.
54 Lope de Vega, *La discreta venganza*, Acto 2.
55 Calderón de la Barca, *Guárdate de la agua mansa*, Jornada 3.
56 Lope de Vega, *Los peligros de la ausencia*, Acto 3. Regarding the insistence upon *indicios* and other proofs as suggestive of an increasingly legalistic mindset in the context of sin, see Kallendorf, *Sins of the Fathers*, 86–7. On the suspension of judgment regarding a given case or moral dilemma, and its consequences for deferring the plot's resolution, see Kallendorf, "*Dilatio*, Deferral, and *Différance*," in *Conscience on Stage*, 192–7.
57 Alarcón, *La crueldad por el honor*, Acto 1.

58 "que el medio más blando elija le aconseja su prudencia" (Moreto, *El desdén con el desdén*, Jornada 1).
59 Calderón de la Barca, *Gustos y disgustos son no más que imaginación*, Jornada 1.
60 Guillén de Castro, *El nacimiento de Montesinos*, Acto 2.
61 "es prudencia prevenir el peligro, queda en paz" (Cervantes, *Pedro de Urdemalas*, Jornada 2).
62 "excusar su prudencia los daños de este peligro" (Moreto, *Lo que puede la aprehensión*, Jornada 1).
63 Cueva, *Comedia del príncipe tirano*, Acto 4.
64 Lope de Vega, *La inocente sangre*, Acto 1.
65 Rojas Zorrilla, *No hay amigo para amigo*, Jornada 2.
66 Tirso de Molina, *Marta la piadosa*, Acto 3.
67 Matos Fragoso, *El hijo de la piedra*, Jornada 2.
68 Alarcón, *Los favores del mundo*, Acto 3.
69 "o cuánto importa la prudencia cana, cuando la juventud se determina" (Lope de Vega, *Los españoles en Flandes*, Acto 3).
70 Alarcón, *El dueño de las estrellas*, Acto 1.
71 Lope de Vega, *Los pleitos de Inglaterra*, Acto 3.
72 Lope de Vega, *El alcalde mayor*, Acto 3.
73 In another example: "¡O quien en tal confusión sin riesgo de la prudencia, imitara la sentencia que hizo sabio a Salomón!" (Tirso de Molina, *Escarmientos para el cuerdo*, Acto 1).
74 Lope de Vega, *El perseguido*, Jornada 2.
75 "el trigo que reservó tu prudencia para los presentes años" (Lope de Vega, *Los trabajos de Jacob*, Jornada 2).
76 Moreto, *Los hermanos encontrados*, Jornada 1. This association is echoed in Tirso de Molina's *Ventura te dé Dios, hijo* in the line "Ulises nuevo me llaman mis engaños, y prudencia" (Jornada 1).
77 Lope de Vega, *La vida de San Pedro Nolasco*, Jornada 2.
78 On this never-painted iconographical program see Kallendorf, "Were the *Arbitristas* Arbitrary?" as well as López Torrijos, "Un manuscrito con instrucciones iconográficas." The proposed design for the ceiling is presented in detail in Valencia, *Descripción de la pintura de las virtudes*.
79 On the circumstances surrounding Rome's third and final (successful) attempt to defeat Carthage, as well as its methods for doing so, see Ridley, "To Be Taken with a Pinch of Salt."
80 Lope de Vega, *La mocedad de Roldán*, Acto 2.
81 "A key part of the myth was that Venice was *potens opibus, sed virtute potentior* ('mighty in her resources but mightier in virtue'), as Petrarch put it; in Burckhardt's rather hyperbolic words, 'no state, indeed, has

ever exercised a greater moral influence over its subjects, whether abroad or at home'. Venetians were supposed to cultivate wisdom, courage, temperance, and justice with unusual diligence, and to comport themselves with dignity at all times" (Craig Kallendorf, *Virgil and the Myth of Venice*, 14).

82 Lope de Vega, *La octava maravilla*, Acto 3.

83 Lope de Vega (attributed), *La ilustre fregona*, Jornada 3. On problems connected to the authorship of this play, see Presotto, "La tradición textual de *La ilustre fregona*."

84 Pérez de Montalbán, *Segunda parte del Séneca de España, Don Felipe Segundo*, Jornada 2.

85 Alarcón, *Ganar amigos*, Acto 1.

86 Alarcón, *La amistad castigada*, Acto 1.

87 The standard biography is still Elliott, *The Count-Duke of Olivares*. Olivares was Baroque poet Francisco de Quevedo's arch-enemy who was probably responsible for placing him under house arrest (Elliott, *The Count-Duke of Olivares*, 554).

88 Calderón de la Barca, *Hado y divisa de Leonido y Marfisa*, Jornada 3.

89 Lope de Vega, *El cuerdo loco*, Acto 1. On the criteria used to formulate these official opinions, see Kallendorf, "Were the *Arbitristas* Arbitrary?"

90 Tirso de Molina, *Ventura te dé Dios, hijo*, Jornada 1.

91 Tirso de Molina, *Ventura te dé Dios, hijo*, Jornada 2.

92 Lope de Vega, *Los españoles en Flandes*, Acto 3.

93 Lope de Vega, *Bamba*, Jornada 2.

94 "guardan su ley, cuando con prudencia el Rey tiene los pueblos contentos" (Lope de Vega, *Porfiando vence amor*, Jornada 3).

95 Lope de Vega, *Mirad a quién alabáis*, Acto 3.

96 "vi que en él cuando entraba cuerdamente competían la prudencia, y la arrogancia" (Guillén de Castro, *La fuerza de la costumbre*, Jornada 1).

97 "a la ira la templanza, y a la crueldad la prudencia" (Rojas Zorrilla, *El más impropio verdugo por la más justa venganza*, Jornada 3).

98 Guillén de Castro, *Los mal casados de Valencia*, Acto 2.

99 Tirso de Molina, *Amar por razón de estado*, Acto 3.

100 Calderón de la Barca, *Antes que todo es mi dama*, Jornada 3.

101 Calderón de la Barca, *La exaltación de la Cruz*, Jornada 2.

102 Rojas Zorrilla, *Peligrar en los remedios*, Jornada 1.

103 Diamante, *El cerco de Zamora*, Jornada 3.

104 Lope de Vega, *La nueva victoria del Marqués de Santa Cruz*, Jornada 3.

105 Lope de Vega, *Los pleitos de Inglaterra*, Acto 1.

106 Calderón de la Barca, *Judás Macabeo*, Acto 1.

107 Calderón de la Barca, *La vida es sueño*, Jornada 3.

108 "La prudencia y la templanza son divinos consejeros, en la república humana" (Lope de Vega, *El valor de las mujeres*, Acto 1).

109 Lope de Vega, *El castigo sin venganza*, Acto 1.

110 "Appetite clearly encompasses both the realm of sex and the realm of food ... These are clearly related concepts which morph ever so slightly in their relationship to each other from one dramatic work to the next according to each particular author's artistic and theological sensibility. In Golden Age literature, food is frequently associated with sex" (Kallendorf, *Sins of the Fathers*, 294, n. 15; the full text of the note offers extensive examples).

111 Guillén de Castro, *Las mocedades del Cid, Comedia primera*, Acto 1.

112 Calderón de la Barca, *El golfo de las Sirenas*, Acto 1.

113 Lope de Vega, *El sembrar en buena tierra*, Acto 1.

114 For a useful survey of the prodigal son theme in Jesuit school drama from this same time period, see Grayson, "The Model Prodigal."

115 Cueva, *La constancia de Arcelina*, Acto 4.

116 Calderón de la Barca, *Auristela y Lisidante*, Jornada 2.

117 Calderón de la Barca, *El Conde Lucanor*, Acto 1.

118 "su paciencia ya pasa a deshonor, si no es prudencia" (Guillén de Castro, *El engañarse engañado*, Jornada 2).

119 Pérez de Montalbán, *La deshonra honrosa*, Jornada 2.

120 Guillén de Castro, *El engañarse engañado*, Jornada 2.

121 On Prudence in Cervantes' works, see González Moreno and Urbina, "Elogio de la prudencia"; and Egido, *El discreto encanto de Cervantes y el crisol de la prudencia*.

122 Calderón de la Barca, *Los cabellos de Absalón*, Jornada 3.

123 Rojas Zorrilla, *Obligados y ofendidos*, Jornada 1.

124 Calderón de la Barca, *Apolo y Climene*, Acto 1. This line may be a direct echo of Machiavelli's *The Prince*: "But prudence consists in knowing how to assess the dangers, and to choose the least bad course of action as being the right one to follow" (Machiavelli, *The Prince*, chapter 21, p. 79). Machiavelli's reception in Spain will be discussed in this book's conclusion.

125 Calderón de la Barca, *Gustos y disgustos son no más que imaginación*, Jornada 1.

126 "Esa razón en un pecho, Flavio, de sustancia, y de prudencia militada" (Calderón de la Barca, *La hija del aire, segunda parte*, Jornada 2).

127 Lope de Vega, *Amor secreto hasta celos*, Acto 2.

128 Rojas Zorrilla, *El profeta falso Mahoma*, Jornada 2.

129 This nationalistic prejudice was in part mitigated by a phenomenon which Barbara Fuchs has designated *maurophilia*. See Fuchs, *Exotic Nation*.
130 Guillén de Castro, *El Conde de Irlos*, Acto 2.
131 Guillén de Castro, *El pretender con pobreza*, Jornada 1.
132 "Bien sé que fuera prudencia, acabar nuestra jornada en paz, pero no valor" (Lope de Vega, *Amar, servir y esperar*, Acto 1).
133 Calderón de la Barca, *Mujer, llora y vencerás*, Jornada 1.
134 Lope de Vega, *La necedad del discreto*, Jornada 2.
135 "llega a derribar mi valor a los pies de tu prudencia" (Lope de Vega, *Las cuentas del Gran Capitán*, Acto 2).
136 Calderón de la Barca, *¿Quién hallará mujer fuerte?* auto sacramental.
137 "ya no puede haber venganza, y será prudencia justa trocar en bodas las armas" (Lope de Vega, *Quien más no puede*, Acto 3).
138 "de reñir deja, porque quiere acompañar el valor de la prudencia" (Calderón de la Barca, *¿Cuál es mayor perfección?* Jornada 2).
139 Guillén de Castro, *El engañarse engañado*, Jornada 2.
140 Diamante, *El Hércules de Ocaña*, Jornada 3.
141 "y así la Oliva le añade los Triunfos de la Prudencia, a los Juicios del valor, políticamente cuerda" (Calderón de la Barca, *Sueños hay que verdad son*, loa for auto sacramental).
142 "ya de la Prudencia viene hollando la senda la Justicia" (Calderón de la Barca, *¿Quién hallará mujer fuerte?* auto sacramental).
143 "Bien es, que alguna templanza dé la prudencia a la ira" (Lope de Vega, *El robo de Dina*, Acto 1).
144 "Moderando inquietudes con sosiegos, y con prudencia enojos" (Guillén de Castro, *El engañarse engañado*, Jornada 3).
145 Rojas Zorrilla, *El profeta falso Mahoma*, Jornada 1.
146 "tened prudencia, que alargáis jurisdicciones de deudo, a mayores deudas" (Tirso de Molina, *Amar por arte mayor*, Acto 2).
147 "al hombro flaco con una prudencia santa debe la virtud perfecta proporcionarle la carga" (Moreto, *Santa Rosa del Perú*, Jornada 2).
148 Lope de Vega, *El príncipe perfecto, parte primera*, Acto 2.
149 Calderón de la Barca, *Mujer, llora y vencerás*, Jornada 1.
150 "tu prudencia, en el mar de mi fortuna, piloto ha de ser" (Calderón de la Barca, *La hija del aire, segunda parte*, Jornada 2).
151 Guillén de Castro, *La justicia en la piedad*, Jornada 1.
152 "soy Ulises atado al árbol de mi prudencia" (Lope de Vega, *Hay verdades que en amor*, Acto 2).
153 Solís, *El doctor Carlino*, Jornada 1.

154 As in "le suplico, y pido abra los ojos de su Real prudencia" and "Si con los ojos de prudencia llegas a mirar, gran señor, cuán importante es tu grandeza" (both in Tirso de Molina, *Averígüelo Vargas*, Jornada 1).
155 Lope de Vega, *Los pleitos de Inglaterra*, Acto 2.
156 Alarcón, *La manganilla de Melilla*, Acto 1.
157 See Cardaillac, "Un aspecto de las relaciones entre moriscos y cristianos."
158 Rojas Zorrilla, *Donde hay agravios no hay celos*, Jornada 2.
159 "es razón que calléis, y que tengáis prudencia en lo que tratáis, y en dejarlo, discreción" (Lope de Vega, *El Duque de Viseo*, Acto 1).
160 "mira que importa ahora, que esté la lengua a la prudencia asida" (Lope de Vega, *La venganza venturosa*, Acto 1).
161 "Guardadnos silencio un día, tenednos prudencia y seso" (Lope de Vega, *Loa en vituperio de la mala lengua*).
162 Lope de Vega, *Del mal lo menos*, Acto 3.
163 Lope de Vega, *La Santa Liga*, preliminares to 1621 edition. Lope seems to be referring to Euripides's *Alcmena*, where he alludes to "schools of swallows." These chattering birds are understood to represent rival poets' barbarisms.
164 "os he comunicado secretos que encerraba la prudencia" (Tirso de Molina, *Del enemigo el primer consejo*, Jornada 1).
165 Lope de Vega, *La mayor victoria de Alemania de Don Gonzalo de Córdoba*, preliminares to 1637 edition.
166 "Viva en mi prudencia fija, el alma de este secreto" (Rojas Zorrilla, *Progne y Filomena*, Jornada 2).
167 Alarcón, *La verdad sospechosa*, Acto 3.
168 "Pase nuestro amor así con prudencia, y con secreto" (Lope de Vega, *La ilustre fregona*, Jornada 3).
169 Pérez de Montalbán, *La toquera vizcaína*, Jornada 1.
170 Lope de Vega, *El gallardo catalán*, Jornada 1.
171 Alarcón, *La prueba de las promesas*, Acto 1.
172 "que es el morir de temor más flaqueza que prudencia" (Alarcón, *Mudarse por mejorarse*, Acto 2).
173 "ya será cobardía lo que hasta ahora prudencia" (Tirso de Molina, *Amazonas en las Indias*, Acto 3).
174 Zamora, *Áspides hay Basiliscos*, Jornada 1.
175 "'No hay prudencia que resista al engaño': Es disparate pensar que pueda el prudente prevenir a quien le acecha" (Alemán, *Guzmán de Alfarache*, 2:135).
176 Rojas Zorrilla, *Donde hay agravios no hay celos*, Jornada 2.
177 Tirso de Molina, *Marta la piadosa*, Acto 3.

178 "No hay allí prudencia humana, porque es el don de Consejo, que a la prudencia aventaja, quien la guía, y la dirige, y la mueve" (Moreto, *Santa Rosa del Perú*, Jornada 2).
179 Lope de Vega, *Amar, servir y esperar*, Acto 1. A Virtue in its own right, Patience makes its way into many canonical Virtues lists from this period.
180 "Crean los celos mis recelos, con advertida prudencia" (Rojas Zorrilla, *Progne y Filomena*, Jornada 2).
181 "la cordura y prudencia consisten en la tardanza" (Tirso de Molina, *Amor y celos hacen discretos*, Jornada 1).
182 Alarcón, *El desdichado en fingir*, Acto 3. If this investigation is not pursued responsibly, the consequence is a lack of Prudence, and tragedy can result: "Mal consejo tomaste, fue desdicha, pues fuera más prudencia informarte mejor de su inocencia" (Lope de Vega, *El valor de las mujeres*, Acto 1).
183 "el tiempo mismo le irá enseñando prudencia" (Moreto, *Las travesuras del Cid, burlesca*, Jornada 2).
184 Alarcón, *Ganar amigos*, Acto 3. For a discussion of this and related passages, see Kallendorf, "*Dilatio*, Deferral, and *Différance*," in *Conscience on Stage*, 195.
185 Tirso de Molina, *La huerta de Juan Fernández*, Jornada 3.
186 "he menester que a los pies ponga grillos la prudencia" (Tirso de Molina, *Averígüelo Vargas*, Jornada 1).
187 Tirso de Molina, *Siempre ayuda la verdad*, Jornada 2. The song was a number-one hit in the United States and Canada in the 1970s and was sung by Roberta Flack.
188 Calderón de la Barca, *El valle de la zarzuela*, loa for auto sacramental.
189 Rojas Zorrilla, *No hay amigo para amigo*, Jornada 2.
190 "la prudencia dora cuanto deslustra una opinión perdida" (Lope de Vega, *La venganza venturosa*, Acto 1).
191 Robbins, "Prudence and the Compass of Deceit," in *Arts of Perception*, 97–130.
192 Lope de Vega, *Del mal lo menos*, Acto 3.
193 Matos Fragoso, *Callar siempre es lo mejor*, Jornada 2.
194 Alarcón, *La amistad castigada*, Acto 1.
195 "Es prudencia, que con alguna mentira quite a mi hermana el amor" (Lope de Vega, *No son todos ruiseñores*, Jornada 3).
196 Lope de Vega, *El Duque de Viseo*, Acto 1.
197 Lope de Vega, *El sembrar en buena tierra*, Acto 1. Equivocation is discussed in Kallendorf, *Conscience on Stage*, 121, and *Sins of the Fathers*, 189–90.
198 Lope de Vega, *Las flores de Don Juan, y rico y pobre trocados*, Acto 2.

199 Derrida, *The Beast & the Sovereign*, 90.
200 For the polyvalence of this trope, extending even to alchemy and the "philosopher's stone," see DeVun, "The Jesus Hermaphrodite."

6 Class Trumps Sex: The (En)gendering of Virtue

1 Shakespeare, *Othello*, I.iii.320–6. Iago speaks these lines to Roderigo.
2 As César Dubler explains regarding the Spanish medical doctor Andrés de Laguna, personal physician to Charles V and Philip II: "Laguna ... además de médico fue filólogo y botánico. En este último aspecto su aportación es muy apreciable. Se dio cuenta de la diferencia de sexos en las plantas y del modo de fecundación" (César E. Dubler, "La Botánica y las demás ciencias de la Naturaleza," in *La "Materia Médica" de Dioscórides: transmisión medieval y renacentista*, vol. 4, *D. Andrés de Laguna y su época* [Barcelona: Emporius, 1955], 284).
3 See Vyskot and Hobza, "Gender in Plants."
4 Lloyd, "Sexual Strategies in Plants."
5 Borges, "Gender in Plants."
6 Harvey, "Medieval Plantsmanship in England," 20; Harvey here cites Friar Henry Daniel's *Little Book of the Virtues of Rosemary* [ca. 1440], of which he compared multiple manuscripts: Trinity College, Cambridge, MS O.I.13, ff. 77v–82v; British Museum, Sloane MS 7, ff. 40–1; Bodleian Library, Oxford, MS Ashmole 1438, ff. 107–9; and British Museum, Sloane MS 962, ff. 79–82).
7 This idea appears in the words of Julio: "Hay una hierba que llaman los latinos *centum capita* ... Tiene la hierba que digo la raíz hermafrodita, y como cae la diferencia a hombre o mujer así hace el efecto" (Lope de Vega, *La Dorotea*, Acto 3, Escena 4, p. 267).
8 On the constructed nature of gender, I refer of course to the groundbreaking work of Butler, *Gender Trouble*, especially "Gender: The Circular Ruins of Contemporary Debate," 11–17, and "Gender Complexity and the Limits of Identification," 84–90; as well as Butler, *Bodies That Matter*, particularly "Gender is Burning: Questions of Appropriation and Subversion," 121–42. See also Jordan, "Sex and Gender," in *Renaissance Feminism*, 134–247. For gender ambiguity in Renaissance Iberia, see Soyer, *Ambiguous Gender*.
9 "The association of *luxuria* with women has as its natural complement the association of *virtus* with men. *Virtus* is the quality which characterizes a *vir*, just as *senectus* is the quality which characterizes a *senex*; it is literally 'manliness,' in all senses of the word. *Virtus* is the quality which

distinguishes *vir* from *femina* (or *mulier*)" (Boyd, "*Virtus Effeminata* and Sallust's Sempronia," 193). Robert Cowan nuances this rather stark distinction with the claim that a *puer*, or young boy, was as much the antithesis of the epic *vir* as a woman ("Thrasymennus' Wanton Wedding," 232, n. 33).

10 López de Meṣa, "Etimología de algunos prenombres," 444. This clarification is listed under the proper name Andrés, which stems from the Greek *andros*.

11 "The Emperor is not worshipped directly in his lifetime – that is reserved for after death, but he is worshipped indirectly through his *Genius* and his 'Virtues.' In one sense, the 'Virtues' may be regarded as distinct parts or aspects of the one good spirit, the *Genius*, that resides in the Emperor. The Emperor, then, even in life is brought very near to the divine world. He is ... compared in bold metaphors to the gods and allowed to borrow their attributes" (Mattingly, "The Roman 'Virtues,'" 111).

12 Cicero, *Tusculan Disputations* (II, 18, 43), 194–5, emphasis mine.

13 "The Derridian notion of 'trace' is, by its very nature, difficult to explicate. Jacques Derrida says in *Of Grammatology* that 'Writing is one of the representatives of the trace in general, it is not the trace itself. *The trace itself does not exist.*' In *Positions*, he states that 'each "element" ... [is] constituted on the basis of the trace within it of the other elements of the chain or system.' The French word *la trace* can be translated variously as 'footprint,' 'mark,' 'trail,' or 'clue.' Ajay Heble relates it both to Ferdinand de Saussure's concept of the sign and Sigmund Freud's theory of memory, but attributes the term primarily to Derridian deconstruction: 'it is the name Derrida gives to the absences, the relations of difference, that are involved in the production of the sign.' Heble's preferred analogy for the trace is that of a footprint, which 'serves as a physical reminder of something which is no longer there: as a trace it mediates between presence and absence, between that which remains and that which is no longer present'" (Kallendorf, *Conscience on Stage*, 39; I cite Derrida, *Of Grammatology*, 167; Derrida, *Positions*, 26; and Heble, "Trace," 647).

14 Alarcón, *Ganar amigos*, Acto 2.

15 Lope de Vega, *La mayor victoria de Alemania de Don Gonzalo de Córdoba*, Jornada 3. In these lines, Pompeyo speaks to Holy Roman Emperor Otto the Great, who in this play invades Florence. The "pensamiento afeminado" in question is Otto's desire for Pompeyo's daughter Casandra.

16 Lope de Vega, *Pobreza no es vileza*, Acto 3.

17 Calderón de la Barca, *Dicha y desdicha del nombre*, Jornada 2.

18 Lope de Vega, *El Amor enamorado*, preliminares to 1637 edition.

19 Once again in Portia we find an ambiguous figure who became synonymous with Virtue in the Renaissance, whether or not she actually merited this distinction. Juan Luis Vives holds her up for Spanish women as a model, but modern commentators are left guessing as to why: "Portia (or Porcia) was the daughter of Marcus Porcius Cato [95–46 BCE]. In 45, she married Brutus, who headed the assassination of Julius Caesar in 44. In the Renaissance, she had become the type of marital love, loyalty, and chastity. Perhaps 'the wisdom' Vives refers to ... which Portia has gathered from her father, is his love of and dedication to republican values, the same values her husband was also believed to have espoused. Her status as a virtuous woman in the Renaissance is somewhat complicated by her suicide, with accounts holding both that she killed herself after and before Brutus's death" (commentary on Vives, *The Instruction of a Christian Woman*, 102, n. 8).

20 Tirso de Molina, *La prudencia en la mujer*, Jornada 3.

21 Lope de Vega, *El sembrar en buena tierra*, Acto 1.

22 Lope de Vega, *El cardenal de Belén*, Acto 3.

23 Lope de Vega, *El bobo del colegio*, Acto 1.

24 Lope de Vega, *La locura por la honra*, Acto 1.

25 Jordan, *Renaissance Feminism*, 8.

26 Lope de Vega, *El ejemplo de casadas y prueba de la paciencia*, Acto 3.

27 Lope de Vega, *La mal casada*, Acto 1.

28 Lope de Vega, *El ejemplo de casadas y prueba de la paciencia*, Acto 3.

29 Lope de Vega, *El mejor mozo de España*, Acto 1.

30 Lope de Vega, *Con su pan se lo coma*, Acto 1.

31 Muir, "'La aoroent lor vertuz,'" 266. For a fuller account of the goddess Virtus as she was celebrated by both the ancient Greeks and Romans, see Hild, "Virtus."

32 "Domitian on his senatorial coinage ... has a prominent place for the goddess, Virtus" (Mattingly, "The Roman 'Virtues,'" 111–12). In his book on Roman coinage, Mattingly explains her iconography: "A second type that will meet us year by year is that of Virtus, the spirit of martial valour, the symbol of that forward military policy, which ruled Domitian from A. D. 83 to almost the close of his reign. Virtus is here, as usually, a goddess, but represented in Amazon attire ... Her characteristic attribute is the short sword, worn at the belt, the *parazonium* – the weapon of hand to hand combat. Virtus has her seat beside the throne of Jupiter, whose missions she executes ... Virtus Augusti is a special aspect of the goddess, the martial spirit that inspires the Emperor's own achievements" (Mattingly, *Coins of the Roman Empire*, xci).

33 Lope de Vega, *De cosario a cosario*, preliminares to 1624 edition.
34 Brownlee, *The Severed Word*, 9–10.
35 Capra, *Della eccellenza e dignità delle donne*, 106.
36 Capra, *Della eccellenza e dignità delle donne*, 107.
37 On the *comedias de santas* as a recognizable subgenre, see Vincent-Cassy, "Casilda, Orosia, Margarita, Juana y la Ninfa."
38 Jordan, *Renaissance Feminism*, 18–19.
39 Rhodes, *Dressed to Kill*, 28.
40 Matos Fragoso, *El hijo de la piedra*, Jornada 3.
41 Lope de Vega, *Los torneos de Aragón*, Acto 1.
42 Lope de Vega, *Si no vieran las mujeres*, Jornada 3.
43 Salomon, "Virtudes económicas y bienes del villano," 222.
44 Lope de Vega, *El perseguido*, Jornada 3.
45 Alarcón, *El dueño de las estrellas*, Acto 1.
46 Calderón de la Barca, *El alcalde de Zalamea*, Jornada 2.
47 Covarrubias Orozco, *Tesoro de la lengua castellana o española*, 697.
48 A recent reassessment of Islamic intellectual impulses for Spain's Renaissance may be found in Doubleday, *The Wise King*.
49 Tirso de Molina, *La mejor espigadera*, Jornada 3.
50 Matos Fragoso, *El hijo de la piedra*, Acto 1.
51 Calderón de la Barca, *La humildad coronada de las plantas*, auto sacramental.
52 Lope de Vega, *El perseguido*, Jornada 3.
53 Matos Fragoso, *El hijo de la piedra*, Jornada 2.
54 Matos Fragoso, *El hijo de la piedra*, Jornada 3.
55 Matos Fragoso, *El hijo de la piedra*, Jornada 2.
56 Lope de Vega, *El caballero de Illescas*, Acto 2.
57 Calderón de la Barca, *El Rey Don Pedro en Madrid*, Jornada 2.
58 Lope de Vega, *El premio del bien hablar*, Acto 2.
59 "la virtud, que es blasón de la nobleza" (Lope de Vega, *El ausente en el lugar*, Acto 1).
60 Lope de Vega, *Los amantes sin amor*, preliminares to 1618 edition.
61 Calderón de la Barca, *El alcalde de Zalamea*, preliminares to 1683 edition.
62 Cascardi, "Civil Society, Virtue, and the Pursuit of Happiness," 219.
63 Anita K. Stoll, "Politics, Patronage, and Lope's *La noche de San Juan*," *Bulletin of the Comediantes* 39 (1987): 131.
64 Lope de Vega, *El alcalde mayor*, Acto 1.
65 Moreto, *El Cristo de los milagros*, Jornada 3.
66 Lope de Vega, *Peribáñez y el Comendador de Ocaña*, Acto 3.
67 Lope de Vega, *El cardenal de Belén*, Acto 2.
68 Moreto, *La confusión de un jardín*, Jornada 1.

69 "la nobleza, de quien tanta virtud tuvo principio" (Lope de Vega, *La hermosura aborrecida*, Acto 1).
70 Lope de Vega, *El postrer godo de España*, Acto 1. Another character remarks later in the play, "Bravas virtudes son éstas" (Acto 2).
71 On the myth of La Cava and her connection in the popular imagination to Helen of Troy, see Grieve, "Spain's Second Helen," in *The Eve of Spain*, 180–5.
72 Pérez de Montalbán, *Los amantes de Teruel*, Jornada 1.
73 "Quien hereda el valor, y la prudencia con la nobleza, y sangre" (Tirso de Molina, *Averígüelo Vargas*, Jornada 1).
74 Lope de Vega, *Virtud, pobreza y mujer*, Acto 1.
75 For a real-life corollary to this questionable decision by a literary character, see the case of Joana Baptista, resident of the port city of Belém do Pará in northeastern Brazil, who sold herself to the Catalan Pedro da Costa around the year 1780 (Ferreira Furtado, "Lives on the Seas," 273).
76 Lope de Vega, *El ejemplo de casadas y prueba de la paciencia*, Acto 3.
77 Lope de Vega, *El blasón de los Chaves de Villalba*, Acto 2.
78 Lope de Vega, *Contra valor no hay desdicha*, Acto 3.
79 Diamante, *Amor es sangre, y no puede engañarse*, Jornada 1.
80 Lope de Vega, *Las bizarrías de Belisa*, preliminares to 1637 edition.
81 Lope de Vega, *El ejemplo de casadas y prueba de la paciencia*, Acto 3.
82 Lope de Vega, *Las mudanzas de Fortuna, y sucesos de Don Beltrán de Aragón*, Acto 1.
83 Lope de Vega, *Lo que hay que fiar del mundo*, Acto 1.
84 "La nobleza verdadera consiste en la virtud sola" (Lope de Vega, *El hidalgo Abencerraje*, Acto 1).
85 Guillén de Castro, *Don Quijote de la Mancha*, Jornada 1.
86 Lope de Vega, *La fortuna merecida*, Acto 2.
87 Pérez de Montalbán, *A lo hecho no hay remedio, y príncipe de los montes*, Jornada 1. *Ejecutorias* could be bought for the right price. Such may have been the case for the family of so illustrious a personage as Saint Teresa of Ávila. On these speculations, see Bilinkoff, *The Avila of Saint Teresa*, 109–10.
88 "La verdadera nobleza, más Real que más altiva, en la virtud propia estriba, que no en la naturaleza" (Lope de Vega, *El primer Fajardo*, Acto 1).
89 Lope de Vega, *La corona merecida*, Acto 3.
90 Mayoralgo y Lodo, *Génesis y evolución histórica del apellido en España*, 29.
91 "Many of Spain's most famous playwrights during the early modern period ... are known to have been educated as young boys in Jesuit *colegios*" (Kallendorf, *Conscience on Stage*, 23–4; for specifics see the section "Mainstream Dramatists Educated by Jesuits," 22–7).

92 Matos Fragoso, *El hijo de la piedra*, Jornada 2.
93 Tirso de Molina, *Esto sí que es negociar*, Jornada 3.
94 Tirso de Molina, *La elección por la virtud*, Jornada 3.
95 Tirso de Molina, *La elección por la virtud*, Jornada 3.
96 On the currency of Italian humanists' ideas in Spain, see Coroleu, "Italian Humanism and the Spanish Vernacular."
97 Trinkaus, *Adversity's Noblemen*, 48. Note 30 on that page explains that he used an edition wrongly attributed to Leonardo Bruni: *Leonardi Aretini opusculum ... de nobilitate* (s.l.a., but the British Museum Catalogue lists it as Milan, 1480). The note further explains that about half of the known editions of this work are attributed to Buonaccorso, to whom Hans Baron also felt it belongs. An English translation of Buonaccorso da Montemagno's *Controversia de nobilitate* (1428) may be found in *Knowledge, Goodness, and Power*, 24–52. For analysis of this text, see Vanderjagt, "Between Court Literature and Civic Rhetoric."
98 Summary by Trinkhaus, *Adversity's Noblemen*, 49.
99 Bracciolini, *De nobilitate* (ca. 1440) in *Opera omnia* (Basel, 1538). Summarized in Trinkhaus, *Adversity's Noblemen*, 55. This treatise has been translated to English in *Knowledge, Goodness, and Power*, 53–89.
100 Francesco Filelfo, *De Morali Disciplina Libri Quinque* (Venice, 1552), 55. Summarized in Trinkhaus, *Adversity's Noblemen*, 99.
101 On this treatise see Egido, "La *Nobleza virtuosa* de la Condesa de Aranda, doña Luisa de Padilla, amiga de Gracián."
102 On legal challenges to aristocratic privilege during this time period, see Hiltpold, "Noble Status and Urban Privilege: Burgos, 1572."
103 These four Virtues form the core of the analysis presented in Pérez Martínez, *El* Quijote *y su idea de virtud*.
104 Cervantes, *Don Quijote*, II, 42, p. 358.
105 Cascardi, "Politics Brought Down to Earth," in *Cervantes, Literature, and the Discourse of Politics*, 141–2.
106 This was the traditional view expounded by José Antonio Maravall in *Teatro y literatura en la sociedad barroca*. This approach has been much criticized in recent years by myself and others, most harshly in Laura Bass's edited special issue of *Bulletin of the Comediantes* 65.1 (2013), which offers a reassessment of his legacy. See in particular Ruth MacKay, "The Maravall Problem."
107 "It is unusual – but not altogether impossible – to find novelistic, autonomous, or even subversive elements in the *comedias*" (Kallendorf, *Sins of the Fathers*, 207).
108 Salomon, "Virtudes económicas y bienes del villano," 229.

109 "Alexander Parker once noted that all the great Spanish dramatists were good theologians. Many of them were also ordained priests. Spain's most famous dramatist, Lope de Vega (1562–1635), was ordained a priest in 1614 ... His contemporary Mira de Amescua (1574?–1644) was a priest who took his vows even more seriously towards the end of his life ... Tirso de Molina (1584?–1648) ... was a *fraile mercedario* (Mercedarian friar) ... One relatively late example of a priest / dramatist was Agustín Moreto (1618–69). The most important dramatist of his generation, Calderón de la Barca (1600–81), studied canon law and theology at Alcalá and Salamanca before becoming a priest in 1651" (Kallendorf, *Conscience on Stage*, 23).

110 Lope de Vega resented his lack of noble status. On his conflicted attitude toward the court, Melveena McKendrick offers the following nuanced analysis: "Where the royal court was concerned, Lope, like the majority of Spaniards, was as deeply ambivalent as he was about Spain's monarchs. In the case of the court, however, the respect and awe inspired by the institution of monarchy ... did not operate and Lope reserved for it his bitterest and most outspoken complaints. The capital and the court – the use of the one word *corte* for both indicates how exact was the identification of one with the other – was the focus of so many ambitions and desires and possessed therefore such irresistible charisma that the reality fell far short of the illusion. One of the reasons for Lope's bitterness about the court was his dependence upon it. His view of it as a nest of corruption, injustice, treachery, hypocrisy, self-interest and deceit ... was the understandable conviction of all those who felt neglected and under-rewarded" (McKendrick, *Playing the King*, 211).

Conclusion

1 *Measure for Measure*, III.i.136–8.
2 Lope de Vega, *El cardenal de Belén*, Acto 1.
3 Lope de Vega, *El cardenal de Belén*, Acto 3.
4 Lope de Vega, *Los prados de León*, Acto 1.
5 Lope de Vega, *Virtud, pobreza y mujer*, Acto 2.
6 Lope de Vega, *El hombre por su palabra*, Acto 3.
7 Matos Fragoso, *El hijo de la piedra*, Acto 1.
8 Diamante, *El negro más prodigioso*, Jornada 3.
9 "Bien es que a un rostro tan grave, las virtudes que decís honestamente acompañen" (Lope de Vega, *El mayor imposible*, Jornada 1).
10 Calderón de la Barca, *Fortunas de Andrómeda y Perseo*, Jornada 3.

11 Calderón de la Barca, *El mágico prodigioso,* Jornada 2; Jornada 3.
12 Moreto, *Santa Rosa del Perú,* Jornada 3. On *beatas* charged with faking visions, see Imirizaldu, *Monjas y beatas embaucadoras.* These charges were levelled against men as well, as in the accusation "que este nuestro hermano, aunque finge santidad, tiene más que caridad, deshonesto amor liviano" (Lope de Vega, *Juan de Dios y Antón Martín,* Acto 3).
13 Alarcón, *El Anticristo,* Acto 1.
14 Lope de Vega, *La inocente Laura,* preliminares of 1621 edition.
15 Tirso de Molina, *Santo y sastre,* Acto 2.
16 Lope de Vega, *Los Ponces de Barcelona,* Acto 3.
17 "de cobardes ser hipócritas, pues vemos, que con capa de virtud, muchos encubren su miedo" (Diamante, *El jubileo de Porciúncula,* Jornada 1).
18 Both of these texts are presented by Enrique Suárez-Figaredo in a modern edition in *Lemir* 15 (2011): 69–166.
19 Tirso de Molina, *Marta la piadosa,* Acto 2.
20 Lope de Vega, *Ello dirá,* Acto 2.
21 Tirso de Molina, *Santo y sastre,* Acto 1. In the same play we find a similar charge lodged against him: "en acciones contrarias cuando virtudes predica, vicios contrarios le infaman" (Acto 1).
22 Lope de Vega, *Los embustes de Zelauro,* Acto 2.
23 Lope de Vega, *El piadoso aragonés,* Acto 1.
24 Available in a modern edition in Thomas More, *Utopia, with Erasmus's* The Sileni of Alcibiades, 169–91.
25 Rabelais, "The Author's Prologue" to *Gargantua,* 3.
26 Calderón de la Barca, *El gran mercado del mundo,* loa for auto sacramental.
27 "debajo de cuyo Velo, Divina Virtud, incluye oculta Salud, haciendo en exteriores señales, interiores los efectos" (Calderón de la Barca, *No hay instante sin milagro,* auto sacramental).
28 Calderón de la Barca, *Los hijos de la Fortuna Teágenes y Cariclea,* Acto 1.
29 Calderón de la Barca, *Las tres justicias en una,* Jornada 1.
30 Zamora, *El lucero de Madrid y divino labrador San Isidro,* Acto 1.
31 "ha de tener mi verdad por mentira, y mi virtud por vicio" (Cervantes, *El vizcaíno fingido,* Acto 1).
32 Moreto, *Primero es la honra,* Jornada 1.
33 Calderón de la Barca, *El año santo de Roma,* auto sacramental.
34 Pérez de Montalbán, *El valiente Nazareno,* Jornada 3.
35 Alarcón, *Los empeños de un engaño,* Acto 2. These words are spoken by Don Juan.
36 Calderón de la Barca, *El escondido y la tapada,* Jornada 3.

37 "The original Latin terms used by the casuists to discuss the circumstances of sin were *qui* (who), *quid* (what), *ubi* (where), *per que* (why), *quoties* (how much), and *quomodo* (how)... These lists of questions regarding *circumstance* – literally, 'what is standing around' – ultimately derive from Aristotle's *Nicomachean Ethics*" (Kallendorf, *Conscience on Stage*, 10).
38 "hurtar para hacer bien, no es virtud, vicio sí" (Calderón de la Barca, *La estatua de Prometeo*, Jornada 3).
39 Calderón de la Barca, *Las tres justicias en una*, Jornada 1.
40 Lope de Vega, *La serrana de Tormes*, Acto 2.
41 Diamante, *Santa Teresa de Jesús*, Jornada 2.
42 Pérez de Montalbán, *Los amantes de Teruel*, Jornada 3.
43 Lope de Vega, *El Amor enamorado*, preliminares to 1637 edition.
44 Calderón de la Barca, *El pastor fido*, auto sacramental.
45 Lope de Vega, *La noche de San Juan*, Acto 2.
46 Lope de Vega, *La bella malmaridada*, Jornada 1.
47 Lope de Vega, *El Perseo*, Acto 2.
48 Calderón de la Barca, *El mayor monstruo del mundo*, Acto 1.
49 Calderón de la Barca, *Lo que va del hombre a Dios*, auto sacramental.
50 Calderón de la Barca, *El árbol del mejor fruto*, auto sacramental.
51 Calderón de la Barca, *La hija del aire, primera parte*, Jornada 3.
52 Diamante, *Santa Teresa de Jesús*, Jornada 2.
53 Calderón de la Barca, *El Joseph de las mujeres*, Jornada 3.
54 Lope de Vega, *Roma abrasada*, Acto 2.
55 Lope de Vega, *La historia de Tobías*, Acto 1.
56 Recent interesting work on conversion narratives has been done by Ruth Fine in "A vueltas con el parlamento de Ricote (*Quijote* II, 54)."
57 "y desde hoy ordena, (si en pecados la imite) en virtud ser Magdalena" (Tirso de Molina, *La Dama del Olivar*, Acto 3).
58 On the context of free will versus determinism as this debate was understood in the drama of Renaissance Spain and earlier periods, see Insúa Ruiz, "Edipo y Segismundo."
59 Lope de Vega, *El castigo sin venganza*, Acto 3.
60 Lope de Vega, *La niña de plata*, Acto 3; Tirso de Molina, *Tanto es lo demás como lo de menos*, Acto 3.
61 Calderón de la Barca, *Las armas de la hermosura*, Jornada 3.
62 Calderón de la Barca, *El maestro de danzar*, Jornada 3.
63 Milton, *Aeropagitica*, 728.
64 Calderón de la Barca, *El médico de su honra*, Acto 1.
65 Calderón de la Barca, *El monstruo de los jardines*, Jornada 3.
66 Calderón de la Barca, *La cena de Baltasar*, auto sacramental.

67 Calderón de la Barca, *No hay cosa como callar*, Jornada 3.
68 "el lícito deseo. El del alma es virtud, pero delito el material" (Tirso de Molina, *La santa Juana*, Acto 1).
69 "Honor aquí, ya es delito, virtud aquí, ya es infamia" (Tirso de Molina, *La mujer que manda en casa*, Acto 3).
70 "El reconocimiento, aunque es virtud, se vicia, cuando afectado muestra" (Calderón de la Barca, *¿Quién hallará mujer fuerte?* auto sacramental).
71 Guillén de Castro, *El vicio en los extremos*, Jornada 3.
72 Lope de Vega, *Amor secreto hasta celos*, Acto 2.
73 Virgil, *Georgics*, 1.505, p. xxv.
74 Wolfgang Saxon, "Bernard Knox, 95, Classics Scholar, Dies."
75 Camões, Rima 118, "Super Flumina," whose first line reads "Sôbolos rios que vão" (1595), p. 121, lines 34–5. Cited in Cruickshank, *Don Pedro Calderón*, 365, note 30.
76 Calderón de la Barca, *El Laurel de Apolo*, Jornada 2.
77 De Brosse (a pseudonym), *Les Innocents coupables* (1645), ed. Pierre Pasquier (Strasbourg: Théâtre National [collection du répertoire] / Cicero Editeurs, 1992).
78 Le Métel de Boisrobert, *Les Apparences trompeuses*.
79 Cruickshank, *Don Pedro Calderón*, 118.
80 Mena, *Laberinto de Fortuna* (1444), 149, emphasis mine.
81 Mena, *Laberinto de Fortuna*, stanza XCIII, lines 737–44, p. 147, emphasis mine.
82 Calderón de la Barca, *La devoción de la Cruz*, Acto 1. These lines are spoken by Julia.
83 Machiavelli, *Discursos sobre la primera década de Tito Livio*, Book II, ch. 2, pp. 198–9. This was the translation, first published in 1552, that circulated in Golden Age Spain.
84 Machiavelli, *The Prince*, trans. Adams, ch. 15, p. 45.
85 Forte Monje, "Pedro Ribadeneyra," 176.
86 Machiavelli, *The Prince*, trans. Adams, ch. 16, p. 45, emphasis mine.
87 Machiavelli, *The Prince*, trans. Adams, ch. 17, p. 47.
88 Machiavelli, *The Discourses*, Part 2, ch. 14, p. 312.
89 "He started out as a weak monarch, but through fame and glory has become the foremost king of Christendom" (Machiavelli, *The Prince*, trans. Peter Constantine, 102–3).
90 Cascardi, *Cervantes, Literature, and the Discourse of Politics*, 17.
91 Forte Monje and López Álvarez, eds, *Maquiavelo y España*, 28.
92 This book, a second edition, is a translation of Machiavelli's *Discorsi sopra la prima deca di Tito Livio*.

93 "En el siglo XVII, al estar prohibida la difusión de la obra de Maquiavelo, lógicamente sólo se dispone de versiones manuscritas" (Capelli, "Panorama [ideológico]," 210. Two of these manuscripts may be found at the Biblioteca Nacional in Madrid: BNM MS 1017, the anonymous "El Prinçipe y el estado de las cossas de Françia y Alemania ..." and BNM MS 1084, another anonymous codex containing a Spanish translation of *The Prince* (ff. 1–90). Another manuscript, BNM ms. 902, contains Juan Vélez de León's "Diuersos tratados Políticos pertenecientes a los Goviernos Monarquico, Aristocratico y Democratico Utiles a Principes, Consejeros, Senadores y Generales de Exercitos," which also contained a version of *The Prince* (Capelli, "Panorama [ideológico]," 210–11).

94 Puigdomenech, "Maquiavelo y maquiavelismo en España," 49. She reiterates, "Maquiavelo era bien conocido por eclesiásticos, políticos, intelectuales, militares y nobles, como acreditan las bibliotecas de muchos de ellos" (49). She further claims that "los grandes personajes de nuestra historia ... conocían bien a Maquiavelo y en muchos casos le seguían" (59).

95 Saavedra Fajardo, *Empresas políticas*, LXI, p. 101.

96 Saavedra Fajardo, *Empresas políticas*, XVIII, p. 335, emphasis mine.

97 Saavedra Fajardo, *Empresas políticas*, XXVI, p. 401.

98 Alvia de Castro, *Verdadera razon de Estado*, V, p. 22, emphasis mine.

99 Pedro Ribadeneyra, *Tratado de la Religion y Virtudes que deue tener el Principe Christiano para gouernar y conseruar sus Estados: contra lo que Nicolas Machiauelo y los Politicos deste tiempo enseñan* (Madrid: P. Madrigal, 1595), cited in Forte Monje, "Pedro Ribadeneyra y las encrucijadas del antimaquiavelismo en España," 171.

100 Robbins, *Arts of Perception*.

101 Sepúlveda, *Demócrates primero*, 283–4, emphasis mine.

102 Maravall, "Sobre Maquiavelo y el Estado moderno," 336. Maravall cites Juan Ginés de Sepúlveda, *De Regno et regis officio*, I, 7.

103 Sepúlveda, *Demócrates primero*, 274. The relevant passage occurs in Aristotle, *Nicomachean Ethics*, 1106b36.

104 Sepúlveda, *Acerca de la monarquía*, 52, emphasis mine.

105 Castilla Urbano offers a subtle comparison of Sepúlveda's and Machiavelli's distinct approaches to Virtue: "Ya hemos visto que tanto Maquiavelo como Sepúlveda aceptan que la gloria se alcanza por aquellos que poseen la virtud. Pero en torno a este concepto parecen darse las mayores diferencias entre ambos. La *virtù* maquiavélica posee un sentido que enlaza con la antigüedad y la aleja del cristianismo; es un conjunto de habilidad, valor, fuerza, poder, determinación y eficacia

para el florentino, mientras que en Sepúlveda ya hemos visto que, sin ser del todo ajena a estas características, no se aparta del cristianismo. Con ser decisiva esta última diferencia, la virtud maquiavélica permite hacer frente a los vaivenes de la Fortuna, mientras que la manejada por Sepúlveda sirve para desenvolverse en el mundo, lo que convierte a ambas en instrumentos para la gloria y el éxito. Tal vez por ello, se hace imprescindible mostrar cómo, a pesar de su distinta consideración del cristianismo, uno y otro alcanzan a diseñar una concepción de la virtud que dista de ser tan opuesta como sus respectivos puntos de partida hacían presagiar" ("Rasgos maquiavélicos," 128).

106 Ghia, "Las piruetas de Quevedo," 75.

107 Ghia, "Las piruetas de Quevedo," 76.

108 Ghia, "Las piruetas de Quevedo," 98.

109 He states unequivocally, "Baltasar Gracián se apropia, sin ninguna duda, de estas problemáticas maquiavelianas para hacer de ellas uno de los núcleos teóricos de su obra" (Ansaldi, "Maquiavelo y Baltasar Gracián," 102). Jeremy Robbins would seem to agree with this assessment: "For Gracián prudence operates in a world of moral relativity, and its evaluative touchstone is not so much a Christian, absolute sense of right or wrong, but rather the notion of self-interest ... In the *Oráculo*, Gracián comes closer than any other Spaniard to endorsing the amoral pragmatism felt to be synonymous with Machiavelli" (*Arts of Perception*, 131, 149).

110 Gracián, *Oráculo manual*, Aforismo 300, p. 230, emphasis mine.

111 Wehner, "The Theology of Donald Trump."

112 Furió Ceriol, "El Consejo y Consejeros del Príncipe," 86.

113 Diego de Salazar, *Tratado de Re Militari*, ed. E. Botella Ordinas (Madrid: Ministerio de Defensa, 2000).

114 Cascardi, *Cervantes, Literature, and the Discourse of Politics*, 15.

115 Rupp, *Allegories of Kingship*, 173–4, emphasis mine.

116 For a well-nuanced assessment of possible Machiavellianism in Lope de Vega, see Herrera Montero, "*Fuenteovejuna* de Lope de Vega y el maquiavelismo." He ultimately concludes that while this drama by Lope is apparently anti-Machiavellian in content, it may be covertly Machiavellian in terms of intention. Forcione draws similar conclusions in *Majesty and Humanity* regarding a different play by Lope de Vega: "*El villano en su rincón* can be said to incorporate Machiavellian insights – for example, 'salutary cruelty' and dissimulation – into political experience and to dramatize their proper separation, as benign methods of governance, from the abuses that were so spectacularly displayed in the

attacks, literary or direct, on Machiavelli and his 'satanic' politics during the age" (*Majesty and Humanity*, 66).

117 Erasmus, *Enquiridion*, 373, emphasis mine. The basis for this edition is a sixteenth-century printed book held at the Biblioteca Nacional de Madrid, R/5079.

118 Erasmus, *Enquiridion*, 165, emphasis mine.

119 Erasmus, *Enquiridion*, 372, emphasis mine.

120 Erasmus, *Enquiridion*, 165–6, italics in original, boldface emphasis mine.

121 Erasmus, *Enquiridion*, 166.

122 Erasmus, *Enquiridion*, 361.

123 Erasmus, *Enquiridion*, 362, italics in original.

124 Erasmus, *Enquiridion*, 400, emphasis mine.

125 Erasmus, *Enquiridion*, 169, emphasis mine.

126 Erasmus, *Enquiridion*, 382.

127 Taylor and Coroleu, *Humanism and Christian Letters*, 3. They cite *Opus Epistolarum Des. Erasmi Roterodami*, ed. Percy S. Allen et al. (Oxford: Oxford University Press, 1906–58), epistle 1904.

128 Coroleu, "Italian Humanism and the Spanish Vernacular," 101.

129 Taylor and Coroleu, *Humanism and Christian Letters*, 3.

130 Coroleu, "Italian Humanism and the Spanish Vernacular," 109.

131 Bataillon, *Erasmo y España*, 165. Bataillon's afterthoughts on this topic were collected about a decade later into a further volume, *Erasmo y el erasmismo*, which may be seen as a supplement to his larger work.

132 Bataillon, *Erasmo y España*, 191. Bataillon reiterates his characterization of "este libro ... en el cual millares de españoles encontraban ahora respuesta a sus más profundas inquietudes" (204).

133 Bataillon, *Erasmo y España*, Lámina VII, between pp. 192 and 193 shows the Inquisitor General's coat of arms still being published in the 1529 edition by the printer Miguel de Eguía.

134 "los impresores lanzan al mercado miles de ejemplares de esta obra sin alcanzar a saciar al público" (Bataillon, *Erasmo y España*, 218).

135 Bataillon says in reference to the *Enchiridion*, "El iluminismo español, al adoptarlo como libro de cabecera, deja de ser un movimiento puramente local" (Bataillon, *Erasmo y España*, 209). He further explains the effect humanism had of elevating the status of the *alumbrados*: "El humanismo da al fervor de los alumbrados un vigor y una libertad nuevos; los pone al mismo nivel de todo el vasto movimiento europeo" (Bataillon, *Erasmo y España*, 211).

136 Bataillon, *Erasmo y España*, 212–13.

137 Bataillon, *Erasmo y España*, 213, n. 15.

138 Bataillon, *Erasmo y España*, 212.
139 On the possible relationship between Erasmianism and the Jesuits, see Bataillon, "De Erasmo a la Compañía de Jesús: Protesta e integración en la Reforma católica del siglo XVI," in *Erasmo y el erasmismo*, 203–44.
140 Bataillon, *Erasmo y España*, 217.
141 Bataillon, *Erasmo y España*, 217.
142 Bataillon, *Erasmo y España*, 217.
143 For discussion of this celebrated phrase, see Bataillon, *Erasmo y España*, 300.
144 Bataillon, *Erasmo y España*, 219.
145 Bataillon, *Erasmo y España*, 223.
146 Bataillon, *Erasmo y España*, 223.
147 Bataillon, *Erasmo y España*, 225.
148 Bataillon, *Erasmo y España*, 237.
149 "En la corte del Emperador, en las ciudades, en las iglesias, en los conventos, aun en las posadas y caminos, todo el mundo tiene el *Enchiridion* de Erasmo en español. Hasta entonces lo leía en latín una minoría de latinistas, y aun éstos no lo entendían por completo. Ahora lo leen en español personas de toda especie, y los que nunca antes habían oído hablar de Erasmo, han sabido ahora de su existencia por este simple libro" (Bataillon, *Erasmo y España*, 280). Bataillon cites a letter, now lost, written by the translator to Erasmus. The letter has been reconstructed from an extract or *pseudógrafo* which was preserved.
150 Bataillon, *Erasmo y España*, 242. The ambassador was otherwise known as Johann Flaxbinder de Dantzig. Bataillon cites as his source for this quote the *Acta Tomiciana*, 12 vols (Poznan: 1855–1906), 9:217. The first reference to this source appears in Bataillon, *Erasmo y España*, 229, n. 10.
151 Bataillon, *Erasmo y España*, 485, n. 5, n. 7. Bataillon cites A.H.N., *Inquisición de Valencia*, leg. 531, n. 38, fol. 6r–v, and gives relevant extracts from the proceedings. In response to these accusations, Mezquita declares: "Yo le dixe [al fraile] que por cierto yo era tan buen christiano como él y que yo no sabía que el dicho libro fuese malo ni reprouado ... y senyaladamente le dixe que sobrese libro se avía fecho ayuntamiento en Valladolid por mandado del Rmo. Cardenal Inquisidor Mayor de muchos letrados, excelentes varones, que no le avían condepnado al libro ni al Erasmo por erético ni reprouaron sus obras ... Otrosy digo que el dicho libro Inquiridion y los Coloquios que los e visto tener y leer a muchas personas y creo que yo los tengo, aunque es verdat que creo a más de dos años que yo no e leydo en ninguno dellos ... y digo que sé que en Zaragoza los leen

en el estudio [él tiene cuatro hijos en esta Universidad] ... y pareciéndome bien las obras que an llegado suyas a mi noticia, que an seydo el dicho Inquiridion y Coloquios y creo el Pater Noster traduzido ... los e tenido por buenos y me pesava que fuese erege ni por tal tenido, y esta voluntad fue porque vi una letra traduzida que dezían las escriuió al Emperador y Rey nuestro Señor en que dezía que peleava por Jesu Cristo y que tenía muy al baxo las eregías de Lutero" (A.H.N., *Inquisición de Valencia*, leg. 531, n. 38, fol. 6r–v, cited in Bataillon, *Erasmo y España*, 485, n. 7).

152 Bataillon, *Erasmo y España*, 715.

153 Bataillon, *Erasmo y España*, 718.

154 "6 *Enquiridiones* de Erasmo en romance" (Bataillon, *Erasmo y España*, 811).

155 Bataillon, *Erasmo y España*, 811.

156 Bataillon, *Erasmo y España*, 314.

157 See primarily Forcione, *Cervantes and the Humanist Vision*.

158 An important exception is Jonathan Thacker, "Lope de Vega, *El cuerdo loco*, and 'la más discreta figura de la comedia,'" which focuses on Erasmus's *Praise of Folly*.

159 I have explored some of this material in Kallendorf, "An Erasmian View of *Lazarillo*'s Fifth *Tratado*," in *Exorcism and Its Texts*, 68–74. See also O'Reilly, "The Erasmianism of *Lazarillo de Tormes*," in *Essays in Honour of Robert Brian Tate from His Colleagues and Pupils*; and Hanrahan, "*Lazarillo de Tormes*." The anonymous *Lazarillo* was first published in 1554.

160 Erasmus, *Encomium Moriae*, ch. XXIX, pp. 21–2, emphasis mine. This text was known in Spain, as we see from its presence on the inventory of Christopher Columbus's son Hernando Colón's library from the time period when he was in residence at the Spanish royal court in Valladolid (*Catalogue of the Library of Ferdinand Columbus*; registry numbers 3679, 2466, 2968, 2982, and 2013 correspond to books he owned which were written by Erasmus). Bataillon also finds evidence of the influence of this work by Erasmus on Juan Maldonado's *El buen pastor* (1529), Alfonso de Valdés's *Diálogo de las cosas ocurridas en Roma* (ca. 1529), and the same author's *Diálogo de Mercurio y Carón* (1528–9), as well as the *Coloquios* or *Diálogos* of Pedro Mexía (1547) (Bataillon, *Erasmo y España*, 335, 380, 388, 648–9). Bataillon returned to this topic to give it a more systematic treatment in "Un problema de influencia de Erasmo en España: El *Elogio de la Locura*," in *Erasmo y el erasmismo*, 327–46. The clearest influence of Erasmus's *Praise of Folly* on Golden Age Spanish literature is undoubtedly Cervantes' *Don Quijote* (Part I, 1605 and Part II, 1615); on this connection, see Antonio Vilanova, *Erasmo y Cervantes*.

161 On casuistical debate over ethical dilemmas in the *comedias* as it was spawned by Catholic playwrights raised on Jesuit student dramas from their school days, see Kallendorf, "The Rise of Casuistry in Spain, the Flowering of Jesuit School Drama, and the Jesuit Education of Spanish Playwrights," in *Conscience on Stage*, 3–37.

162 Curtius, *European Literature and the Latin Middle Ages*, 138–44.

163 For representative studies of this topos applied to Renaissance European and Spanish Golden Age theatre, see Thacker, *Role-play and the World as Stage in the* Comedia (2002), as well as Egginton, *How the World Became a Stage* (2003).

Epilogue: Virtual Virtue

1 Childers, "Baroque Quixote," 423.

2 Cervantes, *Don Quijote*, I.47, pp. 566–7.

3 Childers, "Baroque Quixote," 438. Childers purports to offer a close reading of Gracián's text but without very many specific quotations from Gracián himself. An unusual exception is his citation of Gracián's passage on why warriors predominate in litanies of famous heroes from the past: "Llenan el mundo de aplauso, los siglos de fama, los libros de proezas, porque lo belicoso tiene más de plausible que lo pacífico" (Gracián, *El héroe*, 23).

4 Childers, "Baroque Quixote," 438, 442.

5 Childers, "Baroque Quixote," 439, 442.

6 D.C. Earl, *The Moral and Political Tradition of Rome* (Ithaca: Cornell University Press, 1967), 20.

7 McDonnell, *Roman Manliness*, 5.

8 McDonnell, "Roman Men and Greek Virtue," 235.

9 This is not surprising, considering the fact that "[f]ew societies have ever sent a higher proportion of their citizens to war, and warfare was central and basic to republican Roman values and institutions" (McDonnell, *Roman Manliness*, 62).

10 McDonnell, "Roman Men and Greek Virtue," 248–9.

11 McDonnell explains that semantic *calque* "works by expanding the semantic range of an indigenous word by analogy with a foreign word with wider references but some common meaning" (McDonnell, *Roman Manliness*, 77).

12 McDonnell, *Roman Manliness*, 9.

13 McDonnell, *Roman Manliness*, 110–11, emphasis mine.

14 McDonnell, *Roman Manliness*, 116. He bases these comments on Polybius's description of Scipio's generosity as astonishing to the Romans because they never gave any of their property away to anyone if they could help it.
15 McDonnell, *Roman Manliness*, 157.
16 McDonnell, *Roman Manliness*, 154. McDonnell clarifies this striking visual correspondence: "The numismatic link between *virtus* and the image of the mounted warrior, in fact, mirrors an old connection between *virtus* and Roman cavalrymen. From the mid-fourth century, the principal way in which upper-class Romans displayed *virtus* was in mounted combat. In addition, there were close associations between the cult to Honos and Virtus, the *transvectio equitum*, and Temple of Castor, all of which were political-religious ceremonies and institutions which honored the Roman state cavalry. Finally, the first temple to honor deified Virtus was vowed at the battle of Clastidium, the greatest cavalry victory in Roman history, by M. Claudius Marcellus, who during the battle had engaged in single mounted combat with the enemy's king and won the *spolia opima*" (McDonnell, *Roman Manliness*, 152).
17 McDonnell, *Roman Manliness*, 158.
18 McDonnell, *Roman Manliness*, 202–3.
19 McDonnell, *Roman Manliness*, 205.
20 McDonnell, *Roman Manliness*, 212.
21 McDonnell, *Roman Manliness*, 239.
22 McDonnell, *Roman Manliness*, 255.
23 McDonnell, *Roman Manliness*, 254.
24 McDonnell, *Roman Manliness*, 257.
25 "Ita Virtus, quae dat virtutem" (Varro, frag. 189 Cardauns, *apud* Aug. *CD* 4.24; quoted in McDonnell, *Roman Manliness*, 289).
26 *Attic Nights* 1.6.8, Teubner edition by C. Hosius; quoted in McDonnell, *Roman Manliness*, 288.
27 McDonnell, *Roman Manliness*, 280.
28 McDonnell, *Roman Manliness*, 302–3.
29 McDonnell, *Roman Manliness*, 354.
30 McDonnell, *Roman Manliness*, 351.
31 *Cat*. 2.25, cited in McDonnell, *Roman Manliness*, 350.
32 McDonnell, *Roman Manliness*, 349.
33 Tuck, "The Origins of Roman Imperial Hunting Imagery," 241–2.
34 On Lucan's reception in Spain, see Schlayer, *Spuren Lukans in der spanischen Dichtung*.
35 Sklenář, *The Taste for Nothingness*, 2, 14.

36 Sklenář, *The Taste for Nothingness*, 38.
37 Sklenář, *The Taste for Nothingness*, 49, 57.
38 Sklenář, *The Taste for Nothingness*, 101–2, 106–7, 135, 151, emphasis mine.
39 Lucan, *The Civil War*, III.690, p. 164. I cite the Latin from this edition but have preferred my own version of an English translation by Robert Sklenář in *The Taste for Nothingness*, 22. The only difference in our translations is that he translates *virtus* as *manliness* instead of *virtue*.
40 "We possess indeed simulacra of morality" (MacIntyre, *After Virtue*, 2).
41 See, for example, Coleman, "Android Arete," and Gips, "Towards the Ethical Robot."

Bibliography

Acevedo, Pedro Pablo de. *Bellum virtutum et vitiorum*. In *Teatro escolar latino del siglo XVI: la obra de Pedro Pablo de Acevedo S.J.*, edited by V. Picón et al., 2:55–164. Madrid: Ediciones Clásicas, 2006.

Adams, Robert P. *The Better Part of Valor: More, Erasmus, Colet, and Vives, on Humanism, War, and Peace, 1496–1535*. Seattle: University of Washington Press, 1962.

Agamben, Giorgio. *Il Regno e la Gloria: Per'una genealogia teologica dell'economia e del governo* (*Homo sacer*, II, 2). Vicenza: Neri Pozza, 2007.

Ágreda y Vargas, Diego de. *El premio de la virtud y castigo del vicio* (1620). In *Colección de novelas escogidas compuestas por los mejores ingenios españoles*, 5:69–132. Madrid: González, 1788.

Albarracín Teulón, Agustín. *La medicina en el teatro de Lope de Vega*. Madrid: Consejo Superior de Investigaciones Científicas / Instituto Arnaldo de Vilanova, 1954.

Alday Redonnet, T. "Iconografía española publicada en el Siglo XVI sobre plantas medicinales." *Archivo Iberoamericano de Historia de la Medicina y de Antropología médica* 8 (1956): 389–91.

Alemán, Mateo. *Guzmán de Alfarache*. Edited by José María Micó. 2nd ed. 2 vols. Madrid: Cátedra, 1992.

Aler Ibarz, Cristina, Manuel Camps Clemente, and Manuel Camps Surroca. "Las farmacias de Zaragoza según la inspección de 1590." In *Actas del IX Congreso Nacional de Historia de Medicina*, edited by F. Bujosa i Homar, 2:419–26. Zaragoza: Prensas Universitarias de Zaragoza, 1991.

Alonso-Lasheras, Diego. *Luis de Molina's* De Iustitia et Iure*: Justice as Virtue in an Economic Context*. Studies in the History of Christian Traditions 152. Leiden: Brill, 2011.

Álvarez de Araujo y Cuéllar, Ángel. *Las órdenes militares de Santiago, Calatrava, Alcántara y Montesa: su origen, organización y estado actual.* Madrid: Fernando Cao y Domingo de Val, 1891.

Alvia de Castro, Fernando. *Verdadera razon de Estado: discurso politico de don Fernando Aluia de Castro.* Lisbon: Pedro Craesbeeck, 1616.

Anderson, Sherry Ruth. *The Feminine Face of God: The Unfolding of the Sacred in Women.* New York: Random House, 2010.

Andrade, Alonso de. *Libro de la Guía de la Virtud y de la Imitación de Nuestra Señora para todos los estados.* Madrid, 1642.

Andretta, Elisa. "The Medical Cultures of 'the Spaniards of Italy': Scientific Communication, Learned Practices, and Medicine in the Correspondence of Juan Páez de Castro (1545–1552)." In *Medical Cultures of the Early Modern Spanish Empire*, edited by John Slater, María Luz López-Terrada, and José Pardo Tomás, 129–48. Farnham, Surrey: Ashgate, 2014.

Ansaldi, Saverio. "Maquiavelo y Baltasar Gracián: De la soberanía a la gubernamentalidad." In *Maquiavelo y España*, edited by Juan Manuel Forte Monje and Pablo López Álvarez, 99–110.

Anselm of Canterbury. *De Conceptu Virginali.* Translated by Joseph M. Colleran as *Why God Became Man and the Virgin Conception and Original Sin.* Albany: Magi, 1969.

Antoniou, S.A., et al. "The Rod and the Serpent: History's Ultimate Healing Symbol." *World Journal of Surgery* 35.1 (2011): 217–21.

Añorbe y Corregel, Tomás de. *La virtud vence al destino (comedia nueva).* Madrid: Juan Pérez, 1735.

Aquinas, Thomas. *Treatise on the Virtues* [*Summa Theologiae* questions 49–67]. Translated by John A. Oesterle. Notre Dame: University of Notre Dame Press, 1984.

Arellano, Ignacio. "Emblems at the Golden Age Theater." In *A Companion to Early Modern Hispanic Theater*, edited by Hilaire Kallendorf, 267–82. Leiden: Brill, 2013.

– *Historia del teatro español del siglo XVII.* Madrid: Cátedra, 1995.

– "Masculinidades ansiosas en tratadistas ibéricos de conducta áulica (Siglo de Oro)." *Criticón* 123 (2015): 193–212.

Aristotle. *De sensu* and *De Memoria.* Translated by G.R.T. Ross. Cambridge: Cambridge University Press, 1906.

– *Nicomachean Ethics.* Translated by Robert C. Bartlett. Chicago: University of Chicago Press, 2012.

– *Rhetoric.* Translated by W. Rhys Roberts. New York: Modern Library, 1954.

Arjoon, Surendra. "Virtue Theory as a Dynamic Theory of Business." *Journal of Business Ethics* 28.2 (2000): 159–78.

Asenjo, Julio Alonso. La tragedia de San Hermenegildo *y otras obras del teatro español de colegio.* 2 vols. Valencia: Universidad Nacional de Educación a Distancia, Universidad de Sevilla, and Universitat de València, 1995.

Badhwar, Neera K. "The Limited Unity of Virtue." *Nous* (1996): 306–29.

Baines, Barbara J. "Kyd's Silenus Box and the Limits of Perception." *Journal of Medieval and Renaissance Studies* 10.1 (1980): 41–51.

Bataillon, Marcel. *Erasmo y el erasmismo.* Barcelona: Crítica, 1977.

– *Erasmo y España.* Translated by Antonio Alatorre. 2nd ed. Mexico City: Fondo de Cultura Económica, 1966.

Batllori, Miguel. *Humanismo y Renacimiento.* Barcelona: Ariel, 1987.

Bayliss, Robert. "Lope enamorado: Patrimonio cultural y cine postnacional." *Hispania* 98.4 (2015): 707–17.

Bejczy, István. *The Cardinal Virtues in the Middle Ages: A Study in Moral Thought from the Fourth to the Fourteenth Century.* Leiden: Brill, 2011.

Bejczy, István, and Cary Nederman, eds. *Princely Virtues in the Middle Ages, 1200–1500.* Turnhout, Belgium: Brepols, 2007.

Beltrán, Luis. "The Poet, the King and the Cardinal Virtues in Juan de Mena's *Laberinto.*" *Speculum* 46.2 (1971): 318–32.

Benet Mateu, Pedro. *Liber in examen apothecariorum.* Barcelona: Joan Rosembach, 1521.

Berco, Cristian. *From Body to Community: Venereal Disease and Society in Baroque Spain.* Toronto: University of Toronto Press, 2016.

Bernardino de Laredo. *Modus faciendi cum ordine medicandi.* Seville: Jacob Cromberger, 1527.

Berthoff, Warner. *Literature and the Continuances of Virtue.* Princeton: Princeton University Press, 1986.

Bilinkoff, Jodi. *The Avila of Saint Teresa: Religious Reform in a Sixteenth-Century City.* Ithaca: Cornell University Press, 1992.

Bireley, Robert. *The Counter-Reformation Prince: Anti-Machiavellianism or Catholic Statecraft in Early Modern Europe.* Chapel Hill: University of North Carolina Press, 1990.

Bleznick, D.W. "Spanish Reaction to Machiavelli in the Sixteenth and Seventeenth Centuries." *Journal of the History of Ideas* 19.4 (1958): 542–50.

Bonardi, Marie-Odile. *Les Vertus dans la France baroque: représentations iconographiques et littéraires.* Paris: Honoré Champion, 2010.

Borges, Renee. "Gender in Plants: More About Why and How Plants Change Sex." *Resonance: Journal of Science Education* 3.11 (1998): 30–9.

Bornholdt, Claudia. *Saintly Spouses: Chaste Marriage in Sacred and Secular Narrative from Medieval Germany (12th and 13th Centuries).* Medieval and Renaissance Texts and Studies 411. Tempe, AZ: Arizona Center for Medieval and Renaissance Studies, 2012.

Bosley, Richard, Roger A. Shiner, and Janet D. Sisson, , eds. *Aristotle, Virtue and the Mean*. Cambridge: Cambridge University Press, 1995.

Bouvet, Honoré. *Arbre des Batailles* (1387). Paris: Michel Le Noir, 1515.

– *The Tree of Battles*. Translated by G.W. Coopland. Cambridge: Harvard University Press, 1949.

Boyd, Barbara Weiden. "*Virtus Effeminata* and Sallust's Sempronia." *Transactions of the American Philological Association* 117 (1987): 183–201.

Boyle, Margaret E. *Unruly Women: Performance, Penitence, and Punishment in Early Modern Spain*. Toronto: University of Toronto Press, 2014.

Bracciolini, Poggio. *De nobilitate* (ca. 1440). In *Knowledge, Goodness, and Power: The Debate over Nobility among Quattrocento Italian Humanists*, edited by Albert Rabil Jr, 63–89. Binghamton, NY: Medieval & Renaissance Texts & Studies, 1991.

Breton, Nicholas. "The Praise of Vertuous Ladies." In *A Mad World, My Masters, and Other Prose Works*, edited by Ursula Kentish-Wright, 2:173–4. London: Cresset, 1929.

Brewer, Carolyn. "'Good' and 'Bad' Women: The Virgin and the Whore." In *Shamanism, Catholicism and Gender Relations in Colonial Philippines, 1521–1685*, 40–62. Aldershot: Ashgate, 2004.

Brickhouse, Thomas C., and Nicholas D. Smith. "Socrates and the Unity of the Virtues." *Journal of Ethics* 1.4 (1997): 311–24.

Bright, David S., Bradley A. Winn, and Jason Kanov. "Reconsidering Virtue: Differences of Perspective in Virtue Ethics and the Positive Social Sciences." *Journal of Business Ethics* 119.4 (2014): 445–60.

Brown, David Alan, ed. *Virtue and Beauty: Leonardo's* Ginevra de'Benci *and Renaissance Portraits of Women*. Washington, DC, and Princeton: National Gallery of Art / Princeton University Press, 2001.

Brown, Lesley. "What is 'The Mean Relative to Us' in Aristotle's Ethics?" *Phronesis: A Journal for Ancient Philosophy* 42.1 (1997): 77–93.

Brown, Peter. *The Body and Society: Men, Women, and Sexual Renunciation in Early Christianity*. New York: Columbia University Press, 1988.

Brownlee, Marina Scordilis. *The Severed Word: Ovid's* Heroides *and the* Novela Sentimental. Princeton: Princeton University Press, 1990.

Buonaccorso da Montemagno. *Controversia de nobilitate* (1428). In *Knowledge, Goodness, and Power: The Debate over Nobility among Quattrocento Italian Humanists*, edited by Albert Rabil Jr, 32–52. Binghamton, NY: Medieval & Renaissance Texts & Studies, 1991.

Burton, Arthur. "The Quest for the Golden Mean: A Study in Schizophrenia." In *Psychotherapy of the Psychoses*, edited by Arthur Burton, 172–207. New York: Basic Books, 1961.

Burton, David G. "Virtue Triumphant in Cueva's *La libertad de España por Bernardo del Carpio.*" *Bulletin of the Comediantes* 38.2 (1986): 219–29.

Butler, Judith. *Bodies That Matter: On the Discursive Limits of Sex*. New York: Routledge, 1993.

– *Gender Trouble: Feminism and the Subversion of Identity*. New York: Routledge, 1999.

Byrne, Susan. *Ficino in Spain*. Toronto: University of Toronto Press, 2015.

Cabré, Montserrat. "Women or Healers? Household Practices and the Categories of Health Care in Late Medieval Iberia." *Bulletin of the History of Medicine* 82.1 (2008): 18–51.

Calderón de la Barca, Pedro. *La cura, y la enfermedad: auto sacramental*. In *Autos sacramentales, alegoricos y historiales*, edited by Pedro de Pando y Mier, vol. 3, part 6, 196–227. Madrid: Manuel Ruiz de Murga, 1717.

– *Mejor está que estaba*. Barcelona: Francisco Suriá y Burgada, 17– ?

– *El nuevo hospicio de pobres*. Edited by Ignacio Arellano. Autos Sacramentales Completos 6. Kassel / Pamplona: Reichenberger / Universidad de Navarra, 1995.

– *Las órdenes militares, en metáfora de la piadosa Hermandad del Refugio, discurriendo por calles, y templos de Madrid*. Edited by J.M. Ruano de la Haza. Autos sacramentales completos de Calderón 44. Pamplona / Kassel: Universidad de Navarra / Reichenberger, 2005.

– *Peor está que estaba*. In *Primera parte de comedias de Pedro Calderon de la Barca*, edited by Joseph Calderón de la Barca, 222v–46. Madrid: Viuda de Iuan Sanchez, 1640.

– *La Plazuela de Santa Cruz*. In *Pedro Calderón de la Barca, Entremeses, jácaras y mojigangas*, edited by E. Rodríguez and A. Tordera, 161–71. Madrid: Castalia, 1982.

– *Saber del mal y del bien*. Barcelona: Carlos Safera, 1763.

– *Sueños hay que verdad son*. Edited by M. McGaha. Pamplona / Kassel: Universidad de Navarra / Reichenberger, 1997.

– *Las tres justicias en una*. Barcelona: Francisco Surtá, 1771.

– *El veneno y la triaca* (*auto*). Edited by Juan Manuel Escudero. Pamplona / Kassel: Universidad de Navarra / Reichenberger, 2000.

Calderón de la Barca, Pedro, Luis Vélez de Guevara, and Jerónimo Cáncer y Velasco. *Enfermar con el remedio*. Valladolid: Alonso del Riego, ca. 1730.

Callahan, William J. *La Santa y Real Hermandad del Refugio y Piedad de Madrid, 1618–1832*. Madrid: Instituto de Estudios Madrileños-CSIC, 1980.

Camões, Luís de. *Os Lusiadas*. Edited by Frank Pierce. Oxford: Clarendon, 1973.

– Rima 118, "Sôbolos rios que vão" (1595). In *Rimas*, edited by Álvaro J. da Costa Pimpão, 120–30. Coimbra: Coimbra University, 1953.

Campbell, Jodi. *At the First Table: Food and Social Identity in Early Modern Spain*. Lincoln: University of Nebraska Press, 2017.

Campos Marín, Ricardo, and Rafael Huertas García-Alejo. "Los lugares de la locura: reflexiones historiográficas en torno a los manicomios y su papel en la génesis y el desarrollo de la psiquiatría." *ARBOR: Ciencia, Pensamiento y Cultura* 184.731 (2008): 471–80.

Capelli, Guido. "Panorama (ideológico) de traducciones de Maquiavelo en España." In *Maquiavelo y España*, edited by Juan Manuel Forte Monje and Pablo López Álvarez, 209–15.

Capps, Donald. *Deadly Sins and Saving Virtues*. Philadelphia: Fortress, 1987.

Capra (a.k.a. Capella), Galeazzo Flavio. *Della eccellenza e dignità delle donne* (1525). Edited by Maria Luisa Doglio. Rome: Bulzoni, 1988.

Cardaillac, L. "Un aspecto de las relaciones entre moriscos y cristianos: polémica y 'taqiyya.'" In *Actas del Coloquio Internacional sobre Literatura Aljamiada y Morisca*, edited by A. Galmés, 107–22. Madrid: Gredos, 1978.

Carmona García, Juan Ignacio. *Enfermedad y sociedad en los primeros tiempos modernos*. Seville: Universidad de Sevilla, 2005.

Carr, David. "The Cardinal Virtues and Plato's Moral Psychology." *Philosophical Quarterly* 38 (1988): 186–200.

Carr, David, and Jan Steutel, eds. *Virtue Ethics and Moral Education*. London: Routledge, 2005.

Carranza, Alonso. *Discurso contra los malos trajes y adornos lascivos* (1636). Edited by Enrique Suárez-Figaredo, *Lemir* 15 (2011): 69–131.

Cascardi, Anthony J. *Cervantes, Literature, and the Discourse of Politics*. Toronto: University of Toronto Press, 2012.

Castilla Urbano, Francisco. "Rasgos maquiavélicos en un pensador antimaquiavélico: Juan Ginés de Sepúlveda." In *Maquiavelo y España*, edited by Juan Manuel Forte Monje and Pablo López Álvarez, 111–33.

Castillejo, David. *Guía de ochocientas comedias del Siglo de Oro para el uso de actores y lectores*. Madrid: Ars Millenii, 2002.

Castillo de Villasante, Diego del. *Doctrinal de confesores en casos de restitución*. Biblioteca Nacional, Madrid. MSS / 102.

Castro, Américo. "La justicia." In *El Pensamiento de Cervantes*, 191–5. Barcelona: Noguer, 1972.

Castro, Guillén de. *La piedad en la justicia*. Madrid: Francisco Nieto, 1666.

Catalogue of the Library of Ferdinand Columbus. New York: Hispanic Society of America, 1896.

Cervantes, Miguel de. *Don Quijote*. Edited by Luis Andrés Murillo. 2 vols. Madrid: Castalia, 1982–7.

Cessario, Romanus. *The Moral Virtues and Theological Ethics*. Notre Dame: University of Notre Dame, 1991.

Charro Arias, A., and B. Barreiro Troncoso. "Contribución a la historia de la farmacia en Galicia: una visita de botica en 1614." *Boletín de la Sociedad Española de Historia de la Farmacia* 7(28) (1956): 145–83.

Chevalier, M. "Le médecin dans la littérature du Siècle d'Or." In *Le Personnage dans la littérature du Siècle d'Or: statut et function*, edited by Didier Ozanam, 21–37. Paris: Casa de Velázquez, 1984.

Childers, William. "Baroque Quixote: New World Writing and the Collapse of the Heroic Ideal." In *Baroque New Worlds: Representation, Transculturation, Counterconquest*, edited by Lois Parkinson Zamora and Monika Kaup, 415–49. Durham and London: Duke University Press, 2010.

– "Hispanic Casuistry Studies: Room to Grow." *Hispanic Review* 79.2 (2011): 317–26.

Cicero, Marcus Tullius. *De finibus bonorum et malorum*. Translated by H. Rackham. London: Loeb, 1931.

– *De officiis*. Translated by Walter Miller. London: Loeb, 1947.

– *Tusculan Disputations*. Translated by J.E. King. 2nd ed. Loeb Classical Library. Cambridge, MA: Harvard University Press, 1927.

Clavero, Bartolomé. "*Favor Maioratus, Usus Hispaniae*: Moralidad de Linaje entre Castilla y Europa." In *Marriage, Property, and Succession*, edited by Lloyd Bonfield, 215–54. Berlin: Duncker and Humblot, 1992.

Clemente, Claudio. *El maquiavelismo degollado por la cristiana sabiduría de España y de Austria: Discurso cristiano-político a la católica majestad de Felipe IV, rey de las Españas*. Alcalá: Antonio Vázquez, 1637.

Clouse, Michele L. "The Apothecary's Profession: Cooperation and Professionalization." In *Medicine, Government and Public Health in Philip II's Spain: Shared Interests, Competing Authorities*, 111–42. Farnham, Surrey: Ashgate, 2011.

Coimbra Commentators. "Commentary on the 'Nicomachean Ethics': Disputation III, Question 3." Translated by Jill Kraye. In *Cambridge Translations of Renaissance Philosophical Texts*, edited by Jill Kraye, 1:80–7. Cambridge: Cambridge University Press, 1997.

Coleman, Kari Gwen. "Android Arete: Toward a Virtue Ethic for Computational Agents." *Ethics and Information Technology* 3.4 (2001): 247–65.

Collard, Franck. *Le Crime de poison au moyen âge*. Paris: Presses Universitaires de France, 2003.

Comte-Sponville, André. *A Small Treatise on the Great Virtues: The Uses of Philosophy in Everyday Life*. Translated by Catherine Temerson. New York: Macmillan, 2001.

Continisio, Chiara, and Cesare Mozzarelli, eds. *Repubblica e virtù: Pensiero politico e Monarchia Cattolica fra XVI e XVII secolo* (atti del convegno, ottobre 1993, Università Cattolica di Milano). Rome: Bulzoni, 1995.

Cooper, John M. "The Unity of Virtue." *Social Philosophy and Policy* 15.1 (1998): 233–74.

Corella, Jayme de. "Definiciones de las virtudes." In *Suma de la teología moral*, 45–6. Madrid: Antonio Román, 1695.

Coroleu, Alejandro. "Italian Humanism and the Spanish Vernacular." In *Printing and Reading Italian Latin Humanism in Renaissance Europe (ca. 1470–ca. 1540)*, 90–122. Newcastle upon Tyne: Cambridge Scholars, 2014.

Cortés, Hernán. *Cartas de relación*. Edited by Ángel Delgado. Madrid: Castalia, 1993.

Cotarelo y Mori, Emiliano. *Colección de entremeses, loas, bailes, jácaras y mojigangas desde fines del siglo XVII a mediados del XVIII*. 2 vols. Granada: Universidad de Granada, 2000.

Covarrubias Orozco, Sebastián. *Tesoro de la lengua castellana o española*. Edited by Felipe C.R. Maldonado. Revised by Manuel Camarero. Madrid: Castalia, 1995.

Cowan, Robert. "Thrasymennus' Wanton Wedding: Etymology, Genre, and *Virtus* in Silius Italicus, *Punica*." *Classical Quarterly* (New Series) 59.1 (2009): 226–37.

Cruickshank, Don W. "Calderón's King Pedro: Just or Unjust?" *Gesammelte Aufsätze zur Kultursgeschichte Spaniens* 25 [1970]: 113–32.

– *Don Pedro Calderón*. Cambridge: Cambridge University Press, 2009.

– "'Pongo mi mano en sangre bañada a la puerta': Adultery in *El médico de su honra*." In *Studies in Spanish Literature of the Golden Age Presented to E.M. Wilson*. Ed. R.O. Jones. London: Tamesis, 1973. 45–62.

Cruz, Anne. *Discourses of Poverty: Social Reform and the Picaresque Novel in Early Modern Spain*. Toronto: University of Toronto Press, 1999.

Cubillo de Aragón, Álvaro. *De el engaño hacer virtud (comedia famosa)*. S.l.: s.n., 1730.

Cueva y Silva, Leonor de. *La firmeza en la ausencia*. In *Women's Acts: Plays by Women Dramatists of Spain's Golden Age*, edited by Teresa Scott Soufas, 198–224. Lexington: University Press of Kentucky, 2015.

Cunningham, S.B. "Getting It Right: Aristotle's 'Golden Mean' as Theory Deterioration." *Journal of Mass Media Ethics* 14.1 (1999): 5–15.

Curtius, Ernst Robert. *European Literature and the Latin Middle Ages*. Translated by Willard R. Trask. Introduction by Colin Burrow. Princeton: Princeton University Press, 2013.

Curzer, Howard J. "A Defense of Aristotle's Doctrine that Virtue is a Mean." *Ancient Philosophy* 16.1 (1996): 129–38.

David-Peyre, Yvonne. *Le Personnage du médecin et la relation médecin-malade dans la littérature ibérique, XVIe et XVIIe siècles*. Paris: Ediciones Iberoamericanas, 1971.

Davis, T. Antony, and Rudolf Altevogt. "Golden Mean of the Human Body." *Fibonacci Quarterly* 17.4 (1979): 340–4.

De Brosse (pen name / no first name). *Les Innocents coupables* (1645). Edited by Pierre Pasquier. Strasbourg: Théâtre National (collection du répertoire) / Cicero Editeurs, 1992.

DeGruy, Karma. "Desiring Angels: The Angelic Body in *Paradise Lost.*" *Criticism* 54.1 (2012): 117–49.

De la Cámara, María Luisa. "La mémoire de Bartolomé de Las Casas chez Quevedo: déplacements des enjeux de la guerre juste." In *Penser la guerre au XVIIe siècle*, edited by Ninon Grangé, 197–216. Vincennes: Presses Universitaires de Vincennes, 2012.

"De las virtudes theologales" and "De las virtudes cardinales." In *Arte para bien confessar fecho por un devoto religioso de la orden de Sant Hieronymo*. lx–lxi. Burgos: s.n., 1541.

Del Río Parra, Elena. *Cartografías de conciencia española en la Edad de Oro*. Mexico: Fondo de Cultura Económica, 2008.

Derrida, Jacques. *The Beast & the Sovereign*. Vol. I. Edited by Michel Lisse, Marie-Louise Mallet, and Ginette Michaud. Translated by Geoffrey Bennington. Chicago: University of Chicago Press, 2009.

– *Of Grammatology*. Translated by Gayatri Chakravorty Spivak. Baltimore: Johns Hopkins University Press, 1997.

– "Plato's Pharmacy." In *Dissemination*, translated by Barbara Johnson, 63–172. Chicago: University of Chicago Press, 1981.

– *Positions*. Translated by Alan Bass. Chicago: University of Chicago Press, 1981.

Devereux, Daniel T. "The Unity of the Virtues in Plato's *Protagoras* and *Laches*." *Philosophical Review* 101.4 (1992): 765–89.

DeVun, Leah. "The Jesus Hermaphrodite: Science and Sex Difference in Premodern Europe." *Journal of the History of Ideas* 69.2 (2008): 193–218.

Dickson, Sandra H. "The 'Golden Mean' in Journalism." *Journal of Mass Media Ethics* 3.1 (1988): 33–7.

Diego de Valera, Mosén. *Espejo de verdadera nobleza*. In *Prosistas castellanos del siglo XV*, edited by M. Penna, 77–113. Madrid: Atlas, 1959.

"Documentos relacionados con la farmacia." *Boletín de la Sociedad Española de Historia de la Farmacia* 19.75 (1968): 51–2.

Donnell, Sidney. *Feminizing the Enemy: Imperial Spain, Transvestite Drama, and the Crisis of Masculinity*. Lewisburg, PA: Bucknell University Press, 2003.

Doubleday, Simon R. *The Wise King: A Christian Prince, Muslim Spain, and the Birth of the Renaissance*. New York: Basic Books, 2015.

Eamon, William. "Masters of Fire: Italian Alchemists in the Court of Philip II." In *Chymia: Science and Nature in Early Modern Europe (1450–1750)*, edited by Miguel López Pérez and Didier Kahn, 138–56. Cambridge: Cambridge Scholars Publishing, 2010.

Egginton, William. *How the World Became a Stage: Presence, Theatricality, and the Question of Modernity*. Albany: State University of New York Press, 2003.

Egido, Aurora. *El discreto encanto de Cervantes y el crisol de la prudencia*. Vigo: Academia Editorial del Hispanismo, 2011.

– "La *Nobleza virtuosa* de la Condesa de Aranda, doña Luisa de Padilla, amiga de Gracián." *Archivo de Filología Aragonesa* 54–5 (1998): 9–41.

Eire, Carlos. *From Madrid to Purgatory: The Art and Craft of Dying in Sixteenth-Century Spain*. Cambridge: Cambridge University Press, 1995.

Elliott, Dyan. *Spiritual Marriage: Sexual Abstinence in Medieval Wedlock*. Princeton: Princeton University Press, 1995.

Elliott, J.H. *The Count-Duke of Olivares: The Statesman in an Age of Decline*. New Haven: Yale University Press, 1989.

Elman, Linda L. "Between a Rock and a Hard Place: Armesinda Sets Her Own Parameters in *La firmeza en la ausencia* by Leonor de la Cueva y Silva." In *Engendering the Early Modern Stage: Women Playwrights in the Spanish Empire*, edited by Valerie Hegstrom and Amy R. Williamsen, 165–87. New Orleans: University Press of the South, 1999.

Erasmus, Desiderius. *Encomium Moriae*. Translated as *In Praise of Folly* by John Wilson (1668). Edited by T.N.R. Rogers. Mineola, New York: Dover, 2003.

– *El Enquiridion o manual del caballero cristiano*. Translated by Alfonso Fernández de Madrid. Edited by Dámaso Alonso. *Revista de Filología Española* Anejo XVI. Madrid: S. Aguirre, 1932.

Evagrius of Pontus (d. 399). "On the Vices Opposed to the Virtues." In *The Greek Ascetic Corpus*, edited by Robert E. Sinkewicz, 60–5. Oxford: Oxford University Press, 2003.

Evrigenis, Ioannis D. "The Doctrine of the Mean in Aristotle's Ethical and Political Theory." *History of Political Thought* 20.3 (1999): 393–416.

Exham, G.A. "Aristotle's Doctrine of the Mean." *Hermathena* 13.30 (1904): 110–28.

Exum, F. "Lope's King Pedro: The Divine Right of Kings vs. the Right of Resistence." *Hispania* 57 (1974): 428–33.

Fears, J.R. "The Cult of Virtues and Roman Imperial Ideology." *Aufstieg und Niedergang der römischen Welt II*, 17.2 (1984): 827–948.

Ferejohn, Michael T. "Socratic Thought-Experiments and the Unity of Virtue Paradox." *Phronesis: A Journal for Ancient Philosophy* 29.2 (1984): 105–22.

– "The Unity of Virtue and the Objects of Socratic Inquiry." *Journal of the History of Philosophy* 20.1 (1982): 1–21.

Ferreira Furtado, Júnia. "Lives on the Seas: Women's Trajectories in Port Cities of the Portuguese Overseas Empire." In *Women in Port: Gendering*

Communities, Economies, and Social Networks in Atlantic Port Cities, 1500–1800, edited by Douglas Catterall and Jodi Campbell, 251–86. Leiden: Brill, 2012.

Figueroa y Córdoba, Diego, and José Figueroa y Córdoba. *La dama capitán*. Madrid: Antonio Sanz, 1748.

Fine, Ruth. "A vueltas con el parlamento de Ricote (*Quijote* II, 54): de la conversión y otras paradojas." *Monteagudo: Revista de literatura española, hispanoamericana y teoría de la literatura* 20 (2015): 29–40.

Fink De Backer, Stephanie. *Widowhood in Early Modern Spain: Protectors, Proprietors, and Patrons*. Leiden: Brill, 2010.

Finkelberg, Margalit. "Virtue and Circumstances: On the City-State Concept of *Arête*." *American Journal of Philology* 123.1 (2002): 35–49.

Flynn, Maureen M. "Charitable Ritual in Late Medieval and Early Modern Spain." *Sixteenth Century Journal* 16.3 (1985): 335–48.

– *Sacred Charity: Confraternities and Social Welfare in Spain, 1400–1700*. Ithaca: Cornell University Press, 1989.

Folch Jou, G. "Las drogas en la obra de Fray Agustín Farfán." *Archivo Iberoamericano de la Medicina y de Antropología médica* 9 (1957): 165–72.

Foot, Philippa. "Virtues and Vices." In *Virtues and Vices and Other Essays in Moral Philosophy*, 1–18. Oxford: Clarendon, 2002.

Forcione, Alban. *Cervantes and the Humanist Vision*. Princeton: Princeton University Press, 1982.

– *Majesty and Humanity: Kings and Their Doubles in the Political Drama of the Spanish Golden Age*. New Haven: Yale University Press, 2009.

Ford, Jeremiah. "Félix de Lope de Vega Carpio." *The Catholic Encyclopedia*. Vol. 9. New York: Robert Appleton Company, 1910. http://www.newadvent.org/cathen/09354b.htm.

Forte Monje, Juan Manuel. "Pedro Ribadeneyra y las encrucijadas del antimaquiavelismo en España." In *Maquiavelo y España*, edited by Juan Manuel Forte Monje and Pablo López Álvarez, 167–79.

Forte Monje, Juan Manuel, and Pablo López Álvarez, eds. *Maquiavelo y España: Maquiavelismo y antimaquiavelismo en la cultura española de los siglos XVI y XVII*. Madrid: Biblioteca Nueva, 2008.

Fothergill-Payne, Louise. "La *Psychomachía* de Prudencio y el teatro alegórico pre-calderoniano." *Neophilologus* 59 (1975): 48–62.

Foucault, Michel. *Discipline and Punish: The Birth of the Prison*. Translated by Alan Sheridan. 2nd ed. New York: Vintage, 1995.

– *Madness and Civilization: A History of Insanity in the Age of Reason*. Translated by Richard Howard. New York: Vintage, 1988.

Francis, Eric D. "Virtue, Folly, and Greek Etymology." In *Approaches to Homer*, edited by Carl A. Rubino and Cynthia W. Shelmerdine, 74–121. Austin: University of Texas Press, 1983.

Fuchs, Barbara. *Exotic Nation: Maurophilia and the Construction of Early Modern Spain*. Philadelphia: University of Pennsylvania Press, 2009.

Furió Ceriol, Fadrique. *Obra Completa*. Valencia: Alfons el Magnànim, 1996.

Gabriel, Richard A. *The Madness of Alexander the Great and the Myth of Military Genius*. Barnsley, South Yorkshire: Pen & Sword, 2015.

Gagliardi, Antonio. "La tragedia della virtù." In *Cervantes e l'Umanesimo*, 73–88. Turin: Tirrenia, 2004.

Galindo, Pedro. *Excelencias de la castidad y virginidad*. Madrid: Matheo de Espinosa y Arteaga, 1681.

García Martínez, Sebastián. "El erasmismo en la Corona de Aragón en el siglo XVI." In *Erasmus in Hispania. Vives in Belgio. Acta Colloqui Brugensis, 23/26, IX, 1985*, edited by Jozef Ijsewijn and Ángel Losada, 215–90. Leuven: Peeters, 1986.

Gascón, Christopher D. *The Woman Saint in Spanish Golden Age Drama*. Lewisburg: Bucknell University Press, 2006.

Gert, Bernard. "Virtue and Vice." *Philosophy and Medicine* 17 (1985): 95–109.

Ghia, Walter. *España y Maquiavelo:* El Príncipe *ante el V Centenario*. Vigo: Editorial Academia del Hispanismo, 2013.

– "Las piruetas de Quevedo ante Maquiavelo." In *Maquiavelo y España*, edited by Juan Manuel Forte Monje and Pablo López Álvarez, 71–98.

Giles, Ryan. *The Laughter of the Saints: Parodies of Holiness in Late Medieval and Renaissance Spain*. Toronto: University of Toronto Press, 2009.

Gips, James. "Towards the Ethical Robot." *Android Epistemology* (1995): 243–52.

Girard, René. *Violence and the Sacred*. Translated by Patrick Gregory. Baltimore: Johns Hopkins University Press, 1979.

Gold, Penny S. "The Marriage of Mary and Joseph in the Twelfth-Century Ideology of Marriage." In *Sexual Practices and the Medieval Church*, edited by Vern L. Bullough and James A. Brundage, 102–17. Buffalo and New York: SUNY Press, 1982.

González Manjarrés, Miguel Ángel. *Andrés Laguna y el humanismo médico: estudio filológico*. Valladolid: Junta de Castilla y León, 2000.

González Moreno, Fernando, and Eduardo Urbina. "Elogio de la prudencia: alegorías de la locura en el *Quijote*." In *La locura en la literatura de Cervantes (I Coloquio Internacional de la Sociedad Cervantina de Madrid y el Editorial Academia del Hispanismo, Madrid, 29–30 septiembre 2011)*, edited by Eduardo Urbina and Jesús G. Maestro, 31–56. Vigo: Editorial Academia del Hispanismo, 2012.

Gonzalo, Arias. *Memorial en defensa de las mujeres de España y de los trajes y adornos de que usan* (1636). Edited by Enrique Suárez-Figaredo. *Lemir* 15 (2011): 131–66.

Gottlieb, Paula. "Aristotle on Dividing the Soul and Uniting the Virtues." *Phronesis: A Journal for Ancient Philosophy* 39.3 (1994): 275–90.

– *The Virtue of Aristotle's Ethics*. Cambridge: Cambridge University Press, 2009.

Gracián, Baltasar. *El Criticón*. Edited by Antonio Prieto. Barcelona: Planeta, 1985.

– *El héroe*. In *Obras completes*, edited by Emilio Blanco, 2:1–41. Madrid: Turner, 1993.

– *Oráculo manual y arte de prudencia*. Edited by Luys Santa Marina. Barcelona: Planeta, 1984.

Granjel, Luis S. *La medicina española renacentista*. Salamanca: Universidad de Salamanca, 1980.

– "Médicos y boticarios en un 'coloquio' de Antonio de Torquemada." In *Humanismo y medicina*, 101–11. Salamanca: Universidad de Salamanca, 1968.

– "Los médicos humanistas españoles." In *Capítulos de la medicina Española*, 13–29. Salamanca: Universidad de Salamanca, 1971.

Grayson, Brandan Leigh. "The Model Prodigal: Jesuit School Plays and the Production of Devotion in the Spanish Empire, 1565–1611." PhD dissertation, Washington University in St Louis. 2011.

Greer, Margaret Rich. "Constituting Community: A New Historical Perspective on the Autos of Calderón." In *New Historicism and the Comedia: Poetics, Politics and Praxis*, edited by José A. Madrigal, 41–68. Boulder, CO: Society of Spanish and Spanish-American Studies, 1997.

Grieve, Patricia E. *The Eve of Spain: Myths of Origins in the History of Christian, Muslim, and Jewish Conflict*. Baltimore: Johns Hopkins University Press, 2009.

Guerra, F. "The Paradox of 'The Treasury of Medicines' by Gregorio López (1542–1596)." In *Clío Médica: Acta Academiae Internationalis Historiae Medicinae*, 1:273–88. Oxford: Pergamon, 1965–7.

Gutiérrez de Arévalo, Pedro. *Práctica de boticarios, guía de enfermeros, remedios para pobres*. Madrid: María de Quiñones, 1634.

Hadreas, Peter. "Aristotle on the Vices and Virtue of Wealth." *Journal of Business Ethics* 39.4 (2002): 361–76.

Hamblenne, P. "Cura ut vir sis! ... ou une vir(tus) peu morale." *Latomus* 43 (1984): 369–88.

Hamburger, Max. "Aristotle and Confucius: A Comparison." *Journal of the History of Ideas* (1959): 236–49.

Hanrahan, Thomas. "*Lazarillo de Tormes*: Erasmian Satire or Protestant Reform?" *Hispania* 66.3 (1983): 333–9.

Hardie, William Francis Ross. "Aristotle's Doctrine that Virtue is a 'Mean.'" *Proceedings of the Aristotelian Society* new series 65 (1964–5): 183–204.

Harvey, John H. "Medieval Plantsmanship in England: The Culture of Rosemary." *Garden History* 1.1 (1972): 14–21.

Hawhee, Debra. "Agonism and Arete." *Philosophy and Rhetoric* 35.3 (2002): 185–207.

Haworth, Kenneth R. *Deified Virtues, Demonic Vices, and Descriptive Allegory in Prudentius'* Psychomachia. Amsterdam: Adolf M. Hakkert, 1980.

Heble, Ajay. "Trace." *Encyclopedia of Contemporary Literary Theory*. Edited by Irena R. Makaryk. Toronto: University of Toronto Press, 1997.

Helleman, Wendy. "Homer's Penelope: A Tale of Feminine *Arete*." *Classical Views* 39 (1995): 227–50.

"Here men may se the vertues off herbes": A Middle English Herbal (MS. Bodley 483, ff. 57r–67v). Edited by Pol Grymonprez. Scripta 3. Brussels: Omirel, 1981.

Herrera Montero, Bernal. "*Fuenteovejuna* de Lope de Vega y el maquiavelismo." *Criticón* 45 (1989): 131–53.

Herrero Hinojo, Pilar. "Contratos de aprendizaje en farmacia en el siglo XVI." *Boletín de la Sociedad Española de Historia de la Farmacia* 19 (74) (1968): 73–9.

– "Inventarios de farmacia." *Boletín de la Sociedad Española de Historia de la Farmacia* 19 (75) (1968): 97–110.

Hespanha, A.M. "De la 'iustitia' a la disciplina." In *Sexo barroco y otras transgresiones premodernas*, edited by Francisco Tomás y Valiente, et al., 175–86. Madrid: Alianza Universidad, 1990.

Hild, J.-A. "Virtus." In *Dictionnaire des Antiquités grecques et romaines*, edited by Ch. Daremberg and Edm. Saglio, 5:926–7. Paris: Hachette, 1873–1919.

Hiltpold, Paul. "Noble Status and Urban Privilege: Burgos, 1572." *Sixteenth Century Journal* 12.4 (1981): 21–44.

Holy Bible, Translated from the Latin Vulgate. Edited by Richard Challoner. New York: Douay Bible House, 1941.

Homiak, Marcia L. "Virtue and Self-Love in Aristotle's Ethics." *Canadian Journal of Philosophy* 11.4 (1981): 633–51.

Höpfl, Harro. *Jesuit Political Thought: The Society of Jesus and the State, c.1540–1630*. Cambridge: Cambridge University Press, 2004.

Horace. *Odes and Epodes*. Edited and translated by Niall Rudd. Loeb Classical Library 33. Cambridge, MA: Harvard University Press, 2004.

Hourani, George F. "Thrasymachus' Definition of Justice in Plato's *Republic*." *Phronesis: A Journal for Ancient Philosophy* 7.2 (1962): 110–20.

Houser, R.E. *The Cardinal Virtues: Aquinas, Albert, and Philip the Chancellor*. Medieval Sources in Translation 39 / Studies in Medieval Moral Teaching 4. Toronto: Pontifical Institute of Mediaeval Studies, 2004.

Hubbard, Thomas K. "The Invention of Sulpicia." *Classical Journal* 100.2 (2004): 177–94.

Huguet-Termes, Teresa. "Madrid Hospitals and Welfare in the Context of the Hapsburg Empire." In *Health and Medicine in Hapsburg Spain: Agents, Practices, Representations*, edited by Teresa Huguet-Termes, Jon Arrizabalaga, and Harold J. Cook, 64–85.

Huguet-Termes, Teresa, Jon Arrizabalaga, and Harold J. Cook, eds. *Health and Medicine in Hapsburg Spain: Agents, Practices, Representations. Medical History*, Supplement 29. London: The Wellcome Trust Centre for the History of Medicine at University College London, 2009.

Hull, Suzanne W. *Chaste, Silent, and Obedient: English Books for Women, 1475–1640*. San Marino, CA: Huntington Library, 1982.

Hursthouse, Rosalind. "A False Doctrine of the Mean." *Proceedings of the Aristotelian Society* 81 (1980): 57–72.

Idoya Zorroza, M., ed. *Las virtudes políticas en el Siglo de Oro*. Colección de Pensamiento medieval y renacentista. Pamplona: Universidad de Navarra, 2013.

Imirizaldu, Jesús. *Monjas y beatas embaucadoras*. Madrid: Editora Nacional, 1977.

Insúa Ruiz, Aurora. "Edipo y Segismundo: Predestinación y Libre Albedrío." *Mar Oceana: Revista del humanismo español e iberoamericano* 22 (2007): 137–53.

Ionescu, Arleen, et al. "Apologia de Mediocritate." *Journal of Literary Studies and Linguistics* 3.1 (2013): 65–86.

Jaeger, Werner. "Aristotle's Use of Medicine as Model of Method in His Ethics." *Journal of Hellenic Studies* 77.1 (1957): 54–61.

Jed, Stephanie H. *Chaste Thinking: The Rape of Lucretia and the Birth of Humanism*. Bloomington: Indiana University Press, 1989.

Johnson, Penelope D. "Virtus." *Augustinian Studies* 6 (1975): 117–24.

Jordan, Constance. "Boccaccio's Infamous Women: Gender and Civic Virtue in the *De mulieribus claris*." In *Ambiguous Realities: Women in the Middle Ages and Renaissance*, edited by Carole Levin and Jeanie Watson, 25–47. Detroit: Wayne State University Press, 1987.

– *Renaissance Feminism: Literary Texts and Political Models*. Ithaca: Cornell University Press, 1990.

Joseph & Aseneth. Translated by David Cook. In *The Apocryphal Old Testament*, 473–503. Oxford: Oxford University Press, 1984.

Jütte, R. "The Doctor on the Stage: Performing and Curing in Early Modern Europe." *Ludica* 5–6 (2000): 63–261.

Kagan, Richard L. *Lawsuits and Litigants in Castile, 1500–1700*. Chapel Hill: University of North Carolina Press, 1981.

Kahn, Charles. "Plato on the Unity of the Virtues." In *Facets of Plato's Philosophy*, edited by W.H. Werkmeister, 21–39. Assen: Van Gorcum, 1976.

Kahn, Victoria. *Machiavellian Rhetoric: From the Counter-Reformation to Milton*. Princeton: Princeton University Press, 1994.

– *Rhetoric, Prudence, and Skepticism in the Renaissance*. Ithaca: Cornell University Press, 1985.
– "*Virtù* and the Example of Agathocles in Machiavelli's *Prince*." *Representations* 13 (1986): 63–85.
Kallendorf, Craig. "Boccaccio's Two Didos: Virgil, Petrarca, and 'Il Più Grande Discepolo.'" In *In Praise of Aeneas: Virgil and Epideictic Rhetoric in the Early Italian Renaissance*, 58–76. Hanover, NH: University Press of New England, 1989.
– *Virgil and the Myth of Venice: Books and Readers in the Italian Renaissance*. Oxford: Oxford University Press, 1999.
Kallendorf, Hilaire. "Cervantes' Democratization of Demonic Possession: *El rufián dichoso*, Blasco de Lanuza, and the Death-Bed of Every Christian." *Bulletin of the Comediantes* 56.2 (2004): 311–26.
– *Conscience on Stage: The Comedia as Casuistry in Early Modern Spain*. Toronto: University of Toronto Press, 2007.
– "Dressed to the Sevens, or Sin in Style: Fashion Statements by the Deadly Vices in Spanish Baroque *Autos Sacramentales*." In *The Seven Deadly Sins: From Communities to Individuals*, edited by Richard Newhauser, 145–82. Leiden: Brill, 2007.
– *Exorcism and Its Texts: Subjectivity in Early Modern Literature of England and Spain*. Toronto: University of Toronto Press, 2003.
– *Sins of the Fathers: Moral Economies in Early Modern Spain*. Toronto: University of Toronto Press, 2013.
– "Were the Arbitristas Arbitrary? Criteria for Distinction in Pedro de Valencia." In *Actas del Congreso Internacional «Culturas globalizadas: del Siglo de Oro al siglo XXI»*, edited by Lygia Rodrigues Vianna Peres and Liège Rinaldi de Assis Pacheco, 127–40. Pamplona: Universidad de Navarra, 2017. Colección BIADIG (Biblioteca Áurea Digital), 39/Publicaciones Digitales del GRISO. http://www.unav.edu/publicacion/biblioteca-aurea-digital/biadig-39.
Kappraff, Jay. "The Relationship between Mathematics and Mysticism of the Golden Mean through History." *Fivefold Symmetry* (1992): 33–66.
Kaster, Robert A. "The Taxonomy of Patience, or When is *Patientia* Not a Virtue?" *Classical Philology* 97 (2002): 133–44.
Katzenellenbogen, A. *Allegories of the Virtues and Vices in Medieval Art*. London: Warburg Institute, 1939.
Keiser, George R. "Rosemary: Not Just for Remembrance." In *Health and Healing from the Medieval Garden*, edited by Peter Dendle and Alain Touwaide, 180–204. Woodbridge, Suffolk: Boydell, 2008.
Keys, Mary M. *Aquinas, Aristotle, and the Promise of the Common Good*. Cambridge: Cambridge University Press, 2006.
Kimminich, Eva. "The Way of Vice and Virtue: A Medieval Psychology." *Comparative Drama* (1991): 77–86.

King, Margaret L. *Women of the Renaissance*. Chicago: University of Chicago Press, 1991.

Kirby, Carol Bingham. "Theater and the Quest for Anointment in *El rey don Pedro en Madrid*." *Bulletin of the Comediantes* 33.2 (1981): 149–59.

Kraye, Jill. "Pagan Virtue in Pursuit of Christian Happiness: Renaissance Humanists and the Revival of Classical Ethics." In *Zeichen – Rituale – Werte: Internationales Kolloquium des Sonderforschungsbereichs 496 an der Westfälischen Wilhelms-Universität Münster*, edited by G. Althoff, 55–68. Münster: Rhema, 2004.

– "Renaissance Commentaries on the *Nicomachean Ethics*." In *Vocabulary of Teaching and Research between Middle Ages and Renaissance*, edited by Olga Weijers, 96–117. Turnhout: Brepols, 1995.

Kuefler, M. *The Manly Eunuch: Masculinity, Gender Ambiguity, and Christian Theology in Late Antiquity*. Chicago: University of Chicago Press, 2001.

Laguna, Andrés de. *De virtutibus vere atq; adamantinus libellus / ex Graeco in sermonem Latinum per Andream a Lacuna ... conueruersus [sic]... ; additae sunt ad calcem aliquot in Grynaeum castigations* ... Cologne: Ioan. Aquensis, 1543.

– *Pedacio Dioscórides Anazarbeo, acerca de la materia medicinal y de los venenos mortíferos*. Antwerp: Juan Latio, 1555.

– *Pedacio Dioscórides Anazarbeo, acerca de la materia medicinal y de los venenos mortíferos*. Valencia: Heredero de Benito Mace, 1695.

Landino, Cristoforo. *On True Nobility* (English translation of *De vera nobilitate*). Edited and translated by Albert Rabil, Jr. In *Knowledge, Goodness, and Power: The Debate over Nobility among Quattrocento Italian Humanists*, edited by Albert Rabil Jr, 190–260. Binghamton, NY: Medieval & Renaissance Texts & Studies, 1991.

Langis, Unhae. "Virtuous Viragos: Female Heroism and Ethical Action in Shakespearean Drama." *Literature Compass* 7.6 (2010): 397–411.

Larkin, Deirdre. "The Virtues of Rosemary." In The Medieval Garden Enclosed: The Cloisters Museum & Gardens. Posted Friday, 10 February 2012. http://blog.metmuseum.org/cloistersgardens/2012/02/10/the-virtues-of-rosemary/ Consulted 3 November 2015.

Lauer, A. Robert. *Tyrannicide and Drama*. Archivum Calderonianum 4. Stuttgart: Steiner, 1987.

Lee, Alexander. *Petrarch and St. Augustine: Classical Scholarship, Christian Theology and the Origins of the Renaissance in Italy*. Brill's Studies in Intellectual History 210. Leiden: Brill, 2012.

Lehfeldt, Elizabeth. "Ideal Men: Masculinity and Decline in Seventeenth-Century Spain." *Renaissance Quarterly* 61.2 (2008): 463–94.

León Coloma, M.A. "Iconografía de la Prudencia en España durante los siglos XV y XVI." *Cuadernos de Arte de la Universidad de Granada* 20 (1989): 65–78.

Levin, Carole. "Advice on Women's Behavior in Three Tudor Homilies." *International Journal of Women's Studies* 6.2 (1983): 176–85.

Lida de Malkiel, María Rosa. *Dido en la literatura española: su retrato y defensa.* London: Tamesis, 1974.

Lines, David, and Sabrina Ebbersmeyer, eds. *Rethinking Virtue, Reforming Society: New Directions in Renaissance Ethics, c. 1350–c. 1650.* Turnhout: Brepols, 2013.

Linn, C.F. *The Golden Mean: Mathematics and the Fine Arts.* New York: Doubleday, 1974.

Lipsius, Justus. *De Constantia.* Translated by John Stradling as *Two Bookes of Constancie.* Edited by Rudolf Kirk and Clayton Morris Hall. New Brunswick, NJ: Rutgers University Press, 1939.

Lloyd, David G. "Sexual Strategies in Plants: A Quantitative Method for Describing the Gender of Plants." *New Zealand Journal of Botany* 18.1 (1980): 103–8.

Lobera, Luis. "Antidotario muy singular." In *Remedio de cuerpos humanos,* clxii recto-clxxxiii recto. Alcalá de Henares: Juan de Brocar, 1542.

Lope de Vega. *Arte nuevo de hacer comedias.* Edited by Enrique García Santo-Tomás. Madrid: Cátedra, 2006.

– *La Dorotea.* Edited by Edwin S. Morby. Madrid: Castalia, 1987.

– *El ejemplo de casadas y prueba de la paciencia.* In *Obras de Lope de Vega publicadas por la Real Academia Española.* Vol. 15, *Comedias novelescas,* edited by Marecelino Menéndez y Pelayo, tercera sección, 9–45. Madrid: Sucesores de Rivadeneyra, 1913.

– *Loa en alabanza de la hvmildad.* In *El Fénix de España Lope de Vega Carpio ... septima parte de sus comedias: con loas, entremeses y bayles,* edited by Miguel de Siles, 301v–2r. Madrid: Viuda de Alonso Martín, 1617.

– *Los locos de Valencia.* Edited by Hélène Tropé. Madrid: Castalia, 2003.

– *La mayor virtud de un rey (comedia).* In *La Vega del Parnaso.* Madrid: Imprenta del Reyno, 1637.

– *El triunfo de la humildad, y soberbia abatida* (1618). In *Decima parte de las comedias de Lope de Vega Carpio,* edited by Miguel de Siles, 78v–102r. Madrid: Viuda de Alonso Martin, 1618.

– *Virtud, pobreza y mujer.* Edited by Donald McGrady. Newark, DE: Juan de la Cuesta, 2010.

López, Gregorio. *Tesoro de medicinas para diversas enfermedades.* Mexico City: Instituto Mexicano de Seguro Social, 1990.

López, Marcela, ed. *The Text and Concordance of Biblioteca Universitaria, Salamanca, MS 2262: Propiedades del romero*. Madison, WI: Hispanic Seminary of Medieval Studies, 1986.

López de Mesa, Luis. "Etimología de algunos prenombres." *Boletín Cultural y Bibliográfico* 3.7 (1960): 442–7.

López-Ibor, J.J. "La fundación en Valencia del primer hospital psiquiátrico del mundo." *Actas Españolas Psiquiátricas* 36.1 (2008): 1–9.

López Terrada, María Luz. "The Control of Medical Practice under the Spanish Monarchy during the Sixteenth and Seventeenth Centuries." In *Beyond the Black Legend: Spain and the Scientific Revolution*, edited by Víctor Navarro Brotóns and William Eamon, 281–94. Valencia: Instituto de Historia y Documentación, 2007.

– "Medical Pluralism in the Iberian Kingdoms: The Control of Extra-academic Practitioners in Valencia." In *Health and Medicine in Hapsburg Spain: Agents, Practices, Representations*, edited by Teresa Huguet-Termes et al., 7–25.

– "Médicos, cirujanos, boticarios y albéitares." In *Historia de la ciencia y de la técnica en la Corona de Castilla. Siglos XVI–XVII*, edited by J.M. López Piñero, 161–85. Valladolid: Junta de Castilla y León, 2002.

– "'Sallow-Faced Girl, Either It's Love or You've Been Eating Clay': The Representation of Illness in Golden Age Theater." In *Medical Cultures of the Early Modern Spanish Empire*, edited by John Slater, María Luz López-Terrada, and José Pardo Tomás, 167–87. Farnham, Surrey: Ashgate, 2014.

López Torrijos, Rosa. "Un manuscrito con instrucciones iconográficas a los pintores del Palacio del Pardo." *Cuadernos de arte e iconografía* 2.3 (1989): 400–7.

Lorenz, Philip. *The Tears of Sovereignty: Perspectives of Power in Renaissance Drama*. New York: Fordham University Press, 2013.

Losin, Peter. "Aristotle's Doctrine of the Mean." *History of Philosophy Quarterly* (1987): 329–41.

Lowrie, Michèle. "Lyric's 'Elegos' and the Aristotelian Mean: Horace, 'C.' 1.24, 1.33, and 2.9." *Classical World* (1994): 377–94.

Lucan. *The Civil War*. Translated by J.D. Duff. Loeb Classical Library 220. Cambridge, MA: Harvard University Press, 1928.

Luis de León. *La perfecta casada*. Edited by Félix García and Federico Carlos Sainz de Robles. Madrid: Aguilar, 1967.

Luna, Álvaro de. *Libro de las virtuosas e claras mujeres*. Edited by Julio Vélez-Sáinz. Madrid: Cátedra, 2009.

Machado de Chaves, Juan. "De las tres virtudes Teologales, que son Fè, Esperança, i Caridad, i de los vicios opuestos à ellas." In *Perfeto confessor, y cura de almas*, 1:247–84. Barcelona: Pedro Lacavalleria, 1641.

Machiavelli, Niccolò. *The Discourses*. Edited by Bernard Crick. Translated by Leslie J. Walker. Harmondsworth: Penguin, 1979.

– *Discursos sobre la primera década de Tito Livio*. Translated by Juan Lorenzo Otevante [1552]. Edited by Ana Martínez Arancón. Madrid: Alianza, 1987.

– *The Prince*. Translated and edited by Robert M. Adams. New York: Norton, 1977.

– *The Prince*. Translated by Peter Constantine. Edited by Albert Russell Ascoli. New York: Random House, 2007.

MacIntyre, Alasdair. *After Virtue: A Study in Moral Theory*. 2nd ed. Notre Dame: University of Notre Dame Press, 1984.

MacKay, Ruth. "The Maravall Problem: A Historical Inquiry." *Bulletin of the Comediantes* 65.1 (2013): 45–56.

Malamud, Martha. "Making a Virtue of Perversity: The Poetry of Prudentius." *Ramus* 19.1 (1990): 274–98.

Maravall, José Antonio. "Sobre Maquiavelo y el Estado moderno" (1969). In *Estudios de historia del pensamiento español*. Serie segunda, *La época del Renacimiento*, ch. 11, 331–42. Madrid: Ediciones Cultura Hispánica, 1984.

– *Teatro y literatura en la sociedad barroca*. Madrid: Seminarios y Ediciones, 1972.

Marcela de San Félix. "Loa." In *Teatro breve de mujeres, Siglos XVII–XX*, edited by Fernando Doménech, 27–36. Madrid: Asociación de Directores de Escena de España, 1996.

Markowsky, George. "Misconceptions about the Golden Ratio." *College Mathematics Journal* 23.1 (1992): 2–19.

Marroni, Francesco, interviewed by Gloria Lauri-Lucente and Ivan Callus. "The Average and the Excellent: Literary Possibilities and Cultural Ambiguities." *Word and Text: A Journal of Literary Studies and Linguistics* 3.1 (2013): 93–101.

Martínez, Ángel. "Estudio comparativo de la farmacopeas catalanas o concordias de 1511, 1535 y 1587." *Farmacia nueva* 15.164 (1950): 341–50.

Martz, Linda. *Poverty and Welfare in Habsburg Spain: The Example of Toledo*. Cambridge: Cambridge University Press, 1983.

Mastrangelo, Marc. *The Roman Self in Late Antiquity: Prudentius and the Poetics of the Soul*. Baltimore: Johns Hopkins University Press, 2007.

Mattingly, Harold. *Coins of the Roman Empire in the British Museum*. Vol. 2, *Vespasian to Domitian*. London: British Museum, 1930.

– "The Roman 'Virtues.'" *Harvard Theological Review* 30 (1937): 103–17.

Mayoralgo y Lodo, José Miguel de. *Génesis y evolución histórica del apellido en España*. Madrid: Real Academia Matritense de Heráldica y Genealogía, 1991.

Mcaleer, Sean. "An Aristotelian Account of Virtue Ethics: An Essay in Moral Taxonomy." *Pacific Philosophical Quarterly* 88.2 (2007): 208–25.

McDonnell, Myles. *Roman Manliness: "Virtus" and the Roman Republic*. Cambridge: Cambridge University Press, 2006.

– "Roman Men and Greek Virtue." *Mnemosyne Leiden Supplementum* (2002): 235–62.

McKendrick, Melveena. "The *Mujer Esquiva*: A Measure of the Feminist Sympathies of Seventeenth-Century Spanish Dramatists." *Hispanic Review* 40.2 (1972): 162–97.

– *Playing the King: Lope de Vega and the Limits of Conformity*. London: Tamesis, 2000.

– *Woman and Society in the Spanish Drama of the Golden Age: A Study of the* Mujer Varonil. Cambridge: Cambridge University Press, 2010.

McLeod, Glenda. *Virtue and Venom: Catalogs of Women from Antiquity to the Renaissance*. Ann Arbor: University of Michigan Press, 1991.

Mena, Juan de. *Laberinto de Fortuna*. Edited by Maxim. P.A.M. Kerkhof. Madrid: Castalia, 1997.

Le Métel de Boisrobert, François. *Les Apparences trompeuses*. Paris: Guillaume de Luyne, 1656.

Middlebrook, Leah. *Imperial Lyric: New Poetry and New Subjects in Early Modern Spain*. University Park: Pennsylvania State University Press, 2009.

Miller, Stephen. Arete: *Greek Sports from Ancient Sources*. Berkeley: University of California Press, 2004.

Milton, John. *Aeropagitica*. In *Complete Poems and Major Prose*, edited by Merritt Y. Hughes, 716–49. Indianapolis: Odyssey, 1980.

Monardes, Nicolás. *Diálogo llamado pharmacodilosis*. Seville: J. Cromberger, 1536.

– *Primera y Segvnda y Tercera Partes dela Historia Medicinal*. Seville: Fernando Diaz, 1580.

Moncín, Luis. *La virtud premiada (comedia nueva)*. Madrid: Librería de Castillo, 1791.

Montesinos Castañeda, María. "Los fundamentos de la visualidad de la Prudencia." *IMAGO: Revista de Emblemática y Cultura Visual* 6 (2014): 97–116.

More, Thomas. *Utopia, with Erasmus's* The Sileni of Alcibiades. Edited by David Wootton. Indianapolis: Hackett, 1999.

Moretti, Franco. *Distant Reading*. London: Verso, 2013.

Muir, Lynette R. "'La aoroent lor vertuz': A line in the *Roman de Troie*." *Studia Neophilologica* 38.2 (1966): 263–70.

Mujica, Bárbara. *A New Anthology of Early Modern Spanish Theater.* New Haven: Yale University Press, 2015.

Muñoz, Luis. *Vida y virtudes de la venerable virgin doña Luisa de Carvajal y Mendoza.* Madrid: Casa Real, 1631. Reprint Madrid: Convento de la Encarnación(?), 1897.

Museo de Historia de la Farmacia de Sevilla. http://institucional.us.es/museohistfarm/web/

Museu d'Història de la Farmàcia Catalana, http://www.ub.edu/museufar/elmuseu.htm.

Nader, Helen, ed. *Gender and Power in Early Modern Spain.* Urbana-Champaign: University of Illinois Press, 2004.

Nelson, Daniel Mark. *The Priority of Prudence: Virtue and Natural Law in Thomas Aquinas and the Implications for Modern Ethics.* University Park: Pennsylvania State University Press, 1992.

Newhauser, Richard. "Justice and Liberality: Opposition to Avarice in the Twelfth Century." In *Virtue and Ethics in the Twelfth Century,* edited by István P. Bejczy and Richard G. Newhauser, 295–316. Leiden: Brill, 2005.

– "Preaching the 'Contrary Virtues.'" *Mediaeval Studies* 70 (2008): 135–62.

Nieremberg, Juan Eusebio. *Corona virtuosa y virtud coronada: en que se proponen los frutos de la virtud de vn Principe, juntamente con los heroicos exemplos de virtudes de los Emperadores de la Casa de Austria, y Reyes de España.* Madrid: Francisco Maroto, 1643.

– *Ideas de virtvd en algvnos claros varones de la Compañia de Iesvs: Para los religiosos della.* Madrid: Maria de Quiñones, 1643.

Noble, D.F. *A World without Women: The Christian Clerical Culture of Western Science.* New York: Alfred Knopf, 1992.

Noreña, C.F. "The Communication of the Emperor's Virtues." *Journal of Roman Studies* 91 (2001): 146–68.

North, Helen F. "Canons and Hierarchies of the Cardinal Virtues in Greek and Latin Literature." In *The Classical Tradition: Literary and Historical Studies in Honor of Harry Caplan,* ed. Luitpold Wallach, 165–83. Ithaca: Cornell University Press, 1966.

Nummedal, Tara E. "The Problem of Fraud in Early Modern Alchemy." In *Shell Games: Studies in Scams, Frauds, and Deceits (1300–1650),* edited by Mark Crane, Richard Raiswell, and Margaret Reeves, 38–58. Toronto: Centre for Reformation and Renaissance Studies, 2004.

Núñez de Cepeda, Francisco. *Idea de el buen pastor representada en empresas sacras.* Lyon: Anisson and Posuel, 1682.

Nussbaum, Martha. *The Fragility of Goodness: Luck and Ethics in Greek Tragedy and Philosophy.* Cambridge: Cambridge University Press, 1986.

Oderberg, David S. "On the Cardinality of the Cardinal Virtues." *International Journal of Philosophical Studies* 7.3 (1999): 305–22.

Olmedilla y Puig, Joaquín. *Estudio histórico de la vida y escritos del sabio español Andrés Laguna, médico de Carlos I y Felipe II y célebre escritor y botánico del siglo XVI.* Madrid: El Correo, 1887.

O'Reilly, Terence. "The Erasmianism of *Lazarillo de Tormes*." In *Essays in Honour of Robert Brian Tate from His Colleagues and Pupils*, edited by Richard A. Cardwell, 91–100. Nottingham: University of Nottingham Press, 1984.

Ortner, Sherry B. "The Virgin and the State." *Feminist Studies* 4.3 (1978): 19–35.

Ostwald, Michael J. "Under Siege: The Golden Mean in Architecture." *Nexus Network Journal* 2.1–2 (2000): 75–82.

Oviedo, Luis de. *Méthodo de la recolección y reposición de las medicinas simples, y de su corrección y preparación.* Madrid: Alonso Gómez, 1581.

Owens, J.B. *"By My Absolute Royal Authority": Justice and the Castilian Commonwealth at the Beginning of the First Global Age.* Rochester: University of Rochester Press, 2005.

Padilla, Luisa de. *Nobleza virtuosa* (Zaragoza, 1637). Valencia: Universidad de Valencia, 1998.

Pagden, A.R.D. "The Diffusion of Aristotle's Moral Philosophy in Spain, ca. 1400–ca. 1600." *Traditio* 31 (1975): 287–313.

Palafox y Mendoza, Juan de. *Virtues of the Indian / Virtudes del Indio.* Edited and translated by Nancy H. Fee. Plymouth, UK: Rowman & Littlefield, 2009.

Parker, Geoffrey. *Imprudent King: A New Life of Philip II.* New Haven: Yale University Press, 2015.

Parra Jiménez, Ginés. "La Inquisición en la medicina del siglo XVI." *Clínica y laboratorio* 68.401 (1959): 146–55.

Pastor Bodmer, Beatriz. *The Armature of Conquest: Spanish Accounts of the Discovery of America, 1492–1589.* Stanford: Stanford University Press, 1992.

Pastor Frechoso, Félix Francisco. *Boticas, boticarios y materia médica en Valladolid: siglos XVI y XVII.* Salamanca: Junta de Castilla y León, 1993.

Pelikan, Jaroslav. *Christianity and Classical Culture: The Metamorphosis of Natural Theology in the Christian Encounter with Hellenism.* New Haven: Yale University Press, 1993.

Pellegrino, Edmund D. "The Virtuous Physician, and the Ethics of Medicine." *Philosophy and Medicine* 17 (1985): 237–55.

Penner, Terry. "The Unity of Virtue." *Philosophical Review* (1973): 35–68.

Peña, Margarita. "Los varios tonos de la relación Lope de Vega-Juan Ruiz de Alarcón." http://www.cervantesvirtual.com/nd/ark:/59851/bmc2n5f7.

Peraita, Carmen. "Arte del disimulo y paradoja: la crítica a Felipe III en *Grandes Anales de Quince Días* de Quevedo." In *Actas del XI Congreso de la Asociación Internacional de Hispanistas*, edited by J. Villegas, 3:111–20. Madrid: Asociación Internacional de Hispanistas, 1994.

Pérez, Mirzam Cristina. *The* Comedia *of Virginity: Mary and the Politics of Seventeenth-Century Spanish Theater.* Waco: Baylor University Press, 2012.

Pérez Bautista, Florencio L. "La medicina y los médicos en el teatro de Calderón de la Barca." *Cuadernos de Historia de la Medicina Española* 7 (1968): 149–245.

Pérez de la Canal, Miguel Ángel. "La justicia en la corte de Castilla durante los siglos XIII al XV." *Historia, instituciones, documentos* 2 (1975): 383–482.

Pérez Fuenzalida, F.J. "Un escrito clave de Nicolás Monardes: *Diálogo llamado Pharmacodilosis o Declaración medicinal* (1536)." In *IV Congreso Español de Historia de la Medicina (Granada, 24–26 de abril de 1973). Actas*, 1:81–8. Granada: Universidad de Granada, 1975.

Pérez Martínez, Ángel. *El* Quijote *y su idea de virtud.* Anejos Revista de Literatura 79. Madrid: Consejo Superior de Investigaciones Científicas, 2012.

Perry, Mary Elizabeth. "Magdalens and Jezebels in Counter-Reformation Spain." In *Culture and Control in Counter-Reformation Spain*, edited by Anne J. Cruz and Mary Elizabeth Perry, 124–44. Minneapolis: University of Minnesota Press, 1991.

Peset Llorca, V. "A Note on the Spanish Version of Dioscorides' *Materia medica*." *Journal of the History of Medicine* 9 (1954): 49–58.

Petro del Barrio, Antonia. *La legitimación de la violencia en la comedia española del siglo XVII.* Salamanca: Universidad de Salamanca, 2006.

Pieper, Josef. *The Four Cardinal Virtues: Prudence, Justice, Fortitude, Temperance.* New York: Harcourt, Brace, 1965.

Plata, Fernando. "On Love and Occasion: A Reading of the 'Tale of Inappropriate Curiosity.'" In *Cervantes and Don Quixote: Proceedings of the Delhi Conference on Miguel de Cervantes*, edited by Vibha Maurya and Ignacio Arellano, 195–210. Hyderabad: EMESCO, 2008.

Platina, Bartolomeo. *De vera nobilitate.* In *Knowledge, Goodness, and Power: The Debate over Nobility among Quattrocento Italian Humanists.* Binghamton, NY: Medieval & Renaissance Texts & Studies, 1991.

Plato. *Gorgias.* Translated by W.D. Woodhead. In *The Collected Dialogues*, edited by E. Hamilton and H. Cairns. Princeton: Princeton University Press, 1961.

– *Protagoras.* In *Plato in Twelve Volumes.* Vol. 3. Translated by W.R.M. Lamb. Cambridge, MA: Harvard University Press, 1967.

– *The Republic*. Translated by Francis Macdonald Cornford. Oxford: Oxford University Press, 1945.

Poska, Allyson. "Elusive Virtue: Rethinking the Role of Female Chastity in Early Modern Spain." *Journal of Early Modern History* 8.1–2 (2004): 135–46.

– "When Bigamy Is the Charge: Gallegan Women and the Holy Office." In *Women in the Inquisition: Spain and the New World*, edited by Mary Giles, 189–205. Baltimore: Johns Hopkins University Press, 1998.

El premio de la virtud y castigo en la mentira. Edited by Elena Di Pinto. In *Comedias burlescas del Siglo de Oro*, edited by Ignacio Arellano, 5:391–510. Madrid and Frankfurt: Universidad de Navarra / Iberoamericana, 2004.

Presberg, Charles D. *Adventures in Paradox:* Don Quixote *and the Western Tradition*. University Park: Pennsylvania State University Press, 2001.

Presotto, Marco. "La tradición textual de *La ilustre fregona* atribuida a Lope de Vega." *Criticón* 89 (2003): 697–708.

Puigdomenech, Helena. "Maquiavelo y maquiavelismo en España: Siglos XVI y XVII." In *Maquiavelo y España*, edited by Juan Manuel Forte Monje and Pablo López Álvarez, 41–60.

Quevedo, Francisco de. *Dios hace justicia a todos*. Valencia: Viuda de Joseph de Orga, 1763.

– *Silvas*. Translated by Hilaire Kallendorf. Lima: Universidad Nacional Mayor de San Marcos, 2011.

– *Teatro completo*. Edited by Ignacio Arellano and Carmen García Valdés. Madrid: Cátedra, 2011.

– *Virtud militante. Contra las quatro pestes del mundo, inuidia, ingratitud, soberbia, avarizia*. Edited by Alfonso Rey. Santiago: Universidad de Santiago de Compostela, 1985.

Quiñones de Benavente, Luis. "Entremés famoso: El Boticario." Revised edition. In Emiliano Cotarelo y Mori, *Colección de entremeses, loas, bailes, jácaras y mojigangas desde fines del siglo XVII a mediados del XVIII*, 2:759–61. Granada: Universidad de Granada, 2000.

Quintilian. *Institutio oratoria*. Translated by H.E. Butler as *Institutes of Oratory*. 4 vols. London: Loeb, 1963.

Rabelais, François. *The Complete Works of Rabelais: The Five Books of Gargantua and Pantagruel*. Translated by Jacques Le Clerq. New York: Random House, 1936.

Ramón Vallejo, José, and José Miguel Cobos. "El recetario de la Escuela de Salerno conocido como el 'Antidotarium Nicolai.'" *Medicina Naturista* 7.1 (2013): 35–41.

Ramoutsaki, I.A., Stelios Haniotakis, and Aristides M. Tsatsakis. "The Snake as the Symbol of Medicine, Toxicology and Toxinology." *Veterinary and Human Toxicology* 42.5 (2000): 306–8.

Reeser, Todd W. *Moderating Masculinity in Early Modern Culture*. Chapel Hill: University of North Carolina Press, 2006.

Regan, Lisa K. "Ariosto's Threshold Patron: Isabella d'Este in the *Orlando Furioso*." *Modern Language Notes* 120.1 (2005): 50–69.

Reshotko, Naomi. *Socratic Virtue: Making the Best of the Neither-Good-nor-Bad*. Cambridge: Cambridge University Press, 2006.

Resnick, Irven M. "Marriage in Medieval Culture: Consent Theory and the Case of Joseph and Mary." *Church History* 69.2 (2000): 350–71.

Rey Bueno, Mar. "*La Mayson pour Distiller des Eaües* at El Escorial: Alchemy and Medicine at the Court of Philip II, 1556–1598." In *Health and Medicine in Hapsburg Spain: Agents, Practices, Representations*, edited by Teresa Huguet-Termes et al., 26–39.

Rhodes, Elizabeth. *Dressed to Kill: Death and Meaning in Zayas's* Desengaños. Toronto: University of Toronto Press, 2011.

Ricard, Robert. *Estudios de literatura religiosa española*. Madrid: Gredos, 1964.

Ricciardi, Roberto. "Galeazzo Capra." *Dizionario Biografico degli Italiani*. Vol. 19. http://www.treccani.it/enciclopedia/galeazzo-capra_(Dizionario_Biografico)/.

Ridley, R.T. "To Be Taken with a Pinch of Salt: The Destruction of Carthage." *Classical Philology* 81.2 (1986): 140–6.

Riley, Philip F. *A Lust for Virtue: Louis XIV's Attack on Sin in Seventeenth-Century France*. Westport, CT: Greenwood, 2001.

Robbins, Jeremy. *Arts of Perception: The Epistemological Mentality of the Spanish Baroque, 1580–1720*. New York: Routledge, 2007.

Roberts, Robert C. "Aristotle on Virtues and Emotions." *Philosophical Studies* 56.3 (1989): 293–306.

Roca Traver, Francisco A. "El Hospital dels folls e ignocents. El Padre Gelabert Jofré." *Estudis castellonencs* 11 (2006–8): 691–730.

Rodríguez, Alonso. *Ejercicio de perfección y virtudes cristianas* (1609). Madrid: Testimonio, 1985.

Rodríguez, Juan. "De las obras, y exercicios de virtudes, que conviene imponer por obligacion a el penitente, para satisfacion, y de otras que se deben aconsejar para medicina de vicios, y aumento de gracia" and "De el exercicio de las tres virtudes Theologales." In *Prudente confessor*, 37–8. Écija: Luis Estupiñán, 1644.

Rodríguez González, Ángel. "Información de limpieza de sangre y práctica de oficio de Médicos, Cirujanos y Boticarios del Real Hospital de Santiago de Compostela (Siglos XVII–XIX)." *Boletín de la Universidad Compostelana* 2 (1965–6): 19–49.

Romano, David G. "The Ancient Stadium-Athletes and *Arete*." *Ancient World* 7.1–2 (1983): 9–16.

Romero, T. "La lujuria es hoy una virtud capital (entrevista con Carmen Aldunate)." *Caras* 9 (2002): 38–41.

Rosenfield, Lawrence W. "The Doctrine of the Mean in Aristotle's *Rhetoric*." *Theoria* 31.3 (1965): 191–8.

Ross, Jill. *Figuring the Feminine: The Rhetoric of Female Embodiment in Medieval Hispanic Literature*. Toronto: University of Toronto Press, 2008.

Rupp, Stephen. *Allegories of Kingship: Calderón and the Anti-Machiavellian Tradition*. University Park: Pennsylvania State University Press, 1996.

Saavedra Fajardo, Diego. *Empresas políticas*. Edited by Sagrario López Poza. Madrid: Cátedra, 1999.

Salaverry, Oswaldo. "Una visión histórica de la educación médica." *Anales de la Facultad de Medicina* (Universidad Nacional Mayor de San Marcos) 59.3 (1998): 215–19.

Salkever, Stephen G. *Finding the Mean: Theory and Practice in Aristotelian Political Philosophy*. Princeton: Princeton University Press, 2014.

Salomon, Noël. "Virtudes económicas y bienes del villano." In *Lo villano en el teatro del Siglo de Oro*, 221–68. Madrid: Castalia, 1985.

Sancho de San Román, R. *La medicina y los médicos en la obra de Tirso de Molina*. Salamanca: Librería Cervantes, 1960.

Saxon, Wolfgang. "Bernard Knox, 95, Classics Scholar, Dies." *New York Times*, Tuesday, 17 August 2010. A22.

Scarry, Elaine. *On Beauty and Being Just*. Princeton: Princeton University Press, 1999.

Schäfer, Peter. *Mirror of His Beauty: Feminine Images of God from the Bible to the Early Kabbalah*. Princeton: Princeton University Press, 2002.

Schlayer, Clotilde. *Spuren Lukans in der spanischen Dichtung*. Heidelberg: P. Braus, 1927.

Schneewind, Jerome B. "The Misfortunes of Virtue." *Ethics* (1990): 42–63.

Scodel, Joshua. *Excess and the Mean in Early Modern English Literature*. Princeton: Princeton University Press, 2009.

Seneca. *Epistulae morales* (*Moral Essays*). Translated by R.M. Gummere. 3 vols. London: Loeb, 1961.

Sepúlveda, Juan Ginés de. *Acerca de la monarquía*. Edited by I.J. García Pinilla. In *Obras completas*, VI. Pozoblanco: Excmo. Ayuntamiento de Pozoblanco, 2001.

– *Demócrates primero o Diálogo sobre la compatibilidad entre la milicia y la religión cristiana* (1535). In *Tratados políticos*. Translated by Á. Losada. Madrid: I.E.P., 1963.

Sepúlveda, Lorenzo de. "Romance del Rey Bamba." In *Tesoro de los romanceros y cancioneros españoles, históricos, caballerescos, moriscos y otros*, edited by Eugenio de Ochoa, 78–9. Paris: Baudry, 1838.

Shakespeare, William. *The Riverside Shakespeare*. Edited by G. Blakemore Evans. Boston: Houghton Mifflin, 1974.
Shelp, E.E., ed. *Virtue and Medicine: Explorations in the Character of Medicine. Philosophy and Medicine* 17 (1985). Special monographic issue.
Sigüenza y Góngora, Carlos de. *Teatro de virtudes políticas que constituyen a un príncipe: advertidas en los monarcas antiguos del mexicano imperio* (1680). Prologue by Roberto Moreno de los Arcos. Mexico City: UNAM / Porrúa, 1986.
Siraisi, Nancy G. "Disease and Treatment."In *Medieval and Early Renaissance Medicine: An Introduction to Knowledge and Practice*, 115–52. Chicago: University of Chicago Press, 1990.
Sklenář, Robert. *The Taste for Nothingness: A Study of* Virtus *and Related Themes in Lucan's* Bellum Civile. Ann Arbor: University of Michigan Press, 2003.
Skoie, Mathilde. *Reading Sulpicia: Commentaries 1475–1990*. Oxford: Oxford University Press, 2002.
Slater, John, and María Luz López-Terrada. "Scenes of Mediation: Staging Medicine in the Spanish Interludes." *Social History of Medicine* 24.2 (2011): 226–43.
Slater, John, María Luz López-Terrada, and José Pardo-Tomás, eds. *Medical Cultures of the Early Modern Spanish Empire*. London: Routledge, 2016.
Smith, Macklin. *Prudentius'* Psychomachia*: A Reexamination*. Princeton: Princeton University Press, 2015.
Sorní i Esteva, Xavier, and Josep M. Suñé i Arbussà. *Aproximació a "Theorica y practica de boticarios" de Fra Antoni Castell* (Barcelona, 1592). Barcelona: Universitat de Barcelona, 1992.
Soyer, François. *Ambiguous Gender in Early Modern Spain and Portugal: Inquisitors, Doctors and the Transgression of Gender Norms*. Leiden: Brill, 2012.
Stadter, Philip. *Plutarch's Historical Methods: An Analysis of "Mulierum Virtutes."* Cambridge: Cambridge University Press, 1965.
Stroud, Matthew D. *Fatal Union: A Pluralistic Approach to the Spanish Wife-Murder* Comedias. Lewisburg, PA: Bucknell University Press, 1990.
– "The Play of Means and Ends: Justice in Lope's *Fuenteovejuna*." *Neophilologus* 92.2 (2008): 247–62.
– "The Wife-Murder Plays." In *A Companion to Early Modern Hispanic Theater*, edited by Hilaire Kallendorf, 91–103. Leiden: Brill, 2014.
Stumpf, W.E. "The Dose Makes the Medicine." *Drug Discovery Today* 11.11 (2006): 550–5.
Suárez, Francisco. "A Work on the Three Theological Virtues: Faith, Hope and Charity." In *Selections from Three Works of Francisco Suárez*, translated by Gwladys L. Williams, Ammi Brown, and John Waldron, revised by Henry Davis, 2:729–868. Oxford: Clarendon, 1944.

Sullivan, Henry W. "The Problematic of Tragedy in Calderón's *El médico de su honra*." *Revista canadiense de estudios hispánicos* 5.3 (1981): 355–72.

– "*Las tres justicias en una* and the Question of Christian Catharsis." In *Critical Perspectives on Calderón de la Barca*, edited by Frederick A. de Armas, David M. Gitlitz, and José A. Madrigal, 119–40. Lincoln: University of Nebraska Press, 1981.

Taouk, Raymond. "The Book of Tobias and the Catholic Ideal of Marriage." http://www.catholicapologetics.info/morality/family/tobias.htm.

Tausiet, María. "Healing Virtue: *Saludadores* versus Witches in Early Modern Spain." In *Health and Medicine in Hapsburg Spain: Agents, Practices, Representations*, edited by Teresa Huguet-Termes et al., 40–63.

Taylor, Barry, and Alejandro Coroleu, eds. *Humanism and Christian Letters in Early Modern Iberia (1480–1630)*. Cambridge: Cambridge Scholars, 2010.

Taylor, Scott T. *Honor and Violence in Golden Age Spain*. New Haven: Yale University Press, 2008.

Tejera, Victorino. "Methodology of a Misreading." *International Studies in Philosophy* 10 (1978): 131–6.

Thacker, Jonathan. "Lope de Vega, *El cuerdo loco*, and 'la más discreta figura de la comedia.'" *Bulletin of Hispanic Studies* 81.4 (2004): 463–78.

– *Role-play and the World as Stage in the* Comedia. Liverpool: Liverpool University Press, 2002.

Thomas, Keith. "The Double Standard." *Journal of the History of Ideas* 20 (1959): 195–216.

Tiles, J.E. "The Practical Import of Aristotle's Doctrine of the Mean." *Apeiron* 28.4 (1995): 1–14.

Tirso de Molina. *La elección por la virtud*. Edited by Miguel Galindo Abellán. Vigo: Editorial Academia del Hispanismo, 2013.

– *La lealtad contra la envidia* (1631). Vol. 4 of *La "Trilogía de los Pizarros" de Tirso de Molina*. Vol. 41 of Teatro del Siglo de Oro: Ediciones críticas, edited by Miguel Zugasti. Kassel: Reichenberger, 1993.

– *La prudencia en la mujer*. In *La prudencia en la mujer y El condenado por desconfiado*. Puerto Rico: Cordillera, 1969.

– *La venganza de Tamar*. Edited by A K.G. Paterson. Cambridge: Cambridge University Press, 2011.

Tomar Romero, F. "Ética y política en Platón: la función de la virtud." *Espíritu* 47.118 (1998): 243–67.

Toner, James H. *Morals under the Gun: The Cardinal Virtues, Military Ethics, and American Society*. Lexington: University Press of Kentucky, 2000.

Torquemada, Antonio de. *Los Coloquios satíricos con un Coloquio pastoril* (1553). Edited by Lina Rodríguez Cacho. Madrid: Universidad Autónoma de Madrid, 1990.

Trinkhaus, Charles. *Adversity's Noblemen: The Italian Humanists on Happiness*. Rev. ed. New York: Octagon, 1965.

Tropé, Hélène. *Locura y sociedad en la Valencia de los siglos XV al XVII*. Valencia: Diputació de Valencia, 1994.

– "Teatro y locura en *Los locos de Valencia* de Lope de Vega." In *Compostella aurea: Actas del VIII Congreso de la AISO* (Santiago de Compostela, 7–11 julio 2008), edited by Antonio Azaustre Galiana and Santiago Fernández Mosquera, 477–83. Santiago: Universidade de Santiago de Compostela, 2011.

Truman, R.W. *Spanish Treatises on Government, Society, and Religion in the Time of Philip II*. Leiden: Brill, 1999.

Tuck, Steven L. "The Origins of Roman Imperial Hunting Imagery: Domitian and the Redefinition of *Virtus* under the Principate." *Greece and Rome*, 2nd ser. 52.2 (2005): 221–45.

Urmson, James Opie. "Aristotle's Doctrine of the Mean." *American Philosophical Quarterly* (1973): 223–30.

Valdés Pozueco, Kátherin. "*Los alimentos del hombre*: análisis jurídico del auto sacramental de Don Pedro Calderón de la Barca." *Anuario Jurídico y Económico Escurialense* 39 (2006): 385–408.

Valdéz García, J. "Salerno: la primera escuela de medicina." *Revista Avances* 2.4 (2004): 37–9.

Valencia, Pedro de. *Descripción de la pintura de las virtudes*. In *Obras completas*. Vol. 6, *Escritos varios*, edited by Jesús María Nieto Ibáñez, 183–224. León: Universidad de León, 2012.

– *Tratado acerca de los moriscos de España*. In *Obras completas*. Vol. 4.2, *Escritos políticos*, edited by Rafael González Cañal and Hipólito B. Riesco Álvarez, 67–140. León: Universidad de León, 1999.

Valles, Francisco. *Tratado de las aguas destiladas, pesos, y medidas de que los boticarios deven usar, por nueva ordenanza y mandato de su Magestad y su Real Consejo*. Madrid: Luis Sánchez, 1592.

Vallone, Lynne. *Disciplines of Virtue: Girls' Culture in the Eighteenth and Nineteenth Centuries*. New Haven: Yale University Press, 1995.

Valverde López, José Luis. *Catálogo de documentos de interés histórico-farmacéutico conservados en el Archivo General de Simancas*. Granada: Universidad de Granada, 1976.

Valverde López, José Luis, and María del Carmen Vidal. *Catálogo de documentos de interés histórico-farmacéutico conservados en el Archivo del Palacio Nacional de Madrid*. Granada: Universidad de Granada, 1971.

Valverde López, José Luis, and Rafael García Serrano. *Colección documental de interés histórico-farmacéutico conservada en el Archivo General de Navarra*. Granada: Universidad de Granada, 1979.

Valverde López, José Luis, and A. Llopis González. *Estudio sobre los fueros y privilegios del antiguo colegio de apotecarios de Valencia*. Granada: Universidad de Granada, 1979.

Valverde López, José Luis, and M. Carmen Téllez. "Diego de Cortavila y Sanabria, boticario real (1571–1650." *Boletín de la Sociedad Española de Historia de la Farmacia* 105 (1976): 3–15.

Valverde López, José Luis, M. Carmen Téllez, and M. Angustias González Gómez. *La botica del real sitio de Aranjuez*. Granada: Universidad de Granada, 1979.

Vanderjagt, A.J. "Between Court Literature and Civic Rhetoric: Buonaccorso da Montemagno's *Controversia de nobilitate*." In *Courtly Literature: Culture and Context (Proceedings of the 5th Triennial Congress of the International Courtly Literature Society, Dalfsen, The Netherlands, 9–16 August 1986)*, edited by Keith Busby and Erik Kooper, 561–72. Utrecht: John Benjamins, 1990.

Vélez de Guevara, Luis. *Virtudes vencen señales*. Edited by William R. Manson and C. George Peale. Newark, DE: Juan de la Cuesta, 2010.

Vilanova, Antonio. *Erasmo y Cervantes*. Barcelona: Consejo Superior de Investigaciones Científicas, 1949.

Vilches, Elvira. "Doing Things with Money in Early Modern Spain." In *A Companion to the Spanish Renaissance*, edited by Hilaire Kallendorf. Leiden: Brill, forthcoming.

– *New World Gold: Cultural Anxiety and Monetary Disorder in Early Modern Spain*. Chicago: University of Chicago Press, 2010.

Villalba, Juan Francisco de. "Empresa quarenta y una Del Examinado en Virtud." In *Empresas espirituales y morales*, Parte I, empresa 41, 95r–96v. Baeza: Fernando Díaz de Montoya, 1613.

Vincent-Cassy, Cécile. "Casilda, Orosia, Margarita, Juana y la Ninfa: sobre las comedias de 'santas' de Tirso de Molina." *Criticón* 97–8 (2006): 45–60.

Virgil. *Georgics*. Edited by R.A.B. Mynors. Oxford: Clarendon, 1990.

La virtud consiste en medio, el pródigo y rico avariento (comedia nueva). Valencia: Viuda de Joseph de Orgaz, 1772.

Virtues and Vices: Patience, Anger, Sloth, Diligence. Web exhibition. Koninklijke Bibliotheek (National Library of the Netherlands). http://www.kb.nl/en/web-exhibitions/highlights-from-medieval-manuscripts/virtues-and-vices. Consulted 27 October 2014.

Vives, Juan Luis. *The Instruction of a Christian Woman*. Translated by Richard Hyrde (1529). In *The Broadview Anthology of Sixteenth-Century Poetry and Prose*, edited by Marie Loughlin, Sandra Bell, and Patricia Brace, 96–110. Buffalo: Broadview, 2012.

Vlastos, G. "The Unity of the Virtues." In *Platonic Studies*, 2nd ed., 221–69. Princeton: Princeton University Press, 1981.

– "The Unity of the Virtues in the *Protagoras*." *Review of Metaphysics* 25 (1972): 415–58.

Von Vacano, Diego. *The Art of Power: Machiavelli, Nietzsche and the Making of Aesthetic Political Theory*. Lexington : Rowman & Littlefield, 2006.

Vyskot, Boris, and Roman Hobza. "Gender in Plants: Sex Chromosomes Are Emerging from the Fog." *Trends in Genetics* 20.9 (2004): 432–8.

Warren, Thomas H. "Critical Thinking beyond Reasoning: Restoring Virtue to Thought." In *Re-thinking Reason: New Perspectives in Critical Thinking*, edited by Kerry S. Walters, 221–31. Albany, NY: SUNY Press, 1964.

Watson, A. Irvine. "Peter the Cruel or Peter the Just? A Reappraisal of the Role Played by King Peter in Calderón's *El médico de su honra*." *Romanistisches Jahrbuch* 14 [1963]: 322–46.

Watson, Gary. "Virtues in Excess." *Philosophical Studies* 46.1 (1984): 57–74.

Webb, Lance. *Conquering the Seven Deadly Sins*. New York and Nashville: Abingdon, 1955.

Webster, J.H.D. "Golden-Mean Form in Music." *Music & Letters* (1950): 238–48.

Wehner, Peter. "The Theology of Donald Trump." Op-ed. *The New York Times*. Tuesday, 5 July 2016. A23.

Weimer, C.B. "Desire, Crisis, and Violence in *Fuenteovejuna*: A Girardian Perspective." In *El arte nuevo de estudiar comedias: Literary Theory and Spanish Golden Age Drama*, edited by Barbara Simerka, 162–86. Lewisburg, PA: Bucknell University Press, 1996.

Whitehead, David. "Cardinal Virtues: The Language of Public Approbation in Democratic Athens." *Classica et mediaevalia* 44 (1993): 37–75.

Wicks, Andrew C., Shawn L. Berman, and Thomas M. Jones. "The Structure of Optimal Trust: Moral and Strategic Implications." *Academy of Management Review* 24.1 (1999): 99–116.

Wiesner-Hanks, Merry E. *Women and Gender in Early Modern Europe*. 3rd ed. Cambridge: Cambridge: University Press, 2008.

Young, Charles M. "Aristotle on Temperance." *The Philosophical Review* (1988): 521–42.

Zamorano Rodríguez, María Luisa. *El Hospital de San Juan Bautista de Toledo durante el siglo XVI*. Toledo: Instituto Provincial de Investigaciones y Estudios Toledanos, 1997.

Zayas, María de. *El desengaño amado y premio de la virtud*. In *Novelas ejemplares y amorosas*, edited by Eduardo Rincón, 189–219. Madrid: Alianza, 1990.

Index of *Comedias*

NB: All *comedias* cited are from the Teatro Español del Siglo de Oro database, distributed by ProQuest: http://teso.chadwyck.com. For plot summaries of many of these plays, see David Castillejo, *Guía de ochocientas comedias del Siglo de Oro* (Madrid: Ars Millenii, 2002).

Alarcón, Juan Ruiz de (1581–1639)
- *La amistad castigada*. 134, 215n106, 240n86, 244n194
- *El Anticristo*. 78, 165, 210n157, 221n238, 226n59, 252n13
- *La crueldad por el honor*. 221n240, 238n57
- *La cueva de Salamanca*. 128, 237n24
- *El desdichado en fingir*. 244n182
- *El dueño de las estrellas*. 133, 237n7, 239n70, 248n45
- *Los empeños de un engaño*. 252n35
- *Examen de maridos*. 104, 231n89
- *Los favores del mundo*. 132, 236n92, 239n68
- *Ganar amigos*. 104, 134, 146, 213n41, 217n138, 220n220, 231n90, 238n53, 240n85, 244n184, 246n14
- *La manganilla de Melilla*. 140, 243n156
- *Mudarse por mejorarse*. 243n172
- *Los pechos privilegiados*. 238n48
- *La prueba de las promesas*. 141, 243n171
- *El tejedor de Segovia*. 215n94
- *La verdad sospechosa*. 243n167

Calderón de la Barca, Pedro (1600–81)
- *A Dios por razón de Estado*, auto sacramental. 39, 211n21
- *A tu prójimo como a ti*, auto sacramental. 214n63
- *Agradecer y no amar*. 28, 208n121, 211n8, 217n148, 222n261, 234n38
- *El alcalde de Zalamea*. 58, 154, 156, 202n41, 220n218, 248nn46, 61

– *El alcalde de sí mismo*. 213n47
– *Los alimentos del hombre*, auto sacramental. 63, 66, 211n15, 214nn71, 76–7, 222n293, 223n295
– *Amar después de la muerte*. 216n114, 221n244, 222n274
– *Amar y ser amado, y divina Philotea*, auto sacramental. 3, 200n5, 229n51
– *Amigo amante, y leal*. 238n28
– *El amor, honor y poder*. 214n64
– *Andrómeda y Perseo*, auto sacramental. 215n91, 218nn174, 178
– *Antes que todo es mi dama*. 240n100
– *El año santo de Roma*, auto sacramental. 108, 214n82, 219n183, 233n17, 252n33
– *El año santo en Madrid*, auto sacramental. 108, 221n250, 233n18
– *Apolo y Climene*. 241n124
– *El árbol del mejor fruto*. 169, 253n50
– *Las armas de la hermosura*. 216n121, 217n147, 253n61
– *Auristela y Lisidante*. 241n116
– *Basta callar*. 231n94
– *Los cabellos de Absalón*. 40, 213nn37, 39, 214n65, 222n275, 241n122
– *La cena de Baltasar*, auto sacramental. 171, 218n175, 253n66
– *La cisma de Inglaterra*. 213n43
– *El Conde Lucanor*. 241n117
– *¿Cuál es mayor perfección?* 242n138
– *La cura y la enfermedad*, auto sacramental. 61, 214n68, 221n253
– *Darlo todo, y no dar nada*. 213n54, 216n211
– *La devoción de la Cruz*. 173, 254n82
– *El día mayor de los días*, auto sacramental. 214n80
– *El diablo mudo*, auto sacramental. 35, 62, 211nn165–6, 221n257
– *Dicha y desdicha del nombre*. 246n17
– *Los dos amantes del cielo*. 238n46
– *Duelos de amor y lealtad*. 219n194
– *Eco y Narciso*. 24, 208n97
– *Las espigas de Ruth*, auto sacramental. 211n13
– *El encanto sin encanto*. 218n164
– *Los encantos de la Culpa*, auto sacramental. 208n118
– *Enfermar con el remedio*. 24
– *El escondido y la tapada*. 252n36
– *La estatua de Prometeo*. 211n16, 253n38
– *La exaltación de la Cruz*. 9, 202n36, 240n101
– *La fiera, el rayo y la piedra*. 216n123
– *Fineza contra fineza*. 217n139, 220n216, 222n265
– *Fortunas de Andrómeda y Perseo*. 251n10
– *Fuego de Dios en el querer bien*. 201n26

– *El galán fantasma*. 24, 208n99
– *El golfo de las Sirenas*. 241n112
– *La gran Cenobia*. 28, 81, 208n120, 215n104, 216n126, 222n268, 227n86
– *El gran mercado del mundo*, auto sacramental. 102, 231n85, 252n26
– *El gran príncipe de Fez*. 62, 221n258
– *Guárdate de la agua mansa*. 238n55
– *Gustos y disgustos son no más que imaginación*. 138, 239n59, 241n125
– *Hado y divisa de Leonido y Marfisa*. 219n185, 240n88
– *La hidalga del valle*, auto sacramental. 61, 221n254
– *La hija del aire, primera parte*. 253n51
– *La hija del aire, segunda parte*. 28, 208n122, 215n101, 241n126, 242n150
– *Los hijos de la Fortuna Teágenes y Cariclea*. 167, 252n28
– *La humildad coronada de las plantas*, auto sacramental. 155, 216n112, 227n2, 229n50, 237nn5–6, 27, 248n51
– *La inmunidad del sagrado*, auto sacramental. 66, 200n4, 214n78, 218n170, 223nn296, 298
– *El indulto general*, auto sacramental. 65, 215n92, 216n122, 223nn292–3, 298
– *El Joseph de las mujeres*. 218n165, 253n53
– *Judás Macabeo*. 240n106
– *El laberinto del mundo*, auto sacramental. 214n84, 219n191
– *El laurel de Apolo*. 172, 254n76
– *Lo que va del hombre a Dios*, auto sacramental. 211n22, 222n259, 225n33, 253n49
– *Llamados y escogidos*, auto sacramental. 237n26
– *El maestrazgo del Toyson*, auto sacramental. 208n100
– *El maestro de danzar*. 253n62
– *El mágico prodigioso*. 252n11
– *Mañanas de abril y mayo*. 208n110
– *El mayor monstruo del mundo*. 253n48
– *El médico de su honra*. 142, 170, 217n144, 253n64
– *Mejor está que estaba*. 172, 219n186, 237n9
– *Mística y real Babilonia*, auto sacramental. 225n34
– *El monstruo de la fortuna*. 26, 208n112
– *El monstruo de los jardines*. 253n65
– *Mujer, llora y vencerás*. 215n95, 242nn133, 149
– *Los misterios de la Misa*, auto sacramental. 201n12, 218n179
– *Ni Amor se libra de Amor*. 213n52
– *No hay cosa como callar*. 171, 254n67
– *No hay instante sin milagro*, auto sacramental. 75, 212n32, 216n121, 223n298, 225n40, 231n87, 252n27
– *No hay más fortuna que Dios*, auto sacramental. 214n83, 216n116

– *El nuevo hospicio de pobres*, auto sacramental. 76, 91–2, 214n81, 225n46, 228n30, 229n36
– *El orden de Melchisedech*, auto sacramental. 221n255
– *Las órdenes militares*, auto sacramental. 92, 222n263, 229n40
– *El origen, pérdida y restauración de la Virgen del Sagrario*. 215n102
– *El pastor fido*, auto sacramental. 120, 235n77, 253n44
– *Peor está que estaba*. 28, 172, 208n123
– *La piel de Gedeón*, auto sacramental. 218n172
– *El pintor de su deshonra*, auto sacramental. 202n45, 214nn58, 62, 224n6
– *El postrer duelo de España*. 214n72
– *La primer flor del Carmelo*, auto sacramental. 10, 49, 50, 202n44, 216n119
– *Psiquis y Cupido, que escribió para la ciudad de Toledo*, auto sacramental. 92, 214n57, 229n44
– *Psiquis y Cupido, que escribió para esta villa de Madrid*, loa for auto sacramental. 103, 231n88
– *El purgatorio de San Patricio*. 116, 207n88, 218n180, 234n55
– *¿Quién hallará mujer fuerte?*, auto sacramental. 34, 49, 81, 128, 200n13, 210n162, 214n85, 216n109, 222nn280, 286, 227n84, 238nn30–1, 40, 242nn136, 142, 254n70
– *El Rey Don Pedro en Madrid, e infanzón de Illescas*. 52, 215n103, 217nn136, 150, 222n288, 248n57
– *Saber del mal, y el bien*. 217n151, 238n49
– *El Santo Rey Don Fernando, primera parte*, auto sacramental. 79, 214n60, 222n287, 226n67, 227n5, 229n52, 238n32
– *La segunda esposa, y triunfar muriendo*, auto sacramental. 62, 221n256
– *El segundo blasón del Austria*, auto sacramental. 228n32
– *El segundo Scipión*. 215n105
– *La señora y la criada*. 229n41
– *La serpiente de metal*, auto sacramental. 26, 62, 222n264
– *La sibila del Oriente*. 64, 222n276
– *La siembra del señor*, auto sacramental. 208n101
– *El socorro general*, auto sacramental. 221n252
– *Sueños hay que verdad son*, auto sacramental. 109, 233nn19–20, 237n22, 242n141
– *La torre de Babilonia*, auto sacramental. 202n28
– *Las tres justicias en una*. xiv, 24, 56, 208nn98, 119, 216n131, 218n152, 252n29, 253n39
– *El valle de la zarzuela*, auto sacramental. 244n188
– *La vacante general*, auto sacramental. 219n187
– *El Viático Cordero*, auto sacramental. 215n88
– *La vida es sueño*. 7, 202n30, 241n107
– *La vida es sueño*, auto sacramental. 200n14, 226n63

Castro, Guillén de (1569–1630)
- *El Conde Alarcos*. 217n146
- *El Conde de Irlos*. 222n267, 242n130
- *Cuánto se estima el honor*. 222n266
- *El curioso impertinente*. 122, 127, 236n87
- *Dido y Eneas*. 122, 223n298
- *Don Quijote de la Mancha*. 249n85
- *El engañarse engañado*. 241nn118, 120, 242nn139, 144
- *La fuerza de la costumbre*. 218n162, 240n96
- *La humildad soberbia*. xiv, 33, 218n158
- *La justicia en la piedad*. xiv, 32–3, 48, 54, 63–4, 140, 210n141, 213n49, 215n93, 218nn158, 161, 219n201, 220n226, 222nn271, 284, 242n151
- *Los mal casados de Valencia*. 240n98
- *El mejor esposo*. 79, 106, 115, 226nn65–6, 232nn1–2, 234nn49–51
- *Las mocedades del Cid, Comedia primera*. 72, 128, 218n166, 224n24, 237n21, 241n111
- *Las mocedades del Cid, Comedia segunda*. 72, 215n98, 218n160, 224n24
- *El nacimiento de Montesinos*. 239n60
- *El perfecto caballero*. 72, 218n159, 224n25
- *La piedad en la justicia*. xvi
- *El pretender con pobreza*. 242n131
- *El vicio en los extremos*. 34, 171, 210nn158–9, 254n71

Cervantes, Miguel de (1547–1616)
- *La casa de los celos y selvas de Ardenia*. 237n25
- *La gran Sultana*. 81, 219n211, 227n85
- *Pedro de Urdemalas*. 98, 210n18, 219n199, 230nn54–5, 231n79, 239n61
- *El rufián dichoso*. 170
- *El vizcaíno fingido*. 252n31

Cueva, Juan de la (1550–1609?)
- *Comedia del príncipe tirano*. 41, 132, 213n40, 219n203, 236n2, 239n63
- *La constancia de Arcelina*. 241n115
- *El degollado*. 78, 226n57
- *El Infamador*. 51, 216n127, 233n22
- *La libertad de España por Bernardo del Carpio*. 76–7, 225nn43, 51
- *La libertad de Roma por Mucio Cevola*. 76, 222n269, 225n45
- *La muerte de Ajax Telamón sobre las armas de Aquiles*. 77, 218n168, 219nn204, 209, 226n56
- *La muerte de Virginia y Appio Claudio*. 52, 71, 216n133, 220n227. 224n13
- *La muerte del Rey don Sancho*. 211n7, 213n49
- *Tragedia del príncipe tirano*. 120, 130, 219n189, 235n76, 238n47

Diamante, Juan Bautista (1625–87)
- *Amor es sangre, y no puede engañarse.* 249n79
- *El cerco de Zamora.* 136, 240n103
- *Cuánto mienten los indicios, y el ganapán de desdichas.* 217n140, 218n154
- *El Hércules de Ocaña.* 226n75, 242n140
- *Ir por el riesgo a la dicha.* 211n17, 230n58
- *El jubileo de Porciúncula.* 228n20, 252n17
- *El nacimiento de Cristo,* zarzuela. 114, 234n45
- *El negro más prodigioso.* 164, 222n277, 251n8
- *Santa Teresa de Jesús.* 82, 227n89, 253nn41, 52

Lope de Vega (1562–1635)
- *El acero de Madrid, primera parte.* 61, 201n25, 221n248
- *El alcalde mayor.* 211n11, 216n112, 239n72, 248n64
- *Las almenas de Toro.* 121, 235n80
- *Los amantes sin amor.* 231n69, 248n60
- *Amar, servir y esperar.* 242n132, 244n179
- *El amigo por fuerza.* 216n113
- *El Amor enamorado.* 147, 220n228, 235n68, 246n18, 253n43
- *Amor, pleito y desafío.* 104, 213n41, 214n56, 217n138, 220n220, 231n91
- *Amor secreto hasta celos.* 241n127, 254n72
- *El animal de Hungría.* 214n69, 216n130
- *El anzuelo de Fenisa.* 35, 210n163
- *Arauco domado por el excelentísimo señor don García Hurtado de Mendoza.* 52, 216n132
- *El asalto de Mastrique por el Príncipe de Parma.* 72, 215n98, 224n26
- *El ausente en el lugar.* 248n59
- *Las aventuras de Don Juan de Alarcos.* 231n67
- *Bamba.* 135, 240n93
- *Barlán y Josafa.* 213n44
- *La batalla del honor.* 80, 226n74
- *La bella malmaridada.* 253n46
- *Las bizarrías de Belisa.* 249n80
- *El blasón de los Chaves de Villalba.* 219n205, 249n77
- *La boba para los otros, y discreta para sí.* 213n42, 220n221, 221n242
- *El bobo del colegio.* 238n38, 247n23
- *El caballero de Illescas.* 156, 248n56
- *El caballero del Sacramento.* 223n290
- *El capellán de la Virgen.* 210n153, 232n11
- *La cárcel de Sevilla,* entremés. 93, 229nn47–8
- *El cardenal de Belén.* 148, 247n22, 248n67, 251nn2–3

– *Carlos quinto en Francia*. 212n34
– *El casamiento en la muerte*. 210n143
– *El castigo sin venganza*. 55, 218n167, 237n18, 241n109, 253n59
– *Los cautivos de Argel*. 212n35, 221n236
– *Con su pan se lo coma*. 247n30
– *El conde Fernán González*. 224n5
– *Contra valor no hay desdicha*. 215n96, 223n290, 224n11, 249n78
– *La corona merecida*. 38, 210n164, 211n12, 224n20, 225n42, 249n89
– *Las cuentas del Gran Capitán*. 75, 215n107, 225n39, 242n135
– *El cuerdo loco*. 240n89
– *De cosario a cosario*. 248n33
– *Del mal lo menos*. 142, 212n26, 243n162, 244n192
– *La discreta venganza*. 79, 226n68, 227n1, 238nn45, 54
– *Don Juan de Castro, primera parte*. 98, 104, 231nn77, 92
– *La doncella Teodor*. 106, 232n3
– *El Duque de Viseo*. 217n134, 243n159, 244n196
– *El ejemplo de casadas y prueba de la paciencia*. 148, 153, 224n16, 247nn26, 28, 249nn76, 81
– *Ello dirá*. 225n52, 252n20
– *Los embustes de Zelauro*. 166, 252n22
– *Los embustes de Fabia*. 219n202
– *Los enemigos en casa*. 219n188
– *La esclava de su galán*. 236n93
– *El esclavo de Roma*. 230n59
– *Los españoles en Flandes*. 135, 239n69, 240n92
– *Las famosas asturianas*. 112, 234n37
– *La fe rompida*. 201n23
– *Las ferias de Madrid*. 216n128
– *La Filisarda*. 224n15
– *Las flores de Don Juan, y rico y pobre trocados*. 244n198
– *La fortuna merecida*. 211n24, 249n86
– *La francesilla*. 25, 208n103
– *Fuenteovejuna*. 42, 213n50, 256n116
– *La fuerza lastimosa*. 208n108, 217n135, 218n177, 219n190
– *El galán de la Membrilla*. 238n52
– *El gallardo catalán*. 243n170
– *El genovés liberal*. 201n11, 214n79, 234n36
– *Las grandezas de Alejandro*. 71, 216n115, 218n176, 224n12
– *El halcón de Federico*. 226n64
– *El Hamete de Toledo*. 222n278
– *Hay verdades que en amor*. 242n152

– *La hermosa Alfreda*. 218n169
– *La hermosa Esther*. 208n111
– *La hermosura aborrecida*. 249n69
– *El hidalgo Abencerraje*. 249n84
– *El hijo de Reduán*. 224n7
– *La historia de Tobías*. 85, 117, 170, 227n7, 231n93, 235n58, 253n55
– *El hombre por su palabra*. 217n141, 224n22, 226n61, 237n10, 251n6
– *El honrado hermano*. 105, 232n99
– *La ilustre fregona*. 134, 232n100, 240n83, 243n168
– *La imperial de Otón*. 48, 211n14, 215n95
– *El ingrato arrepentido*. 210n142
– *La inocente Laura*. 225n35, 252n14
– *La inocente sangre*. 132, 213n46, 220n222, 221n243, 239n64
– *Juan de Dios y Antón Martín*. 73, 85, 87, 91–2, 201nn14–15, 225n38, 227nn3, 9–10, 15, 229nn35, 37, 45–6, 231nn72, 74, 252n12
– *El laberinto de Creta*. 78, 221n237, 226n62
– *El labrador venturoso*. 211n25
– *Lo cierto por lo dudoso*. 210n139
– *Lo que hay que fiar del mundo*. 226n73, 249n83
– *Loa en alabanza de la humildad*. xvi
– *Loa en vituperio de la mala lengua*. 140, 243n161
– *Los locos de Valencia*. 88, 227n14, 228nn16, 18
– *Los locos por el cielo*. 116, 225n44, 234n53
– *La locura por la honra*. 148, 247n24
– *La madre de la mejor*. 224n29
– *La mal casada*. 148, 247n27
– *El Marqués de Mantua*. 213nn38, 48, 214n55
– *El mayor imposible*. 225n53
– *La mayor virtud de un rey*. xv, 54, 218n163
– *La mayor victoria de Alemania de Don Gonzalo de Córdoba*. 212n36, 243n165, 246n15
– *El mayorazgo dudoso*. 214n61
– *El mayordomo de la Duquesa de Amalfi*. 110, 233n30
– *El mejor alcalde, el rey*. 216n125, 220n223, 222n285, 235n66
– *El mejor maestro, el tiempo*. 213n51
– *El mejor mozo de España*. 148, 210n148, 247n29
– *Los melindres de Belisa*. 201n18
– *Mirad a quién alabáis*. 220n232, 235n67, 240n95
– *La mocedad de Roldán*. 239n80
– *El molino*. 105, 222n264, 232n97
– *Las mudanzas de Fortuna, y sucesos de Don Beltrán de Aragón*. 249n82

– *Los muertos vivos*. 224n14
– *Nadie se conoce*. 219n193, 226n76
– *La necedad del discreto*. 202n40, 233n33, 242n134
– *La niña de plata*. 94–5, 210n140, 230n61, 253n60
– *El niño inocente de la Guardia*. 201n19, 220n217
– *No son todos ruiseñores*. 244n195
– *La noche de San Juan*. 169, 253n45
– *La nueva victoria del Marqués de Santa Cruz*. 136, 240n104
– *El Nuevo Mundo descubierto por Cristóbal Colón*. 215n87
– *La obediencia laureada, y primer Carlos de Hungría*. 210n145
– *La octava maravilla*. 210n146, 240n82
– *Las paces de los reyes, y Judía de Toledo*. 231n70
– *El padrino desposado*. 202n29
– *Los peligros de la ausencia*. 131, 236n88, 238n56
– *Peribáñez y el Comendador de Ocaña*. 219n184, 248n66
– *El perro del hortelano*. 32, 210n137, 233n23
– *El perseguido*. 235n75, 239n74, 248nn44, 52
– *El Perseo*. 72, 202n42, 220n219, 225n31, 235nn69, 71, 253n47
– *El piadoso aragonés*. 220n233, 227n4, 252n23
– *El piadoso veneciano*. 39, 211n19
– *Los pleitos de Inglaterra*. 133, 136, 212n29, 215n92, 239n71, 240n105, 243n155
– *Pobreza no es vileza*. 20, 70, 72, 205n70, 224nn9, 19, 21, 27, 226n77, 246n16
– *El poder vencido y amor premiado*. 210n142
– *Los Ponces de Barcelona*. 201n24, 232n5, 252n16
– *Los Porceles de Murcia*. 123, 236n90
– *Porfiando vence amor*. 240n94
– *El postrer godo de España (El último godo)*. 46, 157, 249n70
– *Los prados de León*. 235n72, 251n4
– *El premio de la hermosura*. 221n235
– *El premio del bien hablar*. 248n58
– *El primer Fajardo*. 249n88
– *La primera información*. 215n108
– *El príncipe perfecto, parte primera*. 139, 242n148
– *El príncipe perfecto, parte segunda*. 72, 211n25, 214n74, 219n208, 224n23
– *Quien más no puede*. 242n137
– *Los Ramírez de Arellano*. 210n147, 218n152
– *La resistencia honrada y Condesa Matilde*. 211n220
– *El rey sin reino*. 216n117
– *El robo de Dina*. 71, 224n18, 242n143
– *Roma abrasada*. 170, 253n54
– *El ruiseñor de Sevilla*. 201n13

– *El saber por no saber, y vida de San Julián*. 219n196, 221n249, 222n260, 236n1
– *El saber puede dañar*. 220n230
– *San Isidro labrador de Madrid*. 228n21
– *San Nicolás de Tolentino*. 86, 88, 226n79, 227n12, 228n19
– *La Santa Liga*. 75, 225n41, 243n163
– *El sembrar en buena tierra*. 129, 210n144, 230n56, 238n37, 241n113, 244n197, 247n21
– *El serafín humano*. 237n15
– *La serrana de Tormes*. 81, 226n82, 228n28, 253n40
– *Servir a señor discreto*. 210n160
– *El servir con mala estrella*. 231n68
– *Si no vieran las mujeres*. 248n42
– *Si supieran a qué salgo*. 227n93
– *La sortija del olvido*. 216n118
– *El testigo contra sí*. 211n20
– *Los torneos de Aragón*. 248n41
– *Los trabajos de Jacob*. 239n75
– *La traición bien acertada*. 232n98
– *El triunfo de la humildad, y soberbia abatida*. xvi, 10
– *El valiente Céspedes*. 72, 224n28
– *El valor de las mujeres*. 81, 95, 226n80, 230n63, 241n108, 244n182
– *La varona castellana*. 81
– *La vengadora de las mujeres*. 81, 119, 226n81, 235n73
– *La venganza venturosa*. 243n160, 244n190
– *El verdadero amante*. 32, 210n137
– *La vida de San Pedro Nolasco*. 93, 225n36, 229n49, 239n77
– *El villano en su rincón*. 256n116
– *Virtud, pobreza y mujer*. xv, 110–11, 157, 164, 233nn27, 34, 249n74, 251n5
– *La viuda casada y doncella*. 123, 212n28, 236n88

Matos Fragoso, Juan de (1608?–89)
– *Amor, lealtad y ventura*. 220n229, 237n14
– *Callar siempre es lo mejor*. 142, 237n13, 238n41, 244n193
– *Con amor no hay amistad*. 127, 237n11
– *El genízaro de Hungría*. 201n16, 219n195
– *El hijo de la piedra*. 132, 154, 156, 159, 238n39, 239n67, 248nn40, 50, 53–5, 250n92, 251n7
– *Los indicios sin culpa*. 221n245, 237n12

Moreto, Agustín (1618–69)
– *La cautela en la amistad*. 219n206
– *La confusión de un jardín*. 219n192, 248n68
– *El Cristo de los milagros*. 232n6, 248n65

- *De fuera vendrá*. 210n154
- *El desdén con el desdén*. 239n58
- *La fuerza de la ley*. 223n289
- *Los hermanos encontrados*. 224n8, 239n76
- *Industrias contra finezas*. 222n270
- *Los jueces de Castilla*. 218n155, 220n234
- *El licenciado Vidriera*. 128, 237n19
- *Lo que puede la aprehensión*. 239n62
- *El mejor amigo, el rey*. 214n59
- *Primero es la honra*. 167, 252n32
- *Santa Rosa del Perú*. 82, 115, 227n88, 232n7, 234nn48, 56, 237n3, 242n147, 244n178, 252n12
- *Las travesuras del Cid, burlesca*. 244n183
- *El valiente justiciero*. 40, 51, 54–5, 61, 216n124, 218nn153, 171, 219nn198, 200, 221n246, 222n272, 223nn291, 299

Pérez de Montalbán, Juan (1602–38)
- *A lo hecho no hay remedio, y príncipe de los montes*. 249n87
- *Los amantes de Teruel*. 249n72, 253n42
- *Amor, lealtad y amistad*. 212n31
- *Cumplir con su obligación*. 238n51
- *La deshonra honrosa*. 208n109, 241n119
- *El divino portugués, San Antonio de Padua*. 214n85, 218n173
- *Segunda parte del Séneca de España, Don Felipe Segundo*. 134, 215n99, 222n262, 240n84
- *Los templarios*. 235n63
- *La toquera vizcaína*. 243n169
- *El valiente más dichoso, Don Pedro Guiral*. 219n213
- *El valiente Nazareno*. 168, 252n34

Quiñones de Benavente, Luis (1593?–1652)
- *Entremés famoso del abadegillo*. 202n31
- *La verdad*, entremés cantado. 90, 228n24

Rojas Zorrilla, Francisco de (1607–48)
- *Abrir el ojo*. 221n247, 224n22
- *Los áspides de Cleopatra*. 48, 210n155, 214n66, 215n90, 217n149
- *Donde hay agravios no hay celos*. 238n33, 243nn158, 176
- *Entre bobos anda el juego*. 210n151
- *Lo que quería ver el Marqués de Villena*. 211n9
- *El más impropio verdugo por la más justa venganza*. 33, 55, 202n43, 210n152, 222n282, 240n97
- *No hay amigo para amigo*. 239n65, 244n189

– *No hay ser padre siendo rey*. 218n156, 237n23
– *Obligados y ofendidos*. 241n123
– *Peligrar en los remedios*. 240n102
– *Persiles y Sigismunda*. 219n197
– *El profeta falso Mahoma*. 138, 241n128, 242n145
– *Progne y Filomena*. 238n43, 243n166, 244n180
– *Santa Isabel, reina de Portugal*. 89, 228n22
– *Los trabajos de Tobías*. 85, 107, 117, 227n8, 228n25, 233n12, 234n57
– *La traición busca el castigo*. 122, 210n157, 213n45, 236n86, 238n44

Rueda, Lope de (1510–65)
– *Eufemia*. 217n142
– *Prendas de amor*. 217n143

Solís, Antonio de (1610–86)
– *El doctor Carlino*. 242n153
– *La gitanilla de Madrid*. 231n95

Tirso de Molina (1584?–1648)
– *Los amantes de Teruel*. 238n35
– *Amar por arte mayor*. 242n146
– *Amar por razón de estado*. 240n99
– *Amazonas en las Indias*. 201n22, 243n173
– *El amor médico*. 6, 201n17
– *Amor y celos hacen discretos*. 244n181
– *Antona García*. 221n241
– *Averígüelo Vargas*. 225n55, 243n154, 244n186, 249n73
– *El castigo del penséque*. 123, 236n91
– *La Dama del Olivar*. 231n71, 253n57
– *Del enemigo el primer consejo*. 243n164
– *Don Gil de las calzas verdes*. 223n298
– *Doña Beatriz de Silva*. 238n32
– *La elección por la virtud*. 159, 238n50, 250nn94–5
– *Escarmientos para el cuerdo*. 217n145, 239n73
– *Esto sí que es negociar*. 250n93
– *La huerta de Juan Fernández*. 57, 215n89, 238n34, 244n185
– *La lealtad contra la envidia*. 10, 25, 202n46, 208n104, 226nn58, 70
– *Marta la piadosa*. 100, 118, 165, 231nn82–3, 235n64, 239n66, 243n177, 252n19
– *El mayor desengaño*. 208n107, 231n84
– *La mejor espigadera*. 91, 228n33, 248n49
– *La mujer que manda en casa*. 254n69

– *La peña de Francia*. 212n27, 219n212
– *Por el sótano y el torno*. 212n33
– *Próspera fortuna de Don Álvaro de Luna, primera parte*. 211n23
– *La prudencia en la mujer*. xvi, 129, 147, 208n105, 213n51, 217n134, 238n36, 247n19
– *Quien no cae no se levanta*. 233n24
– *La república al revés*. 127, 220n214, 235n65, 237nn16–17
– *La santa Juana*. 95, 215n86, 230n66, 254n68
– *Santo y sastre*. 59, 86, 90, 165–6, 210n138, 220n224, 227n11, 228n26, 252nn15, 21
– *Segunda parte de Santa Juana*. 96, 214n70, 231nn73, 75
– *Siempre ayuda la verdad*. 244n187
– *Tanto es lo demás como lo de menos*. 210n138, 220n231, 253n60
– *La venganza de Tamar*. 41
– *Ventura te dé Dios, hijo*. 239n76, 240nn90–1
– *La vida de Herodes*. 211n10, 238n42
– *La villana de la Sagra*. 220n215, 228n27
– *La villana de Vallecas*. 230n65

Zamora, Antonio de (1662?–1728)
– *Amar es saber vencer, y el arte contra el poder*. 217n134
– *Áspides hay Basiliscos*. 243n174
– *El custodio de la Hungría, San Juan Capistrano*. 73, 219n210, 225n37
– *El hechizado por fuerza*. 6, 201n27
– *El lucero de Madrid y divino labrador San Isidro*. 252n30
– *Mazariegos y Monsalves*. 222n279
– *Todo lo vence el amor*. 225n54

Index

abbess, 95, 111
Abel, 50, 216n112
Absalom, 99, 231n80
abstinence, 107
accounting, 103, 129
Acevedo, Pedro Pablo de, 3
Achilles, 190
Acis, 110
act of contrition, 43
Acteon, 109
actor, 43, 102
adage, 166
Adam, 62, 65–6, 223n293
adelantado mayor, 212n31
adolescence, 133
adultery, 121, 123, 131
advice, 127, 160–1, 244n178
Aeneas, 111, 119–20, 190
afecto, 35
affect, 84–5
Agamben, Giorgio, 46
agency, 161
agravio, 49
Ágreda y Vargas, Diego de, xvi
al-Andalus, 46
Alarcón, Juan Ruiz de, 213n41, 220n220
albarelo, 17 fig. 6. *See also* pharmacy (jar)
Albarracín Teulón, Agustín, 201n8
Alcalá de Henares, 183; University of, 183, 251n109
alcalde, 57, 93
Alcañiz, 187
Alcázar, 47
alchemy, 22, 119, 205n66, 235n70, 245n200
Alcibiades, 188
Alcides, 70
Alcina, 120–1
alcoholism, 91
Alcor, 183–4
Alemán, Mateo, 141, 243n175
Aler Ibarz, Cristina, 206n75
Alexander the Great, 71, 105, 190, 196, 231n96
Alfonso I, King, 81
Alfonso II (El Casto), King, 112, 235n72
Alfonso VI, King, 75
Alfonso X, King, 152
Algiers, 157
allegory, 3, 31, 35, 38, 43–4, 46, 62, 64, 73, 75–6, 92–3, 107–9, 111, 121, 123, 124 fig. 14, 129, 155, 169, 214nn69, 85, 221n257
allergy, xiii
Almanzor, 46

alms, 86, 88, 90, 93, 98, 100, 102, 230n57
Alpujarras, 72
altar, 120–1
alumbrado, 184, 186, 257n135. *See also* Illuminist
Álvarez de Araujo y Cuéllar, Ángel, 229n38
Alvia de Castro, Fernando, 177, 255n98
Amazon, 247n32
ambassador, 37, 94, 134, 141, 172, 186, 211n4, 258n150
Amberes, Index of, 187
ambergris, 167
amethyst, 43
Amnon, 231n80
amomum, 167
Anderson, Sherry Ruth, 230n60
andreia, 80. *See also* courage
Andretta, Elisa, 205n65
androgyny, 125, 129, 143, 189
Andromache, 78
andros, 246n10
anêr, 80
angel, 36, 63–4, 66, 76, 82, 99, 107, 223n293, 232–3n11; Gabriel, 73, 225n32; guardian, 73; Michael, 73, 74 fig. 13, 225n32; Raphael, 73, 117
Anger, 10, 12, 29, 33, 47–8, 55, 130, 135, 182, 238n45, 240n97, 242n143
Anglo-Saxon, 110–11
animal, 6, 70, 89, 141, 143
Annunciation, 225n32
Añorbe y Corregel, Tomás de, xvi
Ansaldi, Saverio, 179
Anselm of Canterbury, Saint, 61, 221n249
Antaeus, 197
Antichrist, 78, 165
antidotario, 7, 12, 14, 203n48
antidote, 12–22, 135–6, 138, 145–6, 166, 182, 188, 206n85, 207n86
anti-Machiavellianism, 177–81, 237n20, 256n116
Antón Martín, 5, 205n62
Antoniou, S.A., 208n117
aperitif, 6
apocrypha, 109, 117
aporia, 29
apothecary, 12, 20–1, 24, 139, 203n56, 203–4n57, 204nn58–9, 205nn62, 64; box, 155, 166, 188–9; brother, 205n62; personal, 205n67; shop, 205n62, 206n75
apotheosis, 44, 50, 55, 61, 63, 135
appetite, 6, 78, 115, 136, 241n110
apple, 200n14
Aquinas, Thomas, Saint, xv, 178, 200n9, 200n6, 236n2
Arabic, 12, 110
Aragon, 14, 52, 81, 125, 131, 157, 186, 202n48
Aranda, Countess of, 160
Aranda Quintanilla, Francisco de, 66, 67 fig. 12
Aranjuez, 18, 205n66
arbitrista, 133–5, 227n6
archdeacon, 183–4
architecture, 4, 29
archive, xvii, 16
Arellano, Ignacio, 226n72
arena, 196
arete, xiv, 191, 195
Arete Initiative, xiv
Arigón, Rafael de, 205n67
Ariosto, Ludovico, 111–12, 120–1, 234n35
aristocracy, 131, 154, 160–1, 178, 194, 250n102

Aristotle, 4, 18, 29–31, 37, 143, 173, 178, 200n6, 209nn125, 129, 253n37, 255n103
arm, 65, 101
armour, 225n32
army, 99, 129, 195
arousal, 125
arrogance, 33–4, 96, 135, 175, 194, 240n96
arrow, 25, 82
arsehole, 167
artillery, 218n177
ascetic, 69
Asclepius, 208n117
Asenath, 109
Asia, 48
Asmodeo, 117
assassination, 111, 147, 247n19
astrologer, 26, 159
atheism, 200n16
Athens, 195
athlete, xiv
attitude, 169
Augustine, Saint, xv, 44, 45 fig. 11, 200n9
Augustinian, 12, 38
Augustus, Emperor, 52, 110, 217n134, 247n32
aurea mediocritas, 28, 30. *See also* Golden Mean
Aurelian, 111
authorship, 217n136, 240n83
auto de fe, 53
auto sacramental, 3, 34, 46, 55, 63–4, 66, 73, 77, 81, 84, 91, 103, 152, 168, 187, 214n69, 216n121, 223n298
autobiography, 145
autonomy, 250n107
Avarice, 58, 101. *See also* Greed
Ave Maria, 101
Avicenna, 18
ayo, 136

baby, 133
Bacchus, 166
Badajoz, 75
balance, 43, 46, 84, 139
balsam, 167
Baltimore, 10
bandage, 90
bandit, 87
Baptista, Joana, 249n75
barbarism, 243n163
Barcelona, 203n48
Baron, Hans, 250n97
Baroque, 26, 31–3, 59, 79, 102, 116, 125, 171, 178–9, 190–1, 226n72, 240n87
Bass, Laura, 250n106
Bataillon, Marcel, 184, 186–7, 257nn131–7, 258–9
bath, 109
baton, 129
battle, 3, 73–5, 111, 129, 186, 261n16; battlefront, 123; field, 195–6; flag, 108; legal, 203n56
bawd, 62
Bayliss, Robert, 233n32, 235n81
beast, 114
beata, 165, 252n12
beauty, 37, 80, 118, 148, 156, 165, 179, 188
bed, 99, 237n23; bedroom, 119–20
beggar, 87–9, 91, 96, 100, 102–3, 105, 188, 227n13; false, 102
beheading, 56. *See also* decapitation
Belém do Pará, 249n75
bellum virtutem et vitiorum, 108
Beltrán, Luis, 200n11
Benedictine, 184

bengala, 129
Bennett, William J., xiii
bequest, 100
Berco, Cristian, 226n79
Bermúdez, Gonzalo, 136
Bernard, Saint, Order of, 18
Bernini, Gian Lorenzo, 82, 227n90
betrayal, 190
bewitchment, 6
Bible, 26, 48; Catholic, 117
bigamy, 123
bilingualism, 192
Bilinkoff, Jodi, 249n87
bird, 49, 89, 215n108; chattering, 243n163
birth: of Christ, 225n32; humble, 156
bishop, 187, 204n59
blade, 57
blindness, 59, 99, 102–3, 220n232
blood, 32, 47, 50, 52, 55–6, 110, 119–21, 128, 156–8, 161, 216n112, 217n137, 222n279, 249n73; draining, 142; purity, 16, 41, 107, 204n59, 223n298, 232n8, 234n44 (see also *limpieza de sangre*)
bloodshed, 73, 132
Boaz, 91
Boccaccio, Giovanni, 119–20
Boisrobert, Le Métel de, 172
boñiga, 6
Bornholdt, Claudia, 116
Bosch, Hieronymus, 227n13
botany, 6, 145, 245n2
botica, 204n59, 206n75. *See also* pharmacy
boticario, 16, 18, 20, 145 *See also* pharmacist
Boticario del Real Hospital, 18
Bourbon, 125
Bouvet, Honoré, 69, 79, 82, 206n85
Boyd, Barbara Weiden, 246n9
Boyle, Margaret, 92
Bracciolini, Poggio, 160
bravery, 148. *See also* valour
Brazil, 5, 249n75
bread, 66, 89–91, 96, 228n31; of Life, 91; riot, 228n29
breakfast, 90
bribe, 57–8, 220n214
bride, 117
Bristol, Earl of, 172
broadside, 202n34
brother, 224n17, 237n23; half brother, 231n80
Brown, Peter, 113, 234n40
Brownlee, Marina, 150
Bruni, Leonardo, 250n97
Brutus, 147, 247n19
Buen Genio, 102–3
bullet, 55
Buonaccorso da Montemagno, 159–60, 250n97
Burckhardt, Jacob, 239n81
Burgos, 220n225
burial, 85, 92, 104; alive, 120
burning: alive, 51, 53–4; in effigy, 51
Bush, George W., 134
business, 127
Butler, Judith, 245n8
Byrne, Susan, 207n89
Byzantine Senate, 127, 237n17

Cabré, Montserrat, 201n25
cadaver, 116. *See also* corpse
Caesar, Julius, 147, 190, 193, 195, 197, 247n19
calaguala, 6
calculus, 155, 167
Calderón de la Barca, Pedro, 16, 25, 38, 94, 112, 137, 147, 169, 180–1, 189, 200n3, 216n121, 217n136, 223n298, 251n109

Calenus, 110
Callahan, William J., 229n39
calque, 192, 260n11
Cambridge University, xvi
Camões, Luis de, 172
Campbell, Jodi, 91
Campos Marín, Ricardo, 228n17
Camps Clemente, Manuel, 206n75
Camps Surroca, Manuel, 206n75
Canada, 244n187
Cáncer, Jerónimo, 25
cape, 165, 167, 252n17. *See also* cloak
Capella, Martianus, 150
Capistrano, Juan, Saint, 73
Capra, Galeazzo Flavio, 37, 94, 108, 152, 211n4, 230n57
Capsia, 20
captain, 72, 224n22
captivity, 78, 121, 157
carat, 43
cardamon, 167
Cardinal Virtue, xv, 69, 110, 161, 178, 200nn10–11, 236n2
Carlos, Prince, 25
Carlos I, King, 18
carnage, 72
Carranza, Alonso, 165
Carranza, Bartolomé, Archbishop, 186
carro, 44, 85, 233n17
carta ejecutoria, 212n25
Carthage, 133, 239n79
Cascardi, Anthony, 9, 30, 156, 175
casino, xiii
Castell, Antonio, 14
Castile, 21, 38–9, 53, 60, 76, 91, 98, 100, 132, 212n25, 218n152, 230n62; Cortes of, 206nn75, 79
Castilla, Alonso de, 187
Castilla Urbano, Francisco, 255n105
Castillo de Villasante, Diego del, 215n100
castration, 113, 234n40
Castro, Álvaro de, 12
casuistry, xiv, xvii, 39, 42, 49, 57, 142, 161, 168, 184, 234n52, 253n37, 260n161
Cataluña, 14, 202n48, 249n75
Catholic, 47, 75, 81, 85, 113, 116, 173, 233n11; Bible, 117; Church, 118; Monarch, 204n59, 212n31
Catilinarian, 196
Cato, Marcus Porcius, 52, 133, 147, 190, 217n134, 247n19
cavalry, 193, 261n16
cave, 94
Celestina, 95, 230n64
celibacy, 113, 116
censorship, 175, 176 fig. 19
centum capita, 245n7
Cerinthus, 110
Cervantes, Miguel de, 75, 122, 161, 187, 190, 220n222, 241n121; *Don Quijote*, 190, 259n160
Céspedes, Alonso de, 72
chain, 51–2, 228n18; gold, 90, 95, 111, 230n64
chair, 46
chamberlain, 157
Chancillería Real (Valladolid), 211n20, 212n31
chapel, 168
chariot race, 196
Charity, xv, 5, 36, 78, 84–105, 107, 112, 119, 129, 155, 177, 193, 227–32, 252n12; True, 93
charlatan, 102
Charles V, Emperor, 21, 183, 187, 209n125, 245n2, 259n151
Charybdis, 97
Chastity, 4 fig. 1, 36, 83, 95, 105–25, 127, 147–8, 155, 168, 232–6, 247n19; lack of, 122; within marriage, 117;

for men, 112; obsession with, 131; permanent, 115
cheese, 91
Chevalier, Maxime, 201n8
Chicago, University of, xiv
chicanery, 204n58
chicken, 89
chicory, 205n66
child, 34, 49, 89, 93, 96, 98, 140, 148
Childers, William, xiv, 77, 190–1, 198, 225n48, 260n3
Chile, 52, 112
chirimías, 46
chivalry, 10, 72; romance of, 111, 120
Christ, 26, 61, 66, 85, 103, 115, 165; birth of, 225n32; Child, 115
Christianity, 177
Cicero, Marcus Tullius, xv, 146, 150, 193, 195–6
cinnamon, 20
circumstance, 53, 63, 168, 171, 207n86, 239n79, 253n37; mitigating, 120; of succession, 196
citizen, 178
civet, 167
civil disobedience, 42, 213n50
class (social), 83, 95, 145–63, 194, 236n85, 245–51, 261n16
classical tradition, 198
Clastidium, 261n16
Clavero, Bartolomé, 211n11
clemency, 64, 66, 190
Clemente, Claudio, 177
Cleopatra, 48
clergy, 95
cloak, 62, 87 92–3, 142, 167
close reading, xvii
cloud, 47
Clouse, Michele, 204nn58–9, 205n64
Clusium, 71
coat of arms, 34, 66, 156, 184, 248n59 (see also *empresa*); Inquisitorial, 223n298
coconut, 101–2
code, 141
coffin, 196
Coimbra: College, 209n125; Commentary, 209n125
coin, 150, 151 fig. 16, 193, 212n25, 227n14, 230n66, 261n16; senatorial, 247n32
coincidentia oppositorum, 31
collateral damage, 206n85
College of Apothecaries, 16
Colleran, Joseph M., 221n249
Colón, Hernando, 259n160
colony, 52, 134
Columbus, Christopher, 259n160
combat: gladiatorial, 196; mounted, 261n16; single, 194, 261n16 (*see also* monomachy)
comedia de santa, 248n37
comedy, 188; Roman, 193
commerce, 127
compassion, 63, 100
Comte-Sponville, André, 3, 37, 64, 70, 78
conceptismo, 31, 179
concordia, 12, 202–3n48
Concordia apothecariorum Barchinonensium, 12, 13 fig. 4
confessor, 40, 117; manual for, 118
confidence, 29
Confirmation, sacrament of, 75
confraternity, 5, 92, 229nn36, 40, 43
Confraternity of the Santa Caridad, 92, 229n43
Congilda, 111
Congress, 63
conquest, 48, 76, 136

conquistador, 76, 123, 135, 225n49
conscience, 57, 99, 179; scruples of, 168; wide, 219n207
consecration, 108
Consejo Real, 39
conspiracy, 196, 204n59
constancy, 128, 138, 237n23
consulado, 220n225
consulship, 195–6
continence, 113
Continental Congress, 150, 151 fig. 17
convent, 88, 95, 116, 205n66, 258n149
conversion, 170, 253n56
converso, 12, 18, 204n59
cooking, 53
copper, 96
Córdoba, 228n29
Córdoba, Juan de, 215n107
cordura, 33
1 Corinthians, xv, 93, 113, 232n4
Cornellana, 16
Coroleu, Alejandro, 183, 250n96
Coronel, Luis, 184
corpse, 110
Corpus Christi, 68, 91, 228n31
Corradini, Antonio, 123, 124 fig. 14
corral, 68
corregidor, 206n75, 212n31
corruption, 251n110
Cortes, 204n59; de Castilla, 206nn75, 80; de León, 206n80; de Madrid, 206nn75, 79; de Valladolid, 206n80
Cortés, Hernán, 76–7, 225n48
cosmetics, 165
Costa, Pedro da, 249n75
costume, 34, 44, 167
Council of Trent, 209n125
counsel, 141
counsellor, 40
counterfeit, 166, 188
courage, 29, 30, 69–83, 156, 161, 199n8, 240n81
court, 38, 92, 101, 112, 180, 183, 187, 205n66, 235n70; heavenly, 66; imperial, 183, 258n149; jester, 53; lady, 234n35; lesser, 212n25; official, 58, 220n214; receiver, 212n25; reporter, 212n25; system, 128
courtesy, xiii, 10, 134
courtier, 59
courtly love, 111, 233n32
courtroom, 68, 122
courtship, 141
Covarrubias, Sebastián de, 154–5
cow, 91; cowboy, 61
Cowan, Robert, 246n9
cowardice, 27 fig. 9, 29, 31, 33–4, 73, 82, 141, 243n173, 252n17
Cremona, 86
Cretan, 60
Crete, 78
crime, 38, 49–51, 53, 56, 62, 123, 130, 168–9, 170–1, 203n57, 217n140, 254nn68–9; hidden, 53
criminal, 92–3, 204n58, 221n238; lawsuit, 128
cripple, 227n13
Cristóbal de la Cruz, 170
Cross, Holy, 26, 66
crown, 38, 41
crucifixion, 26
cruelty, 10, 33, 52–4, 135, 137–8, 143, 148, 217n137, 218n152, 240n97; salutary, 256n116
Cruickshank, Don, 25, 37, 172, 201n17
Crusades, 75
crutch, 90
Cruz, Anne J., 91, 229n43
cruzado, 211n25
Cubillo de Aragón, Álvaro, xvi

Cueva y Silva, Leonor de, 236n88
Culpa, 62, 102–3, 171
cult, 150, 194, 261n16; state-sanctioned, 195
curandera, 6, 201n25
Curio, 197
cymbal, 93
Czech Republic, xiv

dagger, 71, 110
Daniel, Henry, 7, 245n6
daño, 138
Dantisco, Juan, 186
Dares, 173
Darius III, King, 71
daughter, 224n17
David, King, 10, 41, 213n39, 231n80
David-Peyre, Yvonne, 201n8
De Brosse, 172
De la Cámara, María Luisa, 215n97
dead man, 101–2, 104
Deadly Sin, 58, 118, 175
death, 49, 50, 60, 62, 97, 100, 115–16, 120–1, 123, 131, 141–2, 148, 188, 228n29, 233n11, 236n83, 243n172, 246n11; deathbed, 64; dishonourable, 204n58; penalty, 39, 41, 50, 52; scorn of, 146; sentence, 55, 130
Deborah, Judge, 35, 49, 81, 128
debt, 49, 66, 98, 129, 242n146
decapitation, 51, 72, 76, 216n125, 225n44. *See also* beheading
deceit, 141–2, 166–7, 243n175, 251n110
deconstruction, 22, 29, 191, 246n13
deer, 167
deferral, 142, 238n56
deficiency, 209n126
deformity, 188
deification, 146, 261n16
Del Río Parra, Elena, xiv, 234n52
Delilah, 168
democracy, 158, 162
demographics, 236n85
demon, 6, 47, 63–4, 73, 93, 117, 168; demonic possession, 6, 10
dentist, 102
derecho, 38–9. *See also* rights
Derrida, Jacques, 22–4, 26, 118, 143, 146, 246n13
desengaño, 190
D'Este, Isabella, 112
determinism, 253n58
deus ex machina, 66
Devereux, Daniel T., 209n129
devil, 44, 45 fig. 11, 73, 117, 169
DeVun, Leah, 245n200
Diamargariton, 18
diamond, 43, 70
Diana, 109
Dido, 111, 119, 121–2, 235nn74–5, 236n91; chaste, 119–20
diegesis, 150
Digby, George, 172
Digby, John, Sir, 172
dilatio, 42, 142, 238n56
diligence, 182
Dinah, 224n17
Dioscorides, 18, 20
diplomacy, 136
discretion, 134, 141, 243n159
disguise, 93, 103, 188
dissimulation, 140, 142–3, 256n116
Distant Reading, xvii
distillation, 205n66
doctor, 9, 12, 18, 20, 23, 166, 200n1, 204n58, 206nn75, 85, 207nn86, 88, 234n40, 245n2; Jewish, 208n105
dog, 109

dollar, 150, 151 fig. 17
Dolomite, 205n65
Dominican, 7
Domitian, Emperor, 110, 247n32
Don Quijote, 137, 160–1
doncella, 106, 148
Donnell, Sidney, 226n72
door, 43, 86, 90; hinge, 178
doorstep, 99
Dopico Black, Georgina, 122
dosage, 207n86
double standard, 122, 236n82
Doubleday, Simon R., 248n48
doubt, 82, 119, 158
dowry, 94, 107, 155, 230n62
dragon, 53
dream, 109
Drias, 110
drone, 126
drug, 22–3, 139, 145, 167, 206n85; life-threatening, 204n58; magic, 207n96
Dubler, César, 245n2
ducado, 95, 99, 112
duck, 166
duel, 10, 60, 64

Eamon, William, 235n70
ear, 53, 59, 64
Earl, D.C., 191
eclogue, 147
economics, 236n85
economy, 100, 105, 107, 130, 160, 234n35
Edict of 1525, 186
Egginton, William, 260n163
Egido, Aurora, 241n121, 250n101
Eguía, Miguel de, 183, 257n133
Egypt, 48, 109, 111, 133
eighteenth century, xvi, 16
Eire, Carlos, 98
ejecutoria, 158, 249n87
ekphrasis, 34, 166
El Cid, 72
El Escorial, 18, 175, 176 fig. 19, 205n67, 209n125
El Pardo, palace of, 133
El premio de la virtud, xvi
elephant, 18
Elfleda, 111
Elisa, 120, 235n75. *See also* Dido
elixir, 207n86
Elliott, John, 240n87
emblem, 34, 65, 141, 156, 220n222
emotion, 42, 139
emperor, 146, 150, 246n11, 258n149; Holy Roman, 246n15, 259n151
empire, 32, 48, 50, 76, 88; Byzantine, 127, 237n17; Ottoman, 81; Roman, 110; Spanish, 125, 134–5
empresa, 34
enamel, 158, 165
enchantress, 120
England, 7, 48, 236n82
English, 6, 18, 57, 172, 200nn9, 11, 202n37, 233n28, 250n99, 262n39
Ennius, 193
Enrique II, King, 212n25
Entellus, 173
entremés, 201n10
Envy, 10, 12, 175, 182
Ephraim, 109
epic, 195–7, 246n9
epideictic, 120
epigone, 197
epistemology, 177
epistolary, 150, 225n48
epithema, 208n121
epithet, 217n137
epitictima, 208n121

equality, 37
equity, 196, 217n134
equivocation, 143, 184, 244n197
Erasmus, Desiderius, 116, 144, 166, 181–9, 191, 258–9; *Colloquies*, 187, 258n151; *Enchiridion*, 181–7, 258nn149, 151, 259nn151, 154; *Encomium Moriae*, 259nn158, 160
error, 170
eschatology, 165
Escobar y Mendoza, Antonio, 235n60
escudo, 87–9, 227n14
espejo de príncipes, 213n37. *See also* mirror, for princes
Etelfrida, Princess, 111
ethics, 144, 199n1; pagan, 105
ethnic studies, 199n1
Etruscan, 71
etymology, 146
Eucharist, 79
eudaimonia, 29
Eurialio, 190
Euripides, 140, 243n163
Europe, 94, 172, 183, 232n7
Eustoquia, Saint, 148, 149 fig. 15
evil, 145, 169, 206n85, 207n96; lesser, 137
exception, 59; of persons, 41
excess, 209n126
excrement, 6
executioner, 216n125
exemplarity, 191, 233n26
exile, 51, 56, 157, 216n129
exorcism, 117
exorcist, 6
Exum, F., 215n92
eye, 59, 140, 243n154; eyesight, 140

Fabriano, 131
face, 251n9; double-faced, 188
fairness, 37, 42
fairy tale, 96
faith, xv, 55, 62, 75, 77, 84–5, 93, 121, 140, 177, 179, 232n4; alone, 230n53; bad, 166; faithfulness, 123, 128, 138, 190, 237n23; good, 119
famine, 133
fantasy, 121
Farfán, Agustín, 12
father, 132, 166, 247n19
Fault, 62. *See also* Culpa
Faunas, 110
fear, 29, 56–7, 59, 79, 80, 141, 147, 173, 220n232, 243n172, 252n17; fearlessness, 70
femina, 246n9
femininity, 80, 125, 148, 174
feminist, 199n1; feminist theology, 94
fennel, 205n66
Fernández, Mauro, 16
Fernández de Córdoba, Gonzalo, 75
Fernández de Madrid, Alfonso, 183–4, 186
Fernández y Romero, Pedro, 16
Fernando II (el Católico), King, 175
Fernando IV, King, 132, 136, 208n105
Ferrara, 112
Ferreira Furtado, Júnia, 249n75
fertility, 232n7
fiddle, 170, 196
Fierceness, 27 fig. 9, 34
Figueroa y Córdoba, Diego, 81–2
Figueroa y Córdoba, José, 81–2
Filelfo, Francesco, 160
film, 122, 235n81
Fine, Ruth, 253n56
fine arts, 29
Fink de Backer, Stephanie, 51, 230n62
fire, 93, 170, 218n152
First Global Conference on Sins, Vices, and Virtues, xiv

fiscal, 128
Flack, Roberta, 244n187
flag, 129, 150, 151 fig. 17, 156
flattery, 59, 220n232, 234n35
Flaxbinder de Dantzig, Johann, 258n150
Flemish, 183
flirtation, 127
flood, 228n29
Florence, 160, 174, 177, 246n15, 256n105
Flynn, Maureen, 229nn36, 40
food, 90–1, 241n110; food shortage, 89–90
foot, 53, 224n7, 244n186; footprint, 246n13
Forcione, Alban, 187, 217n137, 256n116
Ford, Jeremiah, 236n83
forgiveness, 130
Forte, Juan Manuel, 174
Fortitude, xv, 27 fig. 9, 29, 31, 34–5, 53, 68–83, 110, 113, 123, 136–8, 146–7, 157, 178, 182, 196, 221n243, 224–7
fortress, 47, 107
Fortune, 70, 140, 256n105
Fothergill-Payne, Louise, 200n3
Foucault, Michel, 51, 56–7, 88, 122
Fourth Lateran Council, 9
fox, 143
France, 44, 76, 80, 88, 136, 255n93
Francis, Saint, 89
Franciscan, 38, 73, 184
fraud, 58, 203nn56–7; alchemical, 235n70; pharmaceutical, 204n58
free will, 170, 253n58
French, 22, 75–7, 166, 246n13
Freud, Sigmund, 246n13
friar, 184, 186, 258n151; Mercedarian, 251n109
friendship, 57, 104, 122, 127, 156, 170–1, 190
Fuchs, Barbara, 232n8, 242n129
fuero, 60
funeral, 7; funeral eulogy, 194
Furió Ceriol, Fadrique, 179

Gabriel (archangel), 73, 225n32
Gabriel, Richard A., 232n96
Gaius, 196
Galba, Emperor, 151 fig. 16
Galindo, Pedro, 107
galleys, 51, 216n129
gambling, xiii, 154
García-Alejo, Rafael Huertas, 228n17
García Cuervo, Juan, 16
garden, 107, 145, 205n66; body as a, 232n7; botanical, 18; gardener, 52, 145
Garden of Eden, 62, 81
garlic, 167
Gellius, Aulus, 195
gemstone, 43, 65
gender, 82–3, 95, 109–10, 145–63, 194, 236n82, 245–51; ambiguity, 189, 245n8; constructed, 245n8; of plants, 145; studies, xv
genealogy, xiii–xvii, 144, 146, 159, 190, 193
General Hospital (Madrid), 205n62
Generosity, xiii, 5, 78, 84–105, 174, 231n68, 261n14
Genesis, 61–2, 224n17
genie, 188
Genius, 246n11
genocide, 133
genus, 145
Germany, 116, 255n93
Ghia, Walter, 179
ghost, 98
giant, 197

Girard, René, 68, 207n86
glass, 164
globe, 135
Gluttony, 90, 118, 136
goat, 167
God, 26, 44, 47–8, 50, 56, 62, 66, 71, 73, 75–7, 84, 87, 91, 94, 96, 98–9, 103–4, 107, 115, 118, 168, 179, 206n85, 231n74; feminine, 94
god, 52, 146, 188, 195, 217n134, 246n11; king as, 215n92; of medicine, 208n117; Roman, 192; rural, 188
goddess, 109, 119, 150, 151 figs 16–18, 194–5; Virtus, 247nn31–2
Goes, Emmanuel de, 209n125
gold, 30, 96, 102, 107, 142, 158; chain, 90, 94, 111; coin, 151 fig. 16, 227n14; purity of, 119; refined, 170
Golden Mean, 28–36, 50, 53, 63–4, 79, 105, 137, 139, 170–1, 178, 198
Gomorrah, 206n85
gong, 93
González, Tomás, 16
González Moreno, Fernando, 241n121
Gonzalo, Arias, 165
Good Temper, xiii
goose, 53; horned, 166
gossip, 140
Gottlieb, Paula, 209n129
governor, 111, 148, 151, 161
Grace, 43, 62–3, 65, 179
Gracián, Baltasar, 160, 180, 190, 256n109; *Agudeza y arte de ingenio*, 31; *El Criticón*, 31, 210n134; *El héroe*, 191, 260n3; *Oráculo manual*, 179, 256n109
gracioso, 89–90, 104, 147, 167
grain, 133
grammar, 16, 18
Gran Hospital Real, 16
Granada, 73, 228n29
grandmother, xiii
grandparent, 158
Grayson, Brandan Leigh, 241n114
Greed, 10, 57, 84–105, 135, 230n56
Greek, xiv, 18, 29, 44, 71, 80, 126, 133, 166, 183, 191–3, 196, 207nn86, 96, 232n7, 247n31; etymology, 246n9; god, 208n117; mythology, 110
Grieve, Patricia, 234n44, 249n71
grifter, 10
Grim Reaper, 55
Grimaldi, Benedettina, 112
guadaña, 55
Guevara, Antonio de, 9
guild: of apothecaries, 204n59; of jewellers, 92
Guilelessness, xiii
guillotine, 57
guilt, 47, 56
gusarapa, 109
Guzmán, Gaspar de, 134
Guzmán, Ramiro Felipe de, 128
gypsy, 87

Habsburg, 183
hacienda, 104, 157. *See also* property
hagiographical drama, 73, 85, 115, 148, 152, 170
hair, 99
hand, 53, 55, 61, 65, 75, 76, 89, 94
hanging, 56, 93, 99, 219n189
Hannibal, 71
Hanrahan, Thomas, 259n159
happiness, 29, 179
hare, 166
Harmony, 5
harness, 85, 167

harpy, 166
hart, 167
harvest, 228n29
Harvey, John H., 7, 202n33, 245n6
hatred, 178
Haworth, Kenneth R., 199n7
heart, 82, 99, 101, 217n140; affair of the, 127; divided, 106
heaven, 47–8, 51, 62, 73, 75–6, 84, 87, 91, 97–8, 100, 107, 131, 159, 168, 174; stairway to, 96, 98
Heble, Ajay, 246n13
Hebrew, 48, 55, 85, 109, 115
Hector, 78, 190
Heliodorus, 167
hell, 31, 47
Hellenization, 192, 195
hemlock, 22
herb, 6, 21, 23–4, 146, 205n65, 245n7
Hercules, 70
heresy, 55, 75, 188; Lutheran, 230n53, 259n151
heretic, 51, 85
hermandad, 92, 229n43. *See also* confraternity
Hermandad del Refugio, 92, 229n39
hermaphrodite, 143, 145, 245n7
hermeneutics, 150
hero, 69–83, 105, 117, 133, 140, 150, 152, 156, 179, 190–1, 198, 225n49, 260n3
Herrera Montero, Bernal, 256n116
hiccup, 6
hidalgo, 96, 158
Hild, J.-A., 247n31
Hiltpold, Paul, 250n102
hinge, 178
Hispania Tarraconensis, 151
Hispanic casuistry studies, xiv
historical drama, 132
historical fiction, 122
holiness, 30, 200n8
Hollywood, 52
Holy Family, 115–16
Holy League, 75
Holy Week, 229n43
Holy Writ, 118
homeopathic, 6
homicide, 39, 50, 204n58. *See also* murder
homunculus, 197
honesty, 108, 122, 166, 251n9
honey, 79, 203n57
Honos, 194, 261n16
honour, 5, 29, 49, 53, 60, 71–2, 77, 108, 110, 120, 131–2, 137, 156, 161, 168, 171, 194, 233n17, 241n118, 254n69; temple to, 261n16
hope, xv, 84–5, 232n4
Horace, 29–30, 173, 209n126
horse, 117, 184, 185 fig. 20; horseman, 194; publicly financed, 195; Trojan, 133
hortus conclusus, 232n7
Hospicio de la Congregación del Dulce Nombre de María, 92
hospital, 5, 73, 85, 99, 100, 228n18, 229nn36, 38; for veterans, 88
Hospital de la Misericordia, 5
hospital de los podridos, El, 20
Hospital Tavera, 4
hospitality, 86
hostage, 111
Hourani, George F., 221n241
house, 46, 147, 168; arrest, 240n87; distillation, 205n66; household, 153
Houser, R.E., 200n9
Huarte de San Juan, Juan, 9
Hubbard, Thomas, 110
Huguet-Termes, Teresa, 204–5n62

humanism, 156, 183, 198, 257n135; Christian, 36, 166, 181, 191; secular, 195
humanist, 16, 18, 160, 162, 183, 250n96
Hume, David, 37
humiliation, 148; public, 195
Humility, xiii, 10, 29, 61, 134, 138, 164, 169, 175, 177
humour, 206n85
Hungary, 73
hunger, 90, 228n29
hunter, 109
Hurtado de Mendoza, Diego, 209n125
husband, 114–15, 117, 120–3, 128, 131, 148, 157, 168, 235n60, 236n85, 246n19; absent, 123; dead, 123; kin of, 230n62; prospective, 104
hyacinth, 21
hydra, 188
hyperbole, 116, 239n81
hypocrisy, 164–6, 177, 251n110, 252n17
hyssop, 145

Iago, 145, 245n1
Iberia, 183, 245n8
Iberian Peninsula, 75, 234n44
iconography, xvi, 10, 34, 46, 66, 133, 150, 220n222, 223n298, 225n32, 239n78, 247n32
idolatry, 55
Ignatius, Saint, 62
Illescas, 97
Illuminist, 184, 186, 257n135. See also *alumbrado*
immigrant, 89
immunotherapy, xiii
impalement, 81, 108
imprudence, 53
incest, 41, 213n39
Index, 187; Amberes, 187; of Quiroga, 187; of Valdés, 187; of Venice, 187
India, 111
indicio, 238n56
indulgence, 222n261
industry, 182
infamy, 171, 252n21, 254n69
ingenuity, 155
inheritance, 105
injury, 49, 62
inn, 183
Innocence, 61, 140, 244n182
Inquisition, 51, 53, 66, 67 fig. 12, 68, 183, 186–8, 223n298; coat of arms, 223n298; Mexico, 187; Toledo, 66, 67 fig. 12; trial, 123; Valencia, 186, 258n151
Inquisitor General, 184, 187, 257n133, 258n151
insane asylum, 88
insanity, 78. *See also* madness
Insensitivity, 27 fig. 10, 34
Insúa Ruiz, Aurora, 253n58
Ínsula Barataria, 161
insurance, 98
Intemperance, 27 fig. 10, 34
intention, 52
interés, 58, 220n216
interlude, 20. See also *entremés*
investitute, 68
Ionescu, Arleen, 209n128
Irish, 89
Isabel, Saint, 89–90
Isabel la Católica, Queen, 209n125
Isidore, Saint, 89
Islam, 75, 138, 248n48
Israel, 10, 41; tribe of, 109
Israelite, 26, 128

Italian, 37, 94, 112, 159–60, 162, 207n89, 250n96
Italy, 18, 26, 44, 152, 172–3, 175, 205n65

Jack and the Bean Stalk, 96
Jacob, 38, 71, 224n17
Jael, 35, 81
jail, 109, 123, 229n43. *See also* prison
James, Saint, 114
Janus, 133
Jealousy, 131, 141, 244n180
Jed, Stephanie, 233n26
jerga, 164
Jerome, Saint, 114, 148, 149 fig. 15
Jesuit, xv, 3, 16, 17 fig. 6, 31, 143, 159, 179, 184; college, 209n125, 249n91; Erasmus and, 258n139; school drama, 241n114, 260n161
Jesus, 79, 91, 115; birth of, 114
Jew, 55, 60, 85, 204n59, 208n105, 232n8
jewel, 95
Jewish, 12, 58, 60
Joffre, Juan, 184, 185 fig. 20
John, Gospel of, 9
John of God, Saint, 5, 73, 85, 87, 96
Johnson, Penelope D., 200n9
joke, 6, 122, 168
Jordan, Constance, 148, 153, 245n8
Joseph (patriarch), 109, 133
Joseph, Saint, 79, 114–15
Joseph and Aseneth, 109
journalism, 29
Joy, 91
Judas, 114
judge, 9, 39–40, 42, 44, 58–9, 64, 122, 134, 206n75, 212n30, 220n231, 225n48; female, 49, 128; itinerant, 212n3; male, 214n69
Judges, 227n84
Jupiter, 247n32
jurisdiction, 212n25
jurisprudence, 39, 59
jus, 36
Justice, xv–xvi, 12, 30, 35–69, 102, 105, 128, 130, 132, 135, 137, 139, 146, 161, 171, 177–8, 199n8, 211–23, 225n48, 237n17, 240n81, 242n142; blind, 220n232; commutative, 49; distributive, 50, 58, 105, 129; divine, 214n85; injustice, 251n110; new, 223n290; Original, 61–2, 221nn252, 257; retributive, 50
justicia mayor, 212n31
Justinus, 120

Kagan, Richard, 44, 60, 128, 211n20, 212nn25, 30, 220nn214, 225, 221n239
Kallendorf, Craig, 134, 240n81
Kallendorf, Hilaire: "Cervantes' Democratization of Demonic Possession," 222n281; *Conscience on Stage*, xiv, 57, 142–3, 219n207, 237n8, 238n56, 244nn184, 197, 246n13, 249n91, 251n109, 253n37, 260n161; *Exorcism and Its Texts*, 10, 201n20, 259n159; *Sins of the Fathers*, xiv, xvii, 37, 87, 90, 143, 200n16, 220n222, 225n50, 227n13, 228nn29, 31, 230n56, 233n16, 235n62, 238n56, 241n110, 244n197, 250n107; "Were the Arbitristas Arbitrary?" 239n78, 240n89
Keiser, George R., 7, 207nn91–3
Kindness, xiii
king, 39, 40–3, 48, 50–1, 53–4, 56–8, 60–3, 71, 76–8, 120, 128, 130–5, 140, 142, 156–7, 183, 188, 212n31,

213n49, 215n92, 219n189, 221n243, 240n94, 254n89, 261n16; divine right of, 48, 215n92; kingship, 139, 181; of Palmyra, 111
Kirby, Carol Bingham, 217n136
kitchen, xiii, 168
knife, 57, 182
knight, 72, 93, 141, 184, 185 fig. 20; knight errant, 161
Knox, Bernard, 171
Kraye, Jill, 209n125

laboratory, 205n66
labrador, 156
labyrinth, 60
Lacan, Jacques, 143
La Cava, 157, 249n71
Ladino, 154–5
Laguna, Andrés de, 8 fig. 2, 18, 19 fig. 7, 23, 205n65, 245n2
Laínez, Diego, 136–7
Langis, Unhae, 199n1
Laredo, Bernardino de, 12
Las Casas, Bartolomé de, 177
Las Vegas, xiii
Latin, xiv–xv, 3–4, 30, 37, 57, 69, 80, 145–6, 155, 159–60, 183, 187, 191–3, 198, 199n5, 208n121, 245n7, 253n37, 258n149, 262n39; grammar, 195; macaronic, 20
Lauer, A. Robert, 42
Laura, 111
lavender, 145
law, 37–9, 40, 42, 46, 50, 55–6, 62–3, 85, 98, 104–5, 121, 128, 135, 160, 181, 193, 206n85, 216n118, 217n137, 223n293, 240n94; canon law, 251n109; criminal, 128; law court, 39; lawgiver, 225n48; lawsuit, 21, 39, 40, 44, 122, 212n25, 220n225; natural law, 237n27; Roman law, 192
lawyer, 39, 220n225; fee of, 212n25
laxity, 57, 137, 219n207
Lazarillo, 259n159
ledger, 44, 103
leg, 90
León, 75; Cortes de, 206n80; tribunal of, 215n106
Lepanto, Battle of, 75
leprosy, 112
lethargy, 142
letrado, 38–9, 40, 135
lettuce, 145
Levinas, Emmanuel, 199n1
liar, 166
liberality, 29, 84, 129, 159, 174, 190, 230n56
libertas, 194
Licenciado Vidriera, 137
Lida de Malkiel, María Rosa, 235n74
lie, 142–3, 166–8, 244n195, 252n31
lightning, 47, 214n85
limpieza de sangre, 16, 204n59, 232n8. *See also* blood, purity
lineage, 114, 156, 158
linguistics, 192–3
lion, 70, 79, 224n7
Lipsius, Justus, 209n126
litigant, 60, 212n25
litigation, cost of, 212n25
litmus test, 123
Little Book of the Virtues of Rosemary, 7
loa, 35, 79, 92, 94, 103
Lobera, Luis, 12
Lombardy, 86
Lope de Vega, 77, 150, 162, 213nn41, 50, 215n92, 216n129, 220n220, 228n18, 236n83, 251nn109–10, 256n116; *Arte nuevo*, xv, 3; *La*

Dorotea, 145, 245n7; as womanizer, 121
López, Juan, 18
López, Marcela, 7
López-Ibor, J.J., 228n17
López Terrada, María Luz, 200–1n8, 201n10, 204n58, 226n79
López Torrijos, Rosa, 239n78
Lorenz, Philip, 213n50
love, 33, 57, 59, 84, 93, 137, 168, 220n232, 244n195; affair, 119, 122; Chariot of, 111; dishonest, 252n12; erotic, 110; goddess of, 119; intrigue, 127; love life, 236n83; marital, 114, 123, 247n19; of posterity, 118; paternal, 34
lover, 171; absent, 150; ruse of, 6, 201n20
Low Countries , 173. *See also* Netherlands
Loyalty, 5, 10, 12, 41, 148, 156, 247n19
Loyola, Ignatius, Saint, 184
Lucan, 196–8, 261n34, 262n39
lucid interval, 137
Lucifer, 37
Lucretia, 109–10, 147, 233n26
Lugo, Cristóbal del, 170
lunatic, 228n18
Lust, 4 fig. 1, 108, 113, 117–18, 136, 138, 157, 233nn16–17; within marriage, 118, 235n62
Luther, Martin, 230n53
luxuria, 245n9
Lysimachus, 71

Machiavelli, Niccolò, 144, 173–86, 191, 241n124, 255nn93–4, 105, 256nn105, 109, 256–7n116
machismo, 152
MacIntyre, Alasdair, 262n40
MacKay, Ruth, 250n106
madhouse, 88
madman, 88, 137, 228n18. *See also* lunatic
madness, 105, 116, 137–8, 231n96
Madrid, 5–6, 18, 21, 39, 49, 92, 100, 157, 201n17, 204n59, 205n62; Cortes of, 22, 206nn75, 79
Madrigal, Alfonso de, 9
magic, island of 121
magician, 207n86
magnanimity, 177
maiden name, 159
Malamud, Martha, 199n7
Maldonado, Juan, 259n160
malice, 51, 61–2, 154, 171, 216n121, 222n261
malpractice, 204n58
Malta, 136
Manasseh, 109
mandrake, 6
manna, 91
Manrique, Alonso, 184
Mantua, 112
manuscript, 175, 202nn33–4, 209n125, 215n100, 245n6, 255n93; illumination, 34
Maravall, José Antonio, 178, 250n106
maravedí, 21, 95, 212n25, 230n66
Marcellus, M. Claudius, 261n16
marjoram, 205n66
Mark, Gospel of, 114
market, 102
marriage, 32, 104, 107, 109–11, 113–14, 116–19, 121, 150, 168, 232–3n11, 235n60; consummation of, 115, 117; hatred of, 168; intermarriage, 234n44; medieval, 115
Marroni, Francesco, 209n128

Mars, 70
Martin, Saint, 92
Martínez, Ángel, 14, 202–3n48, 203nn49, 51
Marxist, 154
Mary Magdalene, 170, 253n57
masculinity, 125, 174, 192–8, 226n72, 245n9
mask, 142, 167, 177
mass media ethics, 29
massacre, 121
Mastrangelo, Marc, 199n7
masturbation, 23, 207n87
Mateu, Pedro Benet, 12
mathematics, 29, 35, 103, 139, 155, 170
matron, 148; Roman, 109
Matthew, Gospel of, 85, 103, 114
Mattingly, Harold, 246n11
maurophilia, 242n129
McDonnell, Myles, 192–6, 199n5, 260nn7–13, 261nn14–32
McKendrick, Melveena, 227n87, 251n110
meat, 66
Mecca, 167
Media, 48
medical school, 7, 202n32
Medici, Lorenzo de', 160, 174
medieval, xv, 3, 7, 12, 44, 70, 72, 107–8, 114, 116, 119, 172, 226n72, 232n7; exegesis, 150; marriage, 115
Medina de las Torres, Duke of, 128
Medina del Campo, 175, 205n67
Mediterranean, 7, 75, 232n7; Sea, 75
Medusa, 72
meekness, 79, 177
memento mori, 102
Memnon of Rhodes, 71
Mena, Juan de, xv, 44, 46, 70, 82, 108, 114, 126, 172–3, 200n11
Menander, 105
Mercado, Isabel, 10
mercenary, 71
merchant, 98, 187, 220n225
Mercury, 150
Mercy, 12, 48, 63–6, 67 fig. 12, 99, 148, 213n39, 215n92, 223n298, 230n56; work of, 85, 91–3
meritocracy, 161
metal, 119
Mexía, Pedro, 259n160
Mexico, 76, 187
Mezquita, Miguel, 186, 258–9n151
Michael (archangel), 73, 225n32
Middle Ages, 98, 100, 150
Middle East, 48
Middlebrook, Leah, 226n72
Milan, 57
military, 55, 71–3, 75, 105, 136, 180, 194–8; experience, 196; order, 92; policy, 247n32; service, 195; spectacle, 195; symbol, 120; technology, 218n177; victory, 195–6
milk, 91, 157
Milton, John, 170, 233n11
Minnesota, University of, 24
Minos, King, 78
Mira de Amescua, Antonio, 251n109
miracle, 89, 165
mirror, 164; for princes, 174; play of, 190
miscegenation, 114
miserliness, 29
misogyny, 80–1, 122, 147, 166
mistress, 111, 170
Mithradites, King, 26
Mithraditic cure, 26
moderation, 139
Modesty, 33–4, 108, 111, 123, 124 fig. 14; Temple of, 111
Molina, María de, 132, 208n105

monarchism, 213n50
monarchy, 215n92, 251n110
Monardes, Nicolás, 12, 14, 15 fig. 5
monastery, 16, 88–9, 91, 95, 183, 205n66; cloister, 107; of San Lorenzo, 205n67; of Santa Hilda, 111
Moncín, Luis, xvi
money, 49, 58, 87, 90, 96, 102, 104, 112, 136–7, 157, 168, 230n66
monk, 16, 91, 184
monomachy, 194
monster, 138; green-eyed, 141
mood, 143
Moral (allegorical figure), 155
moral philosophy, 209n125
Moreto, Agustín, 251n109
Moretti, Franco, xvii
morisco, 72, 155, 186, 204n59, 227n6
Moses, 26, 27 fig. 8, 48, 91, 215n89
mother, 109, 129, 132–3, 157
motivation, 93; for sex, 119
mountain, 47, 70, 123, 205n65; mountain woman, 81
mouth, 53, 79, 218n152
Mucius Scaevola, 71
Muhammad, 138
mujer esquiva, 110
mujer varonil, 111, 148, 152
Mujica, Bárbara, 213n50
mule, 117
mulier, 246n9
Muñoz, Miguel Eugenio, 206n73
murder, 50, 71, 120, 157, 168, 204n58, 237n23; legal, 121; mass, 168
music, 29, 31, 66, 180, 190
musk, 167
Muslim, 46–7, 75, 78, 135, 140, 154–5, 157, 204n59, 232n8
muteness, 59
mysticism, 165

Nájera, Duke of, 148, 150
Naples, 123, 124 fig. 14, 125
Napoleon, 83
narcotic, 142
National Endowment for the Humanities, xiv
Nazianzeno, Gregorio, Saint, 164
Near East, 232n7
negligence, 204n58
Nelson, Daniel Mark, 236n2
neo-Stoicism, 177, 209n126
Nero, Emperor, 170, 196
Netherlands, 135
New Testament, 26
"New" World, 76, 98, 102, 123, 177
Newhauser, Richard, xiv
night, 34, 47, 118, 131
nihilism, 197
nipple, 125
nobility, 95, 107, 130, 146, 153, 155–63, 248n59, 249nn69, 73, 84, 88, 251n110
noblesse oblige, 50, 95
Northumbria, 111
notary, 212n25
Notre Dame, University of, 66, 67 fig. 12
novel, 122, 161, 187–8; novella, 187
novelist, xvi, 141, 250n107
nudity, 109–10
Nummedal, Tara E., 235n70
nun, 111
Núñez de Cepeda, Francisco, 31
nymph, 120

obligation, 59, 96, 220n232, 223n293, 230n62; competing, 139; priestly, 236n83
Occasion, 59, 220n222
ocean, 47
odour, 167

Odysseus, xv, 133, 140
Office of Strategic Services, 172
oidor, 40
oil, 66
Old Christian, 204n59
Old Testament, 26, 49, 71, 81, 99, 109, 117, 128, 133, 168
Olivares, Count-Duke of, 25, 134, 209n125, 240n87
olive branch, 65–6, 67 fig. 12, 242n141
onion, 165
opiate, 21
orator, 195
O'Reilly, Terence, 259n159
Orense, 18
Origen, 113, 234n40
Original Sin, 61–2
Osorio, Elena, 216n129
Ospedale di Pammatone, 112
Osubio, King, 111
Otevante, Juan Lorenzo, 175, 176 fig. 19
Otho, 170
Otto the Great, Emperor, 246n15
Ottoman Empire, 81
Ovid, 150, 152
Oviedo, Catalina de, 81
Oviedo, Luis de, 14
ox, 84, 216n118
oxlip, 205n66
oxymoron, 33, 140

PTSD, 88
Pacher, Michael, 44, 45 fig. 11
Padilla, Luisa de, 160
Pagden, A.R.D., 209n125
pain, 146
Palacio Real (Madrid), 17 fig. 6
palm leaf, 107
Palmyra, 81, 111
Palomino, Francisco, 200n3
panacea, 135
panderer, 236n83
Pandora, 188
Panopticon, 122
papal dispensation, 118
paper, 44
parable, 103
parade, 194
paradox, 33, 79, 81, 122, 177
parazonium, 247n32
pardon, 64–6, 131, 223n293
parent, 158
Parker, Alexander, 251n109
Parker, Geoffrey, 134
Parma, 72
passion, 40, 182, 222n265
Pastor Bodmer, Beatriz, 225n49
pastoral, 49, 147
Patience, xiii, 12, 130–1, 238n46, 241n118, 244n179
patriarch, 109, 224n17; patriarchy, 166
patriotism, 134
patron, 112, 236n83; female, 234n35
Paul, Saint, xv, 107, 112
Paula, Saint, 148, 149 fig. 15
peace, 225n48, 239n61, 242n132; peacemaking, 148
pearl, 101
peasant, 131, 148, 154, 162, 164, 188, 213n50
pedagogy, 207n87
Pedro I, King, 52, 54, 217n137
pelvis, 125
Peña, Margarita, 213n41, 220n220
penalty, 55, 204n58
penitence, 164
Penner, Terry, 209n129
Pensamiento, 171
Pepys, Samuel, 172
Pérez, Amador, 206n75
Pérez Bautista, Florencio L., 201n8
Pérez de Montalbán, Juan, 26

Pérez Martínez, Ángel, 250n103
pereza, 33
peripatetic, 182
peripeteia, 170
persecution, 140
Perseus, 72
perseverance, 70
Persia, 48, 71
perspectivism, 169
Peru, 10
perversion, 102, 225n49
Peset, V., 18
Petrarca, Francesco, 111, 119, 239n81
Petro del Barrio, Antonia, 223n30
Pharaoh, 48, 109
pharmacist, 14, 16, 18, 145, 205n62 (*see also* apothecary; *boticario*); shop, 204n58
pharmacology, 12, 14
pharmacopia, 12, 202n48, 203n49
pharmacy, 203n56, 205nn62, 67, 206n76; exam, 18; jar, 16, 17 fig. 6, 21 (see also *albarelo*)
pharmakeus, 207n96
pharmakologos, 26
pharmakon, 22–9, 35–6, 48, 62, 105, 138, 142–3, 171–2, 174, 182, 188, 191, 207nn86–7
pharmakos, 24, 52, 207nn86, 96
Philip II, King, 8 fig. 2, 18, 134–5, 175, 176 fig. 19, 204nn58–9, 205n67, 235n70, 245n2
Philip IV, King, 25, 128, 134, 181
Philistine, 71, 168
philology, xvii, 245n2
philosopher's stone, 245n200
phronēsis, 126
physician, 204n58 (*see also* doctor); God as, 206n85; *morisco*, 204n59
picaresque, 20, 91, 94, 98, 141, 188
Pieper, Josef, 200n10
piety, 190, 200n8
pilgrim, 86–7, 229n38, 230n55
pilot, 242n150
pimp, 62
Pity, 35, 43, 63–5, 102–3, 148, 215nn89, 92, 217n134, 223n298, 230n57
Pius V, Pope, 75, 159
Pizarro, Fernando, 10
plague, 6, 48, 112, 201n17
plaintiff, 49
planet, 70–1
Plasencia, 204n59
Plata, Fernando, 220n222
Plato, xv, 4, 22, 23–4, 30, 79, 105, 173, 199–200n8, 207nn89, 96, 209n129
plausibility, 179
playing doctor, 6
pleasure, 69, 118
pleito, 44. *See also* lawsuit *under* law
plow, 84
poetry, 110
poison, 20–6, 28–9, 35, 171, 181–2, 204nn58, 59, 207n86, 208n105; poisoner, 207n96; sleep-inducing, 142
police, 214n69
polis, 37
political philosophy, 38, 177, 179–80
political science, 174
politician, 195
politics, 161, 175; satanic, 257n116
Polybius, 261n14
pomo, 200n14
Pompey, 197
poor house, 91
Poppea, 170
port, 249n75
Portia, 147, 247n19
Portugal, 90
Portuguese, 73, 172, 177

Poska, Allyson, 123, 236n85
postmodern, 22, 29, 198
potion, 7, 24
Potiphar, 109
poultice, 208n121
poverty, 50, 94, 160, 216n118
pragmática, 206n78
pragmatism, 179–80, 256n109
Prague, xiv
prayer, 75, 93, 99, 100, 230n55
preacher, 40
prejudice, 242n129
prescription, 204n58
President, 63
Presotto, Marco, 240n83
priest, 12, 16, 38, 95, 109, 119, 122, 162, 164, 171, 180, 207n86, 236n83, 251n109; high priest, 115
Pride, 10, 77, 135, 138, 175, 225n50
primogeniture, 38, 66, 211n11
prince, 18, 38, 41, 48, 64, 99, 105, 110, 120, 128, 135, 174–5, 177, 180–1, 237n23; Christian, 177, 237n20; of Fabriano, 131; of Parma, 72
princess, 41, 111
principate, 196
prison, 71, 130; prisoner, 78, 93, 212n25
privado, 134, 181
privy chamber, 128
procreation, 118
prodigal son, 137, 241n114
prodigality, 29, 137
professor, 183
profligacy, 29
promiscuity, 121
prop, 38, 43–4, 46, 55, 64, 91, 129
propaganda, 76, 213n50
propemptikon, 231n76
property, 37, 157, 261n14
prophecy, 159, 165
Propiedades del romero, 7
ProQuest, xvii
prostitute, 73
prostitution, 157
Protestant, 94
protomédico, 204n58
proverb, 23
Proverbs, 226n83
Prudence, xv–xvi, 5, 10, 33, 35–6, 63–4, 77, 79, 105, 125–44, 146–7, 154–5, 157, 161, 175, 177–9, 190, 196, 199n8, 249n73; feminine, 129
Prudentius, xv, 3, 4 fig. 1, 199n7, 200n3
Psalmist, 47
pseudógrafo, 258n149
psychoanalysis, 143
psychology, 232n96
psychomachia, 3, 63
psychotherapy, 29
Pudicizia, 108, 123, 124 fig. 14. *See also* modesty
puer, 246n9
Puigdomenech, Helena, 175
Pujol, Bernardus de, 203n51
Punic War, 71, 133
punishment, 38–9, 43, 51, 54, 64, 78, 119, 130, 139, 203n57, 204n58, 213n39, 219n189, 221n238, 238n46; excessive, 238n46; exemplary, 51–2, 130; proportional, 130; violent, 130, 238n45
purgative, 21
Purgatory, 99

queen, 38, 111, 129, 132, 208n105; of Palmyra, 81, 110; of Portugal, 90; of Sheba, 64
queer studies, 199

querelle des femmes, 94, 152
Quevedo, Francisco de, 59, 179, 209n126, 240n87; *Dios hace justicia a todos*, xiv; *La Hora de todos*, 179–80; *Lince de Italia*, 179; *Migajas*, 179; *Silvas*, 218n177, 231n76; *Sueño del alguacil endemoniado*, 30
quicksand, 97
Quiñones de Benavente, Luis, 20

Ra, 109
Rabelais, François, 166
racism, 41, 75, 89, 232n8
Ramos Solís, Antonio, 16
Ramoutsaki, I.A., 208n117
ransom, 121, 157
rape, 41, 64, 78, 110, 120, 224n17, 231n80
Raphael (archangel), 73, 117
Rawls, John, 211n2
real, 99, 100, 205n67
Real Academia Española, 109
Real Hospital, 18
Real Monasterio de Sobrado, 16, 18
Reason, 5
reason of state, 59
recipe, 14, 18, 20, 22
recompense, 49, 50
Reconquest, 60, 72, 75
rectitude, 57, 59, 220n234
red, 55
Red Sea, 48
redress, 49, 50, 54
Regan, Lisa K., 234n35
regidor, 206n75
Renaissance, xv, 23, 36, 49, 52, 94, 96, 105, 114, 118–19, 145–6, 152–3, 159–60, 162, 174, 191, 198, 207n89, 209nn125–6, 245n8, 247n19, 248n48, 253n58, 260n163; idealism, 191
repentance, 43, 238n45
repertoire, xvii
republic, 31, 39, 110, 136, 241n108; Roman, 192–4, 196, 260n9; values of, 247n19
Resnick, Irven, 115
restitution, 39
retribution, 132
Revelation, 165
revenge, 33, 39, 50, 54–5, 132, 214n85, 218n154, 224n17, 242n137
revolution, 213n50
reward, 43, 51, 72, 98, 139
Rey Bueno, Mar, 205nn6–7
rhetoric, 16, 183, 195, 197, 232n8
Rhodes, Elizabeth, 153
Ribadeneyra, Pedro de, 177, 255n99
Ricard, Robert, 236n83
Ridley, R.T., 239n79
rights, 38, 42
rigour, 43, 52–3, 55, 63, 130–1, 223n290
riot, 52, 228n29
Robbins, Jeremy, 31, 142, 177, 237n20, 256n109
Robin Hood, 168
robot, 198
Roca Traver, Francisco A., 228n17
rock, 47
rod, 44, 46, 48, 55, 58–9, 64
Roderigo, 245n1
Rodríguez, Alonso, 16
Rojas, Fernando de, 230n64
Roland, 76
Roman, xiv, 29, 39, 44, 52, 71, 77, 108–10, 126, 150, 171, 194–8, 247n31, 261n14; cavalry, 261n16; coin, 193; culture, 190; emperor, 150, 151 fig. 16; empire, 110; exemplary, 217n134; Forum, 110;

general, 111; god, 192; history, 109; horseman, 194; language, 155; law, 192; man, 113; matron, 109; mythology, 109; Republic, 192, 196, 260n9; Senate, 133; youth, 194
romance, 141; of chivalry, 111, 120
Rome, 20, 39, 52, 57, 72, 76, 86, 110–11, 146, 192–8, 239n79; decline of, 196
Roncesvalles, Battle of, 76
rosary, 101–2
rose, 119, 235n67; garland, 125; water, 205n66
Rose of Peru, Saint, 116
rosemary, 7, 8 fig. 2, 23, 145, 202n34
Ross, Jill, 232n7
Rotterdam, 181
Ruggiero, 121
Rupp, Stephen, 180–1
Ruth, 91

Saavedra Fajardo, Diego, 30, 175, 177
Sabuco, Miguel, 9
sackcloth, 164
sacrament: of Confirmation, 75; of the Eucharist, 79; of Matrimony, 173
sacrifice: human, 120; state, 195
saddle, 194
sadism, 78
saint, 73, 89, 90, 104, 111, 116, 118, 164–5, 170; female, 82, 153; patron, 92
Salamanca, University of, 7, 183, 251n109
Salazar, Diego de, 180
Salerniano, Nicolás, 203n51
Salerno, 7
Salomon, Noël, 154, 162
salsify, 205n66
salud, 166
Salvador de Bahia, 5
salvation, 26, 98–9, 230n53
Samson, 71, 168
San Lorenzo, monastery of, 205n67
Sánchez, Marina, 230n55
Sánchez de las Brozas, Francisco (El Brocense), 183
Sancho, 161
Sancho, Prince, 136
Sancho IV, King, 208n105
Sancho de San Román, R., 201n8
Sansevero Chapel, 123, 124 fig. 14
Santiago de Compostela, 16, 18; Order of, 229n38
Saracen, 121
Sarah, 117–18
Satan, 73, 225n32
satyr, 166
Saul, King, 10
Saussure, Ferdinand de, 246n13
scale, 40, 43, 46, 139
scammony, 21, 204n58
scandal, 143
scapegoat, 207nn86, 96
Scarry, Elaine, 37
scenery, 46
scepticism, 177
sceptre, 44, 46, 55, 59, 64, 129
Schäfer, Peter, 230n60
Schlayer, Clotilde, 261n34
Scholastic, xv, 29, 60, 234n52, 237n20
Scipio Africanus, Publius Cornelius, 71, 261n14
scorpion, 23, 207n93
scribe, 212n25
scripture, 94, 109, 113
sculpture, 82, 123
scythe, 55
sea monster, 97
sea of fortune, 140, 242n150
Second World War, 172
secrecy, 141, 243nn164, 166, 168
seduction, 109, 125

Segovia, 18
self-fashioning, 76–7
self-interest, 100
semen, 113, 235n60
Senate, 39, 71, 127, 133, 237n17
senator, 111, 127, 193, 195
Seneca, 209n126
senectus, 245n9
senex, 245n9
sensuality, 33
Septimius Odaenathus, 111
Sepúlveda, Juan Ginés de, 177–8, 255n102, 255–6n105
Serna, Gallego de la, 9
servant, 95
Sessa, Duke of, 236n83
Seven Deadly Sins, xiv, 139
Seville, 75, 111, 203n57, 204n59, 212n25, 228n29
sex, 83, 107, 145–63, 241n110; drive, 112; goal of, 118; identification, 145; in plants, 245n2; position, 117, 152, 235n60; strategy, 145; within marriage, 118
Sextus Tarquinius, 110
sexuality, 116, 145, 168; angelic, 232n11; female, 232n7; male, 114
shackles, 244n186
shadow, 47
Shakespeare, William, 189; *Macbeth*, 3, 200n1; *Measure for Measure*, 164; *Othello*, 33, 145; *Romeo and Juliet*, 23–4
shaman, 207n86
sheep, 49, 127, 215n106
shepherd, 49, 50
shield, 55, 82
ship, 98, 111, 231n76; captain, 140; mast, 140, 242n152
shoulder, 89, 135, 140
Shrek, 165
Sicheus, 236n91
Sidonio, 121
Silenus, 155, 166–7, 188
silver, 154
Simon, 114
Simplicity, 62
simulacrum, 191, 198, 262n40
sin, 42, 44, 47, 100, 117, 146, 164, 168, 170, 181, 200n16, 206n85, 235n60, 238n56, 253n57; mortal, 235n60; venial, 235n60
Sincerity, xiii
sinner, 65
Sinón, 190
Siren, 140
Sisera, 81
sister, 231n80, 244n195
Sixtus V, Pope, 159
skirt, 93
Sklenář, Robert, 197, 262n39
Skoie, Mathilde, 233n28
skyscraper, 173
slander, 51, 216n129
Slater, John, 201nn8, 10
slave, 48, 50, 216n118; slavery, 157
sleep, 142
slogan, 195
Sloth, 59, 174
slut, 119
Smith, Macklin, 199n7
snake, 23, 25–6, 48, 62, 141, 207nn92–3, 221n257
Sobrado, 18
Socrates, 22, 166
Sodom, 206n85
sola fide, 230n53
soldier, 50, 71–3, 93, 99, 123, 129, 193, 195, 220n243; Christian, 181–2, 191
soliman, 21
Soloman, King, 64, 79, 133, 239n73
son, 213n39, 215n106, 231n80

song, 142
Song of Songs, 232n7
sonnet, 202n31
soul, 82, 99, 100–1, 104, 108, 159–60, 230n55, 254n68
sovereignty, 44, 181, 213n50
Soyer, François, 245n8
Spanish Match, 172
Sparta, 160
spear, 99
special effects, 65
Speculum Virginum, 10, 11 fig. 3
spice, 21
spider, 56, 141; spider web, 219n193
Spinoza, Benedict de, 37, 211n3
spolia optima, 261n16
spouse, 49, 61, 114, 116, 119, 122, 148, 215n107; absent, 123; test of, 104
spur, 182, 191
stabbing, 110
stag, 109
stage, 47; business, 39; directions, 35, 38, 43–4, 46, 50, 55
star, 140
starvation, 228n29
statecraft, 181
statue, 123, 124 fig. 14; equestrian statue, 193–4
stature, 82
statute, 220n225; of limitations, 50
stewardship, 103
stigmata, 165
stirrup, 194
Stoic, 77
Stoll, Anita K., 156
stone, 72
Stroud, Matthew, 121, 235n79
student, 100, 183
Suárez, Francisco, xv, 200n11
subaltern, 164
subversion, 250n107
suffering, 77
sugar, 203n57
suicide, 22–3, 110, 119, 123, 208n105, 247n19
suitor, 119
Sullivan, Henry, 219n183
Sulpicia, 110
sultan, 81
sumiller de corps, 128
sun, 34, 47, 122, 131; sun god, 109
supplicatio, 195
Supreme Court, 12
Supreme Tribunal, 35
surveillance, 56, 122, 141
swallow, 140, 243n163
sword, xvi, 4, 47, 55–9, 61, 65–6, 67 fig. 12, 78–9, 82, 92, 108, 130–1, 221n243, 238n45; hilt of, 200n14; short, 247n32
symmetry, 37
syphilis, 73
Syria, 81, 110
Syrtes, 97
syrup, 203n57

tableau, 135
Tacitus, 180
taifa, 75
talent, 103
Tamar, 231n80
Taouk, Raymond, 233n11
taqiyya, 140
Tarragona, 151
Tausiet, María, 201n13
tax, 43
taxonomy, xvi
Taylor, Barry, 183
teacher, 40
Teatro Español del Siglo de Oro, xvii
technology, 55

temeridad, 31
Temperance, xv–xvi, 5, 10, 12, 27 fig. 10, 29, 30, 33–5, 63–4, 78–9, 81, 118, 130, 135–7, 139, 148, 161, 178, 196, 199n8, 222n279, 238n45, 240nn81, 97, 241n108, 242n143
temple, 108, 121; of Castor, 261n16; of Modesty, 111; of *Virtus*, 194
Templeton Foundation, xiv
temptation, 232n7
Teresa of Ávila, Saint, 82, 249n87
Tertullian, 114
testator, 100
testimony, 39
Texan, 61
Thacker, Jonathan, 259n158, 260n163
Thapsia, 20
theatrum mundi, 189
theft, 51, 168, 231n74, 253n38
Themis, 217n134
Theological Virtues, xv, 84–5, 107, 200n11
theology, 180, 234n52, 241n110, 251n109; of power, 179
Theseus, 78
Thomas, Keith, 236n82
thorn, 119, 235n67
Thrasymachus, 60
throat, 78
throne, 46–7, 55, 59, 81, 247n32
thunder, 47, 214n85
tightrope, 173
Tirso de Molina, 251n109
Tobias, 85, 104–5, 117–18, 170
Toledo, 4, 12, 47, 75, 112, 136; Canon of, 190–1; Tribunal of, 66, 67 fig. 12
Toledo, García de, 136
Tolentino, Nicholas of, Saint, 87, 89
tolerance, 137
tongue, 140, 243n160
tooth, 53, 101–2
Toronto, University of, xiv
Torquemada, Antonio de, 20
torture, 68
Tovar, Simón de, 14
trace, 146, 246n13
tragedy, 52, 77, 244n182
traitor, 49, 63
Trajan, 52, 190, 217n134
transvectio equitum, 194–5, 261n16
trap door, 47
treachery, 251n110
treasury, 151
tree, 10, 11 fig. 3, 53, 84, 99; family, 157
trench warfare, 75
tribunal, 39; eternal, 99; lesser, 212n25; of León, 215n106; of Toledo, 66, 67 fig. 12
Tribunal del Protomedicato, 21
Trinkhaus, Charles, 159
Tropé, Hélène, 228nn17–18
Troy, 133; Helen of, 249n71
Truman, R.W., 213n37
Trump, Donald, 179
Tuck, Steve, 196
Turingia, 48
Turk, 73, 75, 180
tutor, 136
twin; Siamese, 169; sister, 223n298
tyrannicide, 42, 213n50
tyranny, 38, 41, 49, 63, 110, 120, 131, 178, 219n189

ugliness, 165–7
Ulysses, 190, 239n76, 242n152. *See also* Odysseus
United States, 12, 63, 244n187; Continental Congress, 150, 151 fig. 17
unity of the Virtues, 30–1, 64, 79, 209n129

Unselfishness, xiii
Urbina, Eduardo, 241n121
utilitarianism, 178
uxoricide, 121, 131

vaccine, 138
Valdés, Alfonso de, 183, 259n160
Valdés, Juan de, 183
Valdés Pozueco, Kátherin, 66
Valdéz García, J., 202n32
Valencia, 186, 204nn58–9, 228n18, 258–9n151
Valencia, Pedro de, 133, 227n6, 239n78
Valera, Mosén Diego de, 160
valido, 76
Valladolid, 22, 39, 205n67, 258n151, 259n160; *Chancillería*, 44, 211n20, 212n31; Cortes de, 206n80
Valles, Francisco, 203n53
valour, 33, 69–83, 134, 136–9, 146–8, 157, 179, 190, 192, 221n243, 224nn22, 24, 242n132, 242nn135, 138, 141, 247n32, 249n73, 255n105
Vanderjagt, A.J., 250n97
vanity, 29, 167
Varro, 261n25
vassal, 51, 137, 154, 162, 212n31
Velázquez, Suero, 76
Vélez de Guevara, Luis, xv, 25
Vélez de León, Juan, 255n93
veneer, 81, 97, 119, 142, 164–7
venereal disease, 81, 226n79
Vengador, El, 204n59
Venice, 39, 134, 211n4; Index of, 187; myth of, 239–40n81
venom, 21, 24–6, 141, 171–2
Venus, 119, 172
Verona, 211n4
Vertues off Herbes, 6
Vesta, 119
Vestal virgin, 119
veteran, 88
veto, 63
Vicenzio, Maestro, 20
victim, 50, 53–4, 120–1
Vilanova, Antonio, 259n160
Vilanova, Arnaldo de, 203n51
Vilches, Elvira, 227n14, 230n66
villa, 172
villager, 154
villain, 138
Villaizán, Joseph de, 16
villano, 154–6, 161–2
Vincent-Cassy, Cécile, 248n37
vine, 96
violence, 57, 68, 121, 130, 132, 137, 140, 217n137, 223n299, 238n45; legitimation of, 223n301
vir, xv, 80, 146, 245–6n9
Virgil, 111, 120, 140, 171–3
Virgin Mary, 79, 106, 109, 114–15, 225n32
Virginia, 150, 151 figs 17–18
virginity, 106–7, 117, 148, 232nn7, 11; perpetual, 107, 113–15
virility, 6, 80, 112–13
Virtù, 173–81, 255–6n105
virtud consiste en medio, La, xvi
virtud mayor, 106
Virtue Ethics, xiv
Virtus, xiv, 146, 150, 151 fig. 16, 151 figs 17–18, 184, 185 fig. 20, 191–8, 245n9, 261nn16, 25, 262n39
vision, 252n12
visual art, 125, 133, 225n32
Vivero, Gonzalo, 10
Vives, Juan Luis, 184, 247n19

wager, 103
Walters Art Museum, 10
war, 70, 72–3, 89, 106, 108, 172, 196, 221n243, 226n72, 260n9; civil,

132, 196–8, 206n85; deity of, 194; foreign, 88; holy, 75; just, 48–9, 69; war veteran, 99
warfare, 194, 260n9
warrior, 260n3; female, 4 fig. 1, 108, 111; mounted, 194, 261n16
water: distilled, 205n66; rose, 205n66; well, 133
Watson, A. Irvine, 217n144
wax seal, 38
wealth, 159–61
weapon, 139, 247n32; Chastity as a, 119; spiritual, 82
wedding, 7, 117, 119, 139, 242n137
weed, 53, 145
weights and measures, 14
whale, 167
wheat, 91, 239n75
whip, 46, 48, 55, 147; whiplash, 204n57
widow, 96, 98, 113, 208n105, 230n62, 236n91; assumed, 123
wife, 105, 109, 118, 121–3, 145, 147–8, 170, 235n60; death of, 236n83; murder of, 121, 131
Wilson Rare Books Library, 24
wine, 66, 91
wisdom, 30, 78, 104, 133, 199n8, 240n81, 247n19; of elders, 133; folk, 113; of fools, 116; practical, 126
Wisdom Research Network, xiv
witness, 39; false, 62
wizard, 207n96
wolf, 215n106
womb, 115
worm, 109
wormwood, 205n66
worship, 150; of emperor, 246n11
wound, 119, 207n88, 208n121

Yepes, Antonio de, 111, 233n31
yoke, 61

Zamora, 206n75
Zaragoza, 75, 203n48, 204n59, 206n75, 258n151
Zayas, María de, xvi, 153
zealotry, 69
Zopiro, 190
Zurbarán, Francisco de, 148, 149 fig. 15

Toronto Iberic

1. Anthony J. Cascardi, *Cervantes, Literature, and the Discourse of Politics*
2. Jessica A. Boon, *The Mystical Science of the Soul: Medieval Cognition in Bernardino de Laredo's Recollection Method*
3. Susan Byrne, *Law and History in Cervantes' Don Quixote*
4. Mary E. Barnard and Frederick A. de Armas (eds), *Objects of Culture in the Literature of Imperial Spain*
5. Nil Santiáñez, *Topographies of Fascism: Habitus, Space, and Writing in Twentieth-Century Spain*
6. Nelson Orringer, *Lorca in Tune with Falla: Literary and Musical Interludes*
7. Ana M. Gómez-Bravo, *Textual Agency: Writing Culture and Social Networks in Fifteenth-Century Spain*
8. Javier Irigoyen-García, *The Spanish Arcadia: Sheep Herding, Pastoral Discourse, and Ethnicity in Early Modern Spain*
9. Stephanie Sieburth, *Survival Songs: Conchita Piquer's* Coplas *and Franco's Regime of Terror*
10. Christine Arkinstall, *Spanish Female Writers and the Freethinking Press, 1879–1926*
11. Margaret Boyle, *Unruly Women: Performance, Penitence, and Punishment in Early Modern Spain*

12 Evelina Gužauskytė, *Christopher Columbus's Naming in the* diarios *of the Four Voyages (1492–1504): A Discourse of Negotiation*
13 Mary E. Barnard, *Garcilaso de la Vega and the Material Culture of Renaissance Europe*
14 William Viestenz, *By the Grace of God: Francoist Spain and the Sacred Roots of Political Imagination*
15 Michael Scham, Lector Ludens*: The Representation of Games and Play in* Cervantes
16 Stephen Rupp, *Heroic Forms: Cervantes and the Literature of War*
17 Enrique Fernandez, *Anxieties of Interiority and Dissection in Early Modern Spain*
18 Susan Byrne, *Ficino in Spain*
19 Patricia M. Keller, *Ghostly Landscapes: Film, Photography, and the Aesthetics of Haunting in Contemporary Spanish Culture*
20 Carolyn A. Nadeau, *Food Matters: Alonso Quijano's Diet and the Discourse of Food in Early Modern Spain*
21 Cristian Berco, *From Body to Community: Venereal Disease and Society in Baroque Spain*
22 Elizabeth R. Wright, *The Epic of Juan Latino: Dilemmas of Race and Religion in Renaissance Spain*
23 Ryan D. Giles, *Inscribed Power: Amulets and Magic in Early Spanish Literature*
24 Jorge Pérez, *Confessional Cinema: Religion, Film, and Modernity in Spain's Development Years (1960–1975)*
25 Juan Ramon Resina, *Josep Pla: Life Seen in the Form of Articles*
26 Javier Irigoyen-Garcia, *Moors Dressed as Moors: Clothing, Social Distinction, and Ethnicity in Early Modern Iberia*
27 Jean Dangler, *Edging toward Iberia*
28 Ryan D. Giles and Steven Wagschal (eds), *Beyond Sight: Engaging the Senses in Iberian Literatures and Cultures, 1200–1750*
29 Silvia Bermúdez, *Rocking the Boat: Migration and Race in Contemporary Spanish Music*
30 Hilaire Kallendorf, *Ambiguous Antidotes: Virtue as Vaccine for Vice in Early Modern Spain*

www.ingramcontent.com/pod-product-compliance
Lightning Source LLC
LaVergne TN
LVHW090148080826
844660LV00013B/718/J
* 9 7 8 1 4 8 7 5 0 2 1 3 3 *